Text Processing
in Python

Text Processing
in Python

David Mertz

✦▼Addison-Wesley

Boston • San Francisco • New York • Toronto • Montreal
London • Munich • Paris • Madrid
Capetown • Sydney • Tokyo • Singapore • Mexico City

Many of the designations used by manufacturers and sellers to distinguish their products are claimed as trademarks. Where those designators appear in this book, and Addison-Wesley was aware of the trademark claim, the designations have been printed in initial capital letters or all capital letters.

The author and publisher have taken care in preparation of this book, but make no expressed or implied warranty of any kind and assume no responsibility for errors or omissions. No liability is assumed for incidental or consequential damages in connection with or arising out of the use of the information or programs contained herein.

The publisher offers discounts on this book when ordered in quantity for bulk purchases and special sales. For more information, please contact:

U.S. Corporate and Government Sales
(800) 382-3419
corpsales@pearsontechgroup.com

For sales outside of the U.S., please contact:

International Sales
(317) 581-3793
international@pearsontechgroup.com

Visit Addison-Wesley on the Web: www.awprofessional.com

Library of Congress Cataloging-in-Publication Data

Mertz, David.
    Text processing in Python / David Mertz.
      p. cm.
    Includes bibliographical references and index.
    ISBN 0-321-11254-7 (alk. Paper)
    1. Text processing (Computer science) 2. Python (Computer program language) I.
Title.

QA76.9.T48M47 2003
005.13'—dc21

                                                            2003043686

ISBN: 0-321-11254-7
1 2 3 4 5 6 7 8 9 10—CRS—0706050403
First printing, June 2003

Contents

PREFACE

Beautiful is better than ugly.
Explicit is better than implicit.
Simple is better than complex.
Complex is better than complicated.
Flat is better than nested.
Sparse is better than dense.
Readability counts.
Special cases aren't special enough to break the rules.
Although practicality beats purity.
Errors should never pass silently.
Unless explicitly silenced.
In the face of ambiguity, refuse the temptation to guess.
There should be one—and preferably only one—obvious way to do it.
Although that way may not be obvious at first unless you're Dutch.
Now is better than never.
Although never is often better than **right** now.
If the implementation is hard to explain, it's a bad idea.
If the implementation is easy to explain, it may be a good idea.
Namespaces are one honking great idea—let s do more of those!
—Tim Peters, "The Zen of Python"

0.1   What Is Text Processing?

At the broadest level text processing is simply taking textual information and *doing something* with it. This doing might be restructuring or reformatting it, extracting smaller bits of information from it, algorithmically modifying the content of the information, or performing calculations that depend on the textual information. The lines between "text" and the even more general term "data" are extremely fuzzy; at an approximation, "text" is just data that lives in forms that people can themselves read—at least in principle, and maybe with a bit of effort. Most typically computer "text" is composed of sequences of bits that have a "natural" representation as letters, numerals, and symbols; most often such text is delimited (if delimited at all) by symbols and formatting that can be easily pronounced as "next datum."

The lines are fuzzy, but the data that seems least like text—and that, therefore, this particular book is least concerned with—is the data that makes up "multimedia" (pictures, sounds, video, animation, etc.) and data that makes up UI "events" (draw a window, move the mouse, open an application, etc.). Like I said, the lines are fuzzy, and some representations of the most nontextual data are themselves pretty textual. But in general, the subject of this book is all the stuff on the near side of that fuzzy line.

Text processing is arguably what most programmers spend most of their time doing. The information that lives in business software systems mostly comes down to collections of words about the application domain—maybe with a few special symbols mixed in. Internet communications protocols consist mostly of a few special words used as headers, a little bit of constrained formatting, and message bodies consisting of additional wordish texts. Configuration files, log files, CSV and fixed-length data files, error files, documentation, and source code itself are all just sequences of words with bits of constraint and formatting applied.

Programmers and developers spend so much time with text processing that it is easy to forget that that is what we are doing. The most common text processing application is probably your favorite text editor. Beyond simple entry of new characters, text editors perform such text processing tasks as search/replace and copy/paste, which—given guided interaction with the user—accomplish sophisticated manipulation of textual sources. Many text editors go farther than these simple capabilities and include their own complete programming systems (usually called "macro processing"); in those cases where editors include "Turing-complete" macro languages, text editors suffice, in principle, to accomplish anything that the examples in this book can.

After text editors, a variety of text processing tools are widely used by developers. Tools like "File Find" under Windows, or "grep" on Unix (and other platforms), perform the basic chore of *locating* text patterns. "Little languages" like sed and awk perform basic text manipulation (or even nonbasic). A large number of utilities—especially in Unix-like environments—perform small custom text processing tasks: `wc`, `sort`, `tr`, `md5sum`, `uniq`, `split`, `strings`, and many others.

At the top of the text processing food chain are general-purpose programming languages, such as Python. I wrote this book on Python in large part because Python is such a clear, expressive, and general-purpose language. But for all Python's virtues, text editors and "little" utilities will always have an important place for developers "getting the job done." As simple as Python is, it is still more complicated than you need to achieve many basic tasks. But once you get past the very simple, Python is a perfect language for making the difficult things possible (and it is also good at making the easy things simple).

0.2   The Philosophy of Text Processing

Hang around any Python discussion groups for a little while, and you will certainly be dazzled by the contributions of the Python developer, Tim Peters (and by a number of other Pythonistas). His "Zen of Python" captures much of the reason that I choose

Python as the language in which to solve most programming tasks that are presented to me. But to understand what is most special about *text processing* as a programming task, it is worth turning to Perl creator Larry Wall's cardinal virtues of programming: laziness, impatience, hubris.

What sets text processing most clearly apart from other tasks computer programmers accomplish is the frequency with which we perform text processing on an ad hoc or "one-shot" basis. One rarely bothers to create a one-shot GUI interface for a program. You even less frequently perform a one-shot normalization of a relational database. But every programmer with a little experience has had numerous occasions where she has received a trickle of textual information (or maybe a deluge of it) from another department, from a client, from a developer working on a different project, or from data dumped out of a DBMS; the problem in such cases is always to "process" the text so that it is usable for your own project, program, database, or work unit. Text processing to the rescue. This is where the virtue of impatience first appears—we just want the stuff processed, right now!

But text processing tasks that were obviously one-shot tasks that we knew we would never need again have a habit of coming back like restless ghosts. It turns out that that client needs to update the one-time data they sent last month. Or the boss decides that she would really like a feature of that text summarized in a slightly different way. The virtue of laziness is our friend here—with our foresight not to actually delete those one-shot scripts, we have them available for easy reuse and/or modification when the need arises.

Enough is not enough, however. That script you reluctantly used a second time turns out to be quite similar to a more general task you will need to perform frequently, perhaps even automatically. You imagine that with only a slight amount of extra work you can generalize and expand the script, maybe add a little error checking and some runtime options while you are at it; and do it all in time and under budget (or even as a side project, off the budget). Obviously, this is the voice of that greatest of programmers' virtues: hubris.

The goal of this book is to make its readers a little lazier, a smidgeon more impatient, and a whole bunch more hubristic. Python just happens to be the language best suited to the study of virtue.

0.3   What You'll Need to Use This Book

This book is ideally suited for programmers who are a little bit familiar with Python, and whose daily tasks involve a fair amount of text processing chores. Programmers who have some background in other programming languages—especially with other "scripting" languages—should be able to pick up enough Python to get going by reading Appendix A.

While Python is a rather simple language at heart, this book is not intended as a tutorial on Python for nonprogrammers. Instead, this book is about two other things: getting the job done, pragmatically and efficiently; and understanding why what works works and what doesn't work doesn't work, theoretically and conceptually. As such, we hope this book can be useful both to working programmers and to students of programming at a level just past the introductory.

Many sections of this book are accompanied by problems and exercises, and these in turn often pose questions for users. In most cases, the answers to the listed questions are somewhat open-ended—there are no simple right answers. I believe that working through the provided questions will help both self-directed and instructor-guided learners; the questions can typically be answered at several levels and often have an underlying subtlety. Instructors who wish to use this text are encouraged to contact the author for assistance in structuring a curriculum involving it. All readers are encouraged to consult the book's Web site to see possible answers provided by both the author and other readers; additional related questions will be added to the Web site over time, along with other resources.

The Python language itself is conservative. Almost every Python script written ten years ago for Python 1.0 will run fine in Python 2.3+. However, as versions improve, a certain number of new features have been added. The most significant changes have matched the version number changes—Python 2.0 introduced list comprehensions, augmented assignments, Unicode support, and a standard XML package. Many scripts written in the most natural and efficient manner using Python 2.0+ will not run without changes in earlier versions of Python.

The general target of this book will be users of Python 2.1+, but some 2.2+ specific features will be utilized in examples. Maybe half the examples in this book will run fine on Python 1.5.1+ (and slightly fewer on older versions), but examples will not necessarily indicate their requirement for Python 2.0+ (where it exists). On the other hand, new features introduced with Python 2.1 and above will only be utilized where they make a task significantly easier, or where the feature itself is being illustrated. In any case, examples requiring versions past Python 2.0 will usually indicate this explicitly.

In the case of modules and packages—whether in the standard library or third-party— we will explicitly indicate what Python version is required and, where relevant, which version added the module or package to the standard library. In some cases, it will be possible to use later standard library modules with earlier Python versions. In important cases, this possibility will be noted.

0.4   Conventions Used in This Book

Several typographic conventions are used in main text to guide the readers eye. Both block and inline literals are presented in a fixed font, including names of utilities, URLs, variable names, and code samples. Names of objects in the standard library, however, are presented in italics. Names of modules and packages are printed in a sans serif typeface. Heading come in several different fonts, depending on their level and purpose.

All constants, functions, and classes in discussions and cross-references will be explicitly prepended with their namespace (module). Methods will additionally be prepended with their class. In some cases, code examples will use the local namespace, but a preference for explicit namespace identification will be present in sample code also. For example, a reference might read:

SEE ALSO: email.Generator.DecodedGenerator.flatten() *351*; raw_input() *446*; tempfile.mktemp() *71*;

The first is a class method in the *email.Generator* module; the second, a built-in function; the last, a function in the *tempfile* module.

In the special case of built-in methods on types, the expression for an empty type object will be used in the style of a namespace modifier. For example:

Methods of built-in types include *[].sort()*, *"".islower()*, *{}.keys()*, and *(lambda:1).func_code*.

The file object type will be indicated by the name `FILE` in capitals. A reference to a file object method will appear as, for example:

SEE ALSO: FILE.flush() *16*;

Brief inline illustrations of Python concepts and usage will be taken from the Python interactive shell. This approach allows readers to see the immediate evaluation of constructs, much as they might explore Python themselves. Moreover, examples presented in this manner will be self-sufficient (not requiring external data), and may be entered—with variations—by readers trying to get a grasp on a concept. For example:

```
>>> 13/7  # integer division
1
>>> 13/7. # float division
1.8571428571428572
```

In documentation of module functions, where named arguments are available, they are listed with their default value. Optional arguments are listed in square brackets. These conventions are also used in the *Python Library Reference*. For example:

foobar.spam(s, val=23 [,taste="spicy"])

The function *foobar.spam()* uses the argument s to ...

If a named argument does not have a specifiable default value, the argument is listed followed by an equal sign and ellipsis. For example:

foobar.baz(string=..., maxlen=...)

The *foobar.baz()* function ...

With the introduction of Unicode support to Python, an equivalence between a character and a byte no longer holds in all cases. Where an operation takes a numeric argument affecting a string-like object, the documentation will specify whether characters or bytes are being counted. For example:

Operation A reads `num` bytes from the buffer. Operation B reads `num` characters from the buffer.

The first operation indicates a number of actual 8-bit bytes affected. The second operation indicates an indefinite number of bytes are affected, but that they compose a number of (maybe multibyte) characters.

0.5   A Word on Source Code Examples

First things first. All the source code in this book is hereby released to the public domain. You can use it however you like, without restriction. You can include it in free software, or in commercial/proprietary projects. Change it to your heart's content, and in any manner you want. If you feel like giving credit to the author (or sending him large checks) for code you find useful, that is fine—but no obligation to do so exists.

All the source code in this book, and various other public domain examples, can be found at the book's Web site. If such an electronic form is more convenient for you, we hope this helps you. In fact, if you are able, you might benefit from visiting this location, where you might find updated versions of examples or other useful utilities not mentioned in the book.

First things out of the way, let us turn to second things. Little of the source code in this book is intended as a final say on how to perform a given task. Many of the examples are easy enough to copy directly into your own program, or to use as stand-alone utilities. But the real goal in presenting the examples is educational. We really hope you will *think* about what the examples do, and why they do it the way they do. In fact, we hope readers will think of better, faster, and more general ways of performing the same tasks. If the examples work their best, they should be better as inspirations than as instructions.

0.6   External Resources

0.6.1   General Resources

A good clearinghouse for resources and links related to this book is the book's Web site. Over time, I will add errata and additional examples, questions, answers, utilities, and so on to the site, so check it from time to time:

<http://gnosis.cx/TPiP/>

The first place you should probably turn for *any* question on Python programming (after this book), is:

<http://www.python.org/>

The Python newsgroup <comp.lang.python> is an amazingly useful resource, with discussion that is generally both friendly and erudite. You may also post to and follow the newsgroup via a mirrored mailing list:

<http://mail.python.org/mailman/listinfo/python-list>

0.6.2   Books

This book generally aims at an intermediate reader. Other Python books are better introductory texts (especially for those fairly new to programming generally). Some good introductory texts are:

> *Core Python Programming*, Wesley J. Chun, Prentice Hall, 2001. ISBN: 0-130-26036-3.

> *Learning Python*, Mark Lutz & David Ascher, O'Reilly, 1999. ISBN: 1-56592-464-9.

> *The Quick Python Book*, Daryl Harms & Kenneth McDonald, Manning, 2000. ISBN: 1-884777-74-0.

As introductions, I would generally recommend these books in the order listed, but learning styles vary between readers.

Two texts that overlap this book somewhat, but focus more narrowly on referencing the standard library, are:

> *Python Essential Reference, Second Edition*, David M. Beazley, New Riders, 2001. ISBN: 0-7357-1091-0.

> *Python Standard Library*, Fredrik Lundh, O'Reilly, 2001. ISBN: 0-596-00096-0.

For coverage of XML, at a far more detailed level than this book has room for, is the excellent text:

> *Python & XML*, Christopher A. Jones & Fred L. Drake, Jr., O'Reilly, 2002. ISBN: 0-596-00128-2.

0.6.3   Software Directories

Currently, the best Python-specific directory for software is the Vaults of Parnassus:

> `<http://www.vex.net/parnassus/>`

SourceForge is a general open source software resource. Many projects—Python and otherwise—are hosted at that site, and the site provides search capabilities, keywords, category browsing, and the like:

> `<http://sourceforge.net/>`

Freshmeat is another widely used directory of software projects (mostly open source). Like the Vaults of Parnassus, Freshmeat does not directly host project files, but simply acts as an information clearinghouse for finding relevant projects:

> `<http://freshmeat.net/>`

0.6.4   Specific Software

A number of Python projects are discussed in this book. Most of those are listed in one or more of the software directories mentioned above. A general search engine like Google, <http://google.com>, is also useful in locating project home pages. Below are a number of project URLs that are current at the time of this writing. If any of these fall out of date by the time you read this book, try searching in a search engine or software directory for an updated URL.

The author's *Gnosis Utilities* contains a number of Python packages mentioned in this book, including *gnosis.indexer*, *gnosis.xml.indexer*, *gnosis.xml.pickle*, and others. You can download the most current version from:

    <http://gnosis.cx/download/Gnosis_Utils-current.tar.gz>

eGenix.com provides a number of useful Python extensions, some of which are documented in this book. These include *mx.TextTools*, *mx.DateTime*, severeral new datatypes, and other facilities:

    <http://egenix.com/files/python/eGenix-mx-Extensions.html>

SimpleParse is hosted by SourceForge, at:

    <http://simpleparse.sourceforge.net/>

The *PLY* parsers has a home page at:

    <http://systems.cs.uchicago.edu/ply/ply.html>

ACKNOWLEDGMENTS

Portions of this book are adapted from my column *Charming Python* and other writing first published by *IBM developerWorks*, <http://ibm.com/developerWorks/>. I wish to thank IBM for publishing me, for granting permission to use this material, and most especially for maintaining such a general and useful resource for programmers.

The Python community is a wonderfully friendly place. I made drafts of this book, while in progress, available on the Internet. I received numerous helpful and kind responses, many that helped make the book better than it would otherwise have been.

In particular, the following folks made suggestions and contributions to the book while in draft form. I apologize to any correspondents I may have omitted from the list; your advice was appreciated even if momentarily lost in the bulk of my saved email.

Sam Penrose <sam@ddmweb.com>

UserDict string substitution hacks.

Roman Suzi <rnd@onego.ru>

More on string substitution hacks.

Samuel S. Chessman <chessman@tux.org>

Helpful observations of various typos.

John W. Krahn <krahnj@acm.org>

Helpful observations of various typos.

Terry J. Reedy <tjreedy@udel.edu>

Found lots of typos and made good organizational suggestions.

Amund Tveit <amund.tveit@idi.ntnu.no>

Pointers to word-based Huffman compression for Appendix B.

Pascal Oberndoerfer <oberndoerfer@mac.com>

Suggestions about focus of parser discussion.

Bob Weiner <bob@deepware.com>

Suggestions about focus of parser discussion.

Max M <maxm@mxm.dk>

Thought provocation about XML and Unicode entities.

John Machin <sjmachin@lexicon.net>

Nudging to improve sample regular expression functions.

Magnus Lie Hetland <magnus@hetland.org>

Called use of default "static" arguments "spooky code" and failed to appreciate the clarity of the <> operator.

Tim Andrews <Tim.Andrews@adpro.com.au>

Found lots of typos in Chapters 3 and 2.

Marc-Andre Lemburg <mal@lemburg.com>

Wrote *mx.TextTools* in the first place and made helpful comments on my coverage of it.

Mike C. Fletcher <mcfletch@users.sourceforge.net>

Wrote *SimpleParse* in the first place and made helpful comments on my coverage of it.

Lorenzo M. Catucci <lorenzo@sancho.ccd.uniroma2.it>

Suggested glossary entries for CRC and hash.

David LeBlanc <whisper@oz.net>

Various organizational ideas while in draft. Then he wound up acting as one of my technical reviewers and provided a huge amount of helpful advice on both content and organization.

Mike Dussault <dussault@valvesoftware.com>

Found an error in combinatorial HOFs and made good suggestions on Appendix A.

Guillermo Fernandez <guillermo.fernandez@epfl.ch>

Advice on clarifying explanations of compression techniques.

Roland Gerlach <roland@rkga.com.au>

Typos are boundless, but a bit less for his email.

Antonio Cuni <cuni@programmazione.it>

Found error in original Schwartzian sort example and another in
map()/zip() discussion.

Michele Simionato <mis6+@pitt.edu>

Acted as a nice sounding board for deciding on final organization of the
appendices.

Jesper Hertel <jh@magnus.dk>

Was frustrated that I refused to take his well-reasoned advice for code conventions.

Andrew MacIntyre <andymac@bullseye.apana.org.au>

Did not comment on this book, but has maintained the OS/2 port of Python
for several versions. This made my life easier by letting me test and write
examples on my favorite machine.

Tim Churches <tchur@optushome.com.au>

A great deal of subversive entertainment, despite not actually fixing anything
in this book.

Moshe Zadka <moshez@twistedmatrix.com>

Served as technical reviewer of this book in manuscript and brought both
erudition and an eye for detail to the job.

Sergey Konozenko <sergey_konozenko@ieee.org>

Boosted my confidence in final preparation with the enthusiasm he brought
to his technical review—and even more so with the acuity with which he
"got" my attempts to impose mental challenge on my readers.

Chapter 1

PYTHON BASICS

This chapter discusses Python capabilities that are likely to be used in text processing applications. For an introduction to Python syntax and semantics per se, readers might want to skip ahead to Appendix A (A Selective and Impressionistic Short Review of Python); Guido van Rossum's *Python Tutorial* at `<http://python.org/doc/current/tut/tut.html>` is also quite excellent. The focus here occupies a somewhat higher level: not the Python language narrowly, but also not yet specific to text processing.

In Section 1.1, I look at some programming techniques that flow out of the Python language itself, but that are usually not obvious to Python beginners—and are sometimes not obvious even to intermediate Python programmers. The programming techniques that are discussed are ones that tend to be applicable to text processing contexts—other programming tasks are likely to have their own tricks and idioms that are not explicitly documented in this book.

In Section 1.2, I document modules in the Python standard library that you will probably use in your text processing application, or at the very least want to keep in the back of your mind. A number of other Python standard library modules are far enough afield of text processing that you are unlikely to use them in this type of application. Such remaining modules are documented very briefly with one- or two-line descriptions. More details on each module can be found with Python's standard documentation.

1.1 Techniques and Patterns

1.1.1 Utilizing Higher-Order Functions in Text Processing

This first topic merits a warning. It jumps feet-first into higher-order functions (HOFs) at a fairly sophisticated level and may be unfamiliar even to experienced Python programmers. Do not be too frightened by this first topic—you can understand the rest of the book without it. If the functional programming (FP) concepts in this topic seem unfamiliar to you, I recommend you jump ahead to Appendix A, especially its final section on FP concepts.

In text processing, one frequently acts upon a series of chunks of text that are, in a sense, homogeneous. Most often, these chunks are lines, delimited by newline characters—but sometimes other sorts of fields and blocks are relevant. Moreover, Python has standard functions and syntax for reading in lines from a file (sensitive to platform differences). Obviously, these chunks are not entirely homogeneous—they can contain varying data. But at the level we worry about during processing, each chunk contains a natural parcel of instruction or information.

As an example, consider an imperative style code fragment that selects only those lines of text that match a criterion `isCond()`:

```
selected = []                    # temp list to hold matches
fp = open(filename):
for line in fp.readlines():      # Py2.2 -> "for line in fp:"
    if isCond(line):             # (2.2 version reads lazily)
        selected.append(line)
del line                         # Cleanup transient variable
```

There is nothing *wrong* with these few lines (see *xreadlines* on efficiency issues). But it does take a few seconds to read through them. In my opinion, even this small block of lines does not parse as a *single thought*, even though its operation really is such. Also the variable `line` is slightly superfluous (and it retains a value as a side effect after the loop and also could conceivably step on a previously defined value). In FP style, we could write the simpler:

```
selected = filter(isCond, open(filename).readlines())
# Py2.2 -> filter(isCond, open(filename))
```

In the concrete, a textual source that one frequently wants to process as a list of lines is a log file. All sorts of applications produce log files, most typically either ones that cause system changes that might need to be examined or long-running applications that perform actions intermittently. For example, the PythonLabs Windows installer for Python 2.2 produces a file called `INSTALL.LOG` that contains a list of actions taken during the install. Below is a highly abridged copy of this file from one of my computers:

INSTALL.LOG sample data file

```
Title: Python 2.2
Source: C:\DOWNLOAD\PYTHON-2.2.EXE | 02-23-2002 | 01:40:54 | 7074248
Made Dir: D:\Python22
File Copy: D:\Python22\UNWISE.EXE | 05-24-2001 | 12:59:30 | | ...
RegDB Key: Software\Microsoft\Windows\CurrentVersion\Uninstall\Py...
RegDB Val: Python 2.2
File Copy: D:\Python22\w9xpopen.exe | 12-21-2001 | 12:22:34 | | ...
Made Dir: D:\PYTHON22\DLLs
File Overwrite: C:\WINDOWS\SYSTEM\MSVCRT.DLL | | | | | 295000 | 770c8856
```

```
RegDB Root: 2
RegDB Key: Software\Microsoft\Windows\CurrentVersion\App Paths\Py...
RegDB Val: D:\PYTHON22\Python.exe
Shell Link: C:\WINDOWS\Start Menu\Programs\Python 2.2\Uninstall Py...
Link Info: D:\Python22\UNWISE.EXE | D:\PYTHON22 | | 0 | 1 | 0 |
Shell Link: C:\WINDOWS\Start Menu\Programs\Python 2.2\Python ...
Link Info: D:\Python22\python.exe | D:\PYTHON22 | D:\PYTHON22\...
```

You can see that each action recorded belongs to one of several types. A processing application would presumably handle each type of action differently (especially since each action has different data fields associated with it). It is easy enough to write Boolean functions that identify line types, for example:

```
def isFileCopy(line):
    return line[:10]=='File Copy:' # or line.startswith(...)
def isFileOverwrite(line):
    return line[:15]=='File Overwrite:'
```

The string method *"".startswith()* is less error prone than an initial slice for recent Python versions, but these examples are compatible with Python 1.5. In a slightly more compact functional programming style, you can also write these like:

```
isRegDBRoot = lambda line: line[:11]=='RegDB Root:'
isRegDBKey = lambda line: line[:10]=='RegDB Key:'
isRegDBVal = lambda line: line[:10]=='RegDB Val:'
```

Selecting lines of a certain type is done exactly as above:

```
lines = open(r'd:\python22\install.log').readlines()
regroot_lines = filter(isRegDBRoot, lines)
```

But if you want to select upon multiple criteria, an FP style can initially become cumbersome. For example, suppose you are interested in all the "RegDB" lines; you could write a new custom function for this filter:

```
def isAnyRegDB(line):
    if    line[:11]=='RegDB Root:': return 1
    elif line[:10]=='RegDB Key:':  return 1
    elif line[:10]=='RegDB Val:':  return 1
    else:                          return 0
# For recent Pythons, line.startswith(...) is better
```

Programming a custom function for each combined condition can produce a glut of named functions. More importantly, each such custom function requires a modicum of work to write and has a nonzero chance of introducing a bug. For conditions that should be jointly satisfied, you can either write custom functions or nest several filters within each other. For example:

```
shortline = lambda line: len(line) < 25
short_regvals = filter(shortline, filter(isRegDBVal, lines))
```

In this example, we rely on previously defined functions for the filter. Any error in the filters will be in either `shortline()` or `isRegDBVal()`, but not independently in some third function `isShortRegVal()`. Such nested filters, however, are difficult to read—especially if more than two are involved.

Calls to *map()* are sometimes similarly nested if several operations are to be performed on the same string. For a fairly trivial example, suppose you wished to reverse, capitalize, and normalize whitespace in lines of text. Creating the support functions is straightforward, and they could be nested in *map()* calls:

```
from string import upper, join, split
def flip(s):
    a = list(s)
    a.reverse()
    return join(a,'')
normalize = lambda s: join(split(s),' ')
cap_flip_norms = map(upper, map(flip, map(normalize, lines)))
```

This type of *map()* or *filter()* nest is difficult to read, and should be avoided. Moreover, one can sometimes be drawn into nesting alternating *map()* and *filter()* calls, making matters still worse. For example, suppose you want to perform several operations on each of the lines that meet several criteria. To avoid this trap, many programmers fall back to a more verbose imperative coding style that simply wraps the lists in a few loops and creates some temporary variables for intermediate results.

Within a functional programming style, it is nonetheless possible to avoid the pitfall of excessive call nesting. The key to doing this is an intelligent selection of a few combinatorial *higher-order functions*. In general, a higher-order function is one that takes as argument or returns as result a function object. First-order functions just take some data as arguments and produce a datum as an answer (perhaps a data-structure like a list or dictionary). In contrast, the "inputs" and "outputs" of a HOF are more function objects—ones generally intended to be eventually called somewhere later in the program flow.

One example of a higher-order function is a *function factory*: a function (or class) that returns a function, or collection of functions, that are somehow "configured" at the time of their creation. The "Hello World" of function factories is an "adder" factory. Like "Hello World," an adder factory exists just to show what can be done; it doesn't really *do* anything useful by itself. Pretty much every explanation of function factories uses an example such as:

```
>>> def adder_factory(n):
...     return lambda m, n=n: m+n
...
```

```
>>> add10 = adder_factory(10)
>>> add10
<function <lambda> at 0x00FB0020>
>>> add10(4)
14
>>> add10(20)
30
>>> add5 = adder_factory(5)
>>> add5(4)
9
```

For text processing tasks, simple function factories are of less interest than are *combinatorial* HOFs. The idea of a combinatorial higher-order function is to take several (usually first-order) functions as arguments and return a new function that somehow synthesizes the operations of the argument functions. Below is a simple library of combinatorial higher-order functions that achieve surprisingly much in a small number of lines:

combinatorial.py

```
from operator import mul, add, truth
apply_each = lambda fns, args=[]: map(apply, fns, [args]*len(fns))
bools = lambda lst: map(truth, lst)
bool_each = lambda fns, args=[]: bools(apply_each(fns, args))
conjoin = lambda fns, args=[]: reduce(mul, bool_each(fns, args))
all = lambda fns: lambda arg, fns=fns: conjoin(fns, (arg,))
both = lambda f,g: all((f,g))
all3 = lambda f,g,h: all((f,g,h))
and_ = lambda f,g: lambda x, f=f, g=g: f(x) and g(x)
disjoin = lambda fns, args=[]: reduce(add, bool_each(fns, args))
some = lambda fns: lambda arg, fns=fns: disjoin(fns, (arg,))
either = lambda f,g: some((f,g))
anyof3 = lambda f,g,h: some((f,g,h))
compose = lambda f,g: lambda x, f=f, g=g: f(g(x))
compose3 = lambda f,g,h: lambda x, f=f, g=g, h=h: f(g(h(x)))
ident = lambda x: x
```

Even with just over a dozen lines, many of these combinatorial functions are merely convenience functions that wrap other more general ones. Let us take a look at how we can use these HOFs to simplify some of the earlier examples. The same names are used for results, so look above for comparisons:

> Some examples using higher-order functions

```
# Don't nest filters, just produce func that does both
short_regvals = filter(both(shortline, isRegVal), lines)

# Don't multiply ad hoc functions, just describe need
regroot_lines = \
    filter(some([isRegDBRoot, isRegDBKey, isRegDBVal]), lines)

# Don't nest transformations, make one combined transform
capFlipNorm = compose3(upper, flip, normalize)
cap_flip_norms = map(capFlipNorm, lines)
```

In the example, we bind the composed function `capFlipNorm` for readability. The corresponding *map()* line expresses just the *single thought* of applying a common operation to all the lines. But the binding also illustrates some of the flexibility of combinatorial functions. By condensing the several operations previously nested in several *map()* calls, we can save the combined operation for reuse elsewhere in the program.

As a rule of thumb, I recommend not using more than one *filter()* and one *map()* in any given line of code. If these "list application" functions need to nest more deeply than this, readability is preserved by saving results to intermediate names. Successive lines of such functional programming style calls themselves revert to a more imperative style—but a wonderful thing about Python is the degree to which it allows seamless combinations of different programming styles. For example:

```
intermed = filter(niceProperty, map(someTransform, lines))
final = map(otherTransform, intermed)
```

Any nesting of successive *filter()* or *map()* calls, however, can be reduced to single functions using the proper combinatorial HOFs. Therefore, the number of procedural steps needed is pretty much always quite small. However, the reduction in total lines-of-code is offset by the lines used for giving names to combinatorial functions. Overall, FP style code is usually about one-half the length of imperative style equivalents (fewer lines generally mean correspondingly fewer bugs).

A nice feature of combinatorial functions is that they can provide a complete Boolean algebra for functions that have not been called yet (the use of *operator.add* and *operator.mul* in `combinatorial.py` is more than accidental, in that sense). For example, with a collection of simple values, you might express a (complex) relation of multiple truth values as:

```
satisfied = (this or that) and (foo or bar)
```

In the case of text processing on chunks of text, these truth values are often the results of predicative functions applied to a chunk:

```
satisfied = (thisP(s) or thatP(s)) and (fooP(s) or barP(s))
```

In an expression like the above one, several predicative functions are applied to the same string (or other object), and a set of logical relations on the results are evaluated. But this expression is itself a logical predicate of the string. For naming clarity—and especially if you wish to evaluate the same predicate more than once—it is convenient to create an actual function expressing the predicate:

```
satisfiedP = both(either(thisP,thatP), either(fooP,barP))
```

Using a predicative function created with combinatorial techniques is the same as using any other function:

```
selected = filter(satisfiedP, lines)
```

1.1.2 Exercise: More on combinatorial functions

The module combinatorial.py presented above provides some of the most commonly useful combinatorial higher-order functions. But there is room for enhancement in the brief example. Creating a personal or organization library of useful HOFs is a way to improve the reusability of your current text processing libraries.

QUESTIONS

1. Some of the functions defined in combinatorial.py are not, strictly speaking, combinatorial. In a precise sense, a combinatorial function should take one or several functions as arguments and return one or more function objects that "combine" the input arguments. Identify which functions are not "strictly" combinatorial, and determine exactly what type of thing each one *does* return.

2. The functions both() and and_() do almost the same thing. But they differ in an important, albeit subtle, way. and_(), like the Python operator *and*, uses *shortcutting* in its evaluation. Consider these lines:

```
>>> f = lambda n: n**2 > 10
>>> g = lambda n: 100/n > 10
>>> and_(f,g)(5)
1
>>> both(f,g)(5)
1
>>> and_(f,g)(0)
0
>>> both(f,g)(0)
Traceback (most recent call last):
...
```

The shortcutting and_() can potentially allow the first function to act as a "guard" for the second one. The second function never gets called if the first function returns a false value on a given argument

a. Create a similarly shortcutting combinatorial or_() function for your library.

b. Create general shortcutting functions shortcut_all() and shortcut_some() that behave similarly to the functions all() and some(), respectively.

c. Describe some situations where nonshortcutting combinatorial functions like both(), all(), or anyof3() are more desirable than similar shortcutting functions.

3. The function ident() would appear to be pointless, since it simply returns whatever value is passed to it. In truth, ident() is an almost indispensable function for a combinatorial collection. Explain the significance of ident().

Hint: Suppose you have a list of lines of text, where some of the lines may be empty strings. What filter can you apply to find all the lines that start with a #?

4. The function not_() might make a nice addition to a combinatorial library. We could define this function as:

```
>>> not_ = lambda f: lambda x, f=f: not f(x)
```

Explore some situations where a not_() function would aid combinatoric programming.

5. The function apply_each() is used in combinatorial.py to build some other functions. But the utility of apply_each() is more general than its supporting role might suggest. A trivial usage of apply_each() might look something like:

```
>>> apply_each(map(adder_factory, range(5)),(10,))
[10, 11, 12, 13, 14]
```

Explore some situations where apply_each() simplifies applying multiple operations to a chunk of text.

6. Unlike the functions all() and some(), the functions compose() and compose3() take a fixed number of input functions as arguments. Create a generalized composition function that takes a list of input functions, of any length, as an argument.

7. What other combinatorial higher-order functions that have not been discussed here are likely to prove useful in text processing? Consider other ways of combining first-order functions into useful operations, and add these to your library. What are good names for these enhanced HOFs?

1.1.3   Specializing Python Datatypes

Python comes with an excellent collection of standard datatypes—Appendix A discusses each built-in type. At the same time, an important principle of Python programming makes types less important than programmers coming from other languages tend to expect. According to Python's "principle of pervasive polymorphism" (my own coinage), it is more important what an object *does* than what it *is*. Another common way of putting the principle is: if it walks like a duck and quacks like a duck, treat it like a duck.

Broadly, the idea behind polymorphism is letting the same function or operator work on things of different types. In C++ or Java, for example, you might use signature-based method overloading to let an operation apply to several types of things (acting differently as needed). For example:

C++ signature-based polymorphism

```
#include <stdio.h>
class Print {
public:
  void print(int i)    { printf("int %d\n", i); }
  void print(double d) { printf("double %f\n", d); }
  void print(float f)  { printf("float %f\n", f); }
};
main() {
  Print *p = new Print();
  p->print(37);        /* --> "int 37" */
  p->print(37.0);      /* --> "double 37.000000" */
}
```

The most direct Python translation of signature-based overloading is a function that performs type checks on its argument(s). It is simple to write such functions:

Python "signature-based" polymorphism

```
def Print(x):
    from types import *
    if type(x) is FloatType:  print "float", x
    elif type(x) is IntType:  print "int", x
    elif type(x) is LongType: print "long", x
```

Writing signature-based functions, however, is extremely un-Pythonic. If you find yourself performing these sorts of explicit type checks, you have probably not understood the problem you want to solve correctly! What you *should* (usually) be interested in is not what type x is, but rather whether x can perform the action you need it to perform (regardless of what type of thing it is strictly).

PYTHONIC POLYMORPHISM

Probably the single most common case where pervasive polymorphism is useful is in identifying "file-like" objects. There are many objects that can do things that files can do, such as those created with *urllib*, *cStringIO*, *zipfile*, and by other means. Various objects can perform only subsets of what actual files can: some can read, others can write, still others can seek, and so on. But for many purposes, you have no need to exercise every "file-like" capability—it is good enough to make sure that a specified object has those capabilities you actually need.

Here is a typical example. I have a module that uses DOM to work with XML documents; I would like users to be able to specify an XML source in any of several ways: using the name of an XML file, passing a file-like object that contains XML, or indicating an already-built DOM object to work with (built with any of several XML libraries). Moreover, future users of my module may get their XML from novel places I have not even thought of (an RDBMS, over sockets, etc.). By looking at what a candidate object can *do*, I can just utilize whichever capabilities that object *has*:

Python capability-based polymorphism

```
def toDOM(xml_src=None):
    from xml.dom import minidom
    if hasattr(xml_src, 'documentElement'):
        return xml_src    # it is already a DOM object
    elif hasattr(xml_src,'read'):
        # it is something that knows how to read data
        return minidom.parseString(xml_src.read())
    elif type(xml_src) in (StringType, UnicodeType):
        # it is a filename of an XML document
        xml = open(xml_src).read()
        return minidom.parseString(xml)
    else:
        raise ValueError, "Must be initialized with " +\
                "filename, file-like object, or DOM object"
```

Even simple-seeming numeric types have varying capabilities. As with other objects, you should not usually care about the internal representation of an object, but rather about what it can do. Of course, as one way to assure that an object has a capability, it is often appropriate to coerce it to a type using the built-in functions *complex()*, *dict()*, *float()*, *int()*, *list()*, *long()*, *str()*, *tuple()*, and *unicode()*. All of these functions make a good effort to transform anything that looks a little bit like the type of thing they name into a true instance of it. It is usually not necessary, however, actually to transform values to prescribed types; again we can just check capabilities.

For example, suppose that you want to remove the "least significant" portion of any number—perhaps because they represent measurements of limited accuracy. For whole numbers—ints or longs—you might mask out some low-order bits; for fractional values you might round to a given precision. Rather than testing value types explicitly, you can look for numeric capabilities. One common way to test a capability in Python is to *try* to do something, and catch any exceptions that occur (then try something else). Below is a simple example:

Checking what numbers can do

```
def approx(x):                      # int attributes require 2.2+
    if hasattr(x,'__and__'):        # supports bitwise-and
        return x & ~0x0FL
    try:                            # supports real/imag
        return (round(x.real,2)+round(x.imag,2)*1j)
    except AttributeError:
        return round(x,2)
```

ENHANCED OBJECTS

The reason that the principle of pervasive polymorphism matters is because Python makes it easy to create new objects that behave mostly—but not exactly—like basic datatypes. File-like objects were already mentioned as examples; you may or may not think of a file object as a datatype precisely. But even basic datatypes like numbers, strings, lists, and dictionaries can be easily specialized and/or emulated.

There are two details to pay attention to when emulating basic datatypes. The most important matter to understand is that the capabilities of an object—even those utilized with syntactic constructs—are generally implemented by its "magic" methods, each named with leading and trailing double underscores. Any object that has the right magic methods can act like a basic datatype in those contexts that use the supplied methods. At heart, a basic datatype is just an object with some well-optimized versions of the right collection of magic methods.

The second detail concerns exactly how you get at the magic methods—or rather, how best to make use of existing implementations. There is nothing stopping you from writing your own version of any basic datatype, except for the piddling details of doing so. However, there are quite a few such details, and the easiest way to get the functionality you want is to specialize an existing class. Under all non-ancient versions of Python, the standard library provides the pure-Python modules *UserDict*, *UserList*, and *UserString* as starting points for custom datatypes. You can inherit from an appropriate parent class and specialize (magic) methods as needed. No sample parents are provided for tuples, ints, floats, and the rest, however.

Under Python 2.2 and above, a better option is available. "New-style" Python classes let you inherit from the underlying C implementations of all the Python basic datatypes. Moreover, these parent classes have become the self-same callable objects that are used to coerce types and construct objects: *int()*, *list()*, *unicode()*, and so on. There is a lot of arcana and subtle profundities that accompany new-style classes, but you generally do not need to worry about these. All you need to know is that a class that inherits from *string* is faster than one that inherits from *UserString*; likewise for *list* versus *UserList* and *dict* versus *UserDict* (assuming your scripts all run on a recent enough version of Python).

Custom datatypes, however, need not specialize full-fledged implementations. You are free to create classes that implement "just enough" of the interface of a basic datatype to be used for a given purpose. Of course, in practice, the reason you would create such custom datatypes is either because you want them to contain non-magic methods of their own or because you want them to implement the magic methods associated with multiple basic datatypes. For example, below is a custom datatype that can be passed to the prior `approx()` function, and that also provides a (slightly) useful custom method:

```
>>> class I:  # "Fuzzy" integer datatype
...       def __init__(self, i):  self.i = i
...       def __and__(self, i):    return self.i & i
...       def err_range(self):
...           lbound = approx(self.i)
...           return "Value: [%d, %d)" % (lbound, lbound+0x0F)
...
>>> i1, i2 = I(29), I(20)
>>> approx(i1), approx(i2)
(16L, 16L)
>>> i2.err_range()
'Value: [16, 31)'
```

Despite supporting an extra method and being able to get passed into the `approx()` function, I is not a very versatile datatype. If you try to add, or divide, or multiply using "fuzzy integers," you will raise a `TypeError`. Since there is no module called *UserInt*, under an older Python version you would need to implement every needed magic method yourself.

Using new-style classes in Python 2.2+, you could derive a "fuzzy integer" from the underlying `int` datatype. A partial implementation could look like:

```
>>> class I2(int):    # New-style fuzzy integer
...       def __add__(self, j):
...           vals = map(int, [approx(self), approx(j)])
...           k = int.__add__(*vals)
...           return I2(int.__add__(k, 0x0F))
...       def err_range(self):
...           lbound = approx(self)
...           return "Value: [%d, %d)" %(lbound,lbound+0x0F)
...
>>> i1, i2 = I2(29), I2(20)
>>> print "i1 =", i1.err_range(),": i2 =", i2.err_range()
i1 = Value: [16, 31) : i2 = Value: [16, 31)
>>> i3 = i1 + i2
>>> print i3, type(i3)
47 <class '__main__.I2'>
```

Since the new-style class `int` already supports bitwise-and, there is no need to implement it again. With new-style classes, you refer to data values directly with `self`, rather than as an attribute that holds the data (e.g., `self.i` in class I). As well, it is generally unsafe to use syntactic operators within magic methods that define their operation; for example, I utilize the .__add__() method of the parent int rather than the + operator in the I2.__add__() method.

In practice, you are less likely to want to create number-like datatypes than you are to emulate container types. But it is worth understanding just how and why even plain integers are a fuzzy concept in Python (the fuzziness of the concepts is of a different sort than the fuzziness of I2 integers, though). Even a function that operates on whole numbers need not operate on objects of IntType or LongType—just on an object that satisfies the desired protocols.

1.1.4   Base Classes for Datatypes

There are several magic methods that are often useful to define for *any* custom datatype. In fact, these methods are useful even for classes that do not really define datatypes (in some sense, every object is a datatype since it can contain attribute values, but not every object supports special syntax such as arithmetic operators and indexing). Not quite every magic method that you can define is documented in this book, but most are under the parent datatype each is most relevant to. Moreover, each new version of Python has introduced a few additional magic methods; those covered either have been around for a few versions or are particularly important.

In documenting class methods of base classes, the same general conventions are used as for documenting module functions. The one special convention for these base class methods is the use of self as the first argument to all methods. Since the name self is purely arbitrary, this convention is less special than it might appear. For example, both of the following uses of self are equally legal:

```
>>> import string
>>> self = 'spam'
>>> object.__repr__(self)
'<str object at 0x12c0a0>'
>>> string.upper(self)
'SPAM'
```

However, there is usually little reason to use class methods in place of perfectly good built-in and module functions with the same purpose. Normally, these methods of datatype classes are used only in child classes that override the base classes, as in:

```
>>> class UpperObject(object):
...         def __repr__(self):
...                 return object.__repr__(self).upper()
...
>>> uo = UpperObject()
>>> print uo
<__MAIN__.UPPEROBJECT OBJECT AT 0X1C2C6C>
```

---

object ◇ Ancestor class for new-style datatypes

Under Python 2.2+, `object` has become a base for new-style classes. Inheriting from `object` enables a custom class to use a few new capabilities, such as slots and properties. But usually if you are interested in creating a custom datatype, it is better to inherit from a child of `object`, such as `list`, `float`, or `dict`.

METHODS

object.__eq__(self, other)

Return a Boolean comparison between `self` and `other`. Determines how a datatype responds to the `==` operator. The parent class `object` does not implement `.__eq__()` since by default object equality means the same thing as identity (the `is` operator). A child is free to implement this in order to affect comparisons.

object.__ne__(self, other)

Return a Boolean comparison between `self` and `other`. Determines how a datatype responds to the `!=` and `<>` operators. The parent class `object` does not implement `.__ne__()` since by default object inequality means the same thing as nonidentity (the `is not` operator). Although it might seem that equality and inequality always return opposite values, the methods are not explicitly defined in terms of each other. You could force the relationship with:

```
>>> class EQ(object):
...     # Abstract parent class for equality classes
...     def __eq__(self, o): return not self <> o
...     def __ne__(self, o): return not self == o
...
>>> class Comparable(EQ):
...     # By def'ing inequlty, get equlty (or vice versa)
...     def __ne__(self, other):
...         return someComplexComparison(self, other)
```

object.__nonzero__(self)

Return a Boolean value for an object. Determines how a datatype responds to the Boolean comparisons `or`, `and`, and `not`, and to `if` and `filter(None,...)` tests. An object whose `.__nonzero__()` method returns a true value is itself treated as a true value.

object.__len__(self)
len(object)

Return an integer representing the "length" of the object. For collection types, this is fairly straightforward—how many objects are in the collection? Custom types may change the behavior to some other meaningful value.

object.__repr__(self)
repr(object)
object.__str__(self)
str(object)

Return a string representation of the object `self`. Determines how a datatype responds to the *repr()* and *str()* built-in functions, to the `print` keyword, and to the back-tick operator.

Where feasible, it is desirable to have the `.__repr__()` method return a representation with sufficient information in it to reconstruct an identical object. The goal here is to fulfill the equality `obj==eval(repr(obj))`. In many cases, however, you cannot encode sufficient information in a string, and the `repr()` of an object is either identical to, or slightly more detailed than, the `str()` representation of the same object.

SEE ALSO: repr *96*; operator *47*;

---

file ◇ New-style base class for file objects

Under Python 2.2+, it is possible to create a custom file-like object by inheriting from the built-in class `file`. In older Python versions you may only create file-like objects by defining the methods that define an object as "file-like." However, even in recent versions of Python, inheritance from `file` buys you little—if the data contents come from somewhere other than a native filesystem, you will have to reimplement every method you wish to support.

Even more than for other object types, what makes an object file-like is a fuzzy concept. Depending on your purpose you may be happy with an object that can only read, or one that can only write. You may need to seek within the object, or you may be happy with a linear stream. In general, however, file-like objects are expected to read and write strings. Custom classes only need implement those methods that are meaningful to them and should only be used in contexts where their capabilities are sufficient.

In documenting the methods of file-like objects, I adopt a slightly different convention than for other built-in types. Since actually inheriting from `file` is unusual, I use the capitalized name FILE to indicate a general file-like object. Instances of the actual `file` class are examples (and implement all the methods named), but other types of objects can be equally good FILE instances.

BUILT-IN FUNCTIONS

open(fname [,mode [,buffering]])
file(fname [,mode [,buffering]])

Return a file object that attaches to the filename `fname`. The optional argument `mode` describes the capabilities and access style of the object. An `r` mode is for reading; w for writing (truncating any existing content); a for appending (writing to the end). Each of these modes may also have the binary flag b for platforms like Windows that distinguish text and binary files. The flag + may be used to allow both reading and writing. The argument buffering may be 0 for none, 1 for line-oriented, a larger integer for number of bytes.

```
>>> open('tmp','w').write('spam and eggs\n')
>>> print open('tmp','r').read(),
spam and eggs
>>> open('tmp','w').write('this and that\n')
>>> print open('tmp','r').read(),
this and that
>>> open('tmp','a').write('something else\n')
>>> print open('tmp','r').read(),
this and that
something else
```

METHODS AND ATTRIBUTES

FILE.close()

Close a file object. Reading and writing are disallowed after a file is closed.

FILE.closed

Return a Boolean value indicating whether the file has been closed.

FILE.fileno()

Return a file descriptor number for the file. File-like objects that do not attach to actual files should not implement this method.

FILE.flush()

Write any pending data to the underlying file. File-like objects that do not cache data can still implement this method as pass.

FILE.isatty()

Return a Boolean value indicating whether the file is a TTY-like device. The standard documentation says that file-like objects that do not attach to actual files should not implement this method, but implementing it to always return 0 is probably a better approach.

FILE.mode

Attribute containing the mode of the file, normally identical to the mode argument passed to the object's initializer.

FILE.name

The name of the file. For file-like objects without a filesystem name, some string identifying the object should be put into this attribute.

FILE.read([size=sys.maxint])

Return a string containing up to `size` bytes of content from the file. Stop the read if an EOF is encountered or upon another condition that makes sense for the object type. Move the file position forward immediately past the read in bytes. A negative `size` argument is treated as the default value.

FILE.readline([size=sys.maxint])

Return a string containing one line from the file, including the trailing newline, if any. A maximum of `size` bytes are read. The file position is moved forward past the read. A negative `size` argument is treated as the default value.

FILE.readlines([size=sys.maxint])

Return a list of lines from the file, each line including its trailing newline. If the argument `size` is given, limit the read to *approximately* `size` bytes worth of lines. The file position is moved forward past the read in bytes. A negative `size` argument is treated as the default value.

FILE.seek(offset [,whence=0])

Move the file position by `offset` bytes (positive or negative). The argument `whence` specifies where the initial file position is prior to the move: 0 for BOF; 1 for current position; 2 for EOF.

FILE.tell()

Return the current file position.

FILE.truncate([size=0])

Truncate the file contents (it becomes `size` length).

FILE.write(s)

Write the string `s` to the file, starting at the current file position. The file position is moved forward past the written bytes.

FILE.writelines(lines)

Write the lines in the sequence `lines` to the file. No newlines are added during the write. The file position is moved forward past the written bytes.

FILE.xreadlines()

Memory-efficient iterator over lines in a file. In Python 2.2+, you might implement this as a generator that returns one line per each `yield`.

SEE ALSO: xreadlines 72;

int ◇ New-style base class for integer objects

long ◇ New-style base class for long integers

In Python, there are two standard datatypes for representing integers. Objects of type `IntType` have a fixed range that depends on the underlying platform—usually between plus and minus 2**31. Objects of type `LongType` are unbounded in size. In Python 2.2+, operations on integers that exceed the range of an `int` object results in automatic promotion to `long` objects. However, no operation on a `long` will demote the result back to an `int` object (even if the result is of small magnitude)—with the exception of the *int()* function, of course.

From a user point of view ints and longs provide exactly the same interface. The difference between them is only in underlying implementation, with ints typically being significantly faster to operate on (since they use raw CPU instructions fairly directly). Most of the magic methods integers have are shared by floating point numbers as well and are discussed below. For example, consult the discussion of *float.__mul__()* for information on the corresponding *int.__mul__()* method. The special capability that integers have over floating point numbers is their ability to perform bitwise operations.

Under Python 2.2+, you may create a custom datatype that inherits from `int` or `long`; under earlier versions, you would need to manually define all the magic methods you wished to utilize (generally a lot of work, and probably not worth it).

Each binary bit operation has a left-associative and a right-associative version. If you define both versions and perform an operation on two custom objects, the left-associative version is chosen. However, if you perform an operation with a basic `int` and a custom object, the custom right-associative method will be chosen over the basic operation. For example:

```
>>> class I(int):
...     def __xor__(self, other):
...         return "XOR"
...     def __rxor__(self, other):
...         return "RXOR"
...
>>> 0xFF ^ 0xFF
0
>>> 0xFF ^ I(0xFF)
'RXOR'
>>> I(0xFF) ^ 0xFF
'XOR'
>>> I(0xFF) ^ I(0xFF)
'XOR'
```

METHODS

int.__and__(self, other)
int.__rand__(self, other)

Return a bitwise-and between `self` and `other`. Determines how a datatype responds to the `&` operator.

int.__hex__(self)

Return a hex string representing `self`. Determines how a datatype responds to the built-in *hex()* function.

int.__invert__(self)

Return a bitwise inversion of `self`. Determines how a datatype responds to the `~` operator.

int.__lshift__(self, other)
int.__rlshift__(self, other)

Return the result of bit-shifting `self` to the left by `other` bits. The right-associative version shifts `other` by `self` bits. Determines how a datatype responds to the `<<` operator.

int.__oct__(self)

Return an octal string representing `self`. Determines how a datatype responds to the built-in *oct()* function.

int.__or__(self, other)
int.__ror__(self, other)

Return a bitwise-or between `self` and `other`. Determines how a datatype responds to the `|` operator.

int.__rshift__(self, other)
int.__rrshift__(self, other)

Return the result of bit-shifting `self` to the right by `other` bits. The right-associative version shifts `other` by `self` bits. Determines how a datatype responds to the `>>` operator.

int.__xor__(self, other)
int.__rxor__(self, other)

Return a bitwise-xor between `self` and `other` Determines how a datatype responds to the `^` operator.

SEE ALSO: float *19*; int *421*; long *422*; sys.maxint *50*; operator *47*;

---

float ◇ New-style base class for floating point numbers

Python floating point numbers are mostly implemented using the underlying C floating point library of your platform; that is, to a greater or lesser degree based on the IEEE 754 standard. A complex number is just a Python object that wraps a pair of floats with a few extra operations on these pairs.

DIGRESSION

Although the details are far outside the scope of this book, a general warning is in order. Floating point math is harder than you think! If you think you *understand* just how complex IEEE 754 math is, you are not yet aware of all of the subtleties. By way of indication, Python luminary and erstwhile professor of numeric computing Alex Martelli commented in 2001 (on `<comp.lang.python>`):

> Anybody who thinks he knows what he's doing when floating point is involved IS either naive, or Tim Peters (well, it COULD be W. Kahan I guess, but I don't think he writes here).

Fellow Python guru Tim Peters observed:

> I find it's possible to be both (wink). But **nothing** about fp comes easily to anyone, and even Kahan works his butt off to come up with the amazing things that he does.

Peters illustrated further by way of Donald Knuth (*The Art of Computer Programming, Third Edition*, Addison-Wesley, 1997; ISBN: 0201896842, vol. 2, p. 229):

> Many serious mathematicians have attempted to analyze a sequence of floating point operations rigorously, but found the task so formidable that they have tried to be content with plausibility arguments instead.

The trick about floating point numbers is that although they are extremely useful for representing real-life (fractional) quantities, operations on them do not obey the arithmetic rules we learned in middle school: associativity, transitivity, commutativity; moreover, many very ordinary-seeming numbers can be represented only approximately with floating point numbers. For example:

```
>>> 1./3
0.33333333333333331
>>> .3
0.29999999999999999
>>> 7 == 7./25 * 25
0
>>> 7 == 7./24 * 24
1
```

CAPABILITIES

In the hierarchy of Python numeric types, floating point numbers are higher up the scale than integers, and complex numbers higher than floats. That is, operations on mixed types get promoted upwards. However, the magic methods that make a datatype "float-like" are strictly a subset of those associated with integers. All of the magic methods listed below for floats apply equally to ints and longs (or integer-like custom datatypes). Complex numbers support a few addition methods.

Under Python 2.2+, you may create a custom datatype that inherits from `float` or `complex`; under earlier versions, you would need to manually define all the magic methods you wished to utilize (generally a lot of work, and probably not worth it).

Each binary operation has a left-associative and a right-associative version. If you define both versions and perform an operation on two custom objects, the left-associative version is chosen. However, if you perform an operation with a basic datatype and a custom object, the custom right-associative method will be chosen over the basic operation. See the example under *int*.

METHODS

float.__abs__(self)

> Return the absolute value of `self`. Determines how a datatype responds to the built-in function *abs()*.

float.__add__(self, other)
float.__radd__(self, other)

> Return the sum of `self` and `other`. Determines how a datatype responds to the + operator.

float.__cmp__(self, other)

> Return a value indicating the order of `self` and `other`. Determines how a datatype responds to the numeric comparison operators <, >, <=, >=, ==, <>, and !=. Also determines the behavior of the built-in *cmp()* function. Should return -1 for `self<other`, 0 for `self==other`, and 1 for `self>other`. If other comparison methods are defined, they take precedence over .__cmp__(): .__ge__(), .__gt__(), .__le__(), and .__lt__().

float.__div__(self, other)
float.__rdiv__(self, other)

> Return the ratio of `self` and `other`. Determines how a datatype responds to the / operator. In Python 2.3+, this method will instead determine how a datatype responds to the floor division operator //.

float.__divmod__(self, other)
float.__rdivmod__(self, other)

> Return the pair (div, remainder). Determines how a datatype responds to the built-in *divmod()* function.

float.__floordiv__(self, other)
float.__rfloordiv__(self, other)

> Return the number of whole times `self` goes into `other`. Determines how a datatype responds to the Python 2.2+ floor division operator //.

float.__mod__(self, other)
float.__rmod__(self, other)

Return the modulo division of `self` into `other`. Determines how a datatype responds to the % operator.

float.__mul__(self, other)
float.__rmul__(self, other)

Return the product of `self` and `other`. Determines how a datatype responds to the * operator.

float.__neg__(self)

Return the negative of `self`. Determines how a datatype responds to the unary – operator.

float.__pow__(self, other)
float.__rpow__(self, other)

Return `self` raised to the `other` power. Determines how a datatype responds to the ^ operator.

float.__sub__(self, other)
float.__rsub__(self, other)

Return the difference between `self` and `other`. Determines how a datatype responds to the binary – operator.

float.__truediv__(self, other)
float.__rtruediv__(self, other)

Return the ratio of `self` and `other`. Determines how a datatype responds to the Python 2.3+ true division operator /.

SEE ALSO: complex *22*; int *18*; float *422*; operator *47*;

> **complex** ◇ **New-style base class for complex numbers**

Complex numbers implement all the above documented methods of floating point numbers, and a few additional ones.

Inequality operations on complex numbers are not supported in recent versions of Python, even though they were previously. In Python 2.1+, the methods *complex.__ge__()*, *complex.__gt__()*, *complex.__le__()*, and *complex.__lt__()* all raise `TypeError` rather than return Boolean values indicating the order. There is a certain logic to this change inasmuch as complex numbers do not have a "natural" ordering. But there is also significant breakage with this change—this is one of the few changes in Python, since version 1.4 when I started using it, that I feel was a real mistake. The important breakage comes when you want to sort a list of various things, some of which might be complex numbers:

```
>>> lst = ["string", 1.0, 1, 1L, ('t','u','p')]
>>> lst.sort()
```

```
>>> lst
[1.0, 1, 1L, 'string', ('t', 'u', 'p')]
>>> lst.append(1j)
>>> lst.sort()
Traceback (most recent call last):
  File "<stdin>", line 1, in ?
TypeError: cannot compare complex numbers using <, <=, >, >=
```

It is true that there is no obvious correct ordering between a complex number and another number (complex or otherwise), but there is also no natural ordering between a string, a tuple, and a number. Nonetheless, it is frequently useful to sort a heterogeneous list in order to create a canonical (even if meaningless) order. In Python 2.2+, you can remedy this shortcoming of recent Python versions in the style below (under 2.1 you are largely out of luck):

```
>>> class C(complex):
...     def __lt__(self, o):
...        if hasattr(o, 'imag'):
...           return (self.real,self.imag) < (o.real,o.imag)
...        else:
...           return self.real < o
...     def __le__(self, o): return self < o or self==o
...     def __gt__(self, o): return not (self==o or self < o)
...     def __ge__(self, o): return self > o or self==o
...
>>> lst = ["str", 1.0, 1, 1L, (1,2,3), C(1+1j), C(2-2j)]
>>> lst.sort()
>>> lst
[1.0, 1, 1L, (1+1j), (2-2j), 'str', (1, 2, 3)]
```

Of course, if you adopt this strategy, you have to create all of your complex values using the custom datatype C. And unfortunately, unless you override arithmetic operations also, a binary operation between a C object and another number reverts to a basic complex datatype. The reader can work out the details of this solution if she needs it.

METHODS

complex.conjugate(self)

Return the complex conjugate of self. A quick refresher here: If self is n+mj its conjugate is n-mj.

complex.imag

Imaginary component of a complex number.

complex.real

   Real component of a complex number.

SEE ALSO: float *19*; complex *422*;

> **UserDict ◇ Custom wrapper around dictionary objects**

> **dict ◇ New-style base class for dictionary objects**

Dictionaries in Python provide a well-optimized mapping between immutable objects and other Python objects (see Glossary entry on "immutable"). You may create custom datatypes that respond to various dictionary operations. There are a few syntactic operations associated with dictionaries, all involving indexing with square braces. But unlike with numeric datatypes, there are several regular methods that are reasonable to consider as part of the general interface for dictionary-like objects.

   If you create a dictionary-like datatype by subclassing from *UserDict.UserDict*, all the special methods defined by the parent are proxies to the true dictionary stored in the object's `.data` member. If, under Python 2.2+, you subclass from `dict` itself, the object itself inherits dictionary behaviors. In either case, you may customize whichever methods you wish. Below is an example of the two styles for subclassing a dictionary-like datatype:

```
>>> from sys import stderr
>>> from UserDict import UserDict
>>> class LogDictOld(UserDict):
...     def __setitem__(self, key, val):
...         stderr.write("Set: "+str(key)+"->"+str(val)+"\n")
...         self.data[key] = val
...
>>> ldo = LogDictOld()
>>> ldo['this'] = 'that'
Set: this->that
>>> class LogDictNew(dict):
...     def __setitem__(self, key, val):
...         stderr.write("Set: "+str(key)+"->"+str(val)+"\n")
...         dict.__setitem__(self, key, val)
...
>>> ldn = LogDictOld()
>>> ldn['this'] = 'that'
Set: this->that
```

METHODS

dict.__cmp__(self, other)
UserDict.UserDict.__cmp__(self, other)

Return a value indicating the order of `self` and other. Determines how a datatype responds to the numeric comparison operators `<`, `>`, `<=`, `>=`, `==`, `<>`, and `!=`. Also determines the behavior of the built-in *cmp()* function. Should return -1 for `self<other`, 0 for `self==other`, and 1 for `self>other`. If other comparison methods are defined, they take precedence over `.__cmp__()`: `.__ge__()`, `.__gt__()`, `.__le__()`, and `.__lt__()`.

dict.__contains__(self, x)
UserDict.UserDict.__contains__(self, x)

Return a Boolean value indicating whether `self` "contains" the value `x`. By default, being contained in a dictionary means matching one of its keys, but you can change this behavior by overriding it (e.g., check whether `x` is in a value rather than a key). Determines how a datatype responds to the `in` operator.

dict.__delitem__(self, x)
UserDict.UserDict.__delitem__(self, x)

Remove an item from a dictionary-like datatype. By default, removing an item means removing the pair whose key equals `x`. Determines how a datatype responds to the `del` statement, as in: `del self[x]`.

dict.__getitem__(self, x)
UserDict.UserDict.__getitem__(self, x)

By default, return the value associated with the key `x`. Determines how a datatype responds to indexing with square braces. You may override this method to either search differently or return special values. For example:

```
>>> class BagOfPairs(dict):
...     def __getitem__(self, x):
...         if self.has_key(x):
...             return (x, dict.__getitem__(self,x))
...         else:
...             tmp = dict([(v,k) for k,v in self.items()])
...             return (dict.__getitem__(tmp,x), x)
...
>>> bop = BagOfPairs({'this':'that', 'spam':'eggs'})
>>> bop['this']
('this', 'that')
>>> bop['eggs']
('spam', 'eggs')
>>> bop['bacon'] = 'sausage'
>>> bop
{'this': 'that', 'bacon': 'sausage', 'spam': 'eggs'}
>>> bop['nowhere']
Traceback (most recent call last):
  File "<stdin>", line 1, in ?
  File "<stdin>", line 7, in __getitem__
```

```
KeyError: nowhere
```

dict.__len__(self)
UserDict.UserDict.__len__(self)

Return the length of the dictionary. By default this is simply a count of the key/val pairs, but you could perform a different calculation if you wished (e.g, perhaps you would cache the size of a record set returned from a database query that emulated a dictionary). Determines how a datatype responds to the built-in *len()* function.

dict.__setitem__(self, key, val)
UserDict.UserDict.__setitem__(self, key, val)

Set the dictionary key `key` to value `val`. Determines how a datatype responds to indexed assignment; that is, `self[key]=val`. A custom version might actually perform some calculation based on `val` and/or `key` before adding an item.

dict.clear(self)
UserDict.UserDict.clear(self)

Remove all items from `self`.

dict.copy(self)
UserDict.UserDict.copy(self)

Return a copy of the dictionary `self` (i.e., a distinct object with the same items).

dict.get(self, key [,default=None])
UserDict.UserDict.get(self, key [,default=None])

Return the value associated with the key `key`. If no item with the key exists, return `default` instead of raising a `KeyError`.

dict.has_key(self, key)
UserDict.UserDict.has_key(self, key)

Return a Boolean value indicating whether `self` has the key `key`.

dict.items(self)
UserDict.UserDict.items(self)
dict.iteritems(self)
UserDict.UserDict.iteritems(self)

Return the items in a dictionary, in an unspecified order. The `.items()` method returns a true list of (`key`,`val`) pairs, while the `.iteritems()` method (in Python 2.2+) returns a generator object that successively yields items. The latter method is useful if your dictionary is not a true in-memory structure, but rather some sort of incremental query or calculation. Either method responds externally similarly to a `for` loop:

```
>>> d = {1:2, 3:4}
>>> for k,v in d.iteritems(): print k,v,':',
```

```
...
1 2 : 3 4 :
>>> for k,v in d.items(): print k,v,':',
...
1 2 : 3 4 :
```

dict.keys(self)
UserDict.UserDict.keys(self)
dict.iterkeys(self)
UserDict.UserDict.iterkeys(self)

> Return the keys in a dictionary, in an unspecified order. The .keys() method returns a true list of keys, while the .iterkeys() method (in Python 2.2+) returns a generator object.

> SEE ALSO: dict.items() *26*;

dict.popitem(self)
UserDict.UserDict.popitem(self)

> Return a (key,val) pair for the dictionary, or raise as KeyError if the dictionary is empty. Removes the returned item from the dictionary. As with other dictionary methods, the order in which items are popped is unspecified (and can vary between versions and platforms).

dict.setdefault(self, key [,default=None])
UserDict.UserDict.setdefault(self, key [,default=None])

> If key is currently in the dictionary, return the corresponding value. If key is not currently in the dictionary, set self[key]=default, then return default.

> SEE ALSO: dict.get() *26*;

dict.update(self, other)
UserDict.UserDict.update(self, other)

> Update the dictionary self using the dictionary other. If a key in other already exists in self, the corresponding value from other is used in self. If a (key,val) pair in other is not in self, it is added.

dict.values(self)
UserDict.UserDict.values(self)
dict.itervalues(self)
UserDict.UserDict.itervalues(self)

> Return the values in a dictionary, in an unspecified order. The .values() method returns a true list of keys, while the .itervalues() method (in Python 2.2+) returns a generator object.

> SEE ALSO: dict.items() *26*;

SEE ALSO: dict *428*; list *28*; operator *47*;

UserList ◇ Custom wrapper around list objects

list ◇ New-style base class for list objects

tuple ◇ New-style base class for tuple objects

A Python list is a (possibly) heterogeneous mutable sequence of Python objects. A tuple is a similar immutable sequence (see Glossary entry on "immutable"). Most of the magic methods of lists and tuples are the same, but a tuple does not have those methods associated with internal transformation.

If you create a list-like datatype by subclassing from *UserList.UserList*, all the special methods defined by the parent are proxies to the true list stored in the object's `.data` member. If, under Python 2.2+, you subclass from `list` (or `tuple`) itself, the object itself inherits list (tuple) behaviors. In either case, you may customize whichever methods you wish. The discussion of *dict* and *UserDict* shows an example of the different styles of specialization.

The difference between a list-like object and a tuple-like object runs less deep than you might think. Mutability is only really important for using objects as dictionary keys, but dictionaries only check the mutability of an object by examining the return value of an object's `.__hash__()` method. If this method fails to return an integer, an object is considered mutable (and ineligible to serve as a dictionary key). The reason that tuples are useful as keys is because every tuple composed of the same items has the same hash; two lists (or dictionaries), by contrast, may also have the same items, but only as a passing matter (since either can be changed).

You can easily give a hash value to a list-like datatype. However, there is an obvious and wrong way to do so:

```
>>> class L(list):
...     __hash__ = lambda self: hash(tuple(self))
...
>>> lst = L([1,2,3])
>>> dct = {lst:33, 7:8}
>>> print dct
{[1, 2, 3]: 33, 7: 8}
>>> dct[lst]
33
>>> lst.append(4)
>>> print dct
{[1, 2, 3, 4]: 33, 7: 8}
>>> dct[lst]
Traceback (most recent call last):
  File "<stdin>", line 1, in ?
KeyError: [1, 2, 3, 4]
```

As soon as `lst` changes, its hash changes, and you cannot reach the dictionary item keyed to it. What you need is something that does not change as the object changes:

```
>>> class L(list):
...        __hash__ = lambda self: id(self)
...
>>> lst = L([1,2,3])
>>> dct = {lst:33, 7:8}
>>> dct[lst]
33
>>> lst.append(4)
>>> dct
{[1, 2, 3, 4]: 33, 7: 8}
>>> dct[lst]
33
```

As with most everything about Python datatypes and operations, mutability is merely a protocol that you can choose to support or not support in your custom datatypes.

Sequence datatypes may choose to support order comparisons—in fact they probably should. The methods .__cmp__(), .__ge__(), .__gt__(), .__le__(), and .__lt__() have the same meanings for sequences that they do for other datatypes; see *operator*, *float*, and *dict* for details.

METHODS

list.__add__(self, other)
UserList.UserList.__add__(self, other)
tuple.__add__(self, other)
list.__iadd__(self, other)
UserList.UserList.__iadd__(self, other)

Determine how a datatype responds to the + and += operators. Augmented assignments ("in-place add") are supported in Python 2.0+. For list-like datatypes, normally the statements lst+=other and lst=lst+other have the same effect, but the augmented version might be more efficient.

Under standard meaning, addition of the two sequence objects produces a new (distinct) sequence object with all the items in both self and other. An in-place add (.__iadd__) mutates the left-hand object without creating a new object. A custom datatype might choose to give a special meaning to addition, perhaps depending on the datatype of the object added in. For example:

```
>>> class XList(list):
...        def __iadd__(self, other):
...            if issubclass(other.__class__, list):
...                return list.__iadd__(self, other)
...            else:
...                from operator import add
```

```
...              return map(add, self, [other]*len(self))
...
>>> xl = XList([1,2,3])
>>> xl += [4,5,6]
>>> xl
[1, 2, 3, 4, 5, 6]
>>> xl += 10
>>> xl
[11, 12, 13, 14, 15, 16]
```

list.__contains__(self, x)
UserList.UserList.__contains__(self, x)
tuple.__contains__(self, x)

Return a Boolean value indicating whether self contains the value x. Determines how a datatype responds to the in operator.

list.__delitem__(self, x)
UserList.UserList.__delitem__(self, x)

Remove an item from a list-like datatype. Determines how a datatype responds to the del statement, as in del self[x].

list.__delslice__(self, start, end)
UserList.UserList.__delslice__(self, start, end)

Remove a range of items from a list-like datatype. Determines how a datatype responds to the del statement applied to a slice, as in del self[start:end].

list.__getitem__(self, pos)
UserList.UserList.__getitem__(self, pos)
tuple.__getitem__(self, pos)

Return the value at offset pos in the list. Determines how a datatype responds to indexing with square braces. The default behavior on list indices is to raise an IndexError for nonexistent offsets.

list.__getslice__(self, start, end)
UserList.UserList.__getslice__(self, start, end)
tuple.__getslice__(self, start, end)

Return a subsequence of the sequence self. Determines how a datatype responds to indexing with a slice parameter, as in self[start:end].

list.__hash__(self)
UserList.UserList.__hash__(self)
tuple.__hash__(self)

Return an integer that distinctly identifies an object. Determines how a datatype responds to the built-in *hash()* function—and probably more importantly the hash is used internally in dictionaries. By default, tuples (and other immutable types) will return hash values but lists will raise a TypeError. Dictionaries will handle hash collisions gracefully, but it is best to try to make hashes unique per object.

```
>>> hash(219750523), hash((1,2))
(219750523, 219750523)
>>> dct = {219750523:1, (1,2):2}
>>> dct[219750523]
1
```

list.__len__(self
UserList.UserList.__len__(self
tuple.__len__(self

Return the length of a sequence. Determines how a datatype responds to the built-in
len() function.

list.__mul__(self, num)
UserList.UserList.__mul__(self, num)
tuple.__mul__(self, num)
list.__rmul__(self, num)
UserList.UserList.__rmul__(self, num)
tuple.__rmul__(self, num)
list.__imul__(self, num)
UserList.UserList.__imul__(self, num)

Determine how a datatype responds to the * and *= operators. Augmented assignments ("in-place add") are supported in Python 2.0+. For list-like datatypes,
normally the statements lst*=other and lst=lst*other have the same effect, but
the augmented version might be more efficient.

The right-associative version .__rmul__() determines the value of num*self, the left-
associative .__mul__() determines the value of self*num. Under standard meaning,
the product of a sequence and a number produces a new (distinct) sequence object
with the items in self duplicated num times:

```
>>> [1,2,3] * 3
[1, 2, 3, 1, 2, 3, 1, 2, 3]
```

list.__setitem__(self, pos, val)
UserList.UserList.__setitem__(self, pos, val)

Set the value at offset pos to value value. Determines how a datatype responds
to indexed assignment; that is, self[pos]=val. A custom version might actually
perform some calculation based on val and/or key before adding an item.

list.__setslice__(self, start, end, other)
UserList.UserList.__setslice__(self, start, end, other)

Replace the subsequence self[start:end] with the sequence other. The replaced
and new sequences are not necessarily the same length, and the resulting sequence
might be longer or shorter than self. Determines how a datatype responds to
assignment to a slice, as in self[start:end]=other.

list.append(self, item)
UserList.UserList.append(self, item)

> Add the object `item` to the end of the sequence `self`. Increases the length of `self` by one.

list.count(self, item)
UserList.UserList.count(self, item)

> Return the integer number of occurrences of `item` in `self`.

list.extend(self, seq)
UserList.UserList.extend(self, seq)

> Add each item in `seq` to the end of the sequence `self`. Increases the length of `self` by `len(seq)`.

list.index(self, item)
UserList.UserList.index(self, item)

> Return the offset index of the first occurrence of `item` in `self`.

list.insert(self, pos, item)
UserList.UserList.insert(self, pos, item)

> Add the object `item` to the sequence `self` before the offset `pos`. Increases the length of `self` by one.

list.pop(self [,pos=-1])
UserList.UserList.pop(self [,pos=-1])

> Return the item at offset `pos` of the sequence `self`, and remove the returned item from the sequence. By default, remove the last item, which lets a list act like a stack using the `.pop()` and `.append()` operations.

list.remove(self, item)
UserList.UserList.remove(self, item)

> Remove the first occurrence of `item` in `self`. Decreases the length of `self` by one.

list.reverse(self)
UserList.UserList.reverse(self)

> Reverse the list `self` in place.

list.sort(self [cmpfunc])
UserList.UserList.sort(self [,cmpfunc])

> Sort the list `self` in place. If a comparison function `cmpfunc` is given, perform comparisons using that function.

SEE ALSO: list *427*; tuple *427*; dict *24*; operator *47*;

UserString ◇ Custom wrapper around string objects

str ◇ New-style base class for string objects

A string in Python is an immutable sequence of characters (see Glossary entry on "immutable"). There is special syntax for creating strings—single and triple quoting, character escaping, and so on—but in terms of object behaviors and magic methods, most of what a string does a tuple does, too. Both may be sliced and indexed, and both respond to pseudo-arithmetic operators + and ×.

For the *str* and *UserString* magic methods that are strictly a matter of the sequence quality of strings, see the corresponding *tuple* documentation. These include `str.__add__()`, `str.__getitem__()`, `str.__getslice__()`, `str.__hash__()`, `str.__len__()`, `str.__mul__()`, and `str.__rmul__()`. Each of these methods is also defined in *UserString*. The *UserString* module also includes a few explicit definitions of magic methods that are not in the new-style *str* class: `UserString.__iadd__()`, `UserString.__imul__()`, and `UserString.__radd__()`. However, you may define your own implementations of these methods, even if you inherit from *str* (in Python 2.2+). In any case, internally, in-place operations are still performed on all strings.

Strings have quite a number of nonmagic methods as well. If you wish to create a custom datatype that can be utilized in the same functions that expect strings, you may want to specialize some of these common string methods. The behavior of string methods is documented in the discussion of the *string* module, even for the few string methods that are not also defined in the *string* module. However, inheriting from either *str* or *UserString* provides very reasonable default behaviors for all these methods.

SEE ALSO: `""`.capitalize() *132*; `""`.title() *133*; `""`.center() *133*; `""`.count() *134*; `""`.endswith() *134*; `""`.expandtabs() *134*; `""`.find() *135*; `""`.index() *135*; `""`.isalpha() *136*; `""`.isalnum() *136*; `""`.isdigit() *136*; `""`.islower() *136*; `""`.isspace() *136*; `""`.istitle() *136*; `""`.isupper() *136*; `""`.join() *137*; `""`.ljust() *138*; `""`.lower() *138*; `""`.lstrip() *139*; `""`.replace() *139*; `""`.rfind() *140*; `""`.rindex() *141*; `""`.rjust() *141*; `""`.rstrip() *142*; `""`.split() *142*; `""`.splitlines() *144*; `""`.startswith() *144*; `""`.strip() *144*; `""`.swapcase() *145*; `""`.translate() *145*; `""`.upper() *146*; `""`.encode() *188*;

METHODS

str.__contains__(self, x)
UserString.UserString.__contains__(self, x)

Return a Boolean value indicating whether `self` contains the character x. Determines how a datatype responds to the `in` operator.

In Python versions through 2.2, the `in` operator applied to strings has a semantics that tends to trip me up. Fortunately, Python 2.3+ has the behavior that I expect. In older Python versions, `in` can only be used to determine the presence of a single character in a string—this makes sense if you think of a string as a sequence of characters, but I nonetheless intuitively want something like the code below to work:

```
>>> s = "The cat in the hat"
>>> if "the" in s: print "Has definite article"
...
Traceback (most recent call last):
  File "<stdin>", line 1, in ?
TypeError: 'in <string>' requires character as left operand
```

It is easy to get the "expected" behavior in a custom string-like datatype (while still always producing the same result whenever x is indeed a character):

```
>>> class S(str):
...       def __contains__(self, x):
...            for i in range(len(self)):
...                if self.startswith(x,i): return 1
...
>>> s = S("The cat in the hat")
>>> "the" in s
1
>>> "an" in s
0
```

Python 2.3 strings behave the same way as my datatype S.

SEE ALSO: string *422*; string *129*; operator *47*; tuple *28*;

1.1.5   Exercise: Filling out the forms (or deciding not to)

DISCUSSION

A particular little task that was quite frequent and general before the advent of Web servers has become absolutely ubiquitous for slightly dynamic Web pages. The pattern one encounters is that one has a certain general format that is desired for a document or file, but miscellaneous little details differ from instance to instance. Form letters are another common case where one comes across this pattern, but thematically related collections of Web pages rule the roost of templating techniques.

It turns out that everyone and her sister has developed her own little templating system. Creating a templating system is a very appealing task for users of most scripting languages, just a little while after they have gotten a firm grasp of "Hello World!" Some of these are discussed in Chapter 5, but many others are not addressed. Often, these templating systems will be HTML/CGI oriented and will often include some degree of dynamic calculation of fill-in values—the inspiration in these cases comes from systems like Allaire's ColdFusion, Java Server Pages, Active Server Pages, and PHP, in which some program code gets sprinkled around in documents that are primarily made of HTML.

At the very simplest, Python provides interpolation of special characters in strings, in a style similar to the C `sprintf()` function. So a simple example might appear like:

```
>>> form_letter="""Dear %s %s,
...
... You owe us $%s for account (#%s). Please Pay.
...
... The Company"""
>>> fname = 'David'
>>> lname = 'Mertz'
>>> due = 500
>>> acct = '123-T745'
>>> print form_letter % (fname,lname,due,acct)
Dear David Mertz,

You owe us $500 for account (#123-T745). Please Pay.

The Company
```

This approach does the basic templating, but it would be easy to make an error in composing the tuple of insertion values. And moreover, a slight change to the `form_letter` template—such as the addition or subtraction of a field—would produce wrong results.

A bit more robust approach is to use Python's dictionary-based string interpolation. For example:

```
>>> form_letter="""Dear %(fname)s %(lname)s,
...
... You owe us $%(due)s for account (#%(acct)s). Please Pay.
...
... The Company"""
>>> fields = {'lname':'Mertz', 'fname':'David'}
>>> fields['acct'] = '123-T745'
>>> fields['due'] = 500
>>> fields['last_letter'] = '01/02/2001'
>>> print form_letter % fields
Dear David Mertz,

You owe us $500 for account (#123-T745). Please Pay.

The Company
```

With this approach, the fields need not be listed in a particular order for the insertion. Furthermore, if the order of fields is rearranged in the template, or if the same fields are used for a different template, the `fields` dictionary may still be used for insertion values. If `fields` has unused dictionary keys, it doesn't hurt the interpolation, either.

The dictionary interpolation approach is still subject to failure if dictionary keys are missing. Two improvements using the *UserDict* module can improve matters, in two different (and incompatible) ways. In Python 2.2+ the built-in `dict` type can be a parent for a "new-style class"; if available everywhere you need it to run, `dict` is a better parent than is *UserDict.UserDict*. One approach is to avoid all key misses during dictionary interpolation:

```
>>> form_letter="""%(salutation)s %(fname)s %(lname)s,
...
... You owe us $%(due)s for account (#%(acct)s). Please Pay.
...
... %(closing)s The Company"""
>>> from UserDict import UserDict
>>> class AutoFillingDict(UserDict):
...     def __init__(self,dict={}): UserDict.__init__(self,dict)
...     def __getitem__(self,key):
...         return UserDict.get(self, key, '')
>>> fields = AutoFillingDict()
>>> fields['salutation'] = 'Dear'
>>> fields
{'salutation': 'Dear'}
>>> fields['fname'] = 'David'
>>> fields['due'] = 500
>>> fields['closing'] = 'Sincerely,'
>>> print form_letter % fields
Dear David ,

You owe us $500 for account (#). Please Pay.

Sincerely, The Company
```

Even though the fields `lname` and `acct` are not specified, the interpolation has managed to produce a basically sensible letter (instead of crashing with a KeyError).

Another approach is to create a custom dictionary-like object that will allow for "partial interpolation." This approach is particularly useful to gather bits of the information needed for the final string over the course of the program run (rather than all at once):

```
>>> form_letter="""%(salutation)s %(fname)s %(lname)s,
...
... You owe us $%(due)s for account (#%(acct)s). Please Pay.
...
... %(closing)s The Company"""
>>> from UserDict import UserDict
>>> class ClosureDict(UserDict):
...     def __init__(self,dict={}): UserDict.__init__(self,dict)
...     def __getitem__(self,key):
...         return UserDict.get(self, key, '%('+key+')s')
```

```
>>> name_dict = ClosureDict({'fname':'David','lname':'Mertz'})
>>> print form_letter % name_dict
%(salutation)s David Mertz,

You owe us $%(due)s for account (#%(acct)s). Please Pay.

%(closing)s The Company
```

Interpolating using a `ClosureDict` simply fills in whatever portion of the information it knows, then returns a new string that is closer to being filled in.

SEE ALSO: dict *24*; UserDict *24*; UserList *28*; UserString *33*;

QUESTIONS

1. What are some other ways to provide "smart" string interpolation? Can you think of ways that the *UserList* or *UserString* modules might be used to implement a similar enhanced interpolation?

2. Consider other "magic" methods that you might add to classes inheriting from *UserDict.UserDict*. How might these additional behaviors make templating techniques more powerful?

3. How far do you think you can go in using Python's string interpolation as a templating technique? At what point would you decide you had to apply other techniques, such as regular expression substitutions or a parser? Why?

4. What sorts of error checking might you implement for customized interpolation? The simple list or dictionary interpolation could fail fairly easily, but at least those were trappable errors (they let the application know something is amiss). How would you create a system with both flexible interpolation and good guards on the quality and completeness of the final result?

1.1.6   Problem: Working with lines from a large file

At its simplest, reading a file in a line-oriented style is just a matter of using the `.readline()`, `.readlines()`, and `.xreadlines()` methods of a file object. Python 2.2+ provides a simplified syntax for this frequent operation by letting the file object itself efficiently iterate over lines (strictly in forward sequence). To read in an entire file, you may use the `.read()` method and possibly split it into lines or other chunks using the *string.split()* function. Some examples:

```
>>> for line in open('chap1.txt'): # Python 2.2+
...       # process each line in some manner
...       pass
...
>>> linelist = open('chap1.txt').readlines()
```

```
>>> print linelist[1849],
  EXERCISE: Working with lines from a large file
>>> txt = open('chap1.txt').read()
>>> from os import linesep
>>> linelist2 = txt.split(linesep)
```

For moderately sized files, reading the entire contents is not a big issue. But large files make time and memory issues more important. Complex documents or active log files, for example, might be multiple megabytes, or even gigabytes, in size—even if the contents of such files do not strictly exceed the size of available memory, reading them can still be time consuming. A related technique to those discussed here is discussed in the "Problem: Reading a file backwards by record, line, or paragraph" section of Chapter 2.

Obviously, if you *need* to process every line in a file, you have to read the whole file; *xreadlines* does so in a memory-friendly way, assuming you are able to process them sequentially. But for applications that only need a subset of lines in a large file, it is not hard to make improvements. The most important module to look to for support here is *linecache*.

A CACHED LINE LIST

It is straightforward to read a particular line from a file using *linecache*:

```
>>> import linecache
>>> print linecache.getline('chap1.txt',1850),
  PROBLEM: Working with lines from a large file
```

Notice that *linecache.getline()* uses one-based counting, in contrast to the zero-based list indexing in the prior example. While there is not much to this, it would be even nicer to have an object that combined the efficiency of *linecache* with the interfaces we expect in lists. Existing code might exist to process lists of lines, or you might want to write a function that is agnostic about the source of a list of lines. In addition to being able to enumerate and index, it would be useful to be able to slice *linecache*-based objects, just as we might do to real lists (including with extended slices, which were added to lists in Python 2.3).

cachedlinelist.py

```
import linecache, types
class CachedLineList:
    # Note: in Python 2.2+, it is probably worth including:
    # __slots__ = ('_fname')
    # ...and inheriting from 'object'
    def __init__(self, fname):
        self._fname = fname
```

```
    def __getitem__(self, x):
        if type(x) is types.SliceType:
            return [linecache.getline(self._fname, n+1)
                    for n in range(x.start, x.stop, x.step)]
        else:
            return linecache.getline(self._fname, x+1)
    def __getslice__(self, beg, end):
        # pass to __getitem__ which does extended slices also
        return self[beg:end:1]
```

Using these new objects is almost identical to using a list created by
open(fname).readlines(), but more efficient (especially in memory usage):

```
>>> from cachedlinelist import CachedLineList
>>> cll = CachedLineList('../chap1.txt')
>>> cll[1849]
'  PROBLEM: Working with lines from a large file\r\n'
>>> for line in cll[1849:1851]: print line,
...
  PROBLEM: Working with lines from a large file
  --------------------------------------------------------
>>> for line in cll[1853:1857:2]: print line,
...
  a matter of using the '.readline()', '.readlines()' and
  simplified syntax for this frequent operation by letting the
```

A RANDOM LINE

Occasionally—especially for testing purposes—you might want to check "typical" lines
in a line-oriented file. It is easy to fall into the trap of making sure that a process
works for the first few lines of a file, and maybe for the last few, then assuming it works
everywhere. Unfortunately, the first and last few lines of many files tend to be atypical:
sometimes headers or footers are used; sometimes a log file's first lines were logged
during development rather than usage; and so on. Then again, exhaustive testing of
entire files might provide more data than you want to worry about. Depending on the
nature of the processing, complete testing could be time consuming as well.

On most systems, seeking to a particular position in a file is far quicker than reading
all the bytes up to that position. Even using *linecache*, you need to read a file byte-
by-byte up to the point of a cached line. A fast approach to finding random lines from
a large file is to seek to a random position within a file, then read comparatively few
bytes before and after that position, identifying a line within that chunk.

randline.py

```
#!/usr/bin/python
"""Iterate over random lines in a file (req Python 2.2+)
From command-line use: % randline.py <fname> <numlines>
"""
import sys
from os import stat, linesep
from stat import ST_SIZE
from random import randrange
MAX_LINE_LEN = 4096

#-- Iterable class
class randline(object):
    __slots__ = ('_fp','_size','_limit')
    def __init__(self, fname, limit=sys.maxint):
        self._size = stat(fname)[ST_SIZE]
        self._fp = open(fname,'rb')
        self._limit = limit
    def __iter__(self):
        return self
    def next(self):
        if self._limit <= 0:
            raise StopIteration
        self._limit -= 1
        pos = randrange(self._size)
        priorlen = min(pos, MAX_LINE_LEN)    # maybe near start
        self._fp.seek(pos-priorlen)
        # Add extra linesep at beg/end in case pos at beg/end
        prior = linesep + self._fp.read(priorlen)
        post = self._fp.read(MAX_LINE_LEN) + linesep
        begln = prior.rfind(linesep) + len(linesep)
        endln = post.find(linesep)
        return prior[begln:]+post[:endln]

#-- Use as command-line tool
if __name__=='__main__':
    fname, numlines = sys.argv[1], int(sys.argv[2])
    for line in randline(fname, numlines):
        print line
```

The presented *randline* module may be used either imported into another application or as a command-line tool. In the latter case, you could pipe a collection of random lines to another application, as in:

```
% randline.py reallybig.log 1000 | testapp
```

A couple details should be noted in my implementation. (1) The same line can be chosen more than once in a line iteration. If you choose a small number of lines from a large file, this probably will not happen (but the so-called "birthday paradox" makes an occasional collision more likely than you might expect; see the Glossary). (2) What is selected is "the line that contains a random position in the file," which means that short lines are less likely to be chosen than long lines. That distribution could be a bug or feature, depending on your needs. In practical terms, for testing "enough" typical cases, the precise distribution is not all that important.

SEE ALSO: xreadlines *72*; linecache *64*; random *82*;

1.2 Standard Modules

There are a variety of tasks that many or most text processing applications will perform, but that are not themselves text processing tasks. For example, texts typically live inside files, so for a concrete application you might want to check whether files exist, whether you have access to them, and whether they have certain attributes; you might also want to read their contents. The text processing per se does not happen until the text makes it into a Python value, but getting the text into local memory is a necessary step.

Another task is making Python objects persistent so that final or intermediate processing results can be saved in computer-usable forms. Or again, Python applications often benefit from being able to call external processes and possibly work with the results of those calls.

Yet another class of modules helps you deal with Python internals in ways that go beyond what the inherent syntax does. I have made a judgment call in this book as to which such "Python internal" modules are sufficiently general and frequently used in text processing applications; a number of "internal" modules are given only one-line descriptions under the "Other Modules" topic.

1.2.1 Working with the Python Interpreter

Some of the modules in the standard library contain functionality that is nearly as important to Python as the basic syntax. Such modularity is an important strength of Python's design, but users of other languages may be surprised to find capabilities for reading command-line arguments, catching exceptions, copying objects, or the like in external modules.

copy ◇ Generic copying operations

Names in Python programs are merely bindings to underlying objects; many of these objects are mutable. This point is simple, but it winds up biting almost every beginning Python programmer—and even a few experienced Pythoners get caught, too. The problem is that binding another name (including a sequence position, dictionary entry, or attribute) to an object leaves you with two names bound to the same object. If you change the underlying object using one name, the other name also points to a changed object. Sometimes you want that, sometimes you do not.

One variant of the binding trap is a particularly frequent pitfall. Say you want a 2D table of values, initialized as zeros. Later on, you would like to be able to refer to a row/column position as, for example, `table[2][3]` (as in many programming languages). Here is what you would probably try first, along with its failure:

```
>>> row = [0]*4
>>> print row
[0, 0, 0, 0]
>>> table = [row]*4    # or 'table = [[0]*4]*4
>>> for row in table: print row
...
[0, 0, 0, 0]
[0, 0, 0, 0]
[0, 0, 0, 0]
[0, 0, 0, 0]
>>> table[2][3] = 7
>>> for row in table: print row
...
[0, 0, 0, 7]
[0, 0, 0, 7]
[0, 0, 0, 7]
[0, 0, 0, 7]
>>> id(table[2]), id(table[3])
(6207968, 6207968)
```

The problem with the example is that `table` is a list of four positional bindings to the *exact same* list object. You cannot change just one row, since all four point to just one object. What you need instead is a *copy* of `row` to put in each row of `table`.

Python provides a number of ways to create copies of objects (and bind them to names). Such a copy is a "snapshot" of the state of the object that can be modified independently of changes to the original. A few ways to correct the table problem are:

```
>>> table1 = map(list, [(0,)*4]*4)
>>> id(table1[2]), id(table1[3])
(6361712, 6361808)
>>> table2 = [lst[:] for lst in [[0]*4]*4]
>>> id(table2[2]), id(table2[3])
```

```
(6356720, 6356800)
>>> from copy import copy
>>> row = [0]*4
>>> table3 = map(copy, [row]*4)
>>> id(table3[2]), id(table3[3])
(6498640, 6498720)
```

In general, slices always create new lists. In Python 2.2+, the constructors `list()` and `dict()` likewise construct new/copied lists/dicts (possibly using other sequence or association types as arguments).

But the most general way to make a new copy of *whatever object you might need* is with the *copy* module. If you use the *copy* module you do not need to worry about issues of whether a given sequence is a list, or merely list-like, which the `list()` coercion forces into a list.

FUNCTIONS

copy.copy(obj)

Return a shallow copy of a Python object. Most (but not quite all) types of Python objects can be copied. A shallow copy binds its elements/members to the same objects as bound in the original—but the object itself is distinct.

```
>>> import copy
>>> class C: pass
...
>>> o1 = C()
>>> o1.lst = [1,2,3]
>>> o1.str = "spam"
>>> o2 = copy.copy(o1)
>>> o1.lst.append(17)
>>> o2.lst
[1, 2, 3, 17]
>>> o1.str = 'eggs'
>>> o2.str
'spam'
```

copy.deepcopy(obj)

Return a deep copy of a Python object. Each element or member in an object is itself recursively copied. For nested containers, it is usually more desirable to perform a deep copy—otherwise you can run into problems like the 2D table example above.

```
>>> o1 = C()
>>> o1.lst = [1,2,3]
>>> o3 = copy.deepcopy(o1)
>>> o1.lst.append(17)
```

```
>>> o3.lst
[1, 2, 3]
>>> o1.lst
[1, 2, 3, 17]
```

exceptions ◇ Standard exception class hierarchy

Various actions in Python raise exceptions, and these exceptions can be caught using an except clause. Although strings can serve as exceptions for backwards-compatibility reasons, it is greatly preferable to use class-based exceptions.

When you catch an exception in using an except clause, you also catch any descendent exceptions. By utilizing a hierarchy of standard and user-defined exception classes, you can tailor exception handling to meet your specific code requirements.

```
>>> class MyException(StandardError): pass
...
>>> try:
...     raise MyException
... except StandardError:
...     print "Caught parent"
... except MyException:
...     print "Caught specific class"
... except:
...     print "Caught generic leftover"
...
Caught parent
```

In general, if you need to raise exceptions manually, you should either use a built-in exception close to your situation, or inherit from that built-in exception. The outline in Figure 1.1 shows the exception classes defined in *exceptions*.

getopt ◇ Parser for command line options

Utility applications—whether for text processing or otherwise—frequently accept a variety of command-line switches to configure their behavior. In principle, and frequently in practice, all that you need to do to process command-line options is read through the list sys.argv[1:] and handle each element of the option line. I have certainly written my own small "sys.argv parser" more than once; it is not hard if you do not expect too much.

Exception	Root class for all built-in exceptions
StandardError	Base for "normal" exceptions
ArithmeticError	Base for arithmetic exceptions
OverflowError	Number too large to represent
ZeroDivisionError	Dividing by zero
FloatingPointError	Problem in floating point operation
LookupError	Problem accessing a value in a collection
IndexError	Problem accessing a value in a sequence
KeyError	Problem accessing a value in a mapping
NameError	Problem accessing local or global name
UnboundLocalError	Reference to non-existent name
AttributeError	Problem accessing or setting an attribute
TypeError	Operation or function applied to wrong type
ValueError	Operation or function on unusable value
UnicodeError	Problem encoding or decoding
EnvironmentError	Problem outside of Python itself
IOError	Problem performing I/O
OSError	Error passed from the operating system
WindowsError	Windows-specific OS problem
AssertionError	Failure of an assert statement
EOFError	End-of-file without a read
ImportError	Problem importing a module
ReferenceError	Problem accessing collected weakref
KeyboardInterrupt	User pressed interrupt (`ctrl-c`) key
MemoryError	Operation runs out of memory (try `del`'ing)
SyntaxError	Problem parsing Python code
SystemError	Internal (recoverable) error in Python
RuntimeError	Error not falling under any other category
NotImplementedError	Functionality not yet available
StopIteration	Iterator has no more items available
SystemExit	Raised by `sys.exit()`

Figure 1.1: Standard exceptions

The *getopt* module provides some automation and error handling for option parsing. It takes just a few lines of code to tell *getopt* what options it should handle, and which switch prefixes and parameter styles to use. However, *getopt* is not necessarily the final word in parsing command lines. Python 2.3 includes Greg Ward's *optik* module <http://optik.sourceforge.net/> renamed as *optparse*, and the Twisted Matrix library contains *twisted.python.usage* <http://www.twistedmatrix.com/documents/howto/options>. These modules, and other third-party tools, were written because of perceived limitations in *getopt*.

For most purposes, *getopt* is a perfectly good tool. Moreover, even if some enhanced module is included in later Python versions, either this enhancement will be backwards compatible or *getopt* will remain in the distribution to support existing scripts.

SEE ALSO: sys.argv *49*;

FUNCTIONS

getopt.getopt(args, options [,long_options]])

The argument `args` is the actual list of options being parsed, most commonly `sys.argv[1:]`. The argument `options` and the optional argument `long_options` contain formats for acceptable options. If any options specified in `args` do not match any acceptable format, a *getopt.GetoptError* exception is raised. All options must begin with either a single dash for single-letter options or a double dash for long options (DOS-style leading slashes are not usable, unfortunately).

The return value of *getopt.getopt()* is a pair containing an option list and a list of additional arguments. The latter is typically a list of filenames the utility will operate on. The option list is a list of pairs of the form (`option, value`). Under recent versions of Python, you can convert an option list to a dictionary with `dict(optlist)`, which is likely to be useful.

The `options` format string is a sequence of letters, each optionally followed by a colon. Any option letter followed by a colon takes a (mandatory) value after the option.

The format for `long_options` is a list of strings indicating the option names (excluding the leading dashes). If an option name ends with an equal sign, it requires a value after the option.

It is easiest to see *getopt* in action:

```
>>> import getopt
>>> opts='-a1 -b -c 2 --foo=bar --baz file1 file2'.split()
>>> optlist, args = getopt.getopt(opts,'a:bc:',['foo=','baz'])
>>> optlist
[('-a', '1'), ('-b', ''), ('-c', '2'), ('--foo', 'bar'),
('--baz', '')]
>>> args
['file1', 'file2']
>>> nodash = lambda s: \
...         s.translate(''.join(map(chr,range(256))),'-')
>>> todict = lambda l: \
...         dict([(nodash(opt),val) for opt,val in l])
>>> optdict = todict(optlist)
>>> optdict
{'a': '1', 'c': '2', 'b': '', 'baz': '', 'foo': 'bar'}
```

You can examine options given either by looping through `optlist` or by performing `optdict.get(key, default)` type tests as needed in your program flow.

---

operator ◇ Standard operations as functions

All of the standard Python syntactic operators are available in functional form using the *operator* module. In most cases, it is more clear to use the actual operators, but in a few cases functions are useful. The most common usage for *operator* is in conjunction with functional programming constructs. For example:

```
>>> import operator
>>> lst = [1, 0, (), '', 'abc']
>>> map(operator.not_, lst)    # fp-style negated bool vals
[0, 1, 1, 1, 0]
>>> tmplst = []                # imperative style
>>> for item in lst:
...     tmplst.append(not item)
...
>>> tmplst
[0, 1, 1, 1, 0]
>>> del tmplst                 # must cleanup stray name
```

As well as being shorter, I find the FP style more clear. The source code below provides *sample* implementations of the functions in the *operator* module. The actual implementations are faster and are written directly in C, but the samples illustrate what each function does.

`operator2.py`

```
### Comparison functions
lt = __lt__ = lambda a,b: a < b
le = __le__ = lambda a,b: a <= b
eq = __eq__ = lambda a,b: a == b
ne = __ne__ = lambda a,b: a != b
ge = __ge__ = lambda a,b: a >= b
gt = __gt__ = lambda a,b: a > b
### Boolean functions
not_ = __not__ = lambda o: not o
truth = lambda o: not not o
# Arithmetic functions
abs = __abs__ = abs    # same as built-in function
add = __add__ = lambda a,b: a + b
and_ = __and__ = lambda a,b: a & b  # bitwise, not boolean
div = __div__ = \
        lambda a,b: a/b  # depends on __future__.division
```

```
floordiv = __floordiv__ = lambda a,b: a/b # Only for 2.2+
inv = invert = __inv__ = __invert__ = lambda o: ~o
lshift = __lshift__ = lambda a,b: a << b
rshift = __rshift__ = lambda a,b: a >> b
mod = __mod__ = lambda a,b: a % b
mul = __mul__ = lambda a,b: a * b
neg = __neg__ = lambda o: -o
or_ = __or__ = lambda a,b: a | b     # bitwise, not boolean
pos = __pos__ = lambda o: +o # identity for numbers
sub = __sub__ = lambda a,b: a - b
truediv = __truediv__ = lambda a,b: 1.0*a/b # New in 2.2+
xor = __xor__ = lambda a,b: a ^ b
### Sequence functions (note overloaded syntactic operators)
concat = __concat__ = add
contains = __contains__ = lambda a,b: b in a
countOf = lambda seq,a: len([x for x in seq if x==a])
def delitem(seq,a): del seq[a]
__delitem__ = delitem
def delslice(seq,b,e): del seq[b:e]
__delslice__ = delslice
getitem = __getitem__ = lambda seq,i: seq[i]
getslice = __getslice__ = lambda seq,b,e: seq[b:e]
indexOf = lambda seq,o: seq.index(o)
repeat = __repeat__ = mul
def setitem(seq,i,v): seq[i] = v
__setitem__ = setitem
def setslice(seq,b,e,v): seq[b:e] = v
__setslice__ = setslice
### Functionality functions (not implemented here)
# The precise interfaces required to pass the below tests
#     are ill-defined, and might vary at limit-cases between
#     Python versions and custom data types.
import operator
isCallable = callable     # just use built-in 'callable()'
isMappingType = operator.isMappingType
isNumberType = operator.isNumberType
isSequenceType = operator.isSequenceType
```

sys ◇ Information about current Python interpreter

As with the Python "userland" objects you create within your applications, the Python interpreter itself is very open to introspection. Using the *sys* module, you can examine and modify many aspects of the Python runtime environment. However, as with much of the functionality in the *os* module, some of what *sys* provides is too esoteric to address in this book about text processing. Consult the *Python Library Reference* for information on those attributes and functions not covered here.

The module attributes *sys.exc_type*, *sys.exc_value*, and *sys.exc_traceback* have been deprecated in favor of the function *sys.exc_info()*. All of these, and also *sys.last_type*, *sys.last_value*, *sys.last_traceback*, and *sys.tracebacklimit*, let you poke into exceptions and stack frames to a finer degree than the basic *try* and *except* statements do. *sys.exec_prefix* and *sys.executable* provide information on installed paths for Python.

The functions *sys.displayhook()* and *sys.excepthook()* control where program output goes, and *sys.__displayhook__* and *sys.__excepthook__* retain their original values (e.g., STDOUT and STDERR). *sys.exitfunc* affects interpreter cleanup. The attributes *sys.ps1* and *sys.ps2* control prompts in the Python interactive shell.

Other attributes and methods simply provide more detail than you almost ever need to know for text processing applications. The attributes *sys.dllhandle* and *sys.winver* are Windows specific; *sys.setdlopenflags()*, and *sys.getdlopenflags()* are Unix only. Methods like *sys.builtin_module_names*, *sys.__getframe()*, *sys.prefix*, *sys.getrecursionlimit()*, *sys.setprofile()*, *sys.settrace()*, *sys.setcheckinterval()*, *sys.setrecursionlimit()*, *sys.modules*, and also *sys.warnoptions* concern Python internals. Unicode behavior is affected by the *sys.setdefaultencoding()* method, but is overridable with arguments anyway.

ATTRIBUTES

sys.argv

A list of command-line arguments passed to a Python script. The first item, argv[0], is the script name itself, so you are normally interested in argv[1:] when parsing arguments.

SEE ALSO: getopt *44*; sys.stdin *51*; sys.stdout *51*;

sys.byteorder

The native byte order (endianness) of the current platform. Possible values are big and little. Available in Python 2.0+.

sys.copyright

A string with copyright information for the current Python interpreter.

sys.hexversion

The version number of the current Python interpreter as an integer. This number increases with every version, even nonproduction releases. This attribute is not very human-readable; $sys.version$ or $sys.version\_info$ is generally easier to work with.

SEE ALSO: sys.version *51*; sys.version_info *52*;

sys.maxint

The largest positive integer supported by Python's regular integer type, on most platforms, 2**31-1. The largest negative integer is -sys.maxint-1.

sys.maxunicode

The integer of the largest supported code point for a Unicode character under the current configuration. Unicode characters are stored as UCS-2 or UCS-4.

sys.path

A list of the pathnames searched for modules. You may modify this path to control module loading.

sys.platform

A string identifying the OS platform.

SEE ALSO: os.uname() *81*;

sys.stderr
sys.__stderr__

File object for standard error stream (STDERR). $sys.\_\_stderr\_\_$ retains the original value in case $sys.stderr$ is modified during program execution. Error messages and warnings from the Python interpreter are written to $sys.stderr$. The most typical use of $sys.stderr$ is for application messages that indicate "abnormal" conditions. For example:

```
% cat cap_file.py
#!/usr/bin/env python
import sys, string
if len(sys.argv) < 2:
    sys.stderr.write("No filename specified\n")
else:
    fname = sys.argv[1]
    try:
        input = open(fname).read()
        sys.stdout.write(string.upper(input))
    except:
        sys.stderr.write("Could not read '%s'\n" % fname)
```

```
% ./cap_file.py this > CAPS
% ./cap_file.py nosuchfile > CAPS
Could not read 'nosuchfile'
% ./cap_file.py > CAPS
No filename specified
```

SEE ALSO: sys.argv *49*; sys.stdin *51*; sys.stdout *51*;

sys.stdin
sys.__stdin__

File object for standard input stream (STDIN). *sys.__stdin__* retains the original value in case *sys.stdin* is modified during program execution. *input()* and *raw_input()* are read from *sys.stdin*, but the most typical use of *sys.stdin* is for piped and redirected streams on the command line. For example:

```
% cat cap_stdin.py
#!/usr/bin/env python
import sys, string
input = sys.stdin.read()
print string.upper(input)
% echo "this and that" | ./cap_stdin.py
THIS AND THAT
```

SEE ALSO: sys.argv *49*; sys.stderr *50*; sys.stdout *51*;

sys.stdout
sys.__stdout__

File object for standard output stream (STDOUT). *sys.__stdout__* retains the original value in case *sys.stdout* is modified during program execution. The formatted output of the *print* statement goes to *sys.stdout*, and you may also use regular file methods, such as *sys.stdout.write()*.

SEE ALSO: sys.argv *49*; sys.stderr *50*; sys.stdin *51*;

sys.version

A string containing version information on the current Python interpreter. The form of the string is version (#build_num, build_date, build_time) [compiler]. For example:

```
>>> print sys.version
1.5.2 (#0 Apr 13 1999, 10:51:12) [MSC 32 bit (Intel)]
```

Or:

```
>>> print sys.version
2.2 (#1, Apr 17 2002, 16:11:12)
[GCC 2.95.2 19991024 (release)]
```

This version-independent way to find the major, minor, and micro version components should work for 1.5-2.3.x (at least):

```
>>> from string import split
>>> from sys import version
>>> ver_tup = map(int, split(split(version)[0],'.'))+[0]
>>> major, minor, point = ver_tup[:3]
>>> if (major, minor) >= (1, 6):
...     print "New Way"
... else:
...     print "Old Way"
...
New Way
```

sys.version_info

A 5-tuple containing five components of the version number of the current Python interpreter: (major, minor, micro, releaselevel, serial). releaselevel is a descriptive phrase; the other are integers.

```
>>> sys.version_info
(2, 2, 0, 'final', 0)
```

Unfortunately, this attribute was added to Python 2.0, so its items are not entirely useful in requiring a minimal version for some desired functionality.

SEE ALSO: sys.version *51*;

FUNCTIONS

sys.exit([code=0])

Exit Python with exit code code. Cleanup actions specified by finally clauses of try statements are honored, and it is possible to intercept the exit attempt by catching the SystemExit exception. You may specify a numeric exit code for those systems that codify them; you may also specify a string exit code, which is printed to STDERR (with the actual exit code set to 1).

sys.getdefaultencoding()

Return the name of the default Unicode string encoding in Python 2.0+.

sys.getrefcount(obj)

Return the number of references to the object `obj`. The value returned is one higher than you might expect, because it includes the (temporary) reference passed as the argument.

```
>>> x = y = "hi there"
>>> import sys
>>> sys.getrefcount(x)
3
>>> lst = [x, x, x]
>>> sys.getrefcount(x)
6
```

SEE ALSO: os *74*;

types ◇ Standard Python object types

Every object in Python has a type; you can find it by using the built-in function *type()*. Often Python functions use a sort of *ad hoc* overloading, which is implemented by checking features of objects passed as arguments. Programmers coming from languages like C or Java are sometimes surprised by this style, since they are accustomed to seeing multiple "type signatures" for each set of argument types the function can accept. But that is not the Python way.

Experienced Python programmers try not to rely on the precise types of objects, not even in an inheritance sense. This attitude is also sometimes surprising to programmers of other languages (especially statically typed). What is usually important to a Python program is what an object can *do*, not what it *is*. In fact, it has become much more complicated to describe what many objects *are* with the "type/class unification" in Python 2.2 and above (the details are outside the scope of this book).

For example, you might be inclined to write an overloaded function in the following manner:

Naive overloading of argument

```
import types, exceptions
def overloaded_get_text(o):
    if type(o) is types.FileType:
        text = o.read()
    elif type(o) is types.StringType:
        text = o
    elif type(o) in (types.IntType, types.FloatType,
                     types.LongType, types.ComplexType):
        text = repr(o)
    else:
```

```
        raise exceptions.TypeError
    return text
```

The problem with this rigidly typed code is that it is far more fragile than is necessary. Something need not be an actual `FileType` to read its text, it just needs to be sufficiently "file-like" (e.g., a *urllib.urlopen()* or *cStringIO.StringIO()* object is file-like enough for this purpose). Similarly, a new-style object that descends from *types.StringType* or a *UserString.UserString()* object is "string-like" enough to return as such, and similarly for other numeric types.

A better implementation of the function above is:

```
┌─────────────────────────────────────────────────┐
│ "Quacks like a duck" overloading of argument    │
└─────────────────────────────────────────────────┘
def overloaded_get_text(o):
    if hasattr(o,'read'):
        return o.read()
    try:
        return ""+o
    except TypeError:
        pass
    try:
        return repr(0+o)
    except TypeError:
        pass
    raise
```

At times, nonetheless, it is useful to have symbolic names available to name specific object types. In many such cases, an empty or minimal version of the type of object may be used in conjunction with the *type()* function equally well—the choice is mostly stylistic:

```
>>> type('') == types.StringType
1
>>> type(0.0) == types.FloatType
1
>>> type(None) == types.NoneType
1
>>> type([]) == types.ListType
1
```

BUILT-IN

type(o)

Return the datatype of any object o. The return value of this function is itself an object of the type *types.TypeType*. TypeType objects implement .__str__() and .__repr__() methods to create readable descriptions of object types.

```
>>> print type(1)
<type 'int'>
>>> print type(type(1))
<type 'type'>
>>> type(1) is type(0)
1
```

CONSTANTS

types.BuiltinFunctionType
types.BuiltinMethodType

The type for built-in functions like *abs ()*, *len ()*, and *dir ()*, and for functions in "standard" C extensions like *sys* and *os*. However, extensions like *string* and *re* are actually Python wrappers for C extensions, so their functions are of type *types.FunctionType*. A general Python programmer need not worry about these fussy details.

types.BufferType

The type for objects created by the built-in buffer() function.

types.ClassType

The type for user-defined classes.

```
>>> from operator import eq
>>> from types import *
>>> map(eq, [type(C), type(C()), type(C().foo)],
...          [ClassType, InstanceType, MethodType])
[1, 1, 1]
```

SEE ALSO: types.InstanceType *56*; types.MethodType *56*;

types.CodeType

The type for code objects such as returned by compile().

types.ComplexType

Same as type(0+0j).

types.DictType
types.DictionaryType

Same as type({}).

types.EllipsisType

The type for built-in Ellipsis object.

types.FileType

The type for open file objects.

```
>>> from sys import stdout
>>> fp = open('tst','w')
>>> [type(stdout), type(fp)] == [types.FileType]*2
1
```

types.FloatType

Same as `type(0.0)`.

types.FrameType

The type for frame objects such as `tb.tb_frame` in which `tb` has the type *types.TracebackType*.

types.FunctionType
types.LambdaType

Same as `type(lambda:0)`.

types.GeneratorType

The type for generator-iterator objects in Python 2.2+.

```
>>> from __future__ import generators
>>> def foo(): yield 0
...
>>> type(foo) == types.FunctionType
1
>>> type(foo()) == types.GeneratorType
1
```

SEE ALSO: types.FunctionType *56*;

types.InstanceType

The type for instances of user-defined classes.

SEE ALSO: types.ClassType *55*; types.MethodType *56*;

types.IntType

Same as `type(0)`.

types.ListType

Same as `type()`.

types.LongType

Same as `type(0L)`.

types.MethodType
types.UnboundMethodType

The type for methods of user-defined class instances.

SEE ALSO: types.ClassType *55*; types.InstanceType *56*;

types.ModuleType

The type for modules.

```
>>> import os, re, sys
>>> [type(os), type(re), type(sys)] == [types.ModuleType]*3
1
```

types.NoneType

Same as type(None).

types.StringType

Same as type("").

types.TracebackType

The type for traceback objects found in *sys.exc_traceback*.

types.TupleType

Same as type(()).

types.UnicodeType

Same as type(u"").

types.SliceType

The type for objects returned by slice().

types.StringTypes

Same as (types.StringType,types.UnicodeType).

SEE ALSO: types.StringType *57*; types.UnicodeType *57*;

types.TypeType

Same as type(type(obj)) (for any obj).

types.XRangeType

Same as type(xrange(1)).

1.2.2   Working with the Local Filesystem

dircache ◇ Read and cache directory listings

The *dircache* module is an enhanced version of the *os.listdir()* function. Unlike the *os* function, *dircache* keeps prior directory listings in memory to avoid the need for a new call to the filesystem. Since *dircache* is smart enough to check whether a directory has been touched since last caching, *dircache* is a complete replacement for *os.listdir()* (with possible minor speed gains).

FUNCTIONS

dircache.listdir(path)

Return a directory listing of path `path`. Uses a list cached in memory where possible.

dircache.opendir(path)

Identical to *dircache.listdir()*. Legacy function to support old scripts.

dircache.annotate(path, lst)

Modify the list `lst` in place to indicate which items are directories, and which are plain files. The string `path` should indicate the path to reach the listed files.

```
>>> l = dircache.listdir('/tmp')
>>> l
['501', 'md10834.db']
>>> dircache.annotate('/tmp', l)
>>> l
['501/', 'md10834.db']
```

filecmp ◇ Compare files and directories

The *filecmp* module lets you check whether two files are identical, and whether two directories contain some identical files. You have several options in determining how thorough of a comparison is performed.

FUNCTIONS

filecmp.cmp(fname1, fname2 [,shallow=1 [,use_statcache=0]])

Compare the file named by the string `fname1` with the file named by the string `fname2`. If the default true value of `shallow` is used, the comparison is based only on the mode, size, and modification time of the two files. If `shallow` is a false value, the files are compared byte by byte. Unless you are concerned that someone will deliberately falsify timestamps on files (as in a cryptography context), a shallow comparison is quite reliable. However, `tar` and `untar` can also change timestamps.

```
>>> import filecmp
>>> filecmp.cmp('dir1/file1', 'dir2/file1')
0
>>> filecmp.cmp('dir1/file2', 'dir2/file2', shallow=0)
1
```

The `use_statcache` argument is not relevant for Python 2.2+. In older Python versions, the *statcache* module provided (slightly) more efficient cached access to file stats, but its use is no longer needed.

filecmp.cmpfiles(dirname1, dirname2, fnamelist [,shallow=1 [,use_statcache=0]])

Compare those filenames listed in `fnamelist` if they occur in both the directory `dirname1` and the directory `dirname2`. `filecmp.cmpfiles()` returns a tuple of three lists (some of the lists may be empty): (matches,mismatches,errors). `matches` are identical files in both directories, `mismatches` are nonidentical files in both directories. `errors` will contain names if a file exists in neither, or in only one, of the two directories, or if either file cannot be read for any reason (permissions, disk problems, etc.).

```
>>> import filecmp, os
>>> filecmp.cmpfiles('dir1','dir2',['this','that','other'])
(['this'], ['that'], ['other'])
>>> print os.popen('ls -l dir1').read()
-rwxr-xr-x    1 quilty    staff       169 Sep 27 00:13 this
-rwxr-xr-x    1 quilty    staff       687 Sep 27 00:13 that
-rwxr-xr-x    1 quilty    staff       737 Sep 27 00:16 other
-rwxr-xr-x    1 quilty    staff       518 Sep 12 11:57 spam
>>> print os.popen('ls -l dir2').read()
-rwxr-xr-x    1 quilty    staff       169 Sep 27 00:13 this
-rwxr-xr-x    1 quilty    staff       692 Sep 27 00:32 that
```

The shallow and use_statcache arguments are the same as those to `filecmp.cmp()`.

CLASSES

filecmp.dircmp(dirname1, dirname2 [,ignore=... [,hide=...]])

Create a directory comparison object. `dirname1` and `dirname2` are two directories to compare. The optional argument `ignore` is a sequence of pathnames to ignore and defaults to ["RCS","CVS","tags"]; `hide` is a sequence of pathnames to hide and defaults to [os.curdir,os.pardir] (i.e., [".",".."]).

METHODS AND ATTRIBUTES

The attributes of `filecmp.dircmp` are read-only. Do not attempt to modify them.

filecmp.dircmp.report()

Print a comparison report on the two directories.

```
>>> mycmp = filecmp.dircmp('dir1','dir2')
>>> mycmp.report()
diff dir1 dir2
Only in dir1 : ['other', 'spam']
```

```
Identical files : ['this']
Differing files : ['that']
```

filecmp.dircmp.report_partial_closure()

Print a comparison report on the two directories, including immediate subdirectories. The method name has nothing to do with the theoretical term "closure" from functional programming.

filecmp.dircmp.report_partial_closure()

Print a comparison report on the two directories, recursively including all nested subdirectories.

filecmp.dircmp.left_list

Pathnames in the `dirname1` directory, filtering out the `hide` and `ignore` lists.

filecmp.dircmp.right_list

Pathnames in the `dirname2` directory, filtering out the `hide` and `ignore` lists.

filecmp.dircmp.common

Pathnames in both directories.

filecmp.dircmp.left_only

Pathnames in `dirname1` but not `dirname2`.

filecmp.dircmp.right_only

Pathnames in `dirname2` but not `dirname1`.

filecmp.dircmp.common_dirs

Subdirectories in both directories.

filecmp.dircmp.common_files

Filenames in both directories.

filecmp.dircmp.common_funny

Pathnames in both directories, but of different types.

filecmp.dircmp.same_files

Filenames of identical files in both directories.

filecmp.dircmp.diff_files

Filenames of nonidentical files whose name occurs in both directories.

filecmp.dircmp.funny_files

Filenames in both directories where something goes wrong during comparison.

filecmp.dircmp.subdirs

A dictionary mapping *filecmp.dircmp.common_dirs* strings to corresponding *filecmp.dircmp* objects; for example:

```
>>> usercmp = filecmp.dircmp('/Users/quilty','/Users/dqm')
>>> usercmp.subdirs['Public'].common
['Drop Box']
```

SEE ALSO: os.stat() *79*; os.listdir() *76*;

---

fileinput ◇ Read multiple files or STDIN

Many utilities, especially on Unix-like systems, operate line-by-line on one or more files and/or on redirected input. A flexibility in treating input sources in a homogeneous fashion is part of the "Unix philosophy." The *fileinput* module allows you to write a Python application that uses these common conventions with almost no special programming to adjust to input sources.

A common, minimal, but extremely useful Unix utility is `cat`, which simply writes its input to STDOUT (allowing redirection of STDOUT as needed). Below are a few simple examples of `cat`:

```
% cat a
AAAAA
% cat a b
AAAAA
BBBBB
% cat - b < a
AAAAA
BBBBB
% cat < b
BBBBB
% cat a < b
AAAAA
% echo "XXX" | cat a -
AAAAA
XXX
```

Notice that STDIN is read only if either "-" is given as an argument, or no arguments are given at all. We can implement a Python version of `cat` using the *fileinput* module as follows:

cat.py

```
#!/usr/bin/env python
import fileinput
for line in fileinput.input():
        print line,
```

FUNCTIONS

fileinput.input([files=sys.argv[1:] [,inplace=0 [,backup=".bak"]]])

Most commonly, this function will be used without any of its optional arguments, as in the introductory example of cat.py. However, behavior may be customized for special cases.

The argument files is a sequence of filenames to process. By default, it consists of all the arguments given on the command line. Commonly, however, you might want to treat some of these arguments as flags rather than filenames (e.g., if they start with - or /). Any list of filenames you like may be used as the files argument, whether or not it is built from sys.argv.

If you specify a true value for inplace, output will go into each file specified rather than to STDOUT. Input taken from STDIN, however, will still go to STDOUT. For in-place operation, a temporary backup file is created as the actual input source and is given the extension indicated by the backup argument. For example:

```
% cat a b
AAAAA
BBBBB
% cat modify.py
#!/usr/bin/env python
import fileinput, sys
for line in fileinput.input(sys.argv[1:], inplace=1):
        print "MODIFIED", line,
% echo "XXX" | ./modify.py a b -
MODIFIED XXX
% cat a b
MODIFIED AAAAA
MODIFIED BBBBB
```

fileinput.close()

Close the input sequence.

fileinput.nextfile()

Close the current file, and proceed to the next one. Any unread lines in the current file will not be counted towards the line total.

There are several functions in the *fileinput* module that provide information about the current input state. These tests can be used to process the current line in a context-dependent way.

fileinput.filelineno()

The number of lines read from the current file.

fileinput.filename()

The name of the file from which the last line was read. Before a line is read, the function returns None.

fileinput.isfirstline()

Same as `fileinput.filelineno()==1`.

fileinput.isstdin()

True if the last line read was from STDIN.

fileinput.lineno()

The number of lines read during the input loop, cumulative between files.

CLASSES

fileinput.FileInput([files [,inplace=0 [,backup=".bak"]]])

The methods of *fileinput.FileInput* are the same as the module-level functions, plus an additional `.readline()` method that matches that of file objects. *fileinput.FileInput* objects also have a `.__getitem__()` method to support sequential access.

The arguments to initialize a *fileinput.FileInput* object are the same as those passed to the *fileinput.input()* function. The class exists primarily in order to allow subclassing. For normal usage, it is best to just use the *fileinput* functions.

SEE ALSO: multifile *285*; xreadlines *72*;

glob ◇ Filename globing utility

The *glob* module provides a list of pathnames matching a glob-style pattern. The *fnmatch* module is used internally to determine whether a path matches.

FUNCTIONS

glob.glob(pat)

Both directories and plain files are returned, so if you are only interested in one type of path, use *os.path.isdir()* or *os.path.isfile()*; other functions in *os.path* also support other filters.

Pathnames returned by *glob.glob()* contain as much absolute or relative path information as the pattern **pat** gives. For example:

```
>>> import glob, os.path
>>> glob.glob('/Users/quilty/Book/chap[3-4].txt')
['/Users/quilty/Book/chap3.txt', '/Users/quilty/Book/chap4.txt']
>>> glob.glob('chap[3-6].txt')
['chap3.txt', 'chap4.txt', 'chap5.txt', 'chap6.txt']
>>> filter(os.path.isdir, glob.glob('/Users/quilty/Book/[A-Z]*'))
['/Users/quilty/Book/SCRIPTS', '/Users/quilty/Book/XML']
```

SEE ALSO: fnmatch *232*; os.path *65*;

linecache ◇ Cache lines from files

The module *linecache* can be used to simulate relatively efficient random access to the lines in a file. Lines that are read are cached for later access.

FUNCTIONS

linecache.getline(fname, linenum)

Read line `linenum` from the file named **fname**. If an error occurs reading the line, the function will catch the error and return an empty string. `sys.path` is also searched for the filename if it is not found in the current directory.

```
>>> import linecache
>>> linecache.getline('/etc/hosts', 15)
'192.168.1.108   hermes   hermes.gnosis.lan\n'
```

linecache.clearcache()

Clear the cache of read lines.

linecache.checkcache()

Check whether files in the cache have been modified since they were cached.

---

os.path ◇ Common pathname manipulations

The *os.path* module provides a variety of functions to analyze and manipulate filesystem paths in a cross-platform fashion.

FUNCTIONS

os.path.abspath(pathname)

Return an absolute path for a (relative) pathname.

```
>>> os.path.abspath('SCRIPTS/mk_book')
'/Users/quilty/Book/SCRIPTS/mk_book'
```

os.path.basename(pathname)

Same as os.path.split(pathname)[1].

os .path.commonprefix(pathlist)

Return the path to the most nested parent directory shared by all elements of the sequence pathlist.

```
>>> os.path.commonprefix(['/usr/X11R6/bin/twm',
...                        '/usr/sbin/bash',
...                        '/usr/local/bin/dada'])
'/usr/'
```

os.path.dirname(pathname)

Same as os.path.split(pathname)[0].

os.path.exists(pathname)

Return true if the pathname pathname exists.

os.path.expanduser(pathname)

Expand pathnames that include the tilde character: ∼. Under standard Unix shells, an initial tilde refers to a user's home directory, and a tilde followed by a name refers to the named user's home directory. This function emulates that behavior on other platforms.

```
>>> os.path.expanduser('~dqm')
'/Users/dqm'
>>> os.path.expanduser('~/Book')
'/Users/quilty/Book'
```

os.path.expandvars(pathname)

Expand `pathname` by replacing environment variables in a Unix shell style. While this function is in the *os.path* module, you could equally use it for bash-like scripting in Python, generally (this is not necessarily a good idea, but it is possible).

```
>>> os.path.expandvars('$HOME/Book')
'/Users/quilty/Book'
>>> from os.path import expandvars as ev  # Python 2.0+
>>> if ev('$HOSTTYPE')=='macintosh' and ev('$OSTYPE')=='darwin':
...     print ev("The vendor is $VENDOR, the CPU is $MACHTYPE")
...
The vendor is apple, the CPU is powerpc
```

os.path.getatime(pathname)

Return the last access time of `pathname` (or raise `os.error` if checking is not possible).

os.path.getmtime(pathname)

Return the modification time of `pathname` (or raise `os.error` if checking is not possible).

os.path.getsize(pathname)

Return the size of `pathname` in bytes (or raise `os.error` if checking is not possible).

os.path.isabs(pathname)

Return true if `pathname` is an absolute path.

os.path.isdir(pathname)

Return true if `pathname` is a directory.

os.path.isfile(pathname)

Return true if `pathname` is a regular file (including symbolic links).

os.path.islink(pathname)

Return true if `pathname` is a symbolic link.

os.path.ismount(pathname)

Return true if `pathname` is a mount point (on POSIX systems).

os.path.join(path1 [,path2 [. . .]])

Join multiple path components intelligently.

```
>>> os.path.join('/Users/quilty/','Book','SCRIPTS/','mk_book')
'/Users/quilty/Book/SCRIPTS/mk_book'
```

os.path.normcase(pathname)

Convert `pathname` to canonical lowercase on case-insensitive filesystems. Also convert slashes on Windows systems.

os.path.normpath(pathname)

Remove redundant path information.

```
>>> os.path.normpath('/usr/local/bin/../include/./slang.h')
'/usr/local/include/slang.h'
```

os.path.realpath(pathname)

Return the "real" path to `pathname` after de-aliasing any symbolic links. New in Python 2.2+.

```
>>> os.path.realpath('/usr/bin/newaliases')
'/usr/sbin/sendmail'
```

os.path.samefile(pathname1, pathname2)

Return true if `pathname1` and `pathname2` are the same file.

SEE ALSO: filecmp *58*;

os.path.sameopenfile(fp1, fp2)

Return true if the file handles `fp1` and `fp2` refer to the same file. Not available on Windows.

os.path.split(pathname)

Return a tuple containing the path leading up to the named pathname and the named directory or filename in isolation.

```
>>> os.path.split('/Users/quilty/Book/SCRIPTS')
('/Users/quilty/Book', 'SCRIPTS')
```

os.path.splitdrive(pathname)

Return a tuple containing the drive letter and the rest of the path. On systems that do not use a drive letter, the drive letter is empty (as it is where none is specified on Windows-like systems).

os.path.walk(pathname, visitfunc, arg)

For every directory recursively contained in `pathname`, call `visitfunc(arg, dirname, pathnames)` for each path.

```
>>> def big_files(minsize, dirname, files):
...     for file in files:
...         fullname = os.path.join(dirname,file)
...         if os.path.isfile(fullname):
...             if os.path.getsize(fullname) >= minsize:
...                 print fullname
...
>>> os.path.walk('/usr/', big_files, 5e6)
/usr/lib/libSystem.B_debug.dylib
/usr/lib/libSystem.B_profile.dylib
```

shutil ◇ Copy files and directory trees

The functions in the *shutil* module make working with files a bit easier. There is nothing in this module that you could not do using basic file objects and *os.path* functions, but *shutil* often provides a more direct means and handles minor details for you. The functions in *shutil* match fairly closely the capabilities you would find in Unix filesystem utilities like `cp` and `rm`.

FUNCTIONS

shutil.copy(src, dst)

Copy the file named `src` to the pathname `dst`. If `dst` is a directory, the created file is given the name `os.path.join(dst+os.path.basename(src))`.

SEE ALSO: os.path.join() *66*; os.path.basename() *65*;

shutil.copy2(src, dst)

Same as *shutil.copy()* except that the access and creation time of `dst` are set to the values in `src`.

shutil.copyfile(src, dst)

Copy the file named `src` to the filename `dst` (overwriting `dst` if present). Basically, this has the same effect as `open(dst,"wb").write(open(src,"rb").read())`.

shutil.copyfileobj(fpsrc, fpdst [,buffer=-1])

Copy the file-like object `fpsrc` to the file-like object `fpdst`. If the optional argument `buffer` is given, only the specified number of bytes are read into memory at a time; this allows copying very large files.

shutil.copymode(src, dst)

Copy the permission bits from the file named `src` to the filename `dst`.

shutil.copystat(src, dst)

Copy the permission and timestamp data from the file named `src` to the filename `dst`.

shutil.copytree(src, dst [,symlinks=0])

Copy the directory `src` to the destination `dst` recursively. If the optional argument `symlinks` is a true value, copy symbolic links as links rather than the default behavior of copying the content of the link target. This function may not be entirely reliable on every platform and filesystem.

shutil.rmtree(dirname [ignore [,errorhandler]])

Remove an entire directory tree rooted at `dirname`. If optional argument `ignore` is a true value, errors will be silently ignored. If `errorhandler` is given, a custom error handler is used to catch errors. This function may not be entirely reliable on every platform and filesystem.

SEE ALSO: open() *15*; os.path *65*;

| stat ◇ Constants/functions for os.stat() |

The *stat* module provides two types of support for analyzing the results of *os.stat()*, *os.lstat()*, and *os.fstat()* calls.

Several functions exist to allow you to perform tests on a file. If you simply wish to check one predicate of a file, it is more direct to use one of the *os.path.is*()* functions, but for performing several such tests, it is faster to read the mode once and perform several *stat.S_*()* tests.

As well as helper functions, *stat* defines symbolic constants to access the fields of the 10-tuple returned by *os.stat()* and friends. For example:

```
>>> from stat import *
>>> import os
>>> fileinfo = os.stat('chap1.txt')
>>> fileinfo[ST_SIZE]
68666L
>>> mode = fileinfo[ST_MODE]
>>> S_ISSOCK(mode)
0
>>> S_ISDIR(mode)
0
>>> S_ISREG(mode)
1
```

FUNCTIONS

stat.S_ISDIR(mode)

Mode indicates a directory.

stat.S_ISCHR(mode)

Mode indicates a character special device file.

stat.S_ISBLK(mode)

Mode indicates a block special device file.

stat.S_ISREG(mode)

Mode indicates a regular file.

stat.S_ISFIFO(mode)

Mode indicates a FIFO (named pipe).

stat.S_ISLNK(mode)

Mode indicates a symbolic link.

stat.S_ISSOCK(mode)

Mode indicates a socket.

CONSTANTS

stat.ST_MODE

I-node protection mode.

stat.ST_INO

I-node number.

stat.ST_DEV

Device.

stat.ST_NLINK

Number of links to this i-node.

stat.ST_UID

User id of file owner.

stat.ST_GID

Group id of file owner.

stat.ST_SIZE

Size of file.

stat.ST_ATIME

Last access time.

stat.ST_MTIME

Modification time.

stat.ST_CTIME

Time of last status change.

tempfile ◇ Temporary files and filenames

The *tempfile* module is useful when you need to store transient data using a file-like interface. In contrast to the file-like interface of *StringIO*, *tempfile* uses the actual filesystem for storage rather than simulating the interface to a file in memory. In memory-constrained contexts, therefore, *tempfile* is preferable.

The temporary files created by *tempfile* are as secure against external modification as is supported by the underlying platform. You can be fairly confident that your temporary data will not be read or changed either while your program is running or afterwards (temporary files are deleted when closed). While you should not count on *tempfile* to provide you with cryptographic-level security, it is good enough to prevent accidents and casual inspection.

FUNCTIONS

tempfile.mktemp([suffix=""])

Return an absolute path to a unique temporary filename. If optional argument `suffix` is specified, the name will end with the `suffix` string.

tempfile.TemporaryFile([mode="w+b" [,buffsize=-1 [suffix=""]]])

Return a temporary file object. In general, there is little reason to change the default `mode` argument of `w+b`; there is no existing file to append to before the creation, and it does little good to write temporary data you cannot read. Likewise, the optional `suffix` argument generally will not ever be visible, since the file is deleted when closed. The default `buffsize` uses the platform defaults, but may be modified if needed.

```
>>> tmpfp = tempfile.TemporaryFile()
>>> tmpfp.write('this and that\n')
>>> tmpfp.write('something else\n')
>>> tmpfp.tell()
29L
>>> tmpfp.seek(0)
>>> tmpfp.read()
'this and that\nsomething else\n'
```

SEE ALSO: StringIO *153*; cStringIO *153*;

xreadlines ◇ Efficient iteration over a file

Reading over the lines of a file had some pitfalls in older versions of Python: There was a memory-friendly way, and there was a fast way, but never the twain shall meet. These techniques were:

```
>>> fp = open('bigfile')
>>> line = fp.readline()
>>> while line:
...        # Memory-friendly but slow
...        # ...do stuff...
...        line = fp.readline()

>>> for line in open('bigfile').readlines():
...        # Fast but memory-hungry
...        # ...do stuff...
```

Fortunately, with Python 2.1 a more efficient technique was provided. In Python 2.2+, this efficient technique was also wrapped into a more elegant syntactic form (in keeping with the new iterator). With Python 2.3+, *xreadlines* is officially deprecated in favor of the idiom "`for line in file:`".

FUNCTIONS

xreadlines.xreadlines(fp)

Iterate over the lines of file object `fp` in an efficient way (both speed-wise and in memory usage).

```
>>> for line in xreadlines.xreadlines(open('tmp')):
...        # Efficient all around
...        # ...do stuff...
```

Corresponding to this *xreadlines* module function is the `.xreadlines()` method of file objects.

```
>>> for line in open('tmp').xreadlines():
...        # As a file object method
...        # ...do stuff...
```

If you use Python 2.2 or above, an even nicer version is available:

```
>>> for line in open('tmp'):
...        # ...do stuff...
```

SEE ALSO: linecache *64*; FILE.xreadlines() *17*; os.tmpfile() *80*;

1.2.3   Running External Commands and Accessing OS Features

commands ◇ **Quick access to external commands**

The *commands* module exists primarily as a convenience wrapper for calls to *os.popen*()* functions on Unix-like systems. STDERR is combined with STDOUT in the results.

FUNCTIONS

commands.getoutput(cmd)

Return the output from running cmd. This function could also be implemented as:

```
>>> def getoutput(cmd):
...     import os
...     return os.popen('{ '+cmd+'; } 2>&1').read()
```

commands.getstatusoutput(cmd)

Return a tuple containing the exit status and output from running cmd. This function could also be implemented as:

```
>>> def getstatusoutput(cmd):
...     import os
...     fp = os.popen('{ '+cmd+'; } 2>&1')
...     output = fp.read()
...     status = fp.close()
...     if not status: status=0 # Want zero rather than None
...     return (status, output)
...
>>> getstatusoutput('ls nosuchfile')
(256, 'ls: nosuchfile: No such file or directory\n')
>>> getstatusoutput('ls c*[1-3].txt')
(0, 'chap1.txt\nchap2.txt\nchap3.txt\n')
```

commands.getstatus(filename)

Same as commands.getoutput('ls -ld '+filename).

See Also: os.popen() 77; os.popen2() 77; os.popen3() 78; os.popen4() 78;

os ◇ Portable operating system services

The *os* module contains a large number of functions, attributes, and constants for calling on or determining features of the operating system that Python runs on. In many cases, functions in *os* are internally implemented using modules like *posix*, *os2*, *riscos*, or *mac*, but for portability it is better to use the *os* module.

Not everything in the *os* module is documented in this book. You can read about those features that are unlikely to be used in text processing applications in the *Python Library Reference* that accompanies Python distributions.

Functions and constants not documented here fall into several categories. The functions and attributes *os.confstr()*, *os.confstr_names*, *os.sysconf()*, and *os.sysconf_names* let you probe system configuration. As well, I skip some functions specific to process permissions on Unix-like systems: *os.ctermid()*, *os.getegid()*, *os.geteuid()*, *os.getgid()*, *os.getgroups()*, *os.getlogin()*, *os.getpgrp()*, *os.getppid()*, *os.getuid()*, *os.setegid()*, *os.seteuid()*, *os.setgid()*, *os.setgroups()*, *os.setpgrp()*, *os.setpgid()*, *os.setreuid()*, *os.setregid()*, *os.setsid()*, and *os.setuid(uid)*.

The functions *os.abort()*, *os.exec*()*, *os._exit()*, *os.fork()*, *os.forkpty()*, *os.plock()*, *os.spawn*()*, *os.times()*, *os.wait()*, *os.waitpid()*, *os.WIF*()*, *os.WEXITSTATUS()*, os.WSTOPSIG()', and *os.WTERMSIG()* and the constants *os.P_*￼* and *os.WNOHANG* all deal with process creation and management. These are not documented in this book, since creating and managing multiple processes is not typically central to text processing tasks. However, I briefly document the basic capabilities in *os.kill()*, *os.nice()*, *os.startfile()*, and *os.system()* and in the *os.popen()* family. Some of the omitted functionality can also be found in the *commands* and *sys* modules.

A number of functions in the *os* module allow you to perform low-level I/O using file descriptors. In general, it is simpler to perform I/O using file objects created with the built-in *open()* function or the *os.popen*()* family. These file objects provide methods like *FILE.readline()*, *FILE.write()*, *FILE.seek()*, and *FILE.close()*. Information about files can be determined using the *os.stat()* function or functions in the *os.path* and *shutil* modules. Therefore, the functions *os.close()*, *os.dup()*, *os.dup2()*, *os.fpathconf()*, *os.fstat()*, *os.fstatvfs()*, *os.ftruncate()*, *os.isatty()*, *os.lseek()*, *os.open()*, *os.openpty()*, *os.pathconf()*, *os.pipe()*, *os.read()*, *os.statvfs()*, *os.tcgetpgrp()*, *os.tcsetpgrp()*, *os.ttyname()*, *os.umask()*, and *os.write()* are not covered here. As well, the supporting constants *os.O_*￼* and *os.pathconf_names* are omitted.

SEE ALSO: commands *73*; os.path *65*; shutil *68*; sys *49*;

FUNCTIONS

os.access(pathname, operation)

Check the permission for the file or directory **pathname**. If the type of operation specified is allowed, return a true value. The argument **operation** is a number between 0 and 7, inclusive, and encodes four features: exists, executable, writable, and readable. These features have symbolic names:

```
>>> import os
>>> os.F_OK, os.X_OK, os.W_OK, os.R_OK
(0, 1, 2, 4)
```

To query a specific combination of features, you may add or bitwise-or the individual features.

```
>>> os.access('myfile', os.W_OK | os.R_OK)
1
>>> os.access('myfile', os.X_OK + os.R_OK)
0
>>> os.access('myfile', 6)
1
```

os.chdir(pathname)

Change the current working directory to the path `pathname`.

SEE ALSO: os.getcwd() 75;

os.chmod(pathname, mode)

Change the mode of file or directory `pathname` to numeric mode `mode`. See the `man` page for the `chmod` utility for more information on modes.

os.chown(pathname, uid, gid)

Change the owner and group of file or directory `pathname` to `uid` and `gid` respectively. See the `man` page for the `chown` utility for more information.

os.chroot(pathname)

Change the root directory under Unix-like systems (on Python 2.2+). See the `man` page for the `chroot` utility for more information.

os.getcwd()

Return the current working directory as a string.

```
>>> os.getcwd()
'/Users/quilty/Book'
```

SEE ALSO: os.chdir() 75;

os.getenv(var [,value=None])

Return the value of environment variable `var`. If the environment variable is not defined, return `value`. An equivalent call is `os.environ.get(var, value)`.

SEE ALSO: os.environ *81*; os.putenv() *78*;

os.getpid()

Return the current process id. Possibly useful for calls to external utilities that use process id's.

SEE ALSO: os.kill() *76*;

os.kill(pid, sig)

Kill an external process on Unix-like systems. You will need to determine values for the `pid` argument by some means, such as a call to the `ps` utility. Values for the signal `sig` sent to the process may be found in the *signal* module or with `man signal`. For example:

```
>>> from signal import *
>>> SIGHUP, SIGINT, SIGQUIT, SIGIOT, SIGKILL
(1, 2, 3, 6, 9)
>>> def kill_by_name(progname):
...     pidstr = os.popen('ps|grep '+progname+'|sort').read()
...     pid = int(pidstr.split()[0])
...     os.kill(pid, 9)
...
>>> kill_by_name('myprog')
```

os.link(src, dst)

Create a hard link from path `src` to path `dst` on Unix-like systems. See the `man` page on the `ln` utility for more information.

SEE ALSO: os.symlink() *80*;

os.listdir(pathname)

Return a list of the names of files and directories at path `pathname`. The special entries for the current and parent directories (typically "." and "..") are excluded from the list.

os.lstat(pathname)

Information on file or directory `pathname`. See *os.stat()* for details. *os.lstat()* does not follow symbolic links.

SEE ALSO: os.stat() *79*; stat *69*;

os.mkdir(pathname [,mode=0777])

Create a directory named `pathname` with the numeric mode `mode`. On some operating systems, `mode` is ignored. See the `man` page for the `chmod` utility for more information on modes.

SEE ALSO: os.chmod() 75; os.mkdirs() 77;

os.mkdirs(pathname [,mode=0777])

Create a directory named `pathname` with the numeric mode `mode`. Unlike *os.mkdir()*, this function will create any intermediate directories needed for a nested directory.

SEE ALSO: os.mkdir() 76;

os.mkfifo(pathname [,mode=0666])

Create a named pipe on Unix-like systems.

os.nice(increment)

Decrease the process priority of the current application under Unix-like systems. This is useful if you do not wish for your application to hog system CPU resources.

The four functions in the *os.popen*() family allow you to run external processes and capture their STDOUT and STDERR and/or set their STDIN. The members of the family differ somewhat in how these three pipes are handled.

os.popen(cmd [,mode="r" [,bufsize]])

Open a pipe to or from the external command `cmd`. The return value of the function is an open file object connected to the pipe. The `mode` may be `r` for read (the default) or `w` for write. The exit status of the command is returned when the file object is closed. An optional buffer size `bufsize` may be specified.

```
>>> import os
>>> def ls(pat):
...     stdout = os.popen('ls '+pat)
...     result = stdout.read()
...     status = stdout.close()
...     if status: print "Error status", status
...     else: print result
...
>>> ls('nosuchfile')
ls: nosuchfile: No such file or directory
Error status 256
>>> ls('chap[7-9].txt')
chap7.txt
```

os.popen2(cmd [,mode [,bufsize]])

Open both STDIN and STDOUT pipes to the external command `cmd`. The return value is a pair of file objects connecting to the two respective pipes. `mode` and `bufsize` work as with *os.popen()*.

SEE ALSO: os.popen3() *78*; os.popen() *77*;

os.popen3(cmd [,mode [,bufsize]])

Open STDIN, STDOUT, and STDERR pipes to the external command `cmd`. The return value is a 3-tuple of file objects connecting to the three respective pipes. `mode` and `bufsize` work as with *os.popen()*.

```
>>> import os
>>> stdin, stdout, stderr = os.popen3('sed s/line/LINE/')
>>> print >>stdin, 'line one'
>>> print >>stdin, 'line two'
>>> stdin.write('line three\n')
>>> stdin.close()
>>> stdout.read()
'LINE one\nLINE two\nLINE three\n'
>>> stderr.read()
''
```

os.popen4(cmd [,mode [,bufsize]])

Open STDIN, STDOUT, and STDERR pipes to the external command `cmd`. In contrast to *os.popen3()*, *os.popen4()* combines STDOUT and STDERR on the same pipe. The return value is a pipe of file objects connecting to the two respective pipes. `mode` and `bufsize` work as with *os.popen()*.

SEE ALSO: os.popen3() *78*; os.popen() *77*;

os.putenv(var, value)

Set the environment variable `var` to the value `value`. Changes to the current environment only affect subprocesses of the current process, such as those launched with *os.system()* or *os.popen()*, not the whole OS.

Calls to *os.putenv()* will update the environment, but not the *os.environ* variable. Therefore, it is better to update *os.environ* directly (which also changes the external environment).

SEE ALSO: os.environ *81*; os.getenv() *75*; os.popen() *77*; os.system() *80*;

os.readlink(linkname)

Return a string containing the path symbolic link `linkname` points to. Works on Unix-like systems.

SEE ALSO: os.symlink() *80*;

os.remove(filename)

Remove the file named `filename`. This function is identical to *os.unlink()*. If the file cannot be removed, an `OSError` is raised.

SEE ALSO: os.unlink() *81*;

os.removedirs(pathname)

Remove the directory named `pathname` and any subdirectories of `pathname`. This function will not remove directories with files, and will raise an `OSError` if you attempt to do so.

SEE ALSO: os.rmdir() *79*;

os.rename(src, dst)

Rename the file or directory `src` as `dst`. Depending on the operating system, the operation may raise an `OSError` if `dst` already exists.

SEE ALSO: os.renames() *79*;

os.renames(src, dst)

Rename the file or directory `src` as `dst`. Unlike *os.rename()*, this function will create any intermediate directories needed for a nested directory.

SEE ALSO: os.rename() *79*;

os.rmdir(pathname)

Remove the directory named `pathname`. This function will not remove nonempty directories and will raise an `OSError` if you attempt to do so.

SEE ALSO: os.removedirs() *79*;

os.startfile(path)

Launch an application under Windows system. The behavior is the same as if `path` was double-clicked in a Drives window or as if you typed `start <path>` at a command line. Using Windows associations, a data file can be launched in the same manner as an actual executable application.

SEE ALSO: os.system() *80*;

os.stat(pathname)

Create a `stat_result` object that contains information on the file or directory `pathname`. A `stat_result` object has a number of attributes and also behaves like a tuple of numeric values. Before Python 2.2, only the tuple was provided. The attributes of a `stat_result` object are named the same as the constants in the *stat* module, but in lowercase.

```
>>> import os, stat
>>> file_info = os.stat('chap1.txt')
>>> file_info.st_size
87735L
>>> file_info[stat.ST_SIZE]
87735L
```

On some platforms, additional attributes are available. For example, Unix-like systems usually have `.st_blocks`, `.st_blksize`, and `.st_rdev` attributes; MacOS has `.st_rsize`, `.st_creator`, and `.st_type`; RISCOS has `.st_ftype`, `.st_attrs`, and `.st_obtype`.

SEE ALSO: stat *69*; os.lstat() *76*;

os.strerror(code)

Give a description for a numeric error code `code`, such as that returned by `os.popen(bad_cmd).close()`.

SEE ALSO: os.popen() *77*;

os.symlink(src, dst)

Create a soft link from path `src` to path `dst` on Unix-like systems. See the `man` page on the `ln` utility for more information.

SEE ALSO: os.link() *76*; os.readlink() *78*;

os.system(cmd)

Execute the command `cmd` in a subshell. Unlike execution using *os.popen()* the output of the executed process is not captured (but it may still echo to the same terminal as the current Python application). In some cases, you can use *os.system()* on non-Windows systems to detach an application in a manner similar to *os.startfile()*. For example, under MacOSX, you could launch the TextEdit application with:

```
>>> import os
>>> cmd="/Applications/TextEdit.app/Contents/MacOS/TextEdit &"
>>> os.system(cmd)
0
```

SEE ALSO: os.popen() *77*; os.startfile() *79*; commands *73*;

os.tempnam([dir [,prefix]])

Return a unique filename for a temporary file. If optional argument `dir` is specified, that directory will be used in the path; if `prefix` is specified, the file will have the indicated prefix. For most purposes, it is more secure to use *os.tmpfile()* to directly obtain a file object rather than first generating a name.

SEE ALSO: tempfile *71*; os.tmpfile() *80*;

os.tmpfile()

Return an "invisible" file object in update mode. This file does not create a directory entry, but simply acts as a transient buffer for data on the filesystem.

SEE ALSO: tempfile *71*; StringIO *153*; cStringIO *153*;

os.uname()

Return detailed information about the current operating system on recent Unix-like systems. The returned 5-tuple contains sysname, nodename, release, version, and machine, each as descriptive strings.

os.unlink(filename)

Remove the file named `filename`. This function is identical to *os.remove()*. If the file cannot be removed, an `OSError` is raised.

SEE ALSO: os.remove() *78*;

os.utime(pathname, times)

Set the access and modification timestamps of file `pathname` to the tuple (`atime`, `mtime`) specified in `times`. Alternately, if `times` is `None`, set both timestamps to the current time.

SEE ALSO: time *86*; os.chmod() *75*; os.chown() *75*; os.stat() *79*;

CONSTANTS AND ATTRIBUTES

os.altsep

Usually `None`, but an alternative path delimiter ("/") under Windows.

os.curdir

The string the operating system uses to refer to the current directory; for example, "." on Unix or ":" on Macintosh (before MacOSX).

os.defpath

The search path used by exec*p*() and spawn*p*() absent a PATH environment variable.

os.environ

A dictionary-like object containing the current environment.

```
>>> os.environ['TERM']
'vt100'
>>> os.environ['TERM'] = 'vt220'
>>> os.getenv('TERM')
'vt220'
```

SEE ALSO: os.getenv() *75*; os.putenv() *78*;

os.linesep

> The string that delimits lines in a file; for example "\n" on Unix, "\r" on Macintosh, "\r\n" on Windows.

os.name

> A string identifying the operating system the current Python interpreter is running on. Possible strings include `posix`, `nt`, `dos`, `mac`, `os2`, `ce`, `java`, and `riscos`.

os.pardir

> The string the operating system uses to refer to the parent directory; for example, ".." on Unix or "::" on Macintosh (before MacOSX).

os.pathsep

> The string that delimits search paths; for example, ";" on Windows or ":" on Unix.

os.sep

> The string the operating system uses to refer to path delimiters; for example "/" on Unix, "\" on Windows, ":" on Macintosh.

SEE ALSO: sys *49*; os.path *65*;

1.2.4   Special Data Values and Formats

random ◇ Pseudo-random value generator

Python provides better pseudo-random number generation than do most C libraries with a `rand()` function, but not good enough for cryptographic purposes. The period of Python's Wichmann-Hill generator is about 7 trillion (7e13), but that merely indicates how long it will take a particular seeded generator to cycle; a different seed will produce a different sequence of numbers. Python 2.3 uses the superior Mersenne Twister generator, which has a longer period and has been better analyzed. For practical purposes, pseudo-random numbers generated by Python are more than adequate for random-seeming behavior in applications.

The underlying pseudo-random numbers generated by the *random* module can be mapped into a variety of nonuniform patterns and distributions. Moreover, you can capture and tinker with the state of a pseudo-random generator; you can even subclass the *random.Random* class that operates behind the scenes. However, this latter sort of specialization is outside the scope of this book, and the class *random.Random* and functions *random.getstate()*, *random.jumpahead()*, and *random.setstate()* are omitted from this discussion. The functions *random.whseed()* and *random.randint()* are deprecated.

FUNCTIONS

random.betavariate(alpha, beta)

> Return a floating point value in the range [0.0, 1.0) with a beta distribution.

random.choice(seq)

Select a random element from the nonempty sequence seq.

random.cunifvariate(mean, arc)

Return a floating point value in the range [mean-arc/2, mean+arc/2) with a circular uniform distribution. Arguments and result are expressed in radians.

random.expovariate(lambda_)

Return a floating point value in the range [0.0, +inf) with an exponential distribution. The argument lambda_ gives the *inverse* of the mean of the distribution.

```
>>> import random
>>> t1,t2 = 0,0
>>> for x in range(100):
...     t1 += random.expovariate(1./20)
...     t2 += random.expovariate(20.)
...
>>> print t1/100, t2/100
18.4021962198 0.0558234063338
```

random.gamma(alpha, beta)

Return a floating point value with a gamma distribution (not the gamma function).

random.gauss(mu, sigma)

Return a floating point value with a Gaussian distribution; the mean is mu and the sigma is sigma. *random.gauss()* is slightly faster than *random.normalvariate()*.

random.lognormvariate(mu, sigma)

Return a floating point value with a log normal distribution; the natural logarithm of this distribution is Gaussian with mean mu and sigma sigma.

random.normalvariate(mu, sigma)

Return a floating point value with a Gaussian distribution; the mean is mu and the sigma is sigma.

random.paretovariate(alpha)

Return a floating point value with a Pareto distribution. alpha specifies the shape parameter.

random.random()

Return a floating point value in the range [0.0, 1.0).

random.randrange([start=0,] stop [,step=1])

Return a random element from the specified range. Functionally equivalent to the expression random.choice(range(start,stop,step)), but it does not build the actual range object. Use *random.randrange()* in place of the deprecated *random.randint()*.

random.seed([x=time.time()])

Initialize the Wichmann-Hill generator. You do not necessarily *need* to call `random.seed()`, since the current system time is used to initialize the generator upon module import. But if you wish to provide more entropy in the initial state, you may pass any hashable object as argument x. Your best choice for x is a positive long integer less than 27814431486575L, whose value is selected at random by independent means.

random.shuffle(seq [,random=random.random])

Permute the mutable sequence `seq` in place. An optional argument `random` may be specified to use an alternate random generator, but it is unlikely you will want to use one. Possible permutations get very big very quickly, so even for moderately sized sequences, not every permutation will occur.

random.uniform(min, max)

Return a random floating point value in the range [min, max).

random.vonmisesvariate(mu, kappa)

Return a floating point value with a von Mises distribution. `mu` is the mean angle expressed in radians, and `kappa` is the concentration parameter.

random.weibullvariate(alpha, beta)

Return a floating point value with a Weibull distribution. `alpha` is the scale parameter, and `beta` is the shape parameter.

---

struct ◇ Create and read packed binary strings

The *struct* module allows you to encode compactly Python numeric values. This module may also be used to read C structs that use the same formats; some formatting codes are only useful for reading C structs. The exception *struct.error* is raised if a format does not match its string or values.

A format string consists of a sequence of alphabetic formatting codes. Each code is represented by zero or more bytes in the encoded packed binary string. Each formatting code may be preceded by a number indicating a number of occurrences. The entire format string may be preceded by a global flag. If the flag @ is used, platform-native data sizes and endianness are used. In all other cases, standard data sizes are used. The flag = explicitly indicates platform endianness; < indicates little-endian representations; > or ! indicates big-endian representations.

The available formatting codes are listed below. The standard sizes are given (check your platform for its sizes if platform-native sizes are needed).

```
Formatting codes for struct module
```

x	pad byte	0 bytes
c	char	1 bytes
b	signed char	1 bytes
B	unsigned char	1 bytes
h	short int	2 bytes
H	unsigned short	2 bytes
i	int	4 bytes
I	unsigned int	4 bytes
l	long int	4 bytes
L	unsigned long	4 bytes
q	long long int	8 bytes
Q	unsigned long long	8 bytes
f	float	4 bytes
d	double	8 bytes
s	string	padded to size
p	Pascal string	padded to size
P	char pointer	4 bytes

Some usage examples clarify the encoding:

```
>>> import struct
>>> struct.pack('5s5p2c', 'sss','ppp','c','c')
'sss\x00\x00\x03ppp\x00cc'
>>> struct.pack('h', 1)
'\x00\x01'
>>> struct.pack('I', 1)
'\x00\x00\x00\x01'
>>> struct.pack('l', 1)
'\x00\x00\x00\x01'
>>> struct.pack('<l', 1)
'\x01\x00\x00\x00'
>>> struct.pack('f', 1)
'?\x80\x00\x00'
>>> struct.pack('hil', 1,2,3)
'\x00\x01\x00\x00\x00\x00\x00\x02\x00\x00\x00\x03'
```

FUNCTIONS

struct.calcsize(fmt)

Return the length of the string that corresponds to the format fmt.

struct.pack(fmt, v1 [,v2 [...]])

Return a string with values v1, et alia, packed according to the format fmt.

struct.unpack(fmt, s)

Return a tuple of values represented by string s packed according to the format `fmt`.

| **time** ◇ **Functions to manipulate date/time values** |

The *time* module is useful both for computing and displaying dates and time increments, and for simple benchmarking of applications and functions. For some purposes, eGenix.com's *mx.Date* module is more useful for manipulating datetimes than is *time*. You may obtain *mx.Date* from:

`<http://egenix.com/files/python/eGenix-mx-Extensions.html>`

Time tuples—used by several functions—consist of year, month, day, hour, minute, second, weekday, Julian day, and Daylight Savings flag. All values are integers. Month, day, and Julian day (day of year) are one-based; hour, minute, second, and weekday are zero-based (Monday is 0). The Daylight Savings flag uses 1 for DST, 0 for Standard Time, and -1 for "best guess."

CONSTANTS AND ATTRIBUTES

time.accept2dyear

Boolean to allow two-digit years in date tuples. Default is true value, in which case the first matching date since `time.gmtime(0)` is extrapolated.

```
>>> import time
>>> time.accept2dyear
1
>>> time.localtime(time.mktime((99,1,1,0,0,0,0,0,0)))
(1999, 1, 1, 0, 0, 0, 4, 1, 0)
>>> time.gmtime(0)
(1970, 1, 1, 0, 0, 0, 3, 1, 0)
```

time.altzone
time.daylight
time.timezone
time.tzname

These several constants show information on the current timezone. Different locations use Daylight Savings adjustments during different portions of the year, usually but not always a one-hour adjustment. *time.daylight* indicates only whether such an adjustment is available in *time.altzone*. *time.timezone* indicates how many seconds west of UTC the current zone is; *time.altzone* adjusts that for Daylight Savings if possible. *time.tzname* gives a tuple of strings describing the current zone.

```
>>> time.daylight, time.tzname
(1, ('EST', 'EDT'))
>>> time.altzone, time.timezone
(14400, 18000)
```

FUNCTIONS

time.asctime([tuple=time.localtime()])

Return a string description of a time tuple.

```
>>> time.asctime((2002, 10, 25, 1, 51, 48, 4, 298, 1))
'Fri Oct 25 01:51:48 2002'
```

SEE ALSO: time.ctime() *87*; time.strftime() *88*;

time.clock()

Return the processor time for the current process. The raw value returned has little inherent meaning, but the value is guaranteed to increase roughly in proportion to the amount of CPU time used by the process. This makes *time.clock()* useful for comparative benchmarking of various operations or approaches. The values returned should not be compared between different CPUs, OSs, and so on, but are meaningful on one machine. For example:

```
import time
start1 = time.clock()
approach_one()
time1 = time.clock()-start1
start2 = time.clock()
approach_two()
time2 = time.clock()-start2
if time1 > time2:
    print "The second approach seems better"
else:
    print "The first approach seems better"
```

Always use *time.clock()* for benchmarking rather than *time.time()*. The latter is a low-resolution "wall clock" only.

time.ctime([seconds=time.time()])

Return a string description of seconds since epoch.

```
>>> time.ctime(1035526125)
'Fri Oct 25 02:08:45 2002'
```

SEE ALSO: time.asctime() *87*;

time.gmtime([seconds=time.time()])

Return a time tuple of `seconds` since epoch, giving Greenwich Mean Time.

```
>>> time.gmtime(1035526125)
(2002, 10, 25, 6, 8, 45, 4, 298, 0)
```

SEE ALSO: time.localtime() *88*;

time.localtime([seconds=time.time()])

Return a time tuple of `seconds` since epoch, giving the local time.

```
>>> time.localtime(1035526125)
(2002, 10, 25, 2, 8, 45, 4, 298, 1)
```

SEE ALSO: time.gmtime() *88*; time.mktime() *88*;

time.mktime(tuple)

Return a number of seconds since epoch corresponding to a time tuple.

```
>>> time.mktime((2002, 10, 25, 2, 8, 45, 4, 298, 1))
1035526125.0
```

SEE ALSO: time.localtime() *88*;

time.sleep(seconds)

Suspend execution for approximately `seconds` measured in "wall clock" time (not CPU time). The argument `seconds` is a floating point value (precision subject to system timer) and is fully thread safe.

time.strftime(format [,tuple=time.localtime()])

Return a custom string description of a time tuple. The format given in the string `format` may contain the following fields: `%a/%A/%w` for abbreviated/full/decimal weekday name; `%b/%B/%m` for abbreviated/full/decimal month; `%y/%Y` for abbreviated/full year; `%d` for day-of-month; `%H/%I` for 24/12 clock hour; `%j` for day-of-year; `%M` for minute; `%p` for AM/PM; `%S` for seconds; `%U/%W` for week-of-year (Sunday/Monday start); `%c/%x/%X` for locale-appropriate datetime/date/time; `%Z` for timezone name. Other characters may occur in the format also and will appear as literals (a literal % can be escaped).

```
>>> import time
>>> tuple = (2002, 10, 25, 2, 8, 45, 4, 298, 1)
>>> time.strftime("%A, %B %d '%y (week %U)", tuple)
"Friday, October 25 '02 (week 42)"
```

SEE ALSO: time.asctime() *87*; time.ctime() *87*; time.strptime() *89*;

time.strptime(s [,format="%a %b %d %H:%M:%S %Y"])

Return a time tuple based on a string description of a time. The format given in the string `format` follows the same rules as in *time.strftime()*. Not available on most platforms.

SEE ALSO: time.strftime() *88*;

time.time()

Return the number of seconds since the epoch for the current time. You can specifically determine the epoch using `time.ctime(0)`, but normally you will use other functions in the *time* module to generate useful values. Even though *time.time()* is also generally nondecreasing in its return values, you should use *time.clock()* for benchmarking purposes.

```
>>> time.ctime(0)
'Wed Dec 31 19:00:00 1969'
>>> time.time()
1035585490.484154
>>> time.ctime(1035585437)
'Fri Oct 25 18:37:17 2002'
```

SEE ALSO: time.clock() *87*; time.ctime() *87*;

SEE ALSO: calendar *100*;

1.3   Other Modules in the Standard Library

If your application performs other types of tasks besides text processing, a skim of this module list can suggest where to look for relevant functionality. As well, readers who find themselves maintaining code written by other developers may find that unfamiliar modules are imported by the existing code. If an imported module is not summarized in the list below, nor documented elsewhere, it is probably an in-house or third-party module. For standard library modules, the summaries here will at least give you a sense of the general purpose of a given module.

__builtin__

Access to built-in functions, exceptions, and other objects. Python does a great job of exposing its own internals, but "normal" developers do not need to worry about this.

1.3.1   Serializing and Storing Python Objects

In object-oriented programming (OOP) languages like Python, compound data and structured data is frequently represented at runtime as native objects. At times these objects belong to basic datatypes—lists, tuples, and dictionaries—but more often, once you reach a certain degree of complexity, hierarchies of instances containing attributes become more likely.

For simple objects, especially sequences, serialization and storage is rather straightforward. For example, lists can easily be represented in delimited or fixed-length strings. Lists-of-lists can be saved in line-oriented files, each line containing delimited fields, or in rows of RDBMS tables. But once the dimension of nested sequences goes past two, and even more so for heterogeneous data structures, traditional table-oriented storage is a less-obvious fit.

While it is *possible* to create "object/relational adaptors" that write OOP instances to flat tables, that usually requires custom programming. A number of more general solutions exist, both in the Python standard library and in third-party tools. There are actually two separate issues involved in storing Python objects. The first issue is how to convert them into strings in the first place; the second issue is how to create a general persistence mechanism for such serialized objects. At a minimal level, of course, it is simple enough to store (and retrieve) a serialization string the same way you would any other string—to a file, a database, and so on. The various **dbm* modules create a "dictionary on disk," while the *shelve* module automatically utilizes *cPickle* serialization to write arbitrary objects as values (keys are still strings).

Several third-party modules support object serialization with special features. If you need an XML dialect for your object representation, the modules *gnosis.xml.pickle* and *xmlrpclib* are useful. The YAML format is both human-readable/editable and has support libraries for Python, Perl, Ruby, and Java; using these various libraries, you can exchange objects between these several programming languages.

SEE ALSO: gnosis.xml.pickle *410*; yaml *415*; xmlrpclib *407*;

┌──┐
│ **DBM** ◇ **Interfaces to dbm-style databases** │
└──┘

A dbm-style database is a "dictionary on disk." Using a database of this sort allows you to store a set of key/val pairs to a file, or files, on the local filesystem, and to access and set them as if they were an in-memory dictionary. A dbm-style database, unlike a standard dictionary, always maps strings to strings. If you need to store other types of objects, you will need to convert them to strings (or use the *shelve* module as a wrapper).

Depending on your platform, and on which external libraries are installed, different dbm modules might be available. The performance characteristics of the various modules vary significantly. As well, some DBM modules support some special functionality. Most of the time, however, your best approach is to access the locally supported DBM module using the wrapper module *anydbm*. Calls to this module will select the best available DBM for the current environment without a programmer or user having to worry about the underlying support mechanism.

Functions and methods are documents using the nonspecific capitalized form DEM. In real usage, you would use the name of a specific module. Most of the time, you will get or set DBM values using standard named indexing: for example, db["key"]. A few methods characteristic of dictionaries are also supported, as well as a few methods special to DBM databases.

SEE ALSO: shelve *98*; dict *24*; UserDict *24*;

FUNCTIONS

DBM.open(fname [,flag="r" [,mode=[666]])

Open the filename fname for dbm access. The optional argument flag specifies how the database is accessed. A value of r is for read-only access (on an existing dbm file); w opens an already existing file for read/write access; c will create a database or use an existing one, with read/write access; the option n will always create a new database, erasing the one named in fname if it already existed. The optional mode argument specifies the Unix mode of the file(s) created.

METHODS

DBM.close()

Close the database and flush any pending writes.

DBM.first()

Return the first key/val pair in the DBM. The order is arbitrary but stable. You may use the *DBM.first()* method, combined with repeated calls to *DBM.next()*, to process every item in the dictionary.

In Python 2.2+, you can implement an items() function to emulate the behavior of the .items() method of dictionaries for DBMs:

```
>>> from __future__ import generators
>>> def items(db):
...     try:
...         yield db.first()
...         while 1:
...             yield db.next()
...     except KeyError:
...         raise StopIteration
...
>>> for k,v in items(d):    # typical usage
...     print k,v
```

DBM.has_key(key)

Return a true value if the DBM has the key key.

DBM.keys()

Return a list of string keys in the DBM.

DBM.last()

Return the last key/val pair in the DBM. The order is arbitrary but stable. You may use the *DBM.last()* method, combined with repeated calls to *DBM.previous()*, to process every item in the dictionary in reverse order.

DBM.next()

Return the next key/val pair in the DBM. A pointer to the current position is always maintained, so the methods *DBM.next()* and *DBM.previous()* can be used to access relative items.

DBM.previous()

Return the previous key/val pair in the DBM. A pointer to the current position is always maintained, so the methods *DBM.next()* and *DBM.previous()* can be used to access relative items.

DBM.sync()

Force any pending data to be written to disk.

SEE ALSO: FILE.flush() *16*;

MODULES

anydbm

Generic interface to underlying DBM support. Calls to this module use the functionality of the "best available" DBM module. If you open an existing database file, its type is guessed and used—assuming the current machine supports that style.

SEE ALSO: whichdb *93*;

bsddb

Interface to the Berkeley DB library.

dbhash

Interface to the BSD DB library.

dbm

Interface to the Unix (n)dbm library.

dumbdbm

Interface to slow, but portable pure Python DBM.

gdbm

Interface to the GNU DBM (GDBM) library.

whichdb

Guess which db package to use to open a db file. This module contains the single function *whichdb.whichdb()*. If you open an existing DBM file with *anydbm*, this function is called automatically behind the scenes.

SEE ALSO: shelve *98*;

---

cPickle ◇ **Fast Python object serialization**

---

pickle ◇ **Standard Python object serialization**

The module *cPickle* is a comparatively fast C implementation of the pure Python *pickle* module. The streams produced and read by *cPickle* and *pickle* are interchangeable. The only time you should prefer *pickle* is in the uncommon case where you wish to subclass the pickling base class; *cPickle* is many times faster to use. The class *pickle.Pickler* is not documented here.

The *cPickle* and *pickle* modules support a both binary and an ASCII format. Neither is designed for human readability, but it is not hugely difficult to read an ASCII pickle. Nonetheless, if readability is a goal, *yaml* or *gnosis.xml.pickle* are better choices. Binary format produces smaller pickles that are faster to write or load.

It is possible to fine-tune the pickling behavior of objects by defining the methods .__getstate__(), .__setstate__(), and .__getinitargs__(). The particular black magic invocations involved in defining these methods, however, are not addressed in this book and are rarely necessary for "normal" objects (i.e., those that represent data structures).

Use of the *cPickle* or *pickle* module is quite simple:

```
>>> import cPickle
>>> from somewhere import my_complex_object
>>> s = cPickle.dumps(my_complex_object)
>>> new_obj = cPickle.loads(s)
```

FUNCTIONS

pickle.dump(o, file [,bin=0])
cPickle.dump(o, file [,bin=0])

Write a serialized form of the object o to the file-like object `file`. If the optional argument `bin` is given a true value, use binary format.

pickle.dumps(o [,bin=0])
cPickle.dumps(o [,bin=0])

Return a serialized form of the object o as a string. If the optional argument `bin` is given a true value, use binary format.

pickle.load(file)
cPickle.load(file)

Return an object that was serialized as the contents of the file-like object `file`.

pickle.loads(s)
cPickle.load(s)

Return an object that was serialized in the string `s`.

SEE ALSO: gnosis.xml.pickle *410*; yaml *415*;

marshal

Internal Python object serialization. For more general object serialization, use *pickle*, *cPickle*, or *gnosis.xml.pickle*, or the YAML tools at `<http://yaml.org>`; *marshal* is a limited-purpose serialization to the pseudo-compiled byte-code format used by Python `.pyc` files.

---

pprint ◇ Pretty-print basic datatypes

The module *pprint* is similar to the built-in function *repr()* and the module *repr*. The purpose of *pprint* is to represent objects of basic datatypes in a more readable fashion, especially in cases where collection types nest inside each other. In simple cases *pprint.pformat* and *repr()* produce the same result; for more complex objects, *pprint* uses newlines and indentation to illustrate the structure of a collection. Where possible, the string representation produced by *pprint* functions can be used to re-create objects with the built-in *eval()*.

I find the module *pprint* somewhat limited in that it does not produce a particularly helpful representation of objects of custom types, which might themselves represent compound data. Instance attributes are very frequently used in a manner similar to dictionary keys. For example:

```
>>> import pprint
>>> dct = {1.7:2.5, ('t','u','p'):['l','i','s','t']}
>>> dct2 = {'this':'that', 'num':38, 'dct':dct}
>>> class Container: pass
...
>>> inst = Container()
>>> inst.this, inst.num, inst.dct = 'that', 38, dct
>>> pprint.pprint(dct2)
{'dct': {('t', 'u', 'p'): ['l', 'i', 's', 't'], 1.7: 2.5},
 'num': 38,
 'this': 'that'}
```

```
>>> pprint.pprint(inst)
<__main__.Container instance at 0x415770>
```

In the example, `dct2` and `inst` have the same structure, and either might plausibly be chosen in an application as a data container. But the latter *pprint* representation only tells us the barest information about *what* an object is, not what data it contains. The mini-module below enhances pretty-printing:

pprint2.py

```
from pprint import pformat
import string, sys
def pformat2(o):
    if hasattr(o,'__dict__'):
        lines = []
        klass = o.__class__.__name__
        module = o.__module__
        desc = '<%s.%s instance at )x%x>' % (module, klass, id(o))
        lines.append(desc)
        for k,v in o.__dict__.items():
            lines.append('instance.%s=%s' % (k, pformat(v)))
        return string.join(lines,'\n')
    else:
        return pprint.pformat(o)

def pprint2(o, stream=sys.stdout):
    stream.write(pformat2(o)+'\n')
```

Continuing the session above, we get a more useful report:

```
>>> import pprint2
>>> pprint2.pprint2(inst)
<__main__.Container instance at 0x415770>
instance.this='that'
instance.dct={('t', 'u', 'p'): ['l', 'i', 's', 't'], 1.7: 2.5}
instance.num=38
```

FUNCTIONS

pprint.isreadable(o)

Return a true value if the equality below holds:

```
o == eval(pprint.pformat(o))
```

pprint.isrecursive(o)

Return a true value if the object o contains recursive containers. Objects that contain themselves at any nested level cannot be restored with *eval()*.

pprint.pformat(o)

Return a formatted string representation of the object o.

pprint.pprint(o [,stream=sys.stdout])

Print the formatted representation of the object o to the file-like object `stream`.

CLASSES

pprint.PrettyPrinter(width=80, depth=..., indent=1, stream=sys.stdout)

Return a pretty-printing object that will format using a width of `width`, will limit recursion to depth `depth`, and will indent each new level by `indent` spaces. The method *pprint.PrettyPrinter.pprint()* will write to the file-like object `stream`.

```
>>> pp = pprint.PrettyPrinter(width=30)
>>> pp.pprint(dct2)
{'dct': {1.7: 2.5,
         ('t', 'u', 'p'): ['l',
                           'i',
                           's',
                           't']},
  'num': 38,
  'this': 'that'}
```

METHODS

The class *pprint.PrettyPrinter* has the same methods as the module level functions. The only difference is that the stream used for *pprint.PrettyPrinter.pprint()* is configured when an instance is initialized rather than passed as an optional argument.

SEE ALSO: gnosis.xml.pickle *410*; yaml *415*;

---

repr ◇ Alternative object representation

The module *repr* contains code for customizing the string representation of objects. In its default behavior the function *repr.repr()* provides a length-limited string representation of objects—in the case of large collections, displaying the entire collection can be unwieldy, and unnecessary for merely distinguishing objects. For example:

```
>>> dct = dict([(n,str(n)) for n in range(6)])
>>> repr(dct)     # much worse for, e.g., 1000 item dict
"{0: '0', 1: '1', 2: '2', 3: '3', 4: '4', 5: '5'}"
>>> from repr import repr
>>> repr(dct)
"{0: '0', 1: '1', 2: '2', 3: '3', ...}"
```

```
>>> `dct`
"{0: '0', 1: '1', 2: '2', 3: '3', 4: '4', 5: '5'}"
```

The back-tick operator does not change behavior if the built-in *repr()* function is replaced.

Your can change the behavior of the *repr.repr()* by modifying attributes of the instance object *repr.aRepr*.

```
>>> dct = dict([(n,str(n)) for n in range(6)])
>>> repr(dct)
"{0: '0', 1: '1', 2: '2', 3: '3', 4: '4', 5: '5'}"
>>> import repr
>>> repr.repr(dct)
"{0: '0', 1: '1', 2: '2', 3: '3', ...}"
>>> repr.aRepr.maxdict = 5
>>> repr.repr(dct)
"{0: '0', 1: '1', 2: '2', 3: '3', 4: '4', ...}"
```

In my opinion, the choice of the name for this module is unfortunate, since it is identical to that of the built-in function. You can avoid some of the collision by using the **as** form of importing, as in:

```
>>> import repr as _repr
>>> from repr import repr as newrepr
```

For fine-tuned control of object representation, you may subclass the class *repr.Repr*. Potentially, you could use substitutable **repr()** functions to change the behavior of application output, but if you anticipate such a need, it is better practice to give a name that indicates this; for example, **overridable_repr()**.

CLASSES

repr.Repr()

Base for customized object representations. The instance *repr.aRepr* automatically exists in the module namespace, so this class is useful primarily as a parent class. To change an attribute, it is simplest just to set it in an instance.

ATTRIBUTES

repr.maxlevel

Depth of recursive objects to follow.

repr.maxdict
repr.maxlist
repr.maxtuple

Number of items in a collection of the indicated type to include in the representation. Sequences default to 6, dicts to 4.

repr.maxlong

Number of digits of a long integer to stringify. Default is 40.

repr.maxstring

Length of string representation (e.g., `s[:N]`). Default is 30.

repr.maxother

"Catch-all" maximum length of other representations.

FUNCTIONS

repr.repr(o)

Behaves like built-in *repr()*, but potentially with a different string representation created.

repr.repr_TYPE(o, level)

Represent an object of the type `TYPE`, where the names used are the standard type names. The argument `level` indicates the level of recursion when this method is called (you might want to decide what to print based on how deep within the representation the object is). The *Python Library Reference* gives the example:

```
class MyRepr(repr.Repr):
    def repr_file(self, obj, level):
        if obj.name in ['<stdin>', '<stdout>', '<stderr>']:
            return obj.name
        else:
            return 'obj'
aRepr = MyRepr()
print aRepr.repr(sys.stdin)          # prints '<stdin>'
```

---

shelve ◇ General persistent dictionary

The module *shelve* builds on the capabilities of the DBM modules, but takes things a step forward. Unlike with the DBM modules, you may write arbitrary Python objects as values in a *shelve* database. The keys in *shelve* databases, however, must still be strings.

The methods of *shelve* databases are generally the same as those for their underlying DBMs. However, shelves do not have the `.first()`, `.last()`, `.next()`, or `.previous()` methods; nor do they have the `.items()` method that actual dictionaries do. Most of the time you will simply use name-indexed assignment and access. But from time to time, the available *shelve.get()*, *shelve.keys()*, *shelve.sync()*, *shelve.has_key()*, and *shelve.close()* methods are useful.

Usage of a shelve consists of a few simple steps like the ones below:

```
>>> import shelve
>>> sh = shelve.open('test_shelve')
>>> sh.keys()
['this']
>>> sh['new_key'] = {1:2, 3:4, ('t','u','p'):['l','i','s','t']}
>>> sh.keys()
['this', 'new_key']
>>> sh['new_key']
{1: 2, 3: 4, ('t', 'u', 'p'): ['l', 'i', 's', 't']}
>>> del sh['this']
>>> sh.keys()
['new_key']
>>> sh.close()
```

In the example, I opened an existing shelve, and the previously existing key/value pair was available. Deleting a key/value pair is the same as doing so from a standard dictionary. Opening a new shelve automatically creates the necessary file(s).

Although *shelve* only allows strings to be used as keys, in a pinch it is not difficult to generate strings that characterize other types of immutable objects. For the same reasons that you do not generally want to use mutable objects as dictionary keys, it is also a bad idea to use mutable objects as *shelve* keys. Using the built-in *hash()* method is a good way to generate strings—but keep in mind that this technique does not strictly guarantee uniqueness, so it is possible (but unlikely) to accidentally overwrite entries using this hack:

```
>>> '%x' % hash((1,2,3,4,5))
'866123f4'
>>> '%x' % hash(3.1415)
'6aad0902'
>>> '%x' % hash(38)
'26'
>>> '%x' % hash('38')
'92bb58e3'
```

Integers, notice, are their own hash, and strings of digits are common. Therefore, if you adopted this approach, you would want to hash strings as well, before using them as keys. There is no real problem with doing so, merely an extra indirection step that you need to remember to use consistently:

```
>>> sh['%x' % hash('another_key')] = 'another value'
>>> sh.keys()
['new_key', '8f9ef0ca']
>>> sh['%x' % hash('another_key')]
'another value'
>>> sh['another_key']
Traceback (most recent call last):
```

```
    File "<stdin>", line 1, in ?
    File "/sw/lib/python2.2/shelve.py", line 70, in __getitem__
      f = StringIO(self.dict[key])
KeyError: another_key
```

If you want to go beyond the capabilities of *shelve* in several ways, you might want to investigate the third-party library Zope Object Database (ZODB). ZODB allows arbitrary objects to be persistent, not only dictionary-like objects. Moreover, ZODB lets you store data in ways other than in local files, and also has adaptors for multiuser simultaneous access. Look for details at:

> <http://www.zope.org/Wikis/ZODB/StandaloneZODB>

SEE ALSO: DBM *90*; dict *24*;

○ ·· ○ ·· ○ ·· ○ ·· ○ ·· ○ ·· ○ ·· ○ ·· ○ ·· ○ ·· ○ ·· ○ ·· ○

The rest of the listed modules are comparatively unlikely to be needed in text processing applications. Some modules are specific to a particular platform; if so, this is indicated parenthetically. Recent distributions of Python have taken a "batteries included" approach—much more is included in a base Python distribution than is with other free programming languages (but other popular languages still have a range of existing libraries that can be downloaded separately).

1.3.2   Platform-Specific Operations

_winreg

Access to the Windows registry (Windows).

AE

AppleEvents (Macintosh; replaced by *Carbon.AE*).

aepack

Conversion between Python variables and AppleEvent data containers (Macintosh).

aetypes

AppleEvent objects (Macintosh).

applesingle

Rudimentary decoder for AppleSingle format files (Macintosh).

buildtools

Build MacOS applets (Macintosh).

calendar

Print calendars, much like the Unix `cal` utility. A variety of functions allow you to print or stringify calendars for various time frames. For example,

```
>>> print calendar.month(2002,11)
    November 2002
Mo Tu We Th Fr Sa Su
             1  2  3
 4  5  6  7  8  9 10
11 12 13 14 15 16 17
18 19 20 21 22 23 24
25 26 27 28 29 30
```

Carbon.AE, Carbon.App, Carbon.CF, Carbon.Cm, Carbon.Ctl, Carbon.Dlg, Carbon.Evt, Carbon.Fm, Carbon.Help, Carbon.List, Carbon.Menu, Carbon.Mlte, Carbon.Qd, Carbon.Qdoffs, Carbon.Qt, Carbon.Res, Carbon.Scrap, Carbon.Snd, Carbon.TE, Carbon.Win

Interfaces to Carbon API (Macintosh).

cd

CD-ROM access on SGI systems (IRIX).

cfmfile

Code Fragment Resource module (Macintosh).

ColorPicker

Interface to the standard color selection dialog (Macintosh).

ctb

Interface to the Communications Tool Box (Macintosh).

dl

Call C functions in shared objects (Unix).

EasyDialogs

Basic Macintosh dialogs (Macintosh).

fcntl

Access to Unix `fcntl()` and `iocntl()` system functions (Unix).

findertools

AppleEvents interface to MacOS finder (Macintosh).

fl, FL, flp

Functions and constants for working with the FORMS library (IRIX).

fm, FM

Functions and constants for working with the Font Manager library (IRIX).

fpectl

Floating point exception control (Unix).

FrameWork, MiniAEFrame

Structured development of MacOS applications (Macintosh).

gettext

The module *gettext* eases the development of multilingual applications. While actual translations must be performed manually, this module aids in identifying strings for translation and runtime substitutions of language-specific strings.

grp

Information on Unix groups (Unix).

locale

Control the language and regional settings for an application. The `locale` setting affects the behavior of several functions, such as `time.strftime()` and `string.lower()`. The *locale* module is also useful for creating strings such as number with grouped digits and currency strings for specific nations.

mac, macerrors, macpath

Macintosh implementation of *os* module functionality. It is generally better to use *os* directly and let it call *mac* where needed (Macintosh).

macfs, macfsn, macostools

Filesystem services (Macintosh).

MacOS

Access to MacOS Python interpreter (Macintosh).

macresource

Locate script resources (Macintosh).

macspeech

Interface to Speech Manager (Macintosh).

mactty

Easy access serial to line connections (Macintosh).

mkcwproject

Create CodeWarrior projects (Macintosh).

msvcrt

Miscellaneous Windows-specific functions provided in Microsoft's Visual C++ Runtime libraries (Windows).

Nac

Interface to Navigation Services (Macintosh).

nis

Access to Sun's NIS Yellow Pages (Unix).

pipes

Manage pipes at a finer level than done by *os.popen()* and its relatives. Reliability varies between platforms (Unix).

PixMapWrapper

Wrap PixMap objects (Macintosh).

posix, posixfile

Access to operating system functionality under Unix. The *os* module provides more portable version of the same functionality and should be used instead (Unix).

preferences

Application preferences manager (Macintosh).

pty

Pseudo terminal utilities (IRIX, Linux).

pwd

Access to Unix password database (Unix).

pythonprefs

Preferences manager for Python (Macintosh).

py_resource

Helper to create PYC resources for compiled applications (Macintosh).

quietconsole

Buffered, nonvisible STDOUT output (Macintosh).

resource

Examine resource usage (Unix).

syslog

Interface to Unix syslog library (Unix).

tty, termios, TERMIOS

POSIX tty control (Unix).

W

Widgets for the Mac (Macintosh).

waste

Interface to the WorldScript-Aware Styled Text Engine (Macintosh).

winsound

Interface to audio hardware under Windows (Windows).

xdrlib

Implements (a subset of) Sun eXternal Data Representation (XDR). In concept, *xdrlib* is similar to the *struct* module, but the format is less widely used.

1.3.3   Working with Multimedia Formats

aifc

Read and write AIFC and AIFF audio files. The interface to *aifc* is the same as for the *sunau* and *wave* modules.

al, AL

Audio functions for SGI (IRIX).

audioop

Manipulate raw audio data.

chunk

Read chunks of IFF audio data.

colorsys

Convert between RGB color model and YIQ, HLS, and HSV color spaces.

gl, DEVICE, GL

Functions and constants for working with Silicon Graphics' Graphics Library (IRIX).

imageop

Manipulate image data stored as Python strings. For most operations on image files, the third-party *Python Imaging Library* (usually called "PIL"; see <http://www.pythonware.com/products/pil/>) is a versatile and powerful tool.

imgfile

Support for imglib files (IRIX).

jpeg

Read and write JPEG files on SGI (IRIX). The *Python Imaging Library* (<http://www.pythonware.com/products/pil/>) provides a cross-platform means of working with a large number of image formats and is preferable for most purposes.

rgbimg

Read and write SGI RGB files (IRIX).

sunau

Read and write Sun AU audio files. The interface to *sunau* is the same as for the *aifc* and *wave* modules.

sunaudiodev, SUNAUDIODEV

Interface to Sun audio hardware (SunOS/Solaris).

videoreader

Read QuickTime movies frame by frame (Macintosh).

wave

Read and write WAV audio files. The interface to *wave* is the same as for the *aifc* and *sunau* modules.

1.3.4 Miscellaneous Other Modules

array

Typed arrays of numeric values. More efficient than standard Python lists, where applicable.

atexit

Exit handlers. Same functionality as *sys.exitfunc*, but different interface.

BaseHTTPServer, SimpleHTTPServer, SimpleXMLRPCServer, CGIHTTPServer

HTTP server classes. *BaseHTTPServer* should usually be treated as an abstract class. The other modules provide sufficient customization for usage in the specific context indicated by their names. All may be customized for your application's needs.

Bastion

Restricted object access. Used in conjunction with *rexec*.

bisect

List insertion maintaining sort order.

cmath

Mathematical functions over complex numbers.

cmd

Build line-oriented command interpreters.

code

Utilities to emulate Python's interactive interpreter.

codeop

Compile possibly incomplete Python source code.

compileall

Module/script to compile .py files to cached byte-code files.

compile, compile.ast, compile.visitor

Analyze Python source code and generate Python byte-codes.

copy_reg

Helper to provide extensibility for pickle/cPickle.

curses, curses.ascii, curses.panel, curses.textpad, curses.wrapper

Full-screen terminal handling with the (n)curses library.

dircache

Cached directory listing. This module enhances the functionality of *os.listdir()*.

dis

Disassembler of Python byte-code into mnemonics.

distutils

Build and install Python modules and packages. *distutils* provides a standard mechanism for creating distribution packages of Python tools and libraries, and also for installing them on target machines. Although *distutils* is likely to be useful for text processing applications that are distributed to users, a discussion of the details of working with *distutils* is outside the scope of this book. Useful information can be found in the Python standard documentation, especially Greg Ward's *Distributing Python Modules* and *Installing Python Modules*.

doctest

Check the accuracy of *_doc_* strings.

errno

Standard `errno` system symbols.

fpformat

General floating point formatting functions. Duplicates string interpolation functionality.

gc

Control Python's (optional) cyclic garbage collection.

getpass

Utilities to collect a password without echoing to screen.

imp

Access the internals of the import statement.

inspect

Get useful information from live Python objects for Python 2.1+.

keyword

Check whether string is a Python keyword.

math

Various trigonometric and algebraic functions and constants. These functions generally operate on floating point numbers—use *cmath* for calculations on complex numbers.

mutex

Work with mutual exclusion locks, typically for threaded applications.

new

Create special Python objects in customizable ways. For example, Python hackers can create a module object without using a file of the same name or create an instance while bypassing the normal .__init__() call. "Normal" techniques generally suffice for text processing applications.

pdb

A Python debugger.

popen2

Functions to spawn commands with pipes to STDIN, STDOUT, and optionally STDERR. In Python 2.0+, this functionality is copied to the *os* module in slightly improved form. Generally you should use the *os* module (unless you are running Python 1.52 or earlier).

profile

Profile the performance characteristics of Python code. If speed becomes an issue in your application, your first step in solving any problem issues should be profiling the code. But details of using *profile* are outside the scope of this book. Moreover, it is usually a bad idea to *assume* speed is a problem until it is actually found to be so.

pstats

Print reports on profiled Python code.

pyclbr

Python class browser; useful for implementing code development environments for editing Python.

pydoc

Extremely useful script and module for examining Python documentation. *pydoc* is included with Python 2.1+, but is compatible with earlier versions if downloaded. *pydoc* can provide help similar to Unix `man` pages, help in the interactive shell, and also a Web browser interface to documentation. This tool is worth using frequently while developing Python applications, but its details are outside the scope of this book.

py_compile

"Compile" a .py file to a .pyc (or .pyo) file.

Queue

A multiproducer, multiconsumer queue, especially for threaded programming.

readline, rlcompleter

Interface to GNU readline (Unix).

rexec

Restricted execution facilities.

sched

General event scheduler.

signal

Handlers for asynchronous events.

site, user

Customizable startup module that can be modified to change the behavior of the local Python installation.

statcache

Maintain a cache of *os.stat()* information on files. Deprecated in Python 2.2+.

statvfs

Constants for interpreting the results of *os.statvfs()* and *os.fstatvfs()*.

thread, threading

Create multithreaded applications with Python. Although text processing applications—like other applications—might use a threaded approach, this topic is outside the scope of this book. Most, but not all, Python platforms support threaded applications.

Tkinter, ScrolledText, Tix, turtle

Python interface to TCL/TK and higher-level widgets for TK. Supported on many platforms, but not on all Python installations.

traceback

Extract, format, and print information about Python stack traces. Useful for debugging applications.

unittest

Unit testing framework. Like a number of other documenting, testing, and debugging modules, *unittest* is a useful facility—and its usage is recommended for Python applications in general. But this module is not specific enough to text processing applications to be addressed in this book.

warnings

Python 2.1 added a set of warning messages for conditions a user should be aware of. but that fall below the threshold for raising exceptions. By default, such messages are printed to STDERR, but the *warning* module can be used to modify the behavior of warning messages.

weakref

Create references to objects that do not limit garbage collection. At first brush, weak references seem strange, and the strangeness does not really go away quickly. If you do not know why you would want to use these, do not worry about it—you do not need to.

whrandom

Wichmann-Hill random number generator. Deprecated since Python 2.1, and not necessary to use directly before that—use the module *random* to create pseudo-random values.

Chapter 2

BASIC STRING
OPERATIONS

> The cheapest, fastest and most reliable components of a
> computer system are those that aren't there.
> —Gordon Bell, Encore Computer Corporation

If you are writing programs in Python to accomplish text processing tasks, most of what you need to know is in this chapter. Sure, you will probably need to know how to do some basic things with pipes, files, and arguments to get your text to process (covered in Chapter 1); but for actually *processing* the text you have gotten, the *string* module and string methods—and Python's basic data structures—do most all of what you need done, almost all the time. To a lesser extent, the various custom modules to perform encodings, encryptions, and compressions are handy to have around (and you certainly do not want the work of implementing them yourself). But at the heart of text processing are basic transformations of bits of text. That's what *string* functions and string methods do.

There are a lot of interesting techniques elsewhere in this book. I wouldn't have written about them if I did not find them important. But be cautious before doing interesting things. Specifically, given a fixed task in mind, before cracking this book open to any of the other chapters, consider very carefully whether your problem can be solved using the techniques in this chapter. If you can answer this question affirmatively, you should usually eschew the complications of using the higher-level modules and techniques that other chapters discuss. By all means read all of this book for the insight and edification that I hope it provides; but still focus on the "Zen of Python," and prefer simple to complex when simple is enough.

This chapter does several things. Section 2.1 looks at a number of common problems in text processing that can (and should) be solved using (predominantly) the techniques documented in this chapter. Each of these "Problems" presents working solutions that can often be adopted with little change to real-life jobs. But a larger goal is to provide readers with a starting point for adaptation of the examples. It is not my goal to provide mere collections of packaged utilities and modules—plenty of those exist on the Web, and resources like the Vaults of Parnassus `<http://www.vex.net/parnassus/>` and the Python Cookbook `<http://aspn.activestate.com/ASPN/Python/Cookbook/>` are worth investigating as part of any project/task (and new and better utilities will be written between the time I write this and when you read it). It is better for readers to receive a solid foundation and starting point from which to develop the functionality they need for their own projects and tasks. And even better than spurring adaptation, these examples aim to encourage contemplation. In presenting examples, this book tries to embody a way of thinking about problems and an attitude towards solving them. More than any individual technique, such ideas are what I would most like to share with readers.

Section 2.2 is a "reference with commentary" on the Python standard library modules for doing basic text manipulations. The discussions interspersed with each module try to give some guidance on why you would want to use a given module or function, and the reference documentation tries to contain more examples of actual typical usage than does a plain reference. In many cases, the examples and discussion of individual functions addresses common and productive design patterns in Python. The cross-references are intended to contextualize a given function (or other thing) in terms of related ones (and to help you decide which is right for you). The actual listing of functions, constants, classes, and the like is in alphabetical order within type of thing.

Section 2.3 in many ways continues Section 2.1, but also provides some aids for using this book in a learning context. The problems and solutions presented in Section 2.3 are somewhat more open-ended than those in Section 2.1. As well, each section labeled as "Discussion" is followed by one labeled "Questions." These questions are ones that could be assigned by a teacher to students; but they are also intended to be issues that general readers will enjoy and benefit from contemplating. In many cases, the questions point to limitations of the approaches initially presented, and ask readers to think about ways to address or move beyond these limitations—exactly what readers need to do when writing their own custom code to accomplish outside tasks. However, each Discussion in Section 2.3 should stand on its own, even if the Questions are skipped over by the reader.

2.1   Some Common Tasks

2.1.1   Problem: Quickly sorting lines on custom criteria

Sorting is one of the real meat-and-potatoes algorithms of text processing and, in fact, of most programming. Fortunately for Python developers, the native `[].sort` method is extraordinarily fast. Moreover, Python lists with almost any heterogeneous objects as elements can be sorted—Python cannot rely on the uniform arrays of a language like C (an unfortunate exception to this general power was introduced in recent Python versions where comparisons of complex numbers raise a `TypeError`; and `[1+1j,2+2j].sort()` dies for the same reason; Unicode strings in lists can cause similar problems).

SEE ALSO: complex *22*;

The list sort method is wonderful when you want to sort items in their "natural" order—or in the order that Python considers natural, in the case of items of varying types. Unfortunately, a lot of times, you want to sort things in "unnatural" orders. For lines of text, in particular, any order that is not simple alphabetization of the lines is "unnatural." But often text lines contain meaningful bits of information in positions other than the first character position: A last name may occur as the second word of a list of people (for example, with first name as the first word); an IP address may occur several fields into a server log file; a money total may occur at position 70 of each line; and so on. What if you want to sort lines based on this style of meaningful order that Python doesn't quite understand?

The list sort method *[].sort()* supports an optional custom comparison function argument. The job this function has is to return -1 if the first thing should come first, return 0 if the two things are equal order-wise, and return 1 if the first thing should come second. The built-in function *cmp()* does this in a manner identical to the default *[].sort()* (except in terms of speed, `lst.sort()` is much faster than `lst.sort(cmp)`). For short lists and quick solutions, a custom comparison function is probably the best thing. In a lot of cases, you can even get by with an in-line `lambda` function as the custom comparison function, which is a pleasant and handy idiom.

When it comes to speed, however, use of custom comparison functions is fairly awful. Part of the problem is Python's function call overhead, but a lot of other factors contribute to the slowness. Fortunately, a technique called "Schwartzian Transforms" can make for much faster custom sorts. Schwartzian Transforms are named after Randal Schwartz, who proposed the technique for working with Perl; but the technique is equally applicable to Python.

The pattern involved in the Schwartzian Transform technique consists of three steps (these can more precisely be called the Guttman-Rosler Transform, which is based on the Schwartzian Transform):

1. Transform the list in a reversible way into one that sorts "naturally."

2. Call Python's native *[].sort()* method.

3. Reverse the transformation in (1) to restore the original list items (in new sorted order).

The reason this technique works is that, for a list of size N, it only requires O(2N) transformation operations, which is easy to amortize over the necessary O(N log N) compare/flip operations for large lists. The sort dominates computational time, so anything that makes the sort more efficient is a win in the limit case (this limit is reached quickly).

Below is an example of a simple, but plausible, custom sorting algorithm. The sort is on the fourth and subsequent words of a list of input lines. Lines that are shorter than four words sort to the bottom. Running the test against a file with about 20,000 lines—about 1 megabyte—performed the Schwartzian Transform sort in less than 2 seconds, while taking over 12 seconds for the custom comparison function sort (outputs were verified as identical). Any number of factors will change the exact relative timings, but a better than six times gain can generally be expected.

schwartzian_sort.py

```
# Timing test for "sort on fourth word"
# Specifically, two lines >= 4 words will be sorted
#    lexographically on the 4th, 5th, etc.. words.
#    Any line with fewer than four words will be sorted to
#    the end, and will occur in "natural" order.

import sys, string, time
wrerr = sys.stderr.write

# naive custom sort
def fourth_word(ln1,ln2):
    lst1 = string.split(ln1)
    lst2 = string.split(ln2)
    #-- Compare "long" lines
    if len(lst1) >= 4 and len(lst2) >= 4:
        return cmp(lst1[3:],lst2[3:])
    #-- Long lines before short lines
    elif len(lst1) >= 4 and len(lst2) < 4:
        return -1
    #-- Short lines after long lines
    elif len(lst1) < 4 and len(lst2) >= 4:
        return 1
    else:                         # Natural order
        return cmp(ln1,ln2)

# Don't count the read itself in the time
lines = open(sys.argv[1]).readlines()

# Time the custom comparison sort
start = time.time()
lines.sort(fourth_word)

end = time.time()
wrerr("Custom comparison func in %3.2f secs\n" % (end-start))
# open('tmp.custom','w').writelines(lines)

# Don't count the read itself in the time
lines = open(sys.argv[1]).readlines()
```

```
# Time the Schwartzian sort
start = time.time()
for n in range(len(lines)):          # Create the transform
    lst = string.split(lines[n])
    if len(lst) >= 4:                # Tuple w/ sort info first
        lines[n] = (lst[3:], lines[n])
    else:                            # Short lines to end
        lines[n] = (['\377'], lines[n])

lines.sort()                         # Native sort

for n in range(len(lines)):          # Restore original lines
    lines[n] = lines[n][1]

end = time.time()
wrerr("Schwartzian transform sort in %3.2f secs\n" % (end-start))
# open('tmp.schwartzian','w').writelines(lines)
```

Only one particular example is presented, but readers should be able to generalize this technique to any sort they need to perform frequently or on large files.

2.1.2   Problem: Reformatting paragraphs of text

While I mourn the decline of plaintext ASCII as a communication format—and its eclipse by unnecessarily complicated and large (and often proprietary) formats—there is still plenty of life left in text files full of prose. READMEs, HOWTOs, email, Usenet posts, and this book itself are written in plaintext (or at least something close enough to plaintext that generic processing techniques are valuable). Moreover, many formats like HTML and LaTeX are frequently enough hand-edited that their plaintext appearance is important.

One task that is extremely common when working with prose text files is reformatting paragraphs to conform to desired margins. Python 2.3 adds the module *textwrap*, which performs more limited reformatting than the code below. Most of the time, this task gets done within text editors, which are indeed quite capable of performing the task. However, sometimes it would be nice to automate the formatting process. The task is simple enough that it is slightly surprising that Python has no standard module function to do this. There *is* the class *formatter.DumbWriter*, or the possibility of inheriting from and customizing *formatter.AbstractWriter*. These classes are discussed in Chapter 5; but frankly, the amount of customization and sophistication needed to use these classes and their many methods is way out of proportion for the task at hand.

Below is a simple solution that can be used either as a command-line tool (reading from STDIN and writing to STDOUT) or by import to a larger application.

reformat_para.py

```python
# Simple paragraph reformatter.  Allows specification
# of left and right margins, and of justification style
# (using constants defined in module).

LEFT,RIGHT,CENTER = 'LEFT','RIGHT','CENTER'

def reformat_para(para='',left=0,right=72,just=LEFT):
    words = para.split()
    lines = []
    line  = ''
    word = 0
    end_words = 0
    while not end_words:
        if len(words[word]) > right-left: # Handle very long words
            line = words[word]
            word +=1
            if word >= len(words):
                end_words = 1
        else:                                      # Compose line of words
            while len(line)+len(words[word]) <= right-left:
                line += words[word]+' '
                word += 1
                if word >= len(words):
                    end_words = 1
                    break
        lines.append(line)
        line = ''
    if just==CENTER:
        r, l = right, left
        return '\n'.join([' '*left+ln.center(r-l) for ln in lines])
    elif just==RIGHT:
        return '\n'.join([line.rjust(right) for line in lines])
    else: # left justify
        return '\n'.join([' '*left+line for line in lines])

if __name__=='__main__':
    import sys
    if len(sys.argv) <> 4:
        print "Please specify left_margin, right_marg, justification"
    else:
        left  = int(sys.argv[1])
        right = int(sys.argv[2])
        just  = sys.argv[3].upper()

        # Simplistic approach to finding initial paragraphs
```

```
for p in sys.stdin.read().split('\n\n'):
    print reformat_para(p,left,right,just),'\n'
```

A number of enhancements are left to readers, if needed. You might want to allow hanging indents or indented first lines, for example. Or paragraphs meeting certain criteria might not be appropriate for wrapping (e.g., headers). A custom application might also determine the input paragraphs differently, either by a different parsing of an input file, or by generating paragraphs internally in some manner.

2.1.3 Problem: Column statistics for delimited or flat-record files

Data feeds, DBMS dumps, log files, and flat-file databases all tend to contain ontologically similar records—one per line—with a collection of fields in each record. Usually such fields are separated either by a specified delimiter or by specific column positions where fields are to occur.

Parsing these structured text records is quite easy, and performing computations on fields is equally straightforward. But in working with a variety of such "structured text databases," it is easy to keep writing almost the same code over again for each variation in format and computation.

The example below provides a generic framework for every similar computation on a structured text database.

---
fields_stats.py

```
# Perform calculations on one or more of the
# fields in a structured text database.

import operator
from types import *
from xreadlines import xreadlines # req 2.1, but is much faster...
                                  # could use .readline() meth < 2.1
#-- Symbolic Constants
DELIMITED = 1
FLATFILE = 2

#-- Some sample "statistical" func (in functional programming style)
nillFunc = lambda lst: None
toFloat = lambda lst: map(float, lst)
avg_lst = lambda lst: reduce(operator.add, toFloat(lst))/len(lst)
sum_lst = lambda lst: reduce(operator.add, toFloat(lst))
max_lst = lambda lst: reduce(max, toFloat(lst))

class FieldStats:
    """Gather statistics about structured text database fields
```

```
text_db may be either string (incl. Unicode) or file-like object
style may be in (DELIMITED, FLATFILE)
delimiter specifies the field separator in DELIMITED style text_db
column_positions lists all field positions for FLATFILE style,
                using one-based indexing (first column is 1).
        E.g.: (1, 7, 40) would take fields one, two, three
                from columns 1, 7, 40 respectively.
field_funcs is a dictionary with column positions as keys,
            and functions on lists as values.
      E.g.:  {1:avg_lst, 4:sum_lst, 5:max_lst} would specify the
            average of column one, the sum of column 4, and the
            max of column 5.  All other cols--incl 2,3, >=6--
            are ignored.

"""
def __init__(self,
            text_db='',
            style=DELIMITED,
            delimiter=',',
            column_positions=(1,),
            field_funcs={} ):
    self.text_db = text_db
    self.style = style
    self.delimiter = delimiter
    self.column_positions = column_positions
    self.field_funcs = field_funcs

def calc(self):
    """Calculate the column statistics
    """
    #-- 1st, create a list of lists for data (incl. unused flds)
    used_cols = self.field_funcs.keys()
    used_cols.sort()
    # one-based column naming: column[0] is always unused
    columns = []
    for n in range(1+used_cols[-1]):
        # hint: '[[]]*num' creates refs to same list
        columns.append([])

        #-- 2nd, fill lists used for calculated fields
                # might use a string directly for text_db
        if type(self.text_db) in (StringType,UnicodeType):
            for line in self.text_db.split('\n'):
                fields = self.splitter(line)
                for col in used_cols:
                    field = fields[col-1]    # zero-based index
```

```
                                    columns[col].append(field)
                    else:    # Something file-like for text_db
                        for line in xreadlines(self.text_db):
                            fields = self.splitter(line)
                            for col in used_cols:
                                field = fields[col-1]    # zero-based index
                                columns[col].append(field)

                    #-- 3rd, apply the field funcs to column lists
                    results = [None] * (1+used_cols[-1])
                    for col in used_cols:
                        results[col] = \
                            apply(self.field_funcs[col],(columns[col],))

                    #-- Finally, return the result list
                    return results

        def splitter(self, line):
            """Split a line into fields according to curr inst specs"""
            if self.style == DELIMITED:
                return line.split(self.delimiter)
            elif self.style == FLATFILE:
                fields = []
                # Adjust offsets to Python zero-based indexing,
                # and also add final position after the line
                num_positions = len(self.column_positions)
                offsets = [(pos-1) for pos in self.column_positions]
                offsets.append(len(line))
                for pos in range(num_positions):
                    start = offsets[pos]
                    end = offsets[pos+1]
                    fields.append(line[start:end])
                return fields
            else:
                raise ValueError, \
                    "Text database must be DELIMITED or FLATFILE"

#-- Test data
# First Name, Last Name, Salary, Years Seniority, Department
delim = '''
Kevin,Smith,50000,5,Media Relations
Tom,Woo,30000,7,Accounting
Sally,Jones,62000,10,Management
'''.strip()      # no leading/trailing newlines

# Comment     First     Last      Salary     Years  Dept
flat = '''
```

```
tech note       Kevin     Smith     50000      5      Media Relations
more filler     Tom       Woo       30000      7      Accounting
yet more...     Sally     Jones     62000      10     Management
'''.strip()          # no leading/trailing newlines

#-- Run self-test code
if __name__ == '__main__':
    getdelim = FieldStats(delim, field_funcs={3:avg_lst,4:max_lst})
    print 'Delimited Calculations:'
    results = getdelim.calc()
    print '  Average salary -', results[3]
    print '  Max years worked -', results[4]

    getflat = FieldStats(flat, field_funcs={3:avg_lst,4:max_lst},
                             style=FLATFILE,
                             column_positions=(15,25,35,45,52))
    print 'Flat Calculations:'
    results = getflat.calc()
    print '  Average salary -', results[3]
    print '  Max years worked -', results[4]
```

The example above includes some efficiency considerations that make it a good model for working with large data sets. In the first place, class `FieldStats` can (optionally) deal with a file-like object, rather than keeping the whole structured text database in memory. The generator *xreadlines.xreadlines()* is an extremely fast and efficient file reader, but it requires Python 2.1+—otherwise use *FILE.readline()* or *FILE.readlines()* (for either memory or speed efficiency, respectively). Moreover, only the data that is actually of interest is collected into lists, in order to save memory. However, rather than require multiple passes to collect statistics on multiple fields, as many field columns and summary functions as wanted can be used in one pass.

One possible improvement would be to allow multiple summary functions against the same field during a pass. But that is left as an exercise to the reader, if she desires to do it.

2.1.4   Problem: Counting characters, words, lines, and paragraphs

There is a wonderful utility under Unix-like systems called `wc`. What it does is so basic, and so obvious, that it is hard to imagine working without it. `wc` simply counts the characters, words, and lines of files (or STDIN). A few command-line options control which results are displayed, but I rarely use them.

In writing this chapter, I found myself on a system without `wc`, and felt a remedy was in order. The example below is actually an "enhanced" `wc` since it also counts paragraphs (but it lacks the command-line switches). Unlike the external `wc`, it is easy to use the technique directly within Python and is available anywhere Python is. The main trick—inasmuch as there is one—is a compact use of the *""·join()* and

"".*split()* methods (*string*.*join()* and *string*.*split()* could also be used, for example, to be compatible with Python 1.5.2 or below).

wc.py

```
# Report the chars, words, lines, paragraphs
# on STDIN or in wildcard filename patterns
import sys, glob
if len(sys.argv) > 1:
    c, w, l, p = 0, 0, 0, 0
    for pat in sys.argv[1:]:
        for file in glob.glob(pat):
            s = open(file).read()
            wc = len(s), len(s.split()), \
                len(s.split('\r')), len(s.split('\n\n'))
            print '\t'.join(map(str, wc)),'\t'+file
            c, w, l, p = c+wc[0], w+wc[1], l+wc[2], p+wc[3]
    wc = (c,w,l,p)
    print '\t'.join(map(str, wc)), '\tTOTAL'
else:
    s = sys.stdin.read()
    wc = len(s), len(s.split()), len(s.split('\n')), \
        len(s.split('\n\n'))
    print '\t'.join(map(str, wc)), '\tSTDIN'
```

This little functionality could be wrapped up in a function, but it is almost too compact to bother with doing so. Most of the work is in the interaction with the shell environment, with the counting basically taking only two lines.

The solution above is quite likely the "one obvious way to do it," and therefore Pythonic. On the other hand a slightly more adventurous reader might consider this assignment (if only for fun):

```
>>> wc = map(len,[s]+map(s.split,(None,'\n','\n\n')))
```

A real daredevil might be able to reduce the entire program to a single **print** statement.

2.1.5   Problem: Transmitting binary data as ASCII

Many channels require that the information that travels over them is 7-bit ASCII. Any bytes with a high-order first bit of one will be handled unpredictably when transmitting data over protocols like Simple Mail Transport Protocol (SMTP), Network News Transport Protocol (NNTP), or HTTP (depending on content encoding), or even just when displaying them in many standard tools like editors. In order to encode 8-bit binary data as ASCII, a number of techniques have been invented over time.

An obvious, but obese, encoding technique is to translate each binary byte into its hexadecimal digits. UUencoding is an older standard that developed around the need to

transmit binary files over the Usenet and on BBSs. Binhex is a similar technique from
the MacOS world. In recent years, base64—which is specified by RFC1521—has edged
out the other styles of encoding. All of the techniques are basically 4/3 encodings—that
is, four ASCII bytes are used to represent three binary bytes—but they differ somewhat
in line ending and header conventions (as well as in the encoding as such). Quoted
printable is yet another format, but of variable encoding length. In quoted printable
encoding, most plain ASCII bytes are left unchanged, but a few special characters and
all high-bit bytes are escaped.

Python provides modules for all the encoding styles mentioned. The high-level wrappers *uu*, *binhex*, *base64*, and *quopri* all operate on input and output file-like objects,
encoding the data therein. They also each have slightly different method names and
arguments. *binhex*, for example, closes its output file after encoding, which makes it
unusable in conjunction with a *cStringIO* file-like object. All of the high-level encoders
utilize the services of the low-level C module *binascii*. *binascii*, in turn, implements
the actual low-level block conversions, but assumes that it will be passed the right size
blocks for a given encoding.

The standard library, therefore, does not contain quite the right intermediate-level
functionality for when the goal is just encoding the binary data in arbitrary strings. It
is easy to wrap that up, though:

```
encode_binary.py
```

```python
# Provide encoders for arbitrary binary data
# in Python strings.  Handles block size issues
# transparently, and returns a string.
# Precompression of the input string can reduce
# or eliminate any size penalty for encoding.

import sys
import zlib
import binascii

UU = 45
BASE64 = 57
BINHEX = sys.maxint

def ASCIIencode(s='', type=BASE64, compress=1):
    """ASCII encode a binary string"""
    # First, decide the encoding style
    if type == BASE64:   encode = binascii.b2a_base64
    elif type == UU:     encode = binascii.b2a_uu
    elif type == BINHEX: encode = binascii.b2a_hqx
    else: raise ValueError, "Encoding must be in UU, BASE64, BINHEX"
    # Second, compress the source if specified
    if compress: s = zlib.compress(s)
    # Third, encode the string, block-by-block
```

```
        offset = 0
        blocks = []
        while 1:
            blocks.append(encode(s[offset:offset+type]))
            offset += type
            if offset > len(s):
                break
        # Fourth, return the concatenated blocks
        return ''.join(blocks)

def ASCIIdecode(s='', type=BASE64, compress=1):
    """Decode ASCII to a binary string"""
    # First, decide the encoding style
    if type == BASE64:   s = binascii.a2b_base64(s)
    elif type == BINHEX: s = binascii.a2b_hqx(s)
    elif type == UU:
        s = ''.join([binascii.a2b_uu(line) for line in s.split('\n')])
    # Second, decompress the source if specified
    if compress: s = zlib.decompress(s)
    # Third, return the decoded binary string
    return s

# Encode/decode STDIN for self-test
if __name__ == '__main__':
    decode, TYPE = 0, BASE64
    for arg in sys.argv:
        if   arg.lower()=='-d': decode = 1
        elif arg.upper()=='UU': TYPE=UU
        elif arg.upper()=='BINHEX': TYPE=BINHEX
        elif arg.upper()=='BASE64': TYPE=BASE64
    if decode:
        print ASCIIdecode(sys.stdin.read(),type=TYPE)
    else:
        print ASCIIencode(sys.stdin.read(),type=TYPE)
```

The example above does not attach any headers or delimit the encoded block (by
design); for that, a wrapper like *uu*, *mimify*, or *MimeWriter* is a better choice. Or a
custom wrapper around encode_binary.py.

2.1.6 Problem: Creating word or letter histograms

A histogram is an analysis of the relative occurrence frequency of each of a number
of possible values. In terms of text processing, the occurrences in question are almost
always either words or byte values. Creating histograms is quite simple using Python
dictionaries, but the technique is not always immediately obvious to people thinking
about it. The example below has a good generality, provides several utility functions
associated with histograms, and can be used in a command-line operation mode.

histogram.py

```
# Create occurrence counts of words or characters
# A few utility functions for presenting results
# Avoids requirement of recent Python features

from string import split, maketrans, translate, punctuation, digits
import sys
from types import *
import types

def word_histogram(source):
    """Create histogram of normalized words (no punct or digits)"""
    hist = {}
    trans = maketrans('','')
    if type(source) in (StringType,UnicodeType):  # String-like src
        for word in split(source):
            word = translate(word, trans, punctuation+digits)
            if len(word) > 0:
                hist[word] = hist.get(word,0) + 1
    elif hasattr(source,'read'):                        # File-like src
        try:
            from xreadlines import xreadlines      # Check for module
            for line in xreadlines(source):
                for word in split(line):
                    word = translate(word, trans, punctuation+digits)
                    if len(word) > 0:
                        hist[word] = hist.get(word,0) + 1
        except ImportError:                         # Older Python ver
            line = source.readline()            # Slow but mem-friendly
            while line:
                for word in split(line):
                    word = translate(word, trans, punctuation+digits)
                    if len(word) > 0:
                        hist[word] = hist.get(word,0) + 1
                line = source.readline()
    else:
        raise TypeError, \
            "source must be a string-like or file-like object"
    return hist

def char_histogram(source, sizehint=1024*1024):
    hist = {}
    if type(source) in (StringType,UnicodeType):  # String-like src
        for char in source:
            hist[char] = hist.get(char,0) + 1
    elif hasattr(source,'read'):                        # File-like src
```

```
        chunk = source.read(sizehint)
        while chunk:
            for char in chunk:
                hist[char] = hist.get(char,C) + 1
            chunk = source.read(sizehint)
    else:
        raise TypeError, \
            "source must be a string-like or file-like object"
    return hist

def most_common(hist, num=1):
    pairs = []
    for pair in hist.items():
        pairs.append((pair[1],pair[0]))
    pairs.sort()
    pairs.reverse()
    return pairs[:num]

def first_things(hist, num=1):
    pairs = []
    things = hist.keys()
    things.sort()
    for thing in things:
        pairs.append((thing,hist[thing]))
    pairs.sort()
    return pairs[:num]

if __name__ == '__main__':
    if len(sys.argv) > 1:
        hist = word_histogram(open(sys.argv[1]))
    else:
        hist = word_histogram(sys.stdin)

    print "Ten most common words:"
    for pair in most_common(hist, 10):
        print '\t', pair[1], pair[0]

    print "First ten words alphabetically:"
    for pair in first_things(hist, 10):
        print '\t', pair[0], pair[1]

    # a more practical command-line version might use:
    # for pair in most_common(hist,len(hist)):
    #     print pair[1],'\t',pair[0]
```

Several of the design choices are somewhat arbitrary. Words have all their punctuation stripped to identify "real" words. But on the other hand, words are still case-sensitive, which may not be what is desired. The sorting functions first_things() and `most_common()` only return an initial sublist. Perhaps it would be better to return the whole list, and let the user slice the result. It is simple to customize around these sorts of issues, though.

2.1.7   Problem: Reading a file backwards by record, line, or paragraph

Reading a file line by line is a common task in Python, or in most any language. Files like server logs, configuration files, structured text databases, and others frequently arrange information into logical records, one per line. Very often, the job of a program is to perform some calculation on each record in turn.

Python provides a number of convenient methods on file-like objects for such line-by-line reading. *FILE.readlines()* reads a whole file at once and returns a list of lines. The technique is very fast, but requires the whole contents of the file be kept in memory. For very large files, this can be a problem. *FILE.readline()* is memory-friendly—it just reads a line at a time and can be called repeatedly until the EOF is reached—but it is also much slower. The best solution for recent Python versions is *xreadlines.xreadlines()* or *FILE.xreadlines()* in Python 2.1+. These techniques are memory-friendly, while still being fast and presenting a "virtual list" of lines (by way of Python's new generator/iterator interface).

The above techniques work nicely for reading a file in its natural order, but what if you want to start at the end of a file and work backwards from there? This need is frequently encountered when you want to read log files that have records appended over time (and when you want to look at the most recent records first). It comes up in other situations also. There is a very easy technique if memory usage is not an issue:

```
>>> open('lines','w').write('\n'.join(['n' for n in range(100)]))
>>> fp = open('lines')
>>> lines = fp.readlines()
>>> lines.reverse()
>>> for line in lines[1:5]:
...     # Processing suite here
...     print line,
...
98
97
96
95
```

For large input files, however, this technique is not feasible. It would be nice to have something analogous to *xreadlines* here. The example below provides a good starting point (the example works equally well for file-like objects).

read_backwards.py

```
# Read blocks of a file from end to beginning.
# Blocks may be defined by any delimiter, but the
#  constants LINE and PARA are useful ones.
# Works much like the file object method '.readline()':
#  repeated calls continue to get "next" part, and
#  function returns empty string once BOF is reached.

# Define constants
from os import linesep
LINE = linesep
PARA = linesep*2
READSIZE = 1000

# Global variables
buffer = ''

def read_backwards(fp, mode=LINE, sizehint=READSIZE, _init=[0]):
    """Read blocks of file backwards (return empty string when done)"""
    # Trick of mutable default argument to hold state between calls
    if not _init[0]:
        fp.seek(0,2)
        _init[0] = 1
    # Find a block (using global buffer)
    global buffer
    while 1:
        # first check for block in buffer
        delim = buffer.rfind(mode)
        if delim <> -1:      # block is in buffer, return it
            block = buffer[delim+len(mode):]
            buffer = buffer[:delim]
            return block+mode
        #-- BOF reached, return remainder (or empty string)
        elif fp.tell()==0:
            block = buffer
            buffer = ''
            return block
        else:            # Read some more data into the buffer
            readsize = min(fp.tell(),sizehint)
            fp.seek(-readsize,1)
            buffer = fp.read(readsize) + buffer
            fp.seek(-readsize,1)
```

```
#-- Self test of read_backwards()
if __name__ == '__main__':
    # Let's create a test file to read in backwards
    fp = open('lines','wb')
    fp.write(LINE.join(['--- %d ---'%n for n in range(15)]))
    # Now open for reading backwards
    fp = open('lines','rb')
    # Read the blocks in, one per call (block==line by default)
    block = read_backwards(fp)
    while block:
        print block,
        block = read_backwards(fp)
```

Notice that *anything* could serve as a block delimiter. The constants provided just happened to work for lines and block paragraphs (and block paragraphs only with the current OS's style of line breaks). But other delimiters could be used. It would *not* be immediately possible to read backwards word-by-word—a space delimiter would come close, but would not be quite right for other whitespace. However, reading a line (and maybe reversing its words) is generally good enough.

Another enhancement is possible with Python 2.2+. Using the new `yield` keyword, `read_backwards()` could be programmed as an iterator rather than as a multi-call function. The performance will not differ significantly, but the function might be expressed more clearly (and a "list-like" interface like *FILE.readlines()* makes the application's loop simpler).

QUESTIONS

1. Write a generator-based version of **read_backwards()** that uses the `yield` keyword. Modify the self-test code to utilize the generator instead.

2. Explore and explain some pitfalls with the use of a mutable default value as a function argument. Explain also how the style allows functions to encapsulate data and contrast with the encapsulation of class instances.

2.2   Standard Modules

2.2.1   Basic String Transformations

The module *string* forms the core of Python's text manipulation libraries. That module is certainly the place to look before other modules. Most of the methods in the *string* module, you should note, have been copied to methods of string objects from Python 1.6+. Moreover, methods of string objects are a little bit faster to use than are the corresponding module functions. A few new methods of string objects do not have equivalents in the *string* module, but are still documented here.

SEE ALSO: str *33*; UserString *33*;

> **string** ◇ **A collection of string operations**

There are a number of general things to notice about the functions in the *string* module (which is composed entirely of functions and constants; no classes).

1. Strings are immutable (as discussed in Chapter 1). This means that there is no such thing as changing a string "in place" (as we might do in many other languages, such as C, by changing the bytes at certain offsets within the string). Whenever a *string* module function takes a string object as an argument, it returns a brand-new string object and leaves the original one as is. However, the very common pattern of binding the same name on the left of an assignment as was passed on the right side within the *string* module function somewhat conceals this fact. For example:

```
>>> import string
>>> str = "Mary had a little lamb"
>>> str = string.replace(str, 'had', 'ate')
>>> str
'Mary ate a little lamb'
```

The first string object never gets modified per se; but since the first string object is no longer bound to any name after the example runs, the object is subject to garbage collection and will disappear from memory. In short, calling a *string* module function will not change any existing strings, but rebinding a name can make it look like they changed.

2. Many *string* module functions are now also available as string object methods. To use these string object methods, there is no need to import the *string* module, and the expression is usually slightly more concise. Moreover, using a string object method is usually slightly faster than the corresponding *string* module function. However, the most thorough documentation of each function/method that exists as both a *string* module function and a string object method is contained in this reference to the *string* module.

3. The form `string.join(string.split(...))` is a frequent Python idiom. A more thorough discussion is contained in the reference items for *string.join()* and *string.split()*, but in general, combining these two functions is very often a useful way of breaking down a text, processing the parts, then putting together the pieces.

4. Think about clever *string.replace()* patterns. By combining multiple *string.replace()* calls with use of "place holder" string patterns, a surprising range of results can be achieved (especially when also manipulating the intermediate strings with other techniques). See the reference item for *string.replace()* for some discussion and examples.

5. A mutable string of sorts can be obtained by using built-in lists, or the *array* module. Lists can contain a collection of substrings, each one of which may be replaced or modified individually. The *array* module can define arrays of individual characters, each position modifiable, included with slice notation. The function *string.join()* or the method *"".join()* may be used to re-create true strings; for example:

```
>>> lst = ['spam','and','eggs']
>>> lst[2] = 'toast'
>>> print ''.join(lst)
spamandtoast
>>> print ' '.join(lst)
spam and toast
```

Or:

```
>>> import array
>>> a = array.array('c','spam and eggs')
>>> print ''.join(a)
spam and eggs
>>> a[0] = 'S'
>>> print ''.join(a)
Spam and eggs
>>> a[-4:] = array.array('c','toast')
>>> print ''.join(a)
Spam and toast
```

CONSTANTS

The *string* module contains constants for a number of frequently used collections of characters. Each of these constants is itself simply a string (rather than a list, tuple, or other collection). As such, it is easy to define constants alongside those provided by the *string* module, should you need them. For example:

```
>>> import string
>>> string.brackets = "[]{}()<>"
>>> print string.brackets
[]{}()<>
```

string.digits

The decimal numerals ("0123456789").

string.hexdigits

The hexadecimal numerals ("0123456789abcdefABCDEF").

string.octdigits

The octal numerals ("01234567").

string.lowercase

The lowercase letters; can vary by language. In English versions of Python (most systems):

```
>>> import string
>>> string.lowercase
'abcdefghijklmnopqrstuvwxyz'
```

You should not modify *string.lowercase* for a source text language, but rather define a new attribute, such as `string.spanish_lowercase` with an appropriate string (some methods depend on this constant).

string.uppercase

The uppercase letters; can vary by language. In English versions of Python (most systems):

```
>>> import string
>>> string.uppercase
'ABCDEFGHIJKLMNOPQRSTUVWXYZ'
```

You should not modify *string.uppercase* for a source text language, but rather define a new attribute, such as `string.spanish_uppercase` with an appropriate string (some methods depend on this constant).

string.letters

All the letters (string.lowercase+string.uppercase).

string.punctuation

The characters normally considered as punctuation; can vary by language. In English versions of Python (most systems):

```
>>> import string
>>> string.punctuation
'!"#$%&\'()*+,-./:;<=>?@[\\]^_`{|}~'
```

string.whitespace

The "empty" characters. Normally these consist of tab, linefeed, vertical tab, form-feed, carriage return, and space (in that order):

```
>>> import string
>>> string.whitespace
'\011\012\013\014\015 '
```

You should not modify *string.whitespace* (some methods depend on this constant).

string.printable

All the characters that can be printed to any device; can vary by language (string.digits+string.letters+string.punctuation+string.whitespace).

FUNCTIONS

string.atof(s=...)

Deprecated. Use *float()*.

Converts a string to a floating point value.

SEE ALSO: eval() *445*; float() *422*;

string.atoi(s=...[,base=10])

Deprecated with Python 2.0. Use *int()* if no custom base is needed or if using Python 2.0+.

Converts a string to an integer value (if the string should be assumed to be in a base other than 10, the base may be specified as the second argument).

SEE ALSO: eval() *445*; int() *421*; long() *422*;

string.atol(s=...[,base=10])

Deprecated with Python 2.0. Use *long()* if no custom base is needed or if using Python 2.0+.

Converts a string to an unlimited length integer value (if the string should be assumed to be in a base other than 10, the base may be specified as the second argument).

SEE ALSO: eval() *445*; long() *422*; int() *421*;

string.capitalize(s=...)
"".capitalize()

Return a string consisting of the initial character converted to uppercase (if applicable), and all other characters converted to lowercase (if applicable):

```
>>> import string
>>> string.capitalize("mary had a little lamb!")
'Mary had a little lamb!'
>>> string.capitalize("Mary had a Little Lamb!")
'Mary had a little lamb!'
>>> string.capitalize("2 Lambs had Mary!")
'2 lambs had mary!'
```

For Python 1.6+, use of a string object method is marginally faster and is stylistically preferred in most cases:

```
>>> "mary had a little lamb".capitalize()
'Mary had a little lamb'
```

SEE ALSO: string.capwords() *133*; string.lower() *128*;

string.capwords(s=...)
"".title()

Return a string consisting of the capitalized words. An equivalent expression is:

```
string.join(map(string.capitalize,string.split(s)))
```

But *string.capwords()* is a clearer way of writing it. An effect of this implementation is that whitespace is "normalized" by the process:

```
>>> import string
>>> string.capwords("mary HAD a little lamb!")
'Mary Had A Little Lamb!'
>>> string.capwords("Mary      had a      Little Lamb!")
'Mary Had A Little Lamb!'
```

With the creation of string methods in Python 1.6, the module function *string.capwords()* was renamed as a string method to *"".title()*.

SEE ALSO: string.capitalize() *132*; string.lower() *138*; "".istitle() *136*;

string.center(s=..., width=...)
"".center(width)

Return a string with s padded with symmetrical leading and trailing spaces (but not truncated) to occupy length width (or more).

```
>>> import string
>>> string.center(width=30,s="Mary had a little lamb")
'    Mary had a little lamb    '
>>> string.center("Mary had a little lamb", 5)
'Mary had a little lamb'
```

For Python 1.6+, use of a string object method is stylistically preferred in many cases:

```
>>> "Mary had a little lamb".center(25)
'  Mary had a little lamb '
```

SEE ALSO: string.ljust() *138*; string.rjust() *141*;

string.count(s, sub [,start [,end]])
"".count(sub [,start [,end]])

Return the number of nonoverlapping occurrences of `sub` in `s`. If the optional third or fourth arguments are specified, only the corresponding slice of `s` is examined.

```
>>> import string
>>> string.count("mary had a little lamb", "a")
4
>>> string.count("mary had a little lamb", "a", 3, 10)
2
```

For Python 1.6+, use of a string object method is stylistically preferred in many cases:

```
>>> 'mary had a little lamb'.count("a")
4
```

"".endswith(suffix [,start [,end]])

This string method does not have an equivalent in the *string* module. Return a Boolean value indicating whether the string ends with the suffix `suffix`. If the optional second argument `start` is specified, only consider the terminal substring after offset `start`. If the optional third argument `end` is given, only consider the slice [start:end].

SEE ALSO: "".startswith() *144*; string.find() *135*;

string.expandtabs(s=... [,tabsize=8])
"".expandtabs([,tabsize=8])

Return a string with tabs replaced by a variable number of spaces. The replacement causes text blocks to line up at "tab stops." If no second argument is given, the new string will line up at multiples of 8 spaces. A newline implies a new set of tab stops.

```
>>> import string
>>> s = 'mary\011had a little lamb'
>>> print s
mary    had a little lamb
>>> string.expandtabs(s, 16)
'mary            had a little lamb'
>>> string.expandtabs(tabsize=1, s=s)
'mary had a little lamb'
```

For Python 1.6+, use of a string object method is stylistically preferred in many cases:

```
>>> 'mary\011had a little lamb'.expandtabs(25)
'mary                    had a little lamb'
```

string.find(s, sub [,start [,end]])
"".find(sub [,start [,end]])

Return the index position of the first occurrence of **sub** in **s**. If the optional third or fourth arguments are specified, only the corresponding slice of **s** is examined (but result is position in **s** as a whole). Return -1 if no occurrence is found. Position is zero-based, as with Python list indexing:

```
>>> import string
>>> string.find("mary had a little lamb", "a")
1
>>> string.find("mary had a little lamb", "a", 3, 10)
6
>>> string.find("mary had a little lamb", "b")
21
>>> string.find("mary had a little lamb", "b", 3, 10)
-1
```

For Python 1.6+, use of a string object method is stylistically preferred in many cases:

```
>>> 'mary had a little lamb'.find("ad")
6
```

SEE ALSO: string.index() *135*; string.rfind() *140*;

string.index(s, sub [,start [,end]])
"".index(sub [,start [,end]])

Return the same value as does *string.find()* with same arguments, except raise ValueError instead of returning -1 when sub does not occur in s.

```
>>> import string
>>> string.index("mary had a little lamb", "b")
21
>>> string.index("mary had a little lamb", "b", 3, 10)
Traceback (most recent call last):
  File "<stdin>", line 1, in ?
  File "d:/py20sl/lib/string.py", line 139, in index
    return s.index(*args)
ValueError: substring not found in string.index
```

For Python 1.6+, use of a string object method is stylistically preferred in many cases:

```
>>> 'mary had a little lamb'.index("ad")
6
```

SEE ALSO: string.find() *135*; string.rindex() *141*;

Several string methods that return Boolean values indicating whether a string has a certain property. None of the `.is*()` methods, however, have equivalents in the *string* module:

"".isalpha()

Return a true value if all the characters are alphabetic.

"".isalnum()

Return a true value if all the characters are alphanumeric.

"".isdigit()

Return a true value if all the characters are digits.

"".islower()

Return a true value if all the characters are lowercase and there is at least one cased character:

```
>>> "ab123".islower(), '123'.islower(), 'Ab123'.islower()
(1, 0, 0)
```

SEE ALSO: "".lower() *138*;

"".isspace()

Return a true value if all the characters are whitespace.

"".istitle()

Return a true value if all the string has title casing (each word capitalized).

SEE ALSO: "".title() *133*;

"".isupper()

Return a true value if all the characters are uppercase and there is at least one cased character.

SEE ALSO: "".upper() *146*;

string.join(words=. . . [,sep=" "])
"".join(words)

Return a string that results from concatenating the elements of the list `words` together, with `sep` between each. The function *string.join()* differs from all other *string* module functions in that it takes a list (of strings) as a primary argument, rather than a string.

It is worth noting *string.join()* and *string.split()* are inverse functions if sep is specified to both; in other words, `string.join(string.split(s,sep),sep)==s` for all s and `sep`.

Typically, *string.join()* is used in contexts where it is natural to generate lists of strings. For example, here is a small program to output the list of all-capital words from STDIN to STDOUT, one per line:

```
list_capwords.py
```

```python
import string,sys
capwords = []

for line in sys.stdin.readlines():
    for word in line.split():
        if word == word.upper() and word.isalpha():
            capwords.append(word)
print string.join(capwords, '\n')
```

The technique in the sample `list_capwords.py` script can be considerably more efficient than building up a string by direct concatenation. However, Python 2.0's augmented assignment reduces the performance difference:

```python
>>> import string
>>> s = "Mary had a little lamb"
>>> t = "its fleece was white as snow"
>>> s = s +" "+ t    # relatively "expensive" for big strings
>>> s += " " + t     # "cheaper" than Python 1.x style
>>> lst = [s]
>>> lst.append(t)    # "cheapest" way of building long string
>>> s = string.join(lst)
```

For Python 1.6+, use of a string object method is stylistically preferred in some cases. However, just as *string.join()* is special in taking a list as a first argument, the string object method *"".join()* is unusual in being an operation on the (optional) `sep` string, not on the (required) `words` list (this surprises many new Python programmers).

SEE ALSO: string.split() *142*;

string.joinfields(...)

Identical to *string.join()*.

string.ljust(s=..., width=...)
"".ljust(width)

Return a string with s padded with trailing spaces (but not truncated) to occupy
length width (or more).

```
>>> import string
>>> string.ljust(width=30,s="Mary had a little lamb")
'Mary had a little lamb        '
>>> string.ljust("Mary had a little lamb", 5)
'Mary had a little lamb'
```

For Python 1.6+, use of a string object method is stylistically preferred in many
cases:

```
>>> "Mary had a little lamb".ljust(25)
'Mary had a little lamb   '
```

SEE ALSO: string.rjust() *141*; string.center() *133*;

string.lower(s=...)
"".lower()

Return a string with any uppercase letters converted to lowercase.

```
>>> import string
>>> string.lower("mary HAD a little lamb!")
'mary had a little lamb!'
>>> string.lower("Mary had a Little Lamb!")
'mary had a little lamb!'
```

For Python 1.6+, use of a string object method is stylistically preferred in many
cases:

```
>>> "Mary had a Little Lamb!".lower()
'mary had a little lamb!'
```

SEE ALSO: string.upper() *146*;

string.lstrip(s=. . .)
"".lstrip([chars=string.whitespace])

> Return a string with leading whitespace characters removed. For Python 1.6+, use
> of a string object method is stylistically preferred in many cases:

```
>>> import string
>>> s = """
...     Mary had a little lamb       \011"""
>>> string.lstrip(s)
'Mary had a little lamb       \011'
>>> s.lstrip()
'Mary had a little lamb       \011'
```

> Python 2.3+ accepts the optional argument chars to the string object method. All
> characters in the string chars will be removed.

> SEE ALSO: string.rstrip() *142*; string.strip() *144*;

string.maketrans(from, to)

> Return a translation table string for use with *string.translate()*. The strings
> from and to must be the same length. A translation table is a string of 256 successive
> byte values, where each position defines a translation from the *chr()* value of the
> index to the character contained at that index position.

```
>>> import string
>>> ord('A')
65
>>> ord('z')
122
>>> string.maketrans('ABC','abc')[65:123]
'abcDEFGHIJKLMNOPQRSTUVWXYZ[\\]^_'abcdefghijklmnopqrstuvwxyz'
>>> string.maketrans('ABCxyz','abcXYZ')[65:123]
'abcDEFGHIJKLMNOPQRSTUVWXYZ[\\]^_'abcdefghijklmnopqrstuvwXYZ'
```

> SEE ALSO: string.translate() *145*;

string.replace(s=. . . , old=. . . , new=. . . [,maxsplit=. . .])
"".replace(old, new [,maxsplit])

> Return a string based on s with occurrences of old replaced by new. If the fourth
> argument maxsplit is specified, only replace maxsplit initial occurrences.

```
>>> import string
>>> string.replace("Mary had a little lamb", "a little", "some")
'Mary had some lamb'
```

For Python 1.6+, use of a string object method is stylistically preferred in many cases:

```
>>> "Mary had a little lamb".replace("a little", "some")
'Mary had some lamb'
```

A common "trick" involving *string.replace()* is to use it multiple times to achieve a goal. Obviously, simply to replace several different substrings in a string, multiple *string.replace()* operations are almost inevitable. But there is another class of cases where *string.replace()* can be used to create an intermediate string with "placeholders" for an original substring in a particular context. The same goal can always be achieved with regular expressions, but sometimes staged *string.replace()* operations are both faster and easier to program:

```
>>> import string
>>> line = 'variable = val       # see comments #3 and #4'
>>> # we'd like '#3' and '#4' spelled out within comment
>>> string.replace(line,'#','number ')         # doesn't work
'variable = val       number  see comments number 3 and number 4'
>>> place_holder=string.replace(line,' # ',' !!! ') # insrt plcholder
>>> place_holder
'variable = val       !!! see comments #3 and #4'
>>> place_holder=place_holder.replace('#','number ') # almost there
>>> place_holder
'variable = val       !!! see comments number 3 and number 4'
>>> line = string.replace(place_holder,'!!!','#') # restore orig
>>> line
'variable = val       # see comments number 3 and number 4'
```

Obviously, for jobs like this, a placeholder must be chosen so as not ever to occur within the strings undergoing "staged transformation"; but that should be possible generally since placeholders may be as long as needed.

SEE ALSO: string.translate() *145*; mx.TextTools.replace() *314*;

string.rfind(s, sub [,start [,end]])
"".rfind(sub [,start [,end]])

Return the index position of the last occurrence of sub in s. If the optional third or fourth arguments are specified, only the corresponding slice of s is examined (but result is position in s as a whole). Return -1 if no occurrence is found. Position is zero-based, as with Python list indexing:

```
>>> import string
>>> string.rfind("mary had a little lamb", "a")
```

```
19
>>> string.rfind("mary had a little lamb", "a", 3, 10)
9
>>> string.rfind("mary had a little lamb", "b")
21
>>> string.rfind("mary had a little lamb", "b", 3, 10)
-1
```

For Python 1.6+, use of a string object method is stylistically preferred in many cases:

```
>>> 'mary had a little lamb'.rfind("ad")
6
```

SEE ALSO: string.rindex() *141*; string.find() *135*;

string.rindex(s, sub [,start [,end]])
"".rindex(sub [,start [,end]])

Return the same value as does *string.rfind()* with same arguments, except raise ValueError instead of returning -1 when sub does not occur in s.

```
>>> import string
>>> string.rindex("mary had a little lamb", "b")
21
>>> string.rindex("mary had a little lamb", "b", 3, 10)
Traceback (most recent call last):
  File "<stdin>", line 1, in ?
  File "d:/py20sl/lib/string.py", line 148, in rindex
    return s.rindex(*args)
ValueError: substring not found in string.rindex
```

For Python 1.6+, use of a string object method is stylistically preferred in many cases:

```
>>> 'mary had a little lamb'.index("ad")
6
```

SEE ALSO: string.rfind() *140*; string.index() *135*;

string.rjust(s=..., width=...)
"".rjust(width)

Return a string with s padded with leading spaces (but not truncated) to occupy length width (or more).

```
>>> import string
>>> string.rjust(width=30,s="Mary had a little lamb")
'        Mary had a little lamb'
>>> string.rjust("Mary had a little lamb", 5)
'Mary had a little lamb'
```

For Python 1.6+, use of a string object method is stylistically preferred in many cases:

```
>>> "Mary had a little lamb".rjust(25)
'    Mary had a little lamb'
```

SEE ALSO: string.ljust() *138*; string.center() *133*;

string.rstrip(s=...)
"".rstrip([chars=string.whitespace])

Return a string with trailing whitespace characters removed. For Python 1.6+, use of a string object method is stylistically preferred in many cases:

```
>>> import string
>>> s = """
...      Mary had a little lamb        \011"""
>>> string.rstrip(s)
'\012     Mary had a little lamb'
>>> s.rstrip()
'\012     Mary had a little lamb'
```

Python 2.3+ accepts the optional argument `chars` to the string object method. All characters in the string `chars` will be removed.

SEE ALSO: string.lstrip() *139*; string.strip() *144*;

string.split(s=...[,sep=...[,maxsplit=...]])
"".split([,sep [,maxsplit]])

Return a list of nonoverlapping substrings of s. If the second argument `sep` is specified, the substrings are divided around the occurrences of `sep`. If `sep` is not specified, the substrings are divided around *any* whitespace characters. The dividing strings do not appear in the resultant list. If the third argument `maxsplit` is specified, everything "left over" after splitting `maxsplit` parts is appended to the list, giving the list length 'maxsplit'+1.

```
>>> import string
>>> s = 'mary had a little lamb      ...with a glass of sherry'
>>> string.split(s, ' a ')
```

```
['mary had', 'little lamb     ...with', 'glass of sherry']
>>> string.split(s)
['mary', 'had', 'a', 'little', 'lamb', '...with', 'a', 'glass',
'of', 'sherry']
>>> string.split(s,maxsplit=5)
['mary', 'had', 'a', 'little', 'lamb', '...with a glass of sherry']
```

For Python 1.6+, use of a string object method is stylistically preferred in many cases:

```
>>> "Mary had a Little Lamb!".split()
['Mary', 'had', 'a', 'Little', 'Lamb!']
```

The *string.split()* function (and corresponding string object method) is surprisingly versatile for working with texts, especially ones that resemble prose. Its default behavior of treating all whitespace as a single divider allows *string.split()* to act as a quick-and-dirty word parser:

```
>>> wc = lambda s: len(s.split())
>>> wc("Mary had a Little Lamb")
5
>>> s = """Mary had a Little Lamb
... its fleece as white as snow.
... And everywhere that Mary went  ...  the lamb was sure to go."""
>>> print s
Mary had a Little Lamb
its fleece as white as snow.
And everywhere that Mary went  ...  the lamb was sure to go.
>>> wc(s)
23
```

The function *string.split()* is very often used in conjunction with *string.join()*. The pattern involved is "pull the string apart, modify the parts, put it back together." Often the parts will be words, but this also works with lines (dividing on \n) or other chunks. For example:

```
>>> import string
>>> s = """Mary had a Little Lamb
... its fleece as white as snow.
... And everywhere that Mary went  ...  the lamb was sure to go."""
>>> string.join(string.split(s))
'Mary had a Little Lamb its fleece as white as snow. And everywhere
... that Mary went the lamb was sure to go.'
```

A Python 1.6+ idiom for string object methods expresses this technique compactly:

```
>>> "-".join(s.split())
'Mary-had-a-Little-Lamb-its-fleece-as-white-as-snow.-And-everywhere
...-that-Mary-went--the-lamb-was-sure-to-go.'
```

SEE ALSO: string.join() *137*; mx.TextTools.setsplit() *314*; mx.TextTools.charsplit() *311*; mx.TextTools.splitat() *315*; mx.TextTools.splitlines() *315*;

string.splitfields(...)

Identical to *string.split()*.

"".splitlines([keepends=0])

This string method does not have an equivalent in the *string* module. Return a list of lines in the string. The optional argument `keepends` determines whether line break character(s) are included in the line strings.

"".startswith(prefix [,start [,end]])

This string method does not have an equivalent in the *string* module. Return a Boolean value indicating whether the string begins with the prefix `prefix`. If the optional second argument `start` is specified, only consider the terminal substring after the offset `start`. If the optional third argument `end` is given, only consider the slice [`start:end`].

SEE ALSO: "".endswith() *134*; string.find() *135*;

string.strip(s=...)
"".strip([chars=string.whitespace])

Return a string with leading and trailing whitespace characters removed. For Python 1.6+, use of a string object method is stylistically preferred in many cases:

```
>>> import string
>>> s = """
...     Mary had a little lamb        \011"""
>>> string.strip(s)
'Mary had a little lamb'
>>> s.strip()
'Mary had a little lamb'
```

Python 2.3+ accepts the optional argument `chars` to the string object method. All characters in the string `chars` will be removed.

```
>>> s = "MARY had a LITTLE lamb STEW"
>>> s.strip("ABCDEFGHIJKLMNOPQRSTUVWXYZ") # strip caps
' had a LITTLE lamb '
```

SEE ALSO: string.rstrip() *142*; string.lstrip() *139*;

string.swapcase(s=...)
"".swapcase()

Return a string with any uppercase letters converted to lowercase and any lowercase letters converted to uppercase.

```
>>> import string
>>> string.swapcase("mary HAD a little lamb!")
'MARY had A LITTLE LAMB!'
```

For Python 1.6+, use of a string object method is stylistically preferred in many cases:

```
>>> "Mary had a Little Lamb!".swapcase()
'MARY HAD A LITTLE LAMB!'
```

SEE ALSO: string.upper() *146*; string.lower() *138*;

string.translate(s=..., table=... [,deletechars=""])
"".translate(table [,deletechars=""])

Return a string, based on s, with `deletechars` deleted (if the third argument is specified) and with any remaining characters translated according to the translation `table`.

```
>>> import string
>>> tab = string.maketrans('ABC','abc')
>>> string.translate('MARY HAD a little LAMB', tab, 'Atl')
'MRY HD a ie LMb'
```

For Python 1.6+, use of a string object method is stylistically preferred in many cases. However, if *string.maketrans()* is used to create the translation table, one will need to import the *string* module anyway:

```
>>> 'MARY HAD a little LAMB'.translate(tab, 'Atl')
'MRY HD a ie LMb'
```

The *string.translate()* function is a *very* fast way to modify a string. Setting up the translation table takes some getting used to, but the resultant transformation is much faster than a procedural technique such as:

```
>>> (new,frm,to,dlt) = ("",'ABC','abc','Alt')
>>> for c in 'MARY HAD a little LAMB':
...     if c not in dlt:
...         pos = frm.find(c)
...         if pos == -1: new += c
...         else:         new += to[pos]
...
>>> new
'MRY HD a ie LMb'
```

SEE ALSO: string.maketrans() *139*;

string.upper(s=. . .)
"".upper()

Return a string with any lowercase letters converted to uppercase.

```
>>> import string
>>> string.upper("mary HAD a little lamb!")
'MARY HAD A LITTLE LAMB!'
>>> string.upper("Mary had a Little Lamb!")
'MARY HAD A LITTLE LAMB!'
```

For Python 1.6+, use of a string object method is stylistically preferred in many cases:

```
>>> "Mary had a Little Lamb!".upper()
'MARY HAD A LITTLE LAMB!'
```

SEE ALSO: string.lower() *138*;

string.zfill(s=. . . , width=. . .)

Return a string with s padded with leading zeros (but not truncated) to occupy length width (or more). If a leading sign is present, it "floats" to the beginning of the return value. In general, *string.zfill()* is designed for alignment of numeric values, but no checking is done to see if a string looks number-like.

```
>>> import string
>>> string.zfill("this", 20)
'0000000000000000this'
>>> string.zfill("-37", 20)
'-0000000000000000037'
>>> string.zfill("+3.7", 20)
'+0000000000000003.7'
```

Based on the example of *string.rjust()*, one might expect a string object method *""*.zfill(); however, no such method exists.

SEE ALSO: string.rjust() *141*;

2.2.2 Strings as Files, and Files as Strings

In many ways, strings and files do a similar job. Both provide a storage container for an unlimited amount of (textual) information that is directly structured only by linear position of the bytes. A first inclination is to suppose that the difference between files and strings is one of persistence—files hang around when the current program is no longer running. But that distinction is not really tenable. On the one hand, standard Python modules like *shelve*, *pickle*, and *marshal*—and third-party modules like *xml_pickle* and *ZODB*—provide simple ways of making strings persist (but not thereby correspond in any direct way to a filesystem). On the other hand, many files are not particularly persistent: Special files like STDIN and STDOUT under Unix-like systems exist only for program life; other peculiar files like /dev/cua0 and similar "device files" are really just streams; and even files that live on transient memory disks, or get deleted with program cleanup, are not very persistent.

The real difference between files and strings in Python is no more or less than the set of techniques available to operate on them. File objects can do things like .read() and .seek() on themselves. Notably, file objects have a concept of a "current position" that emulates an imaginary "read-head" passing over the physical storage media. Strings, on the other hand, can be sliced and indexed—for example, str[4:10] or for c in str:—and can be processed with string object methods and by functions of modules like *string* and *re*. Moreover, a number of special-purpose Python objects act "file-like" without quite being files; for example, *gzip.open()* and *urllib.urlopen()*. Of course, Python itself does not impose any strict condition for just how "file-like" something has to be to work in a file-like context. A programmer has to figure that out for each type of object she wishes to apply techniques to (but most of the time things "just work" right).

Happily, Python provides some standard modules to make files and strings easily interoperable.

---

mmap ◇ **Memory-mapped file support**

The *mmap* module allows a programmer to create "memory-mapped" file objects. These special *mmap* objects enable most of the techniques you might apply to "true" file objects and simultaneously most of the techniques you might apply to "true" strings. Keep in mind the hinted caveat about "most," however: Many *string* module functions are implemented using the corresponding string object methods. Since a *mmap* object is only somewhat "string-like," it basically only implements the .find() method and those "magic" methods associated with slicing and indexing. This is enough to support most string object idioms.

When a string-like change is made to a *mmap* object, that change is propagated to the underlying file, and the change is persistent (assuming the underlying file is persistent, and that the object called `.flush()` before destruction). *mmap* thereby provides an efficient route to "persistent strings."

Some examples of working with memory-mapped file objects are worth looking at:

```
>>> # Create a file with some test data
>>> open('test','w').write(' #'.join(map(str, range(1000))))
>>> fp = open('test','r+')
>>> import mmap
>>> mm = mmap.mmap(fp.fileno(),1000)
>>> len(mm)
1000
>>> mm[-20:]
'218 #219 #220 #221 #'
>>> import string    # apply a string module method
>>> mm.seek(string.find(mm, '21'))
>>> mm.read(10)
'21 #22 #23'
>>> mm.read(10)      # next ten bytes
' #24 #25 #'
>>> mm.find('21')    # object method to find next occurrence
402
>>> try: string.rfind(mm, '21')
... except AttributeError: print "Unsupported string function"
...
Unsupported string function
>>> '/'.join(re.findall('..21..',mm))   # regex's work nicely
' #21 #/#121 #/ #210 / #212 / #214 / #216 / #218 /#221 #'
```

It is worth emphasizing that the bytes in a file on disk are in fixed positions. You may use the *mmap.mmap.resize()* method to write into different portions of a file, but you cannot expand the file from the middle, only by adding to the end.

CLASSES

mmap.mmap(fileno, length [,tagname]) (Windows)
mmap.mmap(fileno, length [,flags=MAP_SHARED,
$$\text{prot=PROT\_READ|PROT\_WRITE])}$$

Create a new memory-mapped file object. `fileno` is the numeric file handle to base the mapping on. Generally this number should be obtained using the `.fileno()` method of a file object. `length` specifies the length of the mapping. Under Windows, the value 0 may be given for `length` to specify the current length of the file. If `length` smaller than the current file is specified, only the initial portion of the file will be mapped. If `length` larger than the current file is specified, the file can be extended with additional string content.

The underlying file for a memory-mapped file object must be opened for updating, using the "+" mode modifier.

According to the official Python documentation for Python 2.1, a third argument `tagname` may be specified. If it is, multiple memory-maps against the same file are created. In practice, however, each instance of *mmap.mmap()* creates a new memory-map whether or not a `tagname` is specified. In any case, this allows multiple file-like updates to the same underlying file, generally at different positions in the file.

```
>>> open('test','w').write(' #'.join([str(n) for n in range(1000)]))
>>> fp = open('test','r+')
>>> import mmap
>>> mm1 = mmap.mmap(fp.fileno(),1000)
>>> mm2 = mmap.mmap(fp.fileno(),1000)
>>> mm1.seek(500)
>>> mm1.read(10)
'122 #123 #'
>>> mm2.read(10)
'0 #1 #2 #3'
```

Under Unix, the third argument `flags` may be MAP_PRIVATE or MAP_SHARED. If MAP_SHARED is specified for `flags`, all processes mapping the file will see the changes made to a *mmap* object. Otherwise, the changes are restricted to the current process. The fourth argument, `prot`, may be used to disallow certain types of access by other processes to the mapped file regions.

METHODS

mmap.mmap.close()

Close the memory-mapped file object. Subsequent calls to the other methods of the *mmap* object will raise an exception. Under Windows, the behavior of a *mmap* object after `.close()` is somewhat erratic, however. Note that closing the memory-mapped file object is not the same as closing the underlying file object. Closing the underlying file will make the contents inaccessible, but closing the memory-mapped file object will not affect the underlying file object.

SEE ALSO: FILE.close() *16*;

mmap.mmap.find(sub [,pos])

Similar to *string.find()*. Return the index position of the first occurrence of `sub` in the *mmap* object. If the optional second argument `pos` is specified, the result is the offset returned relative to `pos`. Return -1 if no occurrence is found:

```
>>> open('test','w').write(' #'.join([str(n) for n in range(1000)]))
>>> fp = open('test','r+')
```

```
>>> import mmap
>>> mm = mmap.mmap(fp.fileno(), 0)
>>> mm.find('21')
74
>>> mm.find('21',100)
-26
>>> mm.tell()
0
```

SEE ALSO: mmap.mmap.seek() *152*; string.find() *135*;

mmap.mmap.flush([offset, size])

Writes changes made in memory to *mmap* object back to disk. The first argument `offset` and second argument `size` must either both be specified or both be omitted. If `offset` and `size` are specified, only the position starting at `offset` or length `size` will be written back to disk.

mmap.mmap.flush() is necessary to guarantee that changes are written to disk; however, no guarantee is given that changes *will not* be written to disk as part of normal Python interpreter housekeeping. *mmap* should not be used for systems with "cancelable" changes (since changes may not be cancelable).

SEE ALSO: FILE.flush() *16*;

mmap.mmap.move(target, source, length)

Copy a substring within a memory-mapped file object. The length of the substring is the third argument `length`. The target location is the first argument `target`. The substring is copied from the position `source`. It is allowable to have the substring's original position overlap its target range, but it must not go past the last position of the *mmap* object.

```
>>> open('test','w').write(''.join([c*10 for c in 'ABCDE']))
>>> fp = open('test','r+')
>>> import mmap
>>> mm = mmap.mmap(fp.fileno(),0)
>>> mm[:]
'AAAAAAAAAABBBBBBBBBBCCCCCCCCCCDDDDDDDDDDEEEEEEEEEE'
>>> mm.move(40,0,5)
>>> mm[:]
'AAAAAAAAAABBBBBBBBBBCCCCCCCCCCDDDDDDDDDDAAAAAEEEEE'
```

mmap.mmap.read(num)

Return a string containing `num` bytes, starting at the current file position. The file position is moved to the end of the read string. In contrast to the `.read()` method of file objects, *mmap.mmap.read()* always requires that a byte count be specified, which makes a memory-map file object not fully substitutable for a file object when data is read. However, the following is safe for both true file objects and memory-mapped file objects:

```
>>> open('test','w').write(' #'.join([str(n) for n in range(1000)]))
>>> fp = open('test','r+')
>>> import mmap
>>> mm = mmap.mmap(fp.fileno(),0)
>>> def safe_readall(file):
...     try:
...         length = len(file)
...         return file.read(length)
...     except TypeError:
...         return file.read()
...
>>> s1 = safe_readall(fp)
>>> s2 = safe_readall(mm)
>>> s1 == s2
1
```

SEE ALSO: mmap.mmap.read_byte() *151*; mmap.mmap.readline() *151*; mmap.mmap.write() *153*; FILE.read() *17*;

mmap.mmap.read_byte()

Return a one-byte string from the current file position and advance the current position by one. Same as `mmap.mmap.read(1)`.

SEE ALSO: mmap.mmap.read() *150*; mmap.mmap.readline() *151*;

mmap.mmap.readline()

Return a string from the memory-mapped file object, starting from the current file position and going to the next newline character. Advance the current file position by the amount read.

SEE ALSO: mmap.mmap.read() *150*; mmap.mmap.read_byte() *151*; FILE.readline() *17*;

mmap.mmap.resize(newsize)

Change the size of a memory-mapped file object. This may be used to expand the size of an underlying file or merely to expand the area of a file that is memory-mapped. An expanded file is padded with null bytes (\000) unless otherwise filled with content. As with other operations on *mmap* objects, changes to the underlying file system may not occur until a .flush() is performed.

SEE ALSO: mmap.mmap.flush() *150*;

mmap.mmap.seek(offset [,mode])

Change the current file position. If a second argument `mode` is given, a different seek mode can be selected. The default is 0, absolute file positioning. Mode 1 seeks relative to the current file position. Mode 2 is relative to the end of the memory-mapped file (which may be smaller than the whole size of the underlying file). The first argument `offset` specifies the distance to move the current file position—in mode 0 it should be positive, in mode 2 it should be negative, in mode 1 the current position can be moved either forward or backward.

SEE ALSO: FILE.seek() *17*;

mmap.mmap.size()

Return the length of the underlying file. The size of the actual memory-map may be smaller if less than the whole file is mapped:

```
>>> open('test','w').write('X'*100)
>>> fp = open('test','r+')
>>> import mmap
>>> mm = mmap.mmap(fp.fileno(),50)
>>> mm.size()
100
>>> len(mm)
50
```

SEE ALSO: len() *14*; mmap.mmap.seek() *152*; mmap.mmap.tell() *152*;

mmap.mmap.tell()

Return the current file position.

```
>>> open('test','w').write('X'*100)
>>> fp = open('test','r+')
>>> import mmap
>>> mm = mmap.mmap(fp.fileno(), 0)
>>> mm.tell()
0
>>> mm.seek(20)
>>> mm.tell()
20
>>> mm.read(20)
'XXXXXXXXXXXXXXXXXXXX'
>>> mm.tell()
40
```

SEE ALSO: FILE.tell() *17*; mmap.mmap.seek() *152*;

mmap.mmap.write(s)

Write s into the memory-mapped file object at the current file position. The
current file position is updated to the position following the write. The method
mmap.mmap.write() is useful for functions that expect to be passed a file-like object with a .write() method. However, for new code, it is generally more natural
to use the string-like index and slice operations to write contents. For example:

```
>>> open('test','w').write('X'*50)
>>> fp = open('test','r+')
>>> import mmap
>>> mm = mmap.mmap(fp.fileno(), 0)
>>> mm.write('AAAAA')
>>> mm.seek(10)
>>> mm.write('BBBBB')
>>> mm[30:35] = 'SSSSS'
>>> mm[:]
'AAAAAXXXXXBBBBBXXXXXXXXXXXXXXXXSSSSSXXXXXXXXXXXXXXX'
>>> mm.tell()
15
```

SEE ALSO: FILE.write() *17*; mmap.mmap.read() *150*;

mmap.mmap.write_byte(c)

Write a one-byte string to the current file position, and advance the current position
by one. Same as mmap.mmap.write(c) where c is a one-byte string.

SEE ALSO: mmap.mmap.write() *153*;

StringIO ◇ **File-like objects that read from or write to a string buffer**

cStringIO ◇ **Fast, but incomplete, StringIO replacement**

The *StringIO* and *cStringIO* modules allow a programmer to create "memory files," that
is, "string buffers." These special *StringIO* objects enable most of the techniques you
might apply to "true" file objects, but without any connection to a filesystem.

The most common use of string buffer objects is when some existing techniques for
working with byte-streams in files are to be applied to strings that do not come from
files. A string buffer object behaves in a file-like manner and can "drop in" to most
functions that want file objects.

cStringIO is much faster than *StringIO* and should be used in most cases. Both
modules provide a StringIO class whose instances are the string buffer objects.

cStringIO.StringIO cannot be subclassed (and therefore cannot provide additional methods), and it cannot handle Unicode strings. One rarely needs to subclass *StringIO*, but the absence of Unicode support in *cStringIO* could be a problem for many developers. As well, *cStringIO* does not support write operations, which makes its string buffers less general (the effect of a write against an in-memory file can be accomplished by normal string operations).

A string buffer object may be initialized with a string (or Unicode for *StringIO*) argument. If so, that is the initial content of the buffer. Below are examples of usage (including Unicode handling):

```
>>> from cStringIO import StringIO as CSIO
>>> from StringIO import StringIO as SIO
>>> alef, omega = unichr(1488), unichr(969)
>>> sentence = "In set theory, the Greek "+omega+" represents the \n"+\
...            "ordinal limit of the integers, while the Hebrew \n"+\
...            alef+" represents their cardinality."
>>> sio = SIO(sentence)
>>> try:
...     csio = CSIO(sentence)
...     print "New string buffer from raw string"
... except TypeError:
...     csio = CSIO(sentence.encode('utf-8'))
...     print "New string buffer from ENCODED string"
...
New string buffer from ENCODED string
>>> sio.getvalue() == unicode(csio.getvalue(),'utf-8')
1
>>> try:
...     sio.getvalue() == csio.getvalue()
... except UnicodeError:
...     print "Cannot even compare Unicode with string, in general"
...
Cannot even compare Unicode with string, in general
>>> lines = csio.readlines()
>>> len(lines)
3
>>> sio.seek(0)
>>> print sio.readline().encode('utf-8'),
In set theory, the Greek  represents the ordinal
>>> sio.tell(), csio.tell()
(51, 124)
```

CONSTANTS

cStringIO.InputType

The type of a *cStringIO.StringIO* instance that has been opened in "read" mode. All *StringIO.StringIO* instances are simply InstanceType.

SEE ALSO: cStringIO.StringIO *155*;

cStringIO.OutputType

The type of *cStringIO.StringIO* instance that has been opened in "write" mode (actually read/write). All *StringIO.StringIO* instances are simply InstanceType.

SEE ALSO: cStringIO.StringIO *155*;

CLASSES
StringIO.StringIO([buf=...])
cStringIO.StringIO([buf])

Create a new string buffer. If the first argument buf is specified, the buffer is initialized with a string content. If the *cStringIO* module is used, the presence of the buf argument determines whether write access to the buffer is enabled. A *cStringIO.StringIO* buffer with write access must be initialized with no argument, otherwise it becomes read-only. A *StringIO.StringIO* buffer, however, is always read/write.

METHODS
StringIO.StringIO.close()
cStringIO.StringIO.close()

Close the string buffer. No access is permitted after close.

SEE ALSO: FILE.close() *16*;

StringIO.StringIO.flush()
cStringIO.StringIO.flush()

Compatibility method for file-like behavior. Data in a string buffer is already in memory, so there is no need to finalize a write to disk.

SEE ALSO: FILE.close() *16*;

StringIO.StringIO.getvalue()
cStringIO.StringIO.getvalue()

Return the entire string held by the string buffer. Does not affect the current file position. Basically, this is the way you convert back from a string buffer to a string.

StringIO.StringIO.isatty()
cStringIO.StringIO.isatty()

Return 0. Compatibility method for file-like behavior.

SEE ALSO: FILE.isatty() *16*;

StringIO.StringIO.read([num])
cStringIO.StringIO.read([num])

If the first argument **num** is specified, return a string containing the next **num** characters. If **num** characters are not available, return as many as possible. If **num** is not specified, return all the characters from current file position to end of string buffer. Advance the current file position by the amount read.

SEE ALSO: FILE.read() *17*; mmap.mmap.read() *150*; StringIO.StringIO.readline() *156*;

StringIO.StringIO.readline([length=...])
cStringIO.StringIO.readline([length])

Return a string from the string buffer, starting from the current file position and going to the next newline character. Advance the current file position by the amount read.

SEE ALSO: mmap.mmap.readline() *151*; StringIO.StringIO.read() *156*; StringIO.StringIO.readlines() *156*; FILE.readline() *17*;

StringIO.StringIO.readlines([sizehint=...])
cStringIO.StringIO.readlines([sizehint]

Return a list of strings from the string buffer. Each list element consists of a single line, including the trailing newline character(s). If an argument **sizehint** is specified, only read approximately **sizehint** characters worth of lines (full lines will always be read).

SEE ALSO: StringIO.StringIO.readline() *156*; FILE.readlines() *17*;

cStringIO.StringIO.reset()

Sets the current file position to the beginning of the string buffer. Same as `cStringIO.StringIO.seek(0)`.

SEE ALSO: StringIO.StringIO.seek() *156*;

StringIO.StringIO.seek(offset [,mode=0])
cStringIO.StringIO.seek(offset [,mode])

Change the current file position. If the second argument **mode** is given, a different seek mode can be selected. The default is 0, absolute file positioning. Mode 1 seeks relative to the current file position. Mode 2 is relative to the end of the string buffer. The first argument **offset** specifies the distance to move the current file position—in mode 0 it should be positive, in mode 2 it should be negative, in mode 1 the current position can be moved either forward or backward.

SEE ALSO: FILE.seek() *17*; mmap.mmap.seek() *152*;

StringIO.StringIO.tell()
cStringIO.StringIO.tell()

Return the current file position in the string buffer.

SEE ALSO: StringIO.StringIO.seek() *156*;

StringIO.StringIO.truncate([len=0])
cStringIO.StringIO.truncate([len])

Reduce the length of the string buffer to the first argument `len` characters. Truncation can only reduce characters later than the current file position (an initial `cStringIO.StringIO.reset()` can be used to assure truncation from the beginning).

SEE ALSO: StringIO.StringIO.seek() *156*; cStringIO.StringIO.reset() *156*; StringIO.StringIO.close() *155*;

StringIO.StringIO.write(s=...)
cStringIO.StringIO.write(s)

Write the first argument `s` into the string buffer at the current file position. The current file position is updated to the position following the write.

SEE ALSO: StringIO.StringIO.writelines() *157*; mmap.mmap.write() *153*; StringIO.StringIO.read() *156*; FILE.write() *17*;

StringIO.StringIO.writelines(list=...)
cStringIO.StringIO.writelines(list)

Write each element of `list` into the string buffer at the current file position. The current file position is updated to the position following the write. For the *cStringIO* method, `list` must be an actual list. For the *StringIO* method, other sequence types are allowed. To be safe, it is best to coerce an argument into an actual list first. In either case, `list` must contain only strings, or a `TypeError` will occur.

Contrary to what might be expected from the method name, *StringIO.StringIO.writelines()* never inserts newline characters. For the list elements actually to occupy separate lines in the string buffer, each element string must already have a newline terminator. Consider the following variants on writing a list to a string buffer:

```
>>> from StringIO import StringIO
>>> sio = StringIO()
>>> lst = [c*5 for c in 'ABC']
>>> sio.writelines(lst)
>>> sio.write(''.join(lst))
```

```
>>> sio.write('\n'.join(lst))
>>> print sio.getvalue()
AAAAABBBBBCCCCCAAAAABBBBBCCCCCAAAAA
BBBBB
CCCCC
```

SEE ALSO: FILE.writelines() *17*; StringIO.StringIO.write() *157*;

2.2.3   Converting Between Binary and ASCII

The Python standard library provides several modules for converting between binary data and 7-bit ASCII. At the low level, *binascii* is a C extension to produce fast string conversions. At a high level, *base64*, *binhex*, *quopri*, and *uu* provide file-oriented wrappers to the facilities in *binascii*.

---

base64 ◇ Convert to/from base64 encoding (RFC1521)

The *base64* module is a wrapper around the functions *binascii.a2b_base64()* and *binascii.b2a_base64()*. As well as providing a file-based interface on top of the underlying string conversions, *base64* handles the chunking of binary files into base64 line blocks and provides for the direct encoding of arbitrary input strings. Unlike *uu*, *base64* adds no content headers to encoded data; MIME standards for headers and message-wrapping are handled by other modules that utilize *base64*. Base64 encoding is specified in RFC1521.

FUNCTIONS

base64.encode(input=..., output=...)

Encode the contents of the first argument `input` to the second argument `output`. Arguments `input` and `output` should be file-like objects; `input` must be readable and `output` must be writable.

base64.encodestring(s=...)

Return the base64 encoding of the string passed in the first argument `s`.

base64.decode(input=..., output=...)

Decode the contents of the first argument `input` to the second argument `output`. Arguments `input` and `output` should be file-like objects; `input` must be readable and `output` must be writable.

base64.decodestring(s=...)

Return the decoding of the base64-encoded string passed in the first argument `s`.

SEE ALSO: email *345*; rfc822 *397*; mimetools *396*; mimetypes *374*; MimeWriter *396*; mimify *396*; binascii *159*; quopri *162*;

---

binascii ◇ Convert between binary data and ASCII

The *binascii* module is a C implementation of a number of styles of ASCII encoding of binary data. Each function in the *binascii* module takes either encoded ASCII or raw binary strings as an argument, and returns the string result of converting back or forth. Some restrictions apply to the length of strings passed to some functions in the module (for encodings that operate on specific block sizes).

FUNCTIONS

binascii.a2b_base64(s)

Return the decoded version of a base64-encoded string. A string consisting of one or more encoding blocks should be passed as the argument s.

binascii.a2b_hex(s)

Return the decoded version of a hexadecimal-encoded string. A string consisting of an even number of hexadecimals digits should be passed as the argument s.

binascii.a2b_hqx(s)

Return the decoded version of a binhex-encoded string. A string containing a complete number of encoded binary bytes should be passed as the argument s.

binascii.a2b_qp(s [,header=0])

Return the decoded version of a quoted printable string. A string containing a complete number of encoded binary bytes should be passed as the argument s. If the optional argument header is specified, underscores will be decoded as spaces. New to Python 2.2.

binascii.a2b_uu(s)

Return the decoded version of a UUencoded string. A string consisting of exactly one encoding block should be passed as the argument s (for a full block, 62 bytes input, 45 bytes returned).

binascii.b2a_base64(s)

Return the based64 encoding of a binary string (including the newline after block). A binary string no longer than 57 bytes should be passed as the argument s.

binascii.b2a_hex(s)

Return the hexadecimal encoding of a binary string. A binary string of any length should be passed as the argument s.

binascii.b2a_hqx(s)

Return the binhex4 encoding of a binary string. A binary string of any length should be passed as the argument s. Run-length compression of s is not performed by this function (use *binascii.rlecode_hqx()* first, if needed).

binascii.b2a_qp(s [,quotetabs=0 [,istext=1 [header=0]]])

Return the quoted printable encoding of a binary string. A binary string of any length should be passed as the argument s. The optional argument quotetabs specified whether to escape spaces and tabs; istext specifies *not* to newlines; header specifies whether to encode spaces as underscores (and escape underscores). New to Python 2.2.

binascii.b2a_uu(s)

Return the UUencoding of a binary string (including the initial block specifier— "M" for full blocks—and newline after block). A binary string no longer than 45 bytes should be passed as the argument s.

binascii.crc32(s [,crc])

Return the CRC32 checksum of the first argument s. If the second argument crc is specified, it will be used as an initial checksum. This allows partial computation of a checksum and continuation. For example:

```
>>> import binascii
>>> crc = binascii.crc32('spam')
>>> binascii.crc32(' and eggs', crc)
739139840
>>> binascii.crc32('spam and eggs')
739139840
```

binascii.crc_hqx(s, crc)

Return the binhex4 checksum of the first argument s, using initial checksum value in second argument. This allows partial computation of a checksum and continuation. For example:

```
>>> import binascii
>>> binascii.crc_hqx('spam and eggs', 0)
17918
>>> crc = binascii.crc_hqx('spam', 0)
>>> binascii.crc_hqx(' and eggs', crc)
17918
```

SEE ALSO: binascii.crc32 *160*;

binascii.hexlify(s)

Identical to *binascii.b2a_hex()*.

binascii.rlecode_hqx(s)

Return the binhex4 run-length encoding (RLE) of first argument s. Under this RLE technique, 0x90 is used as an indicator byte. Independent of the binhex4 standard, this is a poor choice of precompression for encoded strings.

SEE ALSO: zlib.compress(*182*;

binascii.rledecode_hqx(s)

Return the expansion of a binhex4 run-length encoded string.

binascii.unhexlify(s)

Identical to *binascii.a2b_hex()*

EXCEPTIONS

binascii.Error

Generic exception that should only result from programming errors.

binascii.Incomplete

Exception raised when a data block is incomplete. Usually this results from programming errors in reading blocks, but it could indicate data or channel corruption.

SEE ALSO: base64 *158*; binhex *161*; uu *163*;

---

binhex ◇ **Encode and decode binhex4 files**

The *binhex* module is a wrapper around the functions *binascii.a2b_hqx()*, *binascii.b2a_hqx()*, *binascii.rlecode_hqx()*, *binascii.rledecode_hqx()*, and *binascii.crc_hqx()*. As well as providing a file-based interface on top of the underlying string conversions, *binhex* handles run-length encoding of encoded files and attaches the needed header and footer information. Under MacOS, the resource fork of a file is encoded along with the data fork (not applicable under other platforms).

FUNCTIONS

binhex.binhex(inp=..., out=...)

Encode the contents of the first argument inp to the second argument out. Argument inp is a filename; out may be either a filename or a file-like object. However, a *cStringIO.StringIO* object is not "file-like" enough since it will be closed after the conversion—and therefore, its value lost. You could override the .close() method in a subclass of *StringIO.StringIO* to solve this limitation.

binhex.hexbin(inp=... [,out=...])

Decode the contents of the first argument to an output file. If the second argument out is specified, it will be used as the output filename, otherwise the filename will be taken from the binhex header. The argument inp may be either a filename or a file-like object.

CLASSES

A number of internal classes are used by *binhex*. They are not documented here, but can be examined in `$PYTHONHOME/lib/binhex.py` if desired (it is unlikely readers will need to do this).

SEE ALSO: binascii *159*;

---

quopri ◇ Convert to/from quoted printable encoding (RFC1521)

The *quopri* module is a wrapper around the functions `binascii.a2b_qp()` and `binascii.b2a_qp()`. The module *quopri* has the same methods as *base64*. Unlike *uu*, *base64* adds no content headers to encoded data; MIME standards for headers and message wrapping are handled by other modules that utilize *quopri*. Quoted printable encoding is specified in RFC1521.

FUNCTIONS

quopri.encode(input, output, quotetabs)

Encode the contents of the first argument `input` to the second argument `output`. Arguments `input` and `output` should be file-like objects; `input` must be readable and `output` must be writable. If `quotetabs` is a true value, escape tabs and spaces.

quopri.encodestring(s [,quotetabs=0])

Return the quoted printable encoding of the string passed in the first argument `s`. If `quotetabs` is a true value, escape tabs and spaces.

quopri.decode(input=..., output=... [,header=0])

Decode the contents of the first argument `input` to the second argument `output`. Arguments `input` and `output` should be file-like objects; `input` must be readable and `output` must be writable. If `header` is a true value, encode spaces as underscores and escape underscores.

quopri.decodestring(s [,header=0])

Return the decoding of the quoted printable string passed in the first argument `s`. If `header` is a true value, decode underscores as spaces.

SEE ALSO: email *345*; rfc822 *397*; mimetools *396*; mimetypes *374*; MimeWriter *396*; mimify *396*; binascii *159*; base64 *158*;

---

uu ◇ UUencode and UUdecode files

The *uu* module is a wrapper around the functions *binascii.a2b_uu()* and *binascii.b2a_uu()*. As well as providing a file-based interface on top of the underlying string conversions, *uu* handles the chunking of binary files into UUencoded line blocks and attaches the needed header and footer.

FUNCTIONS

uu.encode(in, out, [name=... [,mode=0666]])

Encode the contents of the first argument in to the second argument out. Arguments in and out should be file objects, but filenames are also accepted (the latter is deprecated). The special filename "-" can be used to specify STDIN or STDOUT, as appropriate. When file objects are passed as arguments, in must be readable and out must be writable. The third argument name can be used to specify the filename that appears in the UUencoding header; by default it is the name of in. The fourth argument mode is the octal filemode to store in the UUencoding header.

uu.decode(in, [,out_file=... [, mode=...])

Decode the contents of the first argument in to an output file. If the second argument out_file is specified, it will be used as the output file; otherwise, the filename will be taken from the UUencoding header. Arguments in and out_file should be file objects, but filenames are also accepted (the latter is deprecated). If the third argument mode is specified (and if out_file is either unspecified or is a filename), open the created file in mode mode.

SEE ALSO: binascii *159*;

2.2.4 Cryptography

Python does not come with any standard and general cryptography modules. The few included capabilities are fairly narrow in purpose and limited in scope. The capabilities in the standard library consist of several cryptographic hashes and one weak symmetrical encryption algorithm. A quick survey of cryptographic techniques shows what capabilities are absent from the standard library:

Symmetrical Encryption: Any technique by which a plaintext message M is "encrypted" with a key K to produce a cyphertext C. Application of K—or some K′ easily derivable from K—to C is called "decryption" and produces as output M. The standard module *rotor* provides a form of symmetrical encryption.

Cryptographic Hash: Any technique by which a short "hash" H is produced from a plaintext message M that has several additional properties: (1) Given only H, it is difficult to obtain any M′ such that the cryptographic hash of M′ is H; (2) Given two plaintext messages M and M′, there is a very low probability that the cryptographic hashes of M and M′ are the same. Sometimes a third property is included: (3) Given M, its cryptographic hash H, and another hash H′, examining the relationship between

H and H′ does not make it easier to find an M′ whose hash is H′. The standard modules *crypt*, *md5*, and *sha* provide forms of cryptographic hashes.

Asymmetrical Encryption: Also called "public-key cryptography." Any technique by which a pair of keys K_{pub} and K_{priv} can be generated that have several properties. The algorithm for an asymmetrical encryption technique will be called "P(M,K)" in the following. (1) For any plaintext message M, M equals $P(K_{priv},P(M,K_{pub}))$. (2) Given only a public-key K_{pub}, it is difficult to obtain a private-key K_{priv} that assures the equality in (1). (3) Given only $P(M,K_{pub})$, it is difficult to obtain M. In general, in an asymmetrical encryption system, a user generates K_{pub} and K_{priv}, then releases K_{pub} to other users but retains K_{priv} as a secret. There is no support for asymmetrical encryption in the standard library.

Digital Signatures: Digital signatures are really just "public-keys in reverse." In many cases, the same underlying algorithm is used for each. A digital signature is any technique by which a pair of keys K_{ver} and K_{sig} can be generated that have several properties. The algorithm for a digital signature will be called S(M,K) in the following. (1) For any message M, M equals $P(K_{ver},P(M,K_{sig}))$. (2) Given only a verification key K_{ver}, it is difficult to obtain a signature key K_{sig} that assures the equality in (1). (3) Given only $P(M,K_{sig})$, it is difficult to find any C′ such that $P(K_{ver},C)$ is a plausible message (in other words, the signature shows it is not a forgery). In general, in a digital signature system, a user generates K_{ver} and K_{sig}, then releases K_{ver} to other users but retains K_{sig} as a secret. There is no support for digital signatures in the standard library.

∘ · · ∘ · · ∘ · · ∘ · · ∘ · · ∘ · · ∘ · · ∘ · · ∘ · · ∘ · · ∘ · · ∘ · · ∘ · · ∘

Those outlined are the most important cryptographic techniques. More detailed general introductions to cryptology and cryptography can be found at the author's Web site. A first tutorial is *Introduction to Cryptology Concepts I*:

    <http://gnosis.cx/publish/programming/cryptology1.pdf>

Further material is in *Introduction to Cryptology Concepts II*:

    <http://gnosis.cx/publish/programming/cryptology2.pdf>

And more advanced material is in *Intermediate Cryptology: Specialized Protocols*:

    <http://gnosis.cx/publish/programming/cryptology3.pdf>

A number of third-party modules have been created to handle cryptographic tasks; a good guide to these third-party tools is the Vaults of Parnassus Encryption/Encoding index at <http://www.vex.net/parnassus/apyllo.py?i=94738404>. Only the tools in the standard library will be covered here specifically, since all the third-party tools are somewhat far afield of the topic of text processing as such. Moreover, third-party tools often rely on additional non-Python libraries, which will not be present on most platforms, and these tools will not necessarily be maintained as new Python versions introduce changes.

The most important third-party modules are listed below. These are modules that the author believes are likely to be maintained and that provide access to a wide range of cryptographic algorithms.

mxCrypto
amkCrypto

Marc-Andre Lemburg and Andrew Kuchling—both valuable contributors of many Python modules—have played a game of leapfrog with each other by releasing *mxCrypto* and *amkCrypto*, respectively. Each release of either module builds on the work of the other, providing compatible interfaces and overlapping source code. Whatever is newest at the time you read this is the best bet. Current information on both should be obtainable from:

<http://www.amk.ca/python/code/crypto.html>

Python Cryptography

Andrew Kuchling, who has provided a great deal of excellent Python documentation, documents these cryptography modules at:

<http://www.amk.ca/python/writing/pycrypt/>

M2Crypto

The *mxCrypto* and *amkCrypto* modules are most readily available for Unix-like platforms. A similar range of cryptographic capabilities for a Windows platform is available in Ng Pheng Siong's *M2Crypto*. Information and documentation can be found at:

<http://www.post1.com/home/ngps/m2/>

fcrypt

Carey Evans has created *fcrypt*, which is a pure-Python, single-module replacement for the standard library's *crypt* module. While probably orders-of-magnitude slower than a C implementation, *fcrypt* will run anywhere that Python does (and speed is rarely an issue for this functionality). *fcrypt* may be obtained at:

<http://home.clear.net.nz/pages/c.evans/sw/>

crypt ◇ Create and verify Unix-style passwords

The `crypt()` function is a frequently used, but somewhat antiquated, password creation/verification tool. Under Unix-like systems, `crypt()` is contained in system libraries and may be called from wrapper functions in languages like Python. `crypt()` is a form of cryptographic hash based on the Data Encryption Standard (DES). The hash produced by `crypt()` is based on an 8-byte key and a 2-byte "salt." The output of `crypt()` is produced by repeated encryption of a constant string, using the user key as a DES key and the salt to perturb the encryption in one of 4,096 ways. Both the key and the salt are restricted to alphanumerics plus dot and slash.

By using a cryptographic hash, passwords may be stored in a relatively insecure location. An imposter cannot easily produce a false password that will hash to the same value as the one stored in the password file, even given access to the password file. The salt is used to make "dictionary attacks" more difficult. If an imposter has access to the password file, she might try applying `crypt()` to a candidate password and compare the result to every entry in the password file. Without a salt, the chances of matching *some* encrypted password would be higher. The salt (a random value should be used) decreases the chance of such a random guess by 4,096 times.

The *crypt* module is only installed on some Python systems (even only some Unix systems). Moreover, the module, if installed, relies on an underlying system library. For a portable approach to password creation, the third-party *fcrypt* module provides a portable, pure-Python reimplementation.

FUNCTIONS

crypt.crypt(passwd, salt)

Return an ASCII 13-byte encrypted password. The first argument `passwd` must be a string up to eight characters in length (extra characters are truncated and do not affect the result). The second argument `salt` must be a string up to two characters in length (extra characters are truncated). The value of `salt` forms the first two characters of the result.

```
>>> from crypt import crypt
>>> crypt('mypassword','XY')
'XY5XuULXk4pcs'
>>> crypt('mypasswo','XY')
'XY5XuULXk4pcs'
>>> crypt('mypassword...more.characters','XY')
'XY5XuULXk4pcs'
>>> crypt('mypasswo','AB')
'ABO6lnfYxWIKg'
>>> crypt('diffpass','AB')
'ABlO5BopaFYNs'
```

SEE ALSO: fcrypt *165*; md5 *167*; sha *170*;

> **md5** ◇ **Create MD5 message digests**

RSA Data Security, Inc.'s MD5 cryptographic hash is a popular algorithm that is codified by RFC1321. Like *sha*, and unlike *crypt*, *md5* allows one to find the cryptographic hash of arbitrary strings (Unicode strings may not be hashed, however). Absent any other considerations—such as compatibility with other programs—Secure Hash Algorithm (SHA) is currently considered a better algorithm than MD5, and the *sha* module should be used for cryptographic hashes. The operation of *md5* objects is similar to *binascii.crc32()* hashes in that the final hash value may be built progressively from partial concatenated strings. The MD5 algorithm produces a 128-bit hash.

CONSTANTS

md5.MD5Type

The type of an *md5.new* instance.

CLASSES

md5.new([s])

Create an *md5* object. If the first argument s is specified, initialize the MD5 digest buffer with the initial string s. An MD5 hash can be computed in a single line with:

```
>>> import md5
>>> md5.new('Mary had a little lamb').hexdigest()
'e946adb45d4299def2071880d30136d4'
```

md5.md5([s])

Identical to *md5.new*.

METHODS

md5.copy()

Return a new *md5* object that is identical to the current state of the current object. Different terminal strings can be concatenated to the clone objects after they are copied. For example:

```
>>> import md5
>>> m = md5.new('spam and eggs')
>>> m.digest()
'\xb5\x81f\x0c\xff\x17\xe7\x8c\x84\xc3\xa8J\xd0.g\x85'
>>> m2 = m.copy()
>>> m2.digest()
'\xb5\x81f\x0c\xff\x17\xe7\x8c\x84\xc3\xa8J\xd0.g\x85'
>>> m.update(' are tasty')
```

```
>>> m2.update(' are wretched')
>>> m.digest()
'*\x94\xa2\xc5\xceq\x96\xef&\x1a\xc9#\xac98\x16'
>>> m2.digest()
'h\x8c\xfam\xe3\xb0\x90\xe8\x0e\xcb\xbf\xb3\xa7N\xe6\xbc'
```

md5.digest()

Return the 128-bit digest of the current state of the *md5* object as a 16-byte string.
Each byte will contain a full 8-bit range of possible values.

```
>>> import md5              # Python 2.1+
>>> m = md5.new('spam and eggs')
>>> m.digest()
'\xb5\x81f\x0c\xff\x17\xe7\x8c\x84\xc3\xa8J\xd0.g\x85'
```

```
>>> import md5              # Python <= 2.0
>>> m = md5.new('spam and eggs')
>>> m.digest()
'\265\201f\014\377\017\347\214\204\303\250J\320.g\205'
```

md5.hexdigest()

Return the 128-bit digest of the current state of the *md5* object as a 32-
byte hexadecimal-encoded string.   Each byte will contain only values in
string.hexdigits. Each pair of bytes represents 8-bits of hash, and this format
may be transmitted over 7-bit ASCII channels like email.

```
>>> import md5
>>> m = md5.new('spam and eggs')
>>> m.hexdigest()
'b581660cff17e78c84c3a84ad02e6785'
```

md5.update(s)

Concatenate additional strings to the *md5* object. Current hash state is adjusted
accordingly. The number of concatenation steps that go into an MD5 hash does not
affect the final hash, only the actual string that would result from concatenating each
part in a single string. However, for large strings that are determined incrementally,
it may be more practical to call *md5.update()* numerous times. For example:

```
>>> import md5
>>> m1 = md5.new('spam and eggs')
>>> m2 = md5.new('spam')
>>> m2.update(' and eggs')
>>> m3 = md5.new('spam')
>>> m3.update(' and ')
```

```
>>> m3.update('eggs')
>>> m1.hexdigest()
'b581660cff17e78c84c3a84ad02e678E'
>>> m2.hexdigest()
'b581660cff17e78c84c3a84ad02e678E'
>>> m3.hexdigest()
'b581660cff17e78c84c3a84ad02e678E'
```

SEE ALSO: sha *170*; crypt *166*; binascii.crc32() *160*;

---

rotor ◇ Perform Enigma-like encryption and decryption

The *rotor* module is a bit of a curiosity in the Python standard library. The symmetric encryption performed by *rotor* is similar to that performed by the extremely historically interesting and important Enigma algorithm. Given Alan Turing's famous role not just in inventing the theory of computability, but also in cracking German encryption during WWII, there is a nice literary quality to the inclusion of *rotor* in Python. However, *rotor* should not be mistaken for a robust modern encryption algorithm. Bruce Schneier has commented that there are two types of encryption algorithms: those that will stop your little sister from reading your messages, and those that will stop major governments and powerful organization from reading your messages. *rotor* is in the first category—albeit allowing for rather bright little sisters. But *rotor* will not help much against TLAs (three letter agencies). On the other hand, there is nothing else in the Python standard library that performs actual military-grade encryption, either.

CLASSES

rotor.newrotor(key [,numrotors])

Return a *rotor* object with rotor permutations and positions based on the first argument key. If the second argument numrotors is specified, a number of rotors other than the default of 6 can be used (more is stronger). A rotor encryption can be computed in a single line with:

```
>>> rotor.newrotor('mypassword') encrypt('Mary had a lamb')
'\x10\xef\xf1\x1e\xeaor\xe9\xf7\xe5\xad,r\xc6\x9f'
```

Object style encryption and decryption is performed like the following:

```
>>> import rotor
>>> C = rotor.newrotor('pass2').encrypt('Mary had a little lamb')
>>> r1 = rotor.newrotor('mypassword')
>>> C2 = r1.encrypt('Mary had a little lamb')
>>> r1.decrypt(C2)
```

```
'Mary had a little lamb'
>>> r1.decrypt(C)    # Let's try it
'\217R$\217/sE\311\330~#\310\342\200\025F\221\245\263\036\2200'
>>> r1.setkey('pass2')
>>> r1.decrypt(C)    # Let's try it
'Mary had a little lamb'
```

METHODS

rotor.decrypt(s)

Return a decrypted version of cyphertext string s. Prior to decryption, rotors are set to their initial positions.

rotor.decryptmore(s)

Return a decrypted version of cyphertext string s. Prior to decryption, rotors are left in their current positions.

rotor.encrypt(s)

Return an encrypted version of plaintext string s. Prior to encryption, rotors are set to their initial positions.

rotor.encryptmore(s)

Return an encrypted version of plaintext string s. Prior to encryption, rotors are left in their current positions.

rotor.setkey(key)

Set a new key for a *rotor* object.

---

sha ◇ Create SHA message digests

The National Institute of Standards and Technology's (NIST's) Secure Hash Algorithm is the best well-known cryptographic hash for most purposes. Like *md5*, and unlike *crypt*, *sha* allows one to find the cryptographic hash of arbitrary strings (Unicode strings may not be hashed, however). Absent any other considerations—such as compatibility with other programs—SHA is currently considered a better algorithm than MD5, and the *sha* module should be used for cryptographic hashes. The operation of *sha* objects is similar to *binascii.crc32()* hashes in that the final hash value may be built progressively from partial concatenated strings. The SHA algorithm produces a 160-bit hash.

CLASSES

sha.new([s])

Create an *sha* object. If the first argument s is specified, initialize the SHA digest buffer with the initial string s. An SHA hash can be computed in a single line with:

```
>>> import sha
>>> sha.new('Mary had a little lamb').hexdigest()
'bac9388d0498fb378e528d35abd05792291af182'
```

sha.sha([s])

Identical to *sha.new*.

METHODS

sha.copy()

Return a new *sha* object that is identical to the current state of the current object. Different terminal strings can be concatenated to the clone objects after they are copied. For example:

```
>>> import sha
>>> s = sha.new('spam and eggs')
>>> s.digest()
'\276\207\224\213\255\375x\024\245b\036C\322\017\2528 @\017\246'
>>> s2 = s.copy()
>>> s2.digest()
'\276\207\224\213\255\375x\024\245b\036C\322\017\2528 @\017\246'
>>> s.update(' are tasty')
>>> s2.update(' are wretched')
>>> s.digest()
'\013^C\366\253?I\323\206nt\2443\251\227\204-kr6'
>>> s2.digest()
'\013\210\237\216\014\3337X\333\221h&+c\345\007\367\326\274\321'
```

sha.digest()

Return the 160-bit digest of the current state of the *sha* object as a 20-byte string. Each byte will contain a full 8-bit range of possible values.

```
>>> import sha          # Python 2.1+
>>> s = sha.new('spam and eggs')
>>> s.digest()
'\xbe\x87\x94\x8b\xad\xfdx\x14\xa5b\x1eC\xd2\x0f\xaa8 @\x0f\xa6'
```

```
>>> import sha          # Python <= 2.0
>>> s = sha.new('spam and eggs')
>>> s.digest()
'\276\207\224\213\255\375x\024\245b\036C\322\017\2528 @\017\246'
```

sha.hexdigest()

Return the 160-bit digest of the current state of the *sha* object as a 40-byte hexadecimal-encoded string. Each byte will contain only values in *string.hexdigits*. Each pair of bytes represents 8-bits of hash, and this format may be transmitted over 7-bit ASCII channels like email.

```
>>> import sha
>>> s = sha.new('spam and eggs')
>>> s.hexdigest()
'be87948badfd7814a5621e43d20faa3820400fa6'
```

sha.update(s)

Concatenate additional strings to the *sha* object. Current hash state is adjusted accordingly. The number of concatenation steps that go into an SHA hash does not affect the final hash, only the actual string that would result from concatenating each part in a single string. However, for large strings that are determined incrementally, it may be more practical to call *sha.update()* numerous times. For example:

```
>>> import sha
>>> s1 = sha.sha('spam and eggs')
>>> s2 = sha.sha('spam')
>>> s2.update(' and eggs')
>>> s3 = sha.sha('spam')
>>> s3.update(' and ')
>>> s3.update('eggs')
>>> s1.hexdigest()
'be87948badfd7814a5621e43d20faa3820400fa6'
>>> s2.hexdigest()
'be87948badfd7814a5621e43d20faa3820400fa6'
>>> s3.hexdigest()
'be87948badfd7814a5621e43d20faa3820400fa6'
```

SEE ALSO: md5 *167*; crypt *166*; binascii.crc32() *160*;

2.2.5   Compression

Over the history of computers, a large number of data compression formats have been invented, mostly as variants on Lempel-Ziv and Huffman techniques. Compression is useful for all sorts of data streams, but file-level archive formats have been the most widely used and known application. Under MS-DOS and Windows we have seen ARC, PAK, ZOO, LHA, ARJ, CAB, RAR, and other formats—but the ZIP format has become the most widespread variant. Under Unix-like systems, compress (.Z) mostly gave way to gzip (GZ); gzip is still the most popular format on these systems, but bzip (BZ2) generally obtains better compression rates. Under MacOS, the most popular format is

SIT. Other platforms have additional variants on archive formats, but ZIP—and to a lesser extent GZ—are widely supported on a number of platforms.

The Python standard library includes support for several styles of compression. The *zlib* module performs low-level compression of raw string data and has no concept of a file. *zlib* is itself called by the high-level modules below for its compression services.

The modules *gzip* and *zipfile* provide file-level interfaces to compressed archives. However, a notable difference in the operation of *gzip* and *zipfile* arises out of a difference in the underlying GZ and ZIP formats. gzip (GZ) operates exclusively on single files—leaving the work of concatenating collections of files to tools like `tar`. One frequently encounters (especially on Unix-like systems) files like `foo.tar.gz` or `foo.tgz` that are produced by first applying `tar` to a collection of files, then applying `gzip` to the result. ZIP, however, handles both the compression and archiving aspects in a single tool and format. As a consequence, *gzip* is able to create file-like objects based directly on the compressed contents of a GZ file. *ziplib* needs to provide more specialized methods for navigating archive contents and for working with individual compressed file images therein.

Also see Appendix B (A Data Compression Primer).

> **gzip ◇ Functions that read and write gzipped files**

The *gzip* module allows the treatment of the compressed data inside `gzip` compressed files directly in a file-like manner. Uncompressed data can be read out, and compressed data written back in, all without a caller knowing or caring that the file is a GZ-compressed file. A simple example illustrates this:

---

gzip_file.py

```
# Treat a GZ as "just another file"
import gzip, glob
print "Size of data in files:"
for fname in glob.glob('*'):
    try:
        if fname[-3:] == '.gz':
            s = gzip.open(fname).read()
        else:
            s = open(fname).read()
        print ' ',fname,'-',len(s),'bytes'
    except IOError:
        print 'Skipping',file
```

The module *gzip* is a wrapper around *zlib*, with the latter performing the actual compression and decompression tasks. In many respects, *gzip* is similar to *mmap* and *StringIO* in emulating and/or wrapping a file object.

SEE ALSO: mmap *147*; StringIO *153*; cStringIO *152*;

CLASSES

gzip.GzipFile([filename=... [,mode="rb" [,compresslevel=9 [,fileobj=...]]]])

Create a *gzip* file-like object. Such an object supports most file object operations, with the exception of `.seek()` and `.tell()`. Either the first argument `filename` or the fourth argument `fileobj` should be specified (likely by argument name, especially if fourth argument `fileobj`).

The second argument `mode` takes the mode of `fileobj` if specified, otherwise it defaults to `rb` (`r`, `rb`, `a`, `ab`, `w`, or `wb` may be specified with the same meaning as with *FILE.open()* objects). The third argument `compresslevel` specifies the level of compression. The default is the highest level, 9; an integer down to 1 may be selected for less compression but faster operation (compression level of a read file comes from the file itself, however).

gzip.open(filename=... [mode='rb [,compresslevel=9]])

Same as *gzip.GzipFile* but with extra arguments omitted. A GZ file object opened with *gzip.open* is always opened by name, not by underlying file object.

METHODS AND ATTRIBUTES

gzip.close()

Close the *gzip* object. No access is permitted after close. If the object was opened by file object, the underlying file object is not closed, only the *gzip* interface to the file.

SEE ALSO: FILE.close() *16*;

gzip.flush()

Write outstanding data from memory to disk.

SEE ALSO: FILE.close() *16*;

gzip.isatty()

Return 0. Compatibility method for file-like behavior.

SEE ALSO: FILE.isatty() *16*;

gzip.myfileobj

Attribute holding the underlying file object.

gzip.read([num])

If the first argument `num` is specified, return a string containing the next `num` characters. If `num` characters are not available, return as many as possible. If `num` is not specified, return all the characters from current file position to end of string buffer. Advance the current file position by the amount read.

SEE ALSO: FILE.read() *17*;

gzip.readline([length])

Return a string from the *gzip* object, starting from the current file position and going to the next newline character. The argument `length` limits the read if specified. Advance the current file position by the amount read.

SEE ALSO: FILE.readline() *17*;

gzip.readlines([sizehint=...])

Return a list of strings from the *gzip* object. Each list element consists of a single line, including the trailing newline character(s). If an argument `sizehint` is specified, read only approximately `sizehint` characters worth of lines (full lines will always be read).

SEE ALSO: FILE.readlines() *17*;

gzip.write(s)

Write the first argument `s` into the *gzip* object at the current file position. The current file position is updated to the position following the write.

SEE ALSO: FILE.write() *17*;

gzip.writelines(list)

Write each element of `list` into the *gzip* object at the current file position. The current file position is updated to the position following the write. Most sequence types are allowed, but `list` must contain only strings, or a `TypeError` will occur.

Contrary to what might be expected from the method name, *gzip.writelines()* never inserts newline characters. For the list elements actually to occupy separate lines in the string buffer, each element string must already have a newline terminator. See *StringIO.StringIO.writelines()* for an example.

SEE ALSO: FILE.writelines() *17*; StringIO.StringIO.writelines() *157*;

SEE ALSO: zlib *181*; zipfile *176*;

zipfile ◇ Read and write ZIP files

The *zipfile* module enables a variety of operations on ZIP files and is compatible with archives created by applications such as PKZip, Info-Zip, and WinZip. Since the ZIP format allows inclusion of multiple file images within a single archive, the *zipfile* does not behave in a directly file-like manner as *gzip* does. Nonetheless, it is possible to view the contents of an archive, add new file images to one, create a new ZIP archive, or manipulate the contents and directory information of a ZIP file.

An initial example of working with the *zipfile* module gives a feel for its usage.

```
>>> for name in 'ABC':
...     open(name,'w').write(name*1000)
...
>>> import zipfile
>>> z = zipfile.ZipFile('new.zip','w',zipfile.ZIP_DEFLATED) # new archv
>>> z.write('A')                       # write files to archive
>>> z.write('B','B.newname',zipfile.ZIP_STORED)
>>> z.write('C','C.newname')
>>> z.close()                          # close the written archive
>>> z = zipfile.ZipFile('new.zip')     # reopen archive in read mode
>>> z.testzip()                        # 'None' returned means OK
>>> z.namelist()                       # What's in it?
['A', 'B.newname', 'C.newname']
>>> z.printdir()                       # details
File Name                              Modified             Size
A                                      2001-07-18 21:39:36  1000
B.newname                              2001-07-18 21:39:36  1000
C.newname                              2001-07-18 21:39:36  1000
>>> A = z.getinfo('A')                 # bind ZipInfo object
>>> B = z.getinfo('B.newname')         # bind ZipInfo object
>>> A.compress_size
11
>>> B.compress_size
1000
>>> z.read(A.filename)[:40]            # Check what's in A
'AAAAAAAAAAAAAAAAAAAAAAAAAAAAAAAAAAAAAAAA'
>>> z.read(B.filename)[:40]            # Check what's in B
'BBBBBBBBBBBBBBBBBBBBBBBBBBBBBBBBBBBBBBBB'
>>> # For comparison, see what Info-Zip reports on created archive
>>> import os
>>> print os.popen('unzip -v new.zip').read()
Archive:  new.zip
 Length   Method    Size  Ratio   Date   Time   CRC-32    Name
 ------   ------    ----  -----   ----   ----   ------    ----
   1000   Defl:N      11   99%  07-18-01  21:39  51a02e01  A
```

```
1000   Stored      1000    0%  07-18-01  21:39   7d9c564d   B.newname
1000   Defl:N        11   99%  07-18-01  21:39   66778189   C.newname
------              ------   ---                            --------
3000                1022   66%                             3 files
```

The module *gzip* is a wrapper around *zlib*, with the latter performing the actual compression and decompression tasks.

CONSTANTS

Several string constants (*struct* formats) are used to recognize signature identifiers in the ZIP format. These constants are not normally used directly by end-users of *zipfile*.

```
zipfile.stringCentralDir = 'PK\x01\x02'
zipfile.stringEndArchive = 'PK\x05\x06'
zipfile.stringFileHeader = 'PK\x03\x04'
zipfile.structCentralDir = '<4s4B4H3l5H2l'
zipfile.structEndArchive = '<4s4H2l H'
zipfile.structFileHeader = '<4s2B4H3l2H'
```

Symbolic names for the two supported compression methods are also defined.

```
zipfile.ZIP_STORED = 0
zipfile.ZIP_DEFLATED = 8
```

FUNCTIONS

zipfile.is_zipfile(filename=...)

Check if the argument `filename` is a valid ZIP archive. Archives with appended comments are not recognized as valid archives. Return 1 if valid, None otherwise. This function does not guarantee archive is fully intact, but it does provide a sanity check on the file type.

CLASSES

zipfile.PyZipFile(pathname)

Create a *zipfile.ZipFile* object that has the extra method *zipfile.ZipFile.writepy()*. This extra method allows you to recursively add all *.py[oc] files to an archive. This class is not general purpose, but a special feature to aid *distutils*.

zipfile.ZipFile(file=... [,mode='r' [,compression=ZIP_STORED]])

Create a new *zipfile.ZipFile* object. This object is used for management of a ZIP archive. The first argument `file` must be specified and is simply the filename of the archive to be manipulated. The second argument `mode` may have one of three string values: r to open the archive in read-only mode; w to truncate the filename and create a new archive; a to read an existing archive and add to it. The third argument `compression` indicates the compression method—ZIP_DEFLATED requires that *zlib* and the zlib system library be present.

zipfile.ZipInfo()

Create a new *zipfile.ZipInfo* object. This object contains information about an individual archived filename and its file image. Normally, one will not directly instantiate *zipfile.ZipInfo* but only look at the *zipfile.ZipInfo* objects that are returned by methods like *zipfile.ZipFile.infolist()*, *zipfile.ZipFile.getinfo()*, and *zipfile.ZipFile.NameToInfo*. However, in special cases like *zipfile.ZipFile.writestr()*, it is useful to create a *zipfile.ZipInfo* directly.

METHODS AND ATTRIBUTES

zipfile.ZipFile.close()

Close the *zipfile.ZipFile* object, and flush any changes made to it. An object must be explicitly closed to perform updates.

zipfile.ZipFile.getinfo(name=...)

Return the *zipfile.ZipInfo* object corresponding to the filename `name`. If `name` is not in the ZIP archive, a `KeyError` is raised.

zipfile.ZipFile.infolist()

Return a list of *zipfile.ZipInfo* objects contained in the *zipfile.ZipFile* object. The return value is simply a list of instances of the same type. If the filename within the archive is known, *zipfile.ZipFile.getinfo()* is a better method to use. For enumerating over all archived files, however, *zipfile.ZipFile.infolist()* provides a nice sequence.

zipfile.ZipFile.namelist()

Return a list of the filenames of all the archived files (including nested relative directories).

zipfile.ZipFile.printdir()

Print to STDOUT a pretty summary of archived files and information about them. The results are similar to running Info-Zip's `unzip` with the `-1` option.

zipfile.ZipFile.read(name=...)

Return the contents of the archived file with filename `name`.

zipfile.ZipFile.testzip()

Test the integrity of the current archive. Return the filename of the first *zipfile.ZipInfo* object with corruption. If everything is valid, return None.

zipfile.ZipFile.write(filename=... [,arcname=... [,compress_type=...]])

Add the file `filename` to the *zipfile.ZipFile* object. If the second argument `arcname` is specified, use `arcname` as the stored filename (otherwise, use `filename` itself). If the third argument `compress_type` is specified, use the indicated compression method. The current archive must be opened in `w` or `a` mode.

zipfile.ZipFile.writestr(zinfo=..., bytes=...)

Write the data contained in the second argument `bytes` to the *zipfile.ZipFile* object. Directory meta-information must be contained in attributes of the first argument `zinfo` (a filename, data, and time should be included; other information is optional). The current archive must be opened in `w` or `a` mode.

zipfile.ZipFile.NameToInfo

Dictionary that maps filenames in archive to corresponding *zipfile.ZipInfo* objects. The method *zipfile.ZipFile.getinfo()* is simply a wrapper for a dictionary lookup in this attribute.

zipfile.ZipFile.compression

Compression type currently in effect for new *zipfile.ZipFile.write()* operations. Modify with due caution (most likely not at all after initialization).

zipfile.ZipFile.debug = 0

Attribute for level of debugging information sent to STDOUT. Values range from the default 0 (no output) to 3 (verbose). May be modified.

zipfile.ZipFile.filelist

List of *zipfile.ZipInfo* objects contained in the *zipfile.ZipFile* object. The method *zipfile.ZipFile.infolist()* is simply a wrapper to retrieve this attribute. Modify with due caution (most likely not at all).

zipfile.ZipFile.filename

Filename of the *zipfile.ZipFile* object. DO NOT modify!

zipfile.ZipFile.fp

Underlying file object for the *zipfile.ZipFile* object. DO NOT modify!

zipfile.ZipFile.mode

Access mode of current *zipfile.ZipFile* object. DO NOT modify!

zipfile.ZipFile.start_dir

Position of start of central directory. DO NOT modify!

zipfile.ZipInfo.CRC

Hash value of this archived file. DO NOT modify!

zipfile.ZipInfo.comment

Comment attached to this archived file. Modify with due caution (e.g., for use with *zipfile.ZipFile.writestr()*).

zipfile.ZipInfo.compress_size

Size of the compressed data of this archived file. DO NOT modify!

zipfile.ZipInfo.compress_type

Compression type used with this archived file. Modify with due caution (e.g., for use with *zipfile.ZipFile.writestr()*).

zipfile.ZipInfo.create_system

System that created this archived file. Modify with due caution (e.g., for use with *zipfile.ZipFile.writestr()*).

zipfile.ZipInfo.create_version

PKZip version that created the archive. Modify with due caution (e.g., for use with *zipfile.ZipFile.writestr()*).

zipfile.ZipInfo.date_time

Timestamp of this archived file. Modify with due caution (e.g., for use with *zipfile.ZipFile.writestr()*).

zipfile.ZipInfo.external_attr

File attribute of archived file when extracted.

zipfile.ZipInfo.extract_version

PKZip version needed to extract the archive. Modify with due caution (e.g., for use with *zipfile.ZipFile.writestr()*).

zipfile.ZipInfo.file_offset

Byte offset to start of file data. DO NOT modify!

zipfile.ZipInfo.file_size

Size of the uncompressed data in the archived file. DO NOT modify!

zipfile.ZipInfo.filename

Filename of archived file. Modify with due caution (e.g., for use with *zipfile.ZipFile.writestr()*).

zipfile.ZipInfo.header_offset

Byte offset to file header of the archived file. DO NOT modify!

zipfile.ZipInfo.volume

Volume number of the archived file. DO NOT modify!

EXCEPTIONS

zipfile.error

Exception that is raised when corrupt ZIP file is processed.

zipfile.BadZipFile

Alias for *zipfile.error*.

SEE ALSO: zlib *181*; gzip *173*;

---

zlib ◇ Compress and decompress with zlib library

zlib is the underlying compression engine for all Python standard library compression modules. Moreover, *zlib* is extremely useful in itself for compression and decompression of data that does not necessarily live in files (or where data does not map directly to files, even if it winds up in them indirectly). The Python *zlib* module relies on the availability of the zlib system library.

There are two basic modes of operation for *zlib*. In the simplest mode, one can simply pass an uncompressed string to *zlib.compress()* and have the compressed version returned. Using *zlib.decompress()* is symmetrical. In a more complicated mode, one can create compression or decompression objects that are able to receive incremental raw or compressed byte-streams, and return partial results based on what they have seen so far. This mode of operation is similar to the way one uses *sha.sha.update()*, *md5.md5.update()*, *rotor.encryptmore()*, or *binascii.crc32()* (albeit for a different purpose from each of those). For large byte-streams that are determined, it may be more practical to utilize compression/decompression objects than it would be to compress/decompress an entire string at once (for example, if the input or result is bound to a slow channel).

CONSTANTS

zlib.ZLIB_VERSION

The installed zlib system library version.

zlib.Z_BEST_COMPRESSION = 9

Highest compression level.

zlib.Z_BEST_SPEED = 1

Fastest compression level.

zlib.Z_HUFFMAN_ONLY = 2

Intermediate compression level that uses Huffman codes, but not Lempel-Ziv.

FUNCTIONS

zlib.adler32(s [,crc])

Return the Adler-32 checksum of the first argument **s**. If the second argument **crc** is specified, it will be used as an initial checksum. This allows partial computation of a checksum and continuation. An Adler-32 checksum can be computed much more quickly than a CRC32 checksum. Unlike *md5* or *sha*, an Adler-32 checksum is not sufficient for cryptographic hashes, but merely for detection of accidental corruption of data.

SEE ALSO: zlib.crc32() *182*; md5 *167*; sha *170*;

zlib.compress(s [,level])

Return the zlib compressed version of the string in the first argument **s**. If the second argument **level** is specified, the compression technique can be fine-tuned. The compression level ranges from 1 to 9 and may also be specified using symbolic constants such as Z_BEST_COMPRESSION and Z_BEST_SPEED. The default value for **level** is 6 and is usually the desired compression level (usually within a few percent of the speed of Z_BEST_SPEED and within a few percent of the size of Z_BEST_COMPRESSION).

SEE ALSO: zlib.decompress() *182*; zlib.compressobj *183*;

zlib.crc32(s [,crc])

Return the CRC32 checksum of the first argument **s**. If the second argument **crc** is specified, it will be used as an initial checksum. This allows partial computation of a checksum and continuation. Unlike *md5* or *sha*, a CRC32 checksum is not sufficient for cryptographic hashes, but merely for detection of accidental corruption of data.

Identical to *binascii.crc32()* (example appears there).

SEE ALSO: binascii.crc32() *160*; zlib.adler32() *182*; md5 *167*; sha *170*;

zlib.decompress(s [,winsize [,buffsize]])

Return the decompressed version of the zlib compressed string in the first argument **s**. If the second argument **winsize** is specified, it determines the base 2 logarithm of the history buffer size. The default **winsize** is 15. If the third argument **buffsize** is specified, it determines the size of the decompression buffer. The default **buffsize** is 16384, but more is dynamically allocated if needed. One rarely needs to use **winsize** and **buffsize** values other than the defaults.

SEE ALSO: zlib.compress() *182*; zlib.decompressobj *183*;

CLASS FACTORIES

zlib does not define true classes that can be specialized. *zlib.compressobj()* and *zlib.decompressobj()* are actually factory-functions rather than classes. That is, they return instance objects, just as classes do, but they do not have unbound data and methods. For most users, the difference is not important: To get a *zlib.compressobj* or *zlib.decompressobj* object, you just call that factory-function in the same manner you would a class object.

zlib.compressobj([level])

Create a compression object. A compression object is able to incrementally compress new strings that are fed to it while maintaining the seeded symbol table from previously compressed byte-streams. If argument `level` is specified, the compression technique can be fine-tuned. The compression level ranges from 1 to 9. The default value for `level` is 6 and is usually the desired compression level.

SEE ALSO: zlib.compress() *182*; zlib.decompressobj() *183*;

zlib.decompressobj([winsize])

Create a decompression object. A decompression object is able to incrementally decompress new strings that are fed to it while maintaining the seeded symbol table from previously decompressed byte-streams. If the argument `winsize` is specified, it determines the base 2 logarithm of the history buffer size. The default `winsize` is 15.

SEE ALSO: zlib.decompress() *182*; zlib.compressobj() *183*;

METHODS AND ATTRIBUTES

zlib.compressobj.compress(s)

Add more data to the compression object. If the symbol table becomes full, compressed data is returned, otherwise an empty string. All returned output from each repeated call to *zlib.compressobj.compress()* should be concatenated to a decompression byte-stream (either a string or a decompression object). The example below, if run in a directory with some files, lets one examine the buffering behavior of compression objects:

```
zlib_objs.py
```

```
# Demonstrate compression object streams
import zlib, glob
decom = zlib.decompressobj()
com = zlib.compressobj()
for file in glob.glob('*'):
    s = open(file).read()
    c = com.compress(s)
    print 'COMPRESSED:', len(c), 'bytes out'
    d = decom.decompress(c)
    print 'DECOMPRESS:', len(d), 'bytes out'
    print 'UNUSED DATA:', len(decom.unused_data), 'bytes'
    raw_input('-- %s (%s bytes) --' % (file, 'len(s)'))
f = com.flush()
m = decom.decompress(f)
print 'DECOMPRESS:', len(m), 'bytes out'
print 'UNUSED DATA:', len(decom.unused_data), 'byte'
```

SEE ALSO: zlib.compressobj.flush() *184*; zlib.decompressobj.decompress() *185*; zlib.compress() *182*;

zlib.compressobj.flush([mode])

Flush any buffered data from the compression object. As in the example in *zlib.compressobj.compress()*, the output of a *zlib.compressobj.flush()* should be concatenated to the same decompression byte-stream as *zlib.compressobj.compress()* calls are. If the first argument **mode** is left empty, or the default Z_FINISH is specified, the compression object cannot be used further, and one should *delete* it. Otherwise, if Z_SYNC_FLUSH or Z_FULL_FLUSH are specified, the compression object can still be used, but some uncompressed data may not be recovered by the decompression object.

SEE ALSO: zlib.compress() *182*; zlib.compressobj.compress() *183*;

zlib.decompressobj.unused_data

As indicated, *zlib.decompressobj.unused_data* is an instance attribute rather than a method. If any partial compressed stream cannot be decompressed immediately based on the byte-stream received, the remainder is buffered in this instance attribute. Normally, any output of a compression object forms a complete decompression block, and nothing is left in this instance attribute. However, if data is received in bits over a channel, only partial decompression may be possible on a particular *zlib.decompressobj.decompress()* call.

SEE ALSO: zlib.decompress() *182*; zlib.decompressobj.decompress() *185*;

zlib.decompressobj.decompress(s)

Return the decompressed data that may be derived from the current decompression object state and the argument s data passed in. If all of s cannot be decompressed in this pass, the remainder is left in *zlib.decompressobj.unused_data*.

zlib.decompressobj.flush()

Return the decompressed data from any bytes buffered by the decompression object. After this call, the decompression object cannot be used further, and you should *del* it.

EXCEPTIONS

zlib.error

Exception that is raised by compression or decompression errors.

SEE ALSO: gzip *173*; zipfile *176*;

2.2.6 Unicode

Note that Appendix C (Understanding Unicode) also discusses Unicode issues.

Unicode is an enhanced set of character entities, well beyond the basic 128 characters defined in ASCII encoding and the codepage-specific national language sets that contain 128 characters each. The full Unicode character set—evolving continuously, but with a large number of codepoints already fixed—can contain literally millions of distinct characters. This allows the representation of a large number of national character sets within a unified encoding space, even the large character sets of Chinese-Japanese-Korean (CJK) alphabets.

Although Unicode defines a unique codepoint for each distinct character in its range, there are numerous *encodings* that correspond to each character. The encoding called UTF-8 defines ASCII characters as single bytes with standard ASCII values. However, for non-ASCII characters, a variable number of bytes (up to 6) are used to encode characters, with the "escape" to Unicode being indicated by high-bit values in initial bytes of multibyte sequences. UTF-16 is similar, but uses either 2 or 4 bytes to encode each character (but never just 1). UTF-32 is a format that uses a fixed 4-byte value for each Unicode character. UTF-32, however, is not currently supported by Python.

Native Unicode support was added to Python 2.0. On the face of it, it is a happy situation that Python supports Unicode—it brings the world closer to multinational language support in computer applications. But in practice, you have to be careful when working with Unicode, because it is all too easy to encounter glitches like the one below:

```
>>> alef, omega = unichr(1488), unichr(969)
>>> unicodedata.name(alef)
>>> print alef
Traceback (most recent call last):
  File "<stdin>", line 1, in ?
```

```
UnicodeError: ASCII encoding error: ordinal not in range(128)
>>> print chr(170)

>>> if alef == chr(170): print "Hebrew is Roman diacritic"
...
Traceback (most recent call last):
  File "<stdin>", line 1, in ?
UnicodeError: ASCII decoding error: ordinal not in range(128)
```

A Unicode string that is composed of only ASCII characters, however, is considered equal (but not identical) to a Python string of the same characters.

```
>>> u"spam" == "spam"
1
>>> u"spam" is "spam"
0
>>> "spam" is "spam"    # string interning is not guaranteed
1
>>> u"spam" is u"spam" # unicode interning not guaranteed
1
```

Still, the care you take should not discourage you from working with multilanguage strings, as Unicode enables. It is really amazingly powerful to be able to do so. As one says of a talking dog: It is not that he speaks so *well*, but that he speaks at all.

Built-In Unicode Functions/Methods

The Unicode string method *u"".encode()* and the built-in function *unicode()* are inverse operations. The Unicode string method returns a plain string with the 8-bit bytes needed to represent it (using the specified or default encoding). The built-in *unicode()* takes one of these encoded strings and produces the Unicode object represented by the encoding. Specifically, suppose we define the function:

```
>>> chk_eq = lambda u,enc: u == unicode(u.encode(enc),enc)
```

The call *chk_eq(u, enc)* should return 1 for every value of u and enc—as long as enc is a valid encoding name and u is capable of being represented in that encoding.

The set of encodings supported for both built-ins are listed below. Additional encodings may be registered using the *codecs* module. Each encoding is indicated by the string that names it, and the case of the string is normalized before comparison (case-insensitive naming of encodings):

ascii, us-ascii

Encode using 7-bit ASCII.

base64

Encode Unicode strings using the base64 4-to-3 encoding format.

latin-1, iso-8859-1

Encode using common European accent characters in high-bit values of 8-bit bytes. Latin-1 character's *ord()* values are identical to their Unicode codepoints.

quopri

Encode in quoted printable format.

rot13

Not really a Unicode encoding, but "rotate 13 chars" is included with Python 2.2— as an example and convenience.

utf-7

Encode using variable byte-length encoding that is restricted to 7-bit ASCII octets. As with utf-8, ASCII characters encode themselves.

utf-8

Encode using variable byte-length encoding that preserves ASCII value bytes.

utf-16

Encoding using 2/4 byte encoding. Include "endian" lead bytes (platform-specific selection).

utf-16-le

Encoding using 2/4 byte encoding. Assume "little endian," and do not prepend "endian" indicator bytes.

utf-16-be

Encoding using 2/4 byte encoding. Assume "big endian," and do not prepend "endian" indicator bytes.

unicode-escape

Encode using Python-style Unicode string constants (u"\uXXXX").

raw-unicode-escape

Encode using Python-style Unicode raw string constants (ur"\uXXXX").

The error modes for both built-ins are listed below. Errors in encoding transformations may be handled in any of several ways:

strict

Raise UnicodeError for all decoding errors. Default handling.

ignore

Skip all invalid characters.

replace

Replace invalid characters with ? (string target) or u"\xfffd" (Unicode target).

u"".encode([enc [,errmode]])
"".encode([enc [,errmode]])

Return an encoded string representation of a Unicode string (or of a plain string). The representation is in the style of encoding enc (or system default). This string is suitable for writing to a file or stream that other applications will treat as Unicode data. Examples show several encodings:

```
>>> alef = unichr(1488)
>>> s = 'A'+alef
>>> s
u'A\u05d0'
>>> s.encode('unicode-escape')
'A\\u05d0'
>>> s.encode('utf-8')
'A\xd7\x90'
>>> s.encode('utf-16')
'\xff\xfeA\x00\xd0\x05'
>>> s.encode('utf-16-le')
'A\x00\xd0\x05'
>>> s.encode('ascii')
Traceback (most recent call last):
  File "<stdin>", line 1, in ?
UnicodeError: ASCII encoding error: ordinal not in range(128)
>>> s.encode('ascii','ignore')
'A'
```

unicode(s [,enc [,errmode]])

Return a Unicode string object corresponding to the encoded string passed in the first argument s. The string s might be a string that is read from another Unicode-aware application. The representation is treated as conforming to the style of the encoding enc if the second argument is specified, or system default otherwise (usually utf-8). Errors can be handled in the default strict style or in a style specified in the third argument errmode.

unichr(cp)

Return a Unicode string object containing the single Unicode character whose integer codepoint is passed in the argument cp.

codecs ◇ Python Codec Registry, API, and helpers

The *codecs* module contains a lot of sophisticated functionality to get at the internals of Python's Unicode handling. Most of those capabilities are at a lower level than programmers who are just interested in text processing need to worry about. The documentation of this module, therefore, will break slightly with the style of most of the documentation and present only two very useful wrapper functions within the *codecs* module.

codecs.open(filename=... [,mode='rb' [.encoding=... [,errors='strict' [,buffering=1]]]])

This wrapper function provides a simple and direct means of opening a Unicode file, and treating its contents directly as Unicode. In contrast, the contents of a file opened with the built-in *open()* function are written and read as strings; to read/write Unicode data to such a file involves multiple passes through *u"".encode()* and *unicode()*.

The first argument `filename` specifies the name of the file to access. If the second argument `mode` is specified, the read/write mode can be selected. These arguments work identically to those used by *open()*. If the third argument `encoding` is specified, this encoding will be used to interpret the file (an incorrect encoding will probably result in a `UnicodeError`). Error handling may be modified by specifying the fourth argument `errors` (the options are the same as with the built-in *unicode()* function). A fifth argument `buffering` may be specified to use a specific buffer size (on platforms that support this).

An example of usage clarifies the difference between *codecs.open()* and the built-in *open()*:

```
>>> import codecs
>>> alef = unichr(1488)
>>> open('unicode_test','wb').write(('A'+alef).encode('utf-8'))
>>> open('unicode_test').read()    # Read as plain string
'A\xd7\x90'
>>> # Now read directly as Unicode
>>> codecs.open('unicode_test', encoding='utf-8').read()
u'A\u05d0'
```

Data written back to a file opened with *codecs.open()* should likewise be Unicode data.

SEE ALSO: open() *15*;

codecs.EncodedFile(file=. . . , data_encoding=. . . [,file_encoding=. . .
[,errors='strict']])

This function allows an already opened file to be wrapped inside an "encoding translation" layer. The mode and buffering are taken from the underlying file. By specifying a second argument `data_encoding` and a third argument `file_encoding`, it is possible to generate strings in one encoding within an application, then write them directly into the appropriate file encoding. As with *codecs.open()* and *unicode()*, an error handling style may be specified with the fourth argument `errors`.

The most likely purpose for *codecs.EncodedFile()* is where an application is likely to receive byte-streams from multiple sources, encoded according to multiple Unicode encodings. By wrapping file objects (or file-like objects) in an encoding translation layer, the strings coming in one encoding can be transparently written to an output in the format the output expects. An example clarifies:

```
>>> import codecs
>>> alef = unichr(1488)
>>> open('unicode_test','wb').write(('A'+alef).encode('utf-8'))
>>> fp = open('unicode_test','rb+')
>>> fp.read()       # Plain string w/ two-byte UTF-8 char in it
'A\xd7\x90'
>>> utf16_writer = codecs.EncodedFile(fp,'utf-16','utf-8')
>>> ascii_writer = codecs.EncodedFile(fp,'ascii','utf-8')
>>> utf16_writer.tell()    # Wrapper keeps same current position
3
>>> s = alef.encode('utf-16')
>>> s               # Plain string as UTF-16 encoding
'\xff\xfe\xd0\x05'
>>> utf16_writer.write(s)
>>> ascii_writer.write('XYZ')
>>> fp.close()                # File should be UTF-8 encoded
>>> open('unicode_test').read()
'A\xd7\x90\xd7\x90XYZ'
```

SEE ALSO: codecs.open() *189*;

---

unicodedata ◇ Database of Unicode characters

The module *unicodedata* is a database of Unicode character entities. Most of the functions in *unicodedata* take as an argument one Unicode character and return some information about the character contained in a plain (non-Unicode) string. The function of *unicodedata* is essentially informational, rather than transformational. Of course, an application might make decisions about the transformations performed based on the information returned by *unicodedata*. The short utility below provides all the information available for any Unicode codepoint:

---

unichr_info.py

```
# Return all the information [unicodedata] has
# about the single unicode character whose codepoint
# is specified as a command-line argument.
# Arg may be any expression evaluating to an integer
from unicodedata import *
import sys
char = unichr(eval(sys.argv[1]))
print 'bidirectional', bidirectional(char)
print 'category      ', category(char)
print 'combining     ', combining(char)
print 'decimal       ', decimal(char,0)
print 'decomposition', decomposition(char)
print 'digit         ', digit(char,0)
print 'mirrored      ', mirrored(char)
print 'name          ', name(char,'NOT DEFINED')
print 'numeric       ', numeric(char,0)
try: print 'lookup        ', `lookup(name(char))`
except: print "Cannot lookup"
```

The usage of `unichr_info.py` is illustrated below by the runs with two possible arguments:

```
% python unichr_info.py 1488
bidirectional R
category       Lo
combining      0
decimal        0
decomposition
digit          0
mirrored       0
name           HEBREW LETTER ALEF
numeric        0
lookup         u'\u05d0'
```

```
% python unichr_info.py ord('1')
bidirectional EN
category       Nd
combining      0
decimal        1
decomposition
digit          1
mirrored       0
name           DIGIT ONE
numeric        1.0
lookup         u'1'
```

For additional information on current Unicode character codepoints and attributes, consult:

<http://www.unicode.org/Public/UNIDATA/UnicodeData.html>

FUNCTIONS

unicodedata.bidirectional(unichr)

Return the bidirectional characteristic of the character specified in the argument unichr. Possible values are AL, AN, B, BN, CS, EN, ES, ET, L, LRE, LRO, NSM, ON, PDF, R, RLE, RLO, S, and WS. Consult the URL above for details on these. Particularly notable values are L (left-to-right), R (right-to-left), and WS (whitespace).

unicodedata.category(unichr)

Return the category of the character specified in the argument unichr. Possible values are Cc, Cf, Cn, Ll, Lm, Lo, Lt, Lu, Mc, Me, Mn, Nd, Nl, No, Pc, Pd, Pe, Pf, Pi, Po, Ps, Sc, Sk , Sm, So, Zl, Zp, and Zs. The first (capital) letter indicates L (letter), M (mark), N (number), P (punctuation), S (symbol), Z (separator), or C (other). The second letter is generally mnemonic within the major category of the first letter. Consult the URL above for details.

unicodedata.combining(unichr)

Return the numeric combining class of the character specified in the argument unichr. These include values such as 218 (below left) or 210 (right attached). Consult the URL above for details.

unicodedata.decimal(unichr [,default])

Return the numeric decimal value assigned to the character specified in the argument unichr. If the second argument default is specified, return that if no value is assigned (otherwise raise ValueError).

unicodedata.decomposition(unichr)

Return the decomposition mapping of the character specified in the argument unichr, or empty string if none exists. Consult the URL above for details. An example shows that some characters may be broken into component characters:

```
>>> from unicodedata import *
>>> name(unichr(190))
'VULGAR FRACTION THREE QUARTERS'
>>> decomposition(unichr(190))
'<fraction> 0033 2044 0034'
>>> name(unichr(0x33)), name(unichr(0x2044)), name(unichr(0x34))
('DIGIT THREE', 'FRACTION SLASH', 'DIGIT FOUR')
```

unicodedata.digit(unichr [,default])

Return the numeric digit value assigned to the character specified in the argument unichr. If the second argument default is specified, return that if no value is assigned (otherwise raise ValueError).

unicodedata.lookup(name)

Return the Unicode character with the name specified in the first argument name. Matches must be exact, and ValueError is raised if no match is found. For example:

```
>>> from unicodedata import *
>>> lookup('GREEK SMALL LETTER ETA')
u'\u03b7'
>>> lookup('ETA')
Traceback (most recent call last):
  File "<stdin>", line 1, in ?
KeyError: undefined character name
```

SEE ALSO: unicodedata.name() *193*;

unicodedata.mirrored(unichr)

Return 1 if the character specified in the argument unichr is a mirrored character in bidirection text. Return 0 otherwise.

unicodedata.name(unichr)

Return the name of the character specified in the argument unichr. Names are in all caps and have a regular form by descending category importance. Consult the URL above for details.

SEE ALSO: unicodedata.lookup() *193*;

unicodedata.numeric(unichr [,default])

Return the floating point numeric value assigned to the character specified in the argument unichr. If the second argument default is specified, return that if no value is assigned (otherwise raise ValueError).

2.3   Solving Problems

2.3.1   Exercise: Many ways to take out the garbage

DISCUSSION

Recall, if you will, the dictum in "The Zen of Python" that "There should be one—and preferably only one—obvious way to do it." As with most dictums, the real world sometimes fails our ideals. Also as with most dictums, this is not necessarily such a bad thing.

A discussion on the newsgroup `<comp.lang.python>` in 2001 posed an apparently rather simple problem. The immediate problem was that one might encounter telephone numbers with a variety of dividers and delimiters inside them. For example, (123) 456-7890, 123-456-7890, or 123/456-7890 might all represent the same telephone number, and all forms might be encountered in textual data sources (such as ones entered by users of a free-form entry field. For purposes of this problem, the canonical form of this number should be 1234567890.

The problem mentioned here can be generalized in some natural ways: Maybe we are interested in only some of the characters within a longer text field (in this case, the digits), and the rest is simply filler. So the general problem is how to extract the content out from the filler.

The first and "obvious" approach might be a procedural loop through the initial string. One version of this approach might look like:

```
>>> s = '(123)/456-7890'
>>> result = ''
>>> for c in s:
...     if c in '0123456789':
...         result = result + c
...
>>> result
'1234567890'
```

This first approach works fine, but it might seem a bit bulky for what is, after all, basically a single action. And it might also seem odd that you need to loop though character-by-character rather than just transform the whole string.

One possibly simpler approach is to use a regular expression. For readers who have skipped to the next chapter, or who know regular expressions already, this approach seems obvious:

```
>>> import re
>>> s = '(123)/456-7890'
>>> re.sub(r'\D', '', s)
'1234567890'
```

The actual work done (excluding defining the initial string and importing the *re* module) is just one short expression. Good enough, but one catch with regular expressions is that they are frequently far slower than basic string operations. This makes no difference for the tiny example presented, but for processing megabytes, it could start to matter.

Using a functional style of programming is one way to express the "filter" in question rather tersely, and perhaps more efficiently. For example:

```
>>> s = '(123)/456-7890'
>>> filter(lambda c:c.isdigit(), s)
'1234567890'
```

We also get something short, without needing to use regular expressions. Here is another technique that utilizes string object methods and list comprehensions, and also pins some hopes on the great efficiency of Python dictionaries:

```
>>> isdigit = {'0':1,'1':1,'2':1,'3':1,'4':1,
...            '5':1,'6':1,'7':1,'8':1,'9':1}.has_key
>>> ''.join([x for x in s if isdigit(x)])
'1234567890'
```

QUESTIONS

1. Which content extraction technique seems most natural to you? Which would you prefer to use? Explain why.

2. What intuitions do you have about the performance of these different techniques, if applied to large data sets? Are there differences in comparative efficiency of techniques between operating on one single large string input and operating on a large number of small string inputs?

3. Construct a program to verify or refute your intuitions about performance of the constructs.

4. Can you think of ways of combining these techniques to maximize efficiency? Are there any other techniques available that might be even better (hint: think about what *string.translate()* does)? Construct a faster technique, and demonstrate its efficiency.

5. Are there reasons other than raw processing speed to prefer some of these techniques over others? Explain these reasons, if they exist.

2.3.2   Exercise: Making sure things are what they should be

DISCUSSION

The concept of a "digital signature" was introduced in Section 2.2.4. As was mentioned, the Python standard library does not include (directly) any support for digital signatures. One way to characterize a digital signature is as some information that *proves* or *verifies* that some other information really is what it purports to be. But this characterization actually applies to a broader set of things than just digital signatures. In cryptology literature one is accustomed to talk about the "threat model" a crypto-system defends against. Let us look at a few.

Data may be altered by malicious tampering, but it may also be altered by packet loss, storage-media errors, or by program errors. The threat of accidental damage to data is the easiest threat to defend against. The standard technique is to use a hash of the correct data and send that also. The receiver of the data can simply calculate the hash of the data herself—using the same algorithm—and compare it with the hash sent. A very simple utility like the one below does this:

crc32.py

```
# Calculate CRC32 hash of input files or STDIN
# Incremental read for large input sources
# Usage:      python crc32.py [file1 [file2 [...]]]
#    or:      python crc32.py < STDIN

import binascii
import fileinput
filelist = []
crc = binascii.crc32('')
for line in fileinput.input():
    if fileinput.isfirstline():
        if fileinput.isstdin():
            filelist.append('STDIN')
        else:
            filelist.append(fileinput.filename())
    crc = binascii.crc32(line,crc)
print 'Files:', ' '.join(filelist)
print 'CRC32:', crc
```

A slightly faster version could use *zlib.adler32()* instead of *binascii.crc32*. The chance that a randomly corrupted file would have the right CRC32 hash is approximately $(2**-32)$—unlikely enough not to worry about most times.

A CRC32 hash, however, is far too weak to be used cryptographically. While random data error will almost surely not create a chance hash collision, a malicious tamperer—Mallory, in crypto-parlance—can find one relatively easily. Specifically, suppose the true message is M, Mallory can find an M' such that CRC32(M) equals CRC32(M'). Moreover, even imposing the condition that M' appears plausible as a message to the receiver does not make Mallory's tasks particularly difficult.

To thwart fraudulent messages, it is necessary to use a cryptographically strong hash, such as *SHA* or *MD5*. Doing so is almost the same utility as above:

sha.py

```
# Calculate SHA hash of input files or STDIN
# Usage:     python sha.py [file1 [file2 [...]]]
#    or:     python sha.py < STDIN

import sha, fileinput, os, sys
filelist = []
sha = sha.sha()
for line in fileinput.input():
    if fileinput.isfirstline():
        if fileinput.isstdin():
            filelist.append('STDIN')
        else:
            filelist.append(fileinput.filename())
    sha.update(line[:-1]+os.linesep)   # same as binary read
sys.stderr.write('Files: '+' '.join(filelist)+'\nSHA: ')
print sha.hexdigest()
```

An SHA or MD5 hash cannot be forged practically, but if our threat model includes a malicious tamperer, we need to worry about whether the hash itself is authentic. Mallory, our tamperer, can produce a false SHA hash that matches her false message. With CRC32 hashes, a very common procedure is to attach the hash to the data message itself—for example, as the first or last line of the data file, or within some wrapper lines. This is called an "in band" or "in channel" transmission. One alternative is "out of band" or "off channel" transmission of cryptographic hashes. For example, a set of cryptographic hashes matching data files could be placed on a Web page. Merely transmitting the hash off channel does not guarantee security, but it does require Mallory to attack both channels effectively.

By using encryption, it is possible to transmit a secured hash in channel. The key here is to encrypt the hash and attach that encrypted version. If the hash is appended with some identifying information before the encryption, that can be recovered to prove identity. Otherwise, one could simply include both the hash and its encrypted version. For the encryption of the hash, an asymmetrical encryption algorithm is ideal; however, with the Python standard library, the best we can do is to use the (weak) symmetrical encryption in *rotor*. For example, we could use the utility below:

hash_rotor.py

```
#!/usr/bin/env python
# Encrypt hash on STDIN using sys.argv[1] as password
import rotor, sys, binascii
cipher = rotor.newrotor(sys.argv[1])
hexhash = sys.stdin.read()[:-1]  # no newline
print hexhash
hash = binascii.unhexlify(hexhash)
```

```
sys.stderr.write('Encryption: ')
print binascii.hexlify(cipher.encrypt(hash))
```

The utilities could then be used like:

```
% cat mary.txt
Mary had a little lamb
% python sha.py mary.txt | hash_rotor.py mypassword >> mary.txt
Files: mary.txt
SHA: Encryption:
% cat mary.txt
Mary had a little lamb
c49bf9a7840f6c07ab00b164413d7958e0945941
63a9d3a2f4493d957397178354f21915cb36f8f8
```

The penultimate line of the file now has its SHA hash, and the last line has an encryption of the hash. The password used will somehow need to be transmitted securely for the receiver to validate the appended document (obviously, the whole system make more sense with longer and more proprietary documents than in the example).

QUESTIONS

1. How would you wrap up the suggestions in the small utilities above into a more robust and complete "digital_signatures.py" utility or module? What concerns would come into a completed utility?

2. Why is CRC32 not suitable for cryptographic purposes? What sets SHA and MD5 apart (you should not need to know the details of the algorithm for this answer)? Why is uniformity of coverage of hash results important for any hash algorithm?

3. Explain in your own words why hashes serve to verify documents. If you were actually the malicious attacker in the scenarios above, how would you go about interfering with the crypto-systems outlined here? What lines of attack are left open by the system you sketched out or programmed in (1)?

4. If messages are subject to corruptions, including accidental corruption, so are hashes. The short length of hashes may make problems in them less likely, but not impossible. How might you enhance the document verification systems above to detect corruption within a hash itself? How might you allow more accurate targeting of corrupt versus intact portions of a large document (it may be desirable to recover as much as possible from a corrupt document)?

5. Advanced: The RSA public-key algorithm is actually quite simple; it just involves some modulo exponentiation operations and some large primes. An explanation can be found, among other places, at the author's *Introduction to Cryptology Concepts II*: <http://gnosis.cx/publish/programming/cryptology2.pdf>.

   Try implementing an RSA public-key algorithm in Python, and use this to enrich the digital signature system you developed above.

2.3.3   Exercise: Finding needles in haystacks (full-text indexing)

DISCUSSION

Many texts you deal with are loosely structured and prose-like, rather than composed of well-ordered records. For documents of that sort, a very frequent question you want answered is, "What is (or isn't) in the documents?"—at a more general level than the semantic richness you might obtain by actually *reading* the documents. In particular, you often want to check a large collection of documents to determine the (comparatively) small subset of them that are relevant to a given area of interest.

A certain category of questions about document collections has nothing much to do with text processing. For example, to locate all the files modified within a certain time period, and having a certain file size, some basic use of the *os.path* module suffices. Below is a sample utility to do such a search, which includes some typical argument parsing and help screens. The search itself is only a few lines of code:

findfile1.py

```
# Find files matching date and size
_usage = """
Usage:
   python findfile1.py [-start=days_ago] [-end=days_ago]
                       [-small=min_size] [-large=max_size] [pattern]
 Example:
   python findfile1.py -start=10 -end=5 -small=1000 -large=5000 *.txt
"""
import os.path
import time
import glob
import sys

def parseargs(args):
    """Somewhat flexible argument parser for multiple platforms.

    Switches can start with - or /, keywords can end with = or :.
    No error checking for bad arguments is performed, however.
    """
    now = time.time()
    secs_in_day = 60*60*24
    start = 0           # start of epoch
    end = time.time()   # right now
    small = 0           # empty files
    large = sys.maxint  # max file size
    pat = '*'           # match all
    for arg in args:
        if arg[0] in '-/':
            if   arg[1:6]=='start': start = now-(secs_in_day*int(arg[7:]))
```

```
            elif arg[1:4]=='end':    end   = now-(secs_in_day*int(arg[5:]))
            elif arg[1:6]=='small': small = int(arg[7:])
            elif arg[1:6]=='large': large = int(arg[7:])
            elif arg[1] in 'h?': print _usage
        else:
            pat = arg
    return (start,end,small,large,pat)


if __name__ == '__main__':
    if len(sys.argv) > 1:
        (start,end,small,large,pat) = parseargs(sys.argv[1:])
        for fname in glob.glob(pat):
            if not os.path.isfile(fname):
                continue              # don't check directories
            modtime = os.path.getmtime(fname)
            size = os.path.getsize(fname)
            if small <= size <= large and start <= modtime <= end:
                print time.ctime(modtime),'%8d '%size,fname
    else: print _usage
```

What about searching for text inside files? The *string.find()* function is good for locating contents quickly and could be used to search files for contents. But for large document collections, hits may be common. To make sense of search results, ranking the results by number of hits can help. The utility below performs a match-accuracy ranking (for brevity, without the argument parsing of `findfile1.py`):

findfile2.py

```
# Find files that contain a word
_usage = "Usage: python findfile.py word"
import os.path
import glob
import sys

if len(sys.argv) == 2:
    search_word = sys.argv[1]
    results = []
    for fname in glob.glob('*'):
        if os.path.isfile(fname):   # don't check directories
            text = open(fname).read()
            fsize = len(text)
            hits = text.count(search_word)
            density = (fsize > 0) and float(hits)/(fsize)
            if density > 0:          # consider when density==0
                results.append((density,fname))
    results.sort()
```

```
        results.reverse()
        print 'RANKING  FILENAME'
        print '-------  --------------------------'
        for match in results:
            print '%6d  '%int(match[0]*1000000), match[1]
    else:
        print _usage
```

Variations on these are, of course, possible. But generally you could build pretty sophisticated searches and rankings by adding new search options incrementally to `findfile2.py`. For example, adding some regular expression options could give the utility capabilities similar to the `grep` utility.

The place where a word search program like the one above falls terribly short is in speed of locating documents in *very* large document collections. Even something as fast, and well optimized, as `grep` simply takes a while to search a lot of source text. Fortunately, it is possible to *shortcut* this search time, as well as add some additional capabilities.

A technique for rapid searching is to perform a generic search just once (or periodically) and create an index—i.e., database—of those generic search results. Performing a later search need not *really* search contents, but only check the abstracted and structured index of possible searches. The utility `indexer.py` is a functional example of such a computed search index. The most current version may be downloaded from the book's Web site <http://gnosis.cx/TPiP/>.

The utility `indexer.py` allows very rapid searching for the simultaneous occurrence of multiple words within a file. For example, one might want to locate all the document files (or other text sources, such as VARCHAR database fields) that contain the words `Python`, `index`, and `search`. Supposing there are many thousands of candidate documents, searching them on an ad hoc basis could be slow. But `indexer.py` creates a comparatively compact collection of persistent dictionaries that provide answers to such inquiries.

The full source code to `indexer.py` is worth reading, but most of it deals with a variety of persistence mechanisms and with an object-oriented programming (OOP) framework for reuse. The underlying idea is simple, however. Create three dictionaries based on scanning a collection of documents:

```
*Indexer.fileids:   fileid --> filename
*Indexer.files:     filename --> (fileid, wordcount)
*Indexer.words:     word --> {fileid1:occurs, fileid2:occurs, ...}
```

The essential mapping is `*Indexer.words`. For each word, what files does it occur in and how often? The mappings `*Indexer.fileids` and `*Indexer.files` are ancillary. The first just allows shorter numeric aliases to be used instead of long filenames in the `*Indexer.words` mapping (a performance boost and storage saver). The second, `*Indexer.files`, also holds a total wordcount for each file. This allows a ranking of the importance of different matches. The thought is that a megabyte file with ten occurrences of `Python` is less focused on the topic of Python than is a kilobyte file with the same ten occurrences.

Both generating and utilizing the mappings above is straightforward. To search multiple words, one basically simply needs the intersection of the results of several values of the *Indexer.words dictionary, one value for each word key. Generating the mappings involves incrementing counts in the nested dictionary of *Indexer.words, but is not complicated.

QUESTIONS

1. One of the most significant—and surprisingly subtle—concerns in generating useful word indexes is figuring out just what a "word" is. What considerations would you bring to determine word identities? How might you handle capitalization? Punctuation? Whitespace? How might you disallow binary strings that are not "real" words. Try performing word-identification tests against real-world documents. How successful were you?

2. Could other data structures be used to store word index information than those proposed above? If other data structures are used, what efficiency (speed) advantages or disadvantages do you expect to encounter? Are there other data structures that would allow for additional search capabilities than the multiword search of indexer.py? If so, what other indexed search capabilities would have the most practical benefit?

3. Consider adding integrity guarantees to index results. What if an index falls out of synchronization with the underlying documents? How might you address referential integrity? Hint: consider binascii.crc32, sha, and md5. What changes to the data structures would be needed for integrity checks? Implement such an improvement.

4. The utility indexer.py has some ad hoc exclusions of nontextual files from inclusion in an index, based simply on some file extensions. How might one perform accurate exclusion of nontextual data? What does it mean for a document to contain text? Try writing a utility istextual.py that will identify text and nontext real-world documents. Does it work to your satisfaction?

5. Advanced: indexer.py implements several different persistence mechanisms. What other mechanisms might you use from those implemented? Benchmark your mechanism. Does it do better than SlicedZPickleIndexer (the best variant ncluded in both speed and space)?

Chapter 3

REGULAR EXPRESSIONS

Regular expressions allow extremely valuable text processing techniques, but ones that warrant careful explanation. Python's *re* module, in particular, allows numerous enhancements to basic regular expressions (such as named backreferences, lookahead assertions, backreference skipping, non-greedy quantifiers, and others). A solid introduction to the subtleties of regular expressions is valuable to programmers engaged in text processing tasks.

The prequel of this chapter contains a tutorial on regular expressions that allows a reader unfamiliar with regular expressions to move quickly from simple to complex elements of regular expression syntax. This tutorial is aimed primarily at beginners, but programmers familiar with regular expressions in other programming tools can benefit from a quick read of the tutorial, which explicates the particular regular expression dialect in Python.

It is important to note up-front that regular expressions, while very powerful, also have limitations. In brief, regular expressions cannot match patterns that nest to arbitrary depths. If that statement does not make sense, read Chapter 4, which discusses parsers—to a large extent, parsing exists to address the limitations of regular expressions. In general, if you have doubts about whether a regular expression is sufficient for your task, try to understand the examples in Chapter 4, particularly the discussion of how you might spell a floating point number.

Section 3.1 examines a number of text processing problems that are solved most naturally using regular expressions. As in other chapters, the solutions presented to problems can generally be adopted directly as little utilities for performing tasks. However, as elsewhere, the larger goal in presenting problems and solutions is to address a style of thinking about a wider class of problems than those whose solutions are presented directly in this book. Readers who are interested in a range of ready utilities and modules will probably want to check additional resources on the Web, such as the Vaults of Parnassus <http://www.vex.net/parnassus/> and the Python Cookbook <http://aspn.activestate.com/ASPN/Python/Cookbook/>.

Section 3.2 is a "reference with commentary" on the Python standard library modules for doing regular expression tasks. Several utility modules and backward-compatibility regular expression engines are available, but for most readers, the only important module will be *re* itself. The discussions interspersed with each module try to give some guidance on why you would want to use a given module or function, and the reference documentation tries to contain more examples of actual typical usage than does a plain reference. In many cases, the examples and discussion of individual functions address common and productive design patterns in Python. The cross-references are intended to contextualize a given function (or other thing) in terms of related ones (and to help a reader decide which is right for her). The actual listing of functions, constants, classes, and the like are in alphabetical order within each category.

3.1   A Regular Expression Tutorial

> Some people, when confronted with a problem, think "I know,
> I'll use regular expressions." Now they have two problems.
> —Jamie Zawinski, <alt.religion.emacs> (08/12/1997)

3.1.1   Just What Is a Regular Expression, Anyway?

Many readers will have some background with regular expressions, but some will not have any. Those with experience using regular expressions in other languages (or in Python) can probably skip this tutorial section. But readers new to regular expressions (affectionately called `regexes` by users) should read this section; even some with experience can benefit from a refresher.

A regular expression is a compact way of describing complex patterns in texts. You can use them to search for patterns and, once found, to modify the patterns in complex ways. They can also be used to launch programmatic actions that depend on patterns.

Jamie Zawinski's tongue-in-cheek comment in the epigram is worth thinking about. Regular expressions are amazingly powerful and deeply expressive. That is the very reason that writing them is just as error-prone as writing any other complex programming code. It is always better to solve a genuinely simple problem in a simple way; when you go beyond simple, think about regular expressions.

A large number of tools other than Python incorporate regular expressions as part of their functionality. Unix-oriented command-line tools like `grep`, `sed`, and `awk` are mostly wrappers for regular expression processing. Many text editors allow search and/or replacement based on regular expressions. Many programming languages, especially other scripting languages such as Perl and TCL, build regular expressions into the heart of the language. Even most command-line shells, such as Bash or the Windows-console, allow restricted regular expressions as part of their command syntax.

There are some variations in regular expression syntax between different tools that use them, but for the most part regular expressions are a "little language" that gets embedded inside bigger languages like Python. The examples in this tutorial section (and the documentation in the rest of the chapter) will focus on Python syntax, but most of this chapter transfers easily to working with other programming languages and tools.

As with most of this book, examples will be illustrated by use of Python interactive shell sessions that readers can type themselves, so that they can play with variations on the examples. However, the *re* module has little reason to include a function that simply illustrates matches in the shell. Therefore, the availability of the small wrapper program below is implied in the examples:

re_show.py

```
import re
def re_show(pat, s):
    print re.compile(pat, re.M).sub("{\g<0>}", s.rstrip()),'\n'

s = '''Mary had a little lamb
And everywhere that Mary
went, the lamb was sure
to go'''
```

Place the code in an external module and `import` it. Those new to regular expressions need not worry about what the above function does for now. It is enough to know that the first argument to `re_show()` will be a regular expression pattern, and the second argument will be a string to be matched against. The matches will treat each line of the string as a separate pattern for purposes of matching beginnings and ends of lines. The illustrated matches will be whatever is contained between curly braces.

3.1.2   Matching Patterns in Text: The Basics

The very simplest pattern matched by a regular expression is a literal character or a sequence of literal characters. Anything in the target text that consists of exactly those characters in exactly the order listed will match. A lowercase character is not identical with its uppercase version, and vice versa. A space in a regular expression, by the way, matches a literal space in the target (this is unlike most programming languages or command-line tools, where a variable number of spaces separate keywords).

```
>>> from re_show import re_show, s
>>> re_show('a', s)
M{a}ry h{a}d {a} little l{a}mb.
And everywhere th{a}t M{a}ry
went, the l{a}mb w{a}s sure
to go.

>>> re_show('Mary', s)
{Mary} had a little lamb.
And everywhere that {Mary}
went, the lamb was sure
to go.
```

○ · · ○ · · ○ · · ○ · · ○ · · ○ · · ○ · · ○ · · ○ · · ○ · · ○ · · ○ · · ○

A number of characters have special meanings to regular expressions. A symbol with a special meaning can be matched, but to do so it must be prefixed with the backslash character (this includes the backslash character itself: To match one backslash in the target, the regular expression should include \\). In Python, a special way of quoting a string is available that will not perform string interpolation. Since regular expressions use many of the same backslash-prefixed codes as do Python strings, it is usually easier to compose regular expression strings by quoting them as "raw strings" with an initial "r".

```
>>> from re_show import re_show
>>> s = '''Special characters must be escaped.*'''
>>> re_show(r'.*', s)
{Special characters must be escaped.*}

>>> re_show(r'\.\*', s)
Special characters must be escaped{.*}

>>> re_show('\\\\', r'Python \ escaped \ pattern')
Python {\} escaped {\} pattern

>>> re_show(r'\\', r'Regex \ escaped \ pattern')
Regex {\} escaped {\} pattern
```

○ · · ○ · · ○ · · ○ · · ○ · · ○ · · ○ · · ○ · · ○ · · ○ · · ○ · · ○ · · ○

Two special characters are used to mark the beginning and end of a line: caret ("^") and dollar sign ("$"). To match a caret or dollar sign as a literal character, it must be escaped (i.e., precede it by a backslash "\").

An interesting thing about the caret and dollar sign is that they match zero-width patterns. That is, the length of the string matched by a caret or dollar sign by itself is zero (but the rest of the regular expression can still depend on the zero-width match). Many regular expression tools provide another zero-width pattern for word-boundary ("\b"). Words might be divided by whitespace like spaces, tabs, newlines, or other characters like nulls; the word-boundary pattern matches the actual point where a word starts or ends, not the particular whitespace characters.

```
>>> from re_show import re_show, s
>>> re_show(r'^Mary', s)
{Mary} had a little lamb
And everywhere that Mary
went, the lamb was sure
to go

>>> re_show(r'Mary$', s)
Mary had a little lamb
And everywhere that {Mary}
went, the lamb was sure
to go
```

```
>>> re_show(r'$','Mary had a little lamb')
Mary had a little lamb{}
```

o · · o · · o · · o · · o · · c · · c · · o · · o · · o · · o · · o · · o · · o

In regular expressions, a period can stand for any character. Normally, the newline character is not included, but optional switches can force inclusion of the newline character also (see later documentation of *re* module functions). Using a period in a pattern is a way of requiring that "something" occurs here, without having to decide what.

Readers who are familiar with DOS command-line wildcards will know the question mark as filling the role of "some character" in command masks. But in regular expressions, the question mark has a different meaning, and the period is used as a wildcard.

```
>>> from re_show import re_show, s
>>> re_show(r'.a', s)
{Ma}ry {ha}d{ a} little {la}mb
And everywhere t{ha}t {Ma}ry
went, the {la}mb {wa}s sure
to go
```

o · · o · · o · · o · · o · · c · · c · · o · · o · · o · · o · · o · · o · · o

A regular expression can have literal characters in it and also zero-width positional patterns. Each literal character or positional pattern is an atom in a regular expression. One may also group several atoms together into a small regular expression that is part of a larger regular expression. One might be inclined to call such a grouping a "molecule," but normally it is also called an atom.

In older Unix-oriented tools like grep, subexpressions must be grouped with escaped parentheses; for example, \(Mary\). In Python (as with most more recent tools), grouping is done with bare parentheses, but matching a literal parenthesis requires escaping it in the pattern.

```
>>> from re_show import re_show, s
>>> re_show(r'(Mary)( )(had)', s)
{Mary had} a little lamb
And everywhere that Mary
went, the lamb was sure
to go

>>> re_show(r'\(.*\)', 'spam (and eggs)')
spam {(and eggs)}
```

o · · o · · o · · o · · o · · c · · c · · o · · o · · o · · o · · o · · o · · o

Rather than name only a single character, a pattern in a regular expression can match any of a set of characters.

A set of characters can be given as a simple list inside square brackets; for example, [aeiou] will match any single lowercase vowel. For letter or number ranges it may also have the first and last letter of a range, with a dash in the middle; for example, [A-Ma-m] will match any lowercase or uppercase letter in the first half of the alphabet.

Python (as with many tools) provides escape-style shortcuts to the most commonly used character class, such as \s for a whitespace character and \d for a digit. One could always define these character classes with square brackets, but the shortcuts can make regular expressions more compact and more readable.

```
>>> from re_show import re_show, s
>>> re_show(r'[a-z]a', s)
Mary {ha}d a little {la}mb
And everywhere t{ha}t Mary
went, the {la}mb {wa}s sure
to go
```

            o · · o · · o · · o · · o · · o · · o · · o · · o · · o · · o · · o · · o · · o

The caret symbol can actually have two different meanings in regular expressions. Most of the time, it means to match the zero-length pattern for line beginnings. But if it is used at the beginning of a character class, it reverses the meaning of the character class. Everything not included in the listed character set is matched.

```
>>> from re_show import re_show, s
>>> re_show(r'[^a-z]a', s)
{Ma}ry had{ a} little lamb
And everywhere that {Ma}ry
went, the lamb was sure
to go
```

            o · · o · · o · · o · · o · · o · · o · · o · · o · · o · · o · · o · · o · · o

Using character classes is a way of indicating that either one thing or another thing can occur in a particular spot. But what if you want to specify that either of two whole subexpressions occur in a position in the regular expression? For that, you use the alternation operator, the vertical bar ("|"). This is the symbol that is also used to indicate a pipe in Unix/DOS shells and is sometimes called the pipe character.

The pipe character in a regular expression indicates an alternation between everything in the group enclosing it. What this means is that even if there are several groups to the left and right of a pipe character, the alternation greedily asks for everything on both sides. To select the scope of the alternation, you must define a group that encompasses the patterns that may match. The example illustrates this:

```
>>> from re_show import re_show
>>> s2 = 'The pet store sold cats, dogs, and birds.'
>>> re_show(r'cat|dog|bird', s2)
The pet store sold {cat}s, {dog}s, and {bird}s.

>>> s3 = '=first first= # =second second= # =first= # =second='
>>> re_show(r'=first|second=', s3)
{=first} first= # =second {second=} # {=first}= # ={second=}
```

```
>>> re_show(r'(=)(first)|(second)(=)', s3)
{=first} first= # =second {second=} # {=first}= # ={second=}

>>> re_show(r'=(first|second)=', s3)
=first first= # =second second= # {=first=} # {=second=}
```

o · · o · · o · · o · · o · · ɔ · · o · · o · · ɔ · · o · · o · · o · · o

One of the most powerful and common things you can do with regular expressions is to specify how many times an atom occurs in a complete regular expression. Sometimes you want to specify something about the occurrence of a single character, but very often you are interested in specifying the occurrence of a character class or a grouped subexpression.

There is only one quantifier included with "basic" regular expression syntax, the asterisk ("*"); in English this has the meaning "some or none" or "zero or more." If you want to specify that any number of an atom may occur as part of a pattern, follow the atom by an asterisk.

Without quantifiers, grouping expressions doesn't really serve as much purpose, but once we can add a quantifier to a subexpression we can say something about the occurrence of the subexpression as a whole. Take a look at the example:

```
>>> from re_show import re_show
>>> s = '''Match with zero in the middle: @@
... Subexpression occurs, but...: @=!=ABC@
... Lots of occurrences: @=!==!==!==!=@
... Must repeat entire pattern: @=!==!=!==!=@'''
>>> re_show(r'@(=!=)*@', s)
Match with zero in the middle: {@@}
Subexpression occurs, but...: @=!=ABC@
Lots of occurrences: {@=!==!==!==!=@}
Must repeat entire pattern: @=!==!=!==!=@
```

3.1.3 Matching Patterns in Text: Intermediate

In a certain way, the lack of any quantifier symbol after an atom quantifies the atom anyway: It says the atom occurs exactly once. Extended regular expressions add a few other useful numbers to "once exactly" and "zero or more times." The plus sign ("+") means "one or more times" and the question mark ("?") means "zero or one times." These quantifiers are by far the most common enumerations you wind up using.

If you think about it, you can see that the extended regular expressions do not actually let you "say" anything the basic ones do not. They just let you say it in a shorter and more readable way. For example, (ABC)+ is equivalent to (ABC)(ABC)*, and X(ABC)?Y is equivalent to XABCY|XY. If the atoms being quantified are themselves complicated grouped subexpressions, the question mark and plus sign can make things a lot shorter.

```
>>> from re_show import re_show
>>> s = '''AAAD
```

```
...  ABBBBCD
...  BBBCD
...  ABCCD
...  AAABBBC''’
>>> re_show(r'A+B*C?D', s)
{AAAD}
{ABBBBCD}
BBBCD
ABCCD
AAABBBC
```

○ · · ○ · · ○ · · ○ · · ○ · · ○ · · ○ · · ○ · · ○ · · ○ · · ○ · · ○ · · ○

Using extended regular expressions, you can specify arbitrary pattern occurrence counts using a more verbose syntax than the question mark, plus sign, and asterisk quantifiers. The curly braces ("{" and "}") can surround a precise count of how many occurrences you are looking for.

The most general form of the curly-brace quantification uses two range arguments (the first must be no larger than the second, and both must be non-negative integers). The occurrence count is specified this way to fall between the minimum and maximum indicated (inclusive). As shorthand, either argument may be left empty: If so, the minimum/maximum is specified as zero/infinity, respectively. If only one argument is used (with no comma in there), exactly that number of occurrences are matched.

```
>>> from re_show import re_show
>>> s2 = '''aaaaa bbbbb ccccc
... aaa bbb ccc
... aaaaa bbbbbbbbbbbbbb ccccc'''
>>> re_show(r'a{5} b{,6} c{4,8}', s2)
{aaaaa bbbbb ccccc}
aaa bbb ccc
aaaaa bbbbbbbbbbbbbb ccccc

>>> re_show(r'a+ b{3,} c?', s2)
{aaaaa bbbbb c}cccc
{aaa bbb c}cc
{aaaaa bbbbbbbbbbbbbb c}cccc

>>> re_show(r'a{5} b{6,} c{4,8}', s2)
aaaaa bbbbb ccccc
aaa bbb ccc
{aaaaa bbbbbbbbbbbbbb ccccc}
```

○ · · ○ · · ○ · · ○ · · ○ · · ○ · · ○ · · ○ · · ○ · · ○ · · ○ · · ○ · · ○

One powerful option in creating search patterns is specifying that a subexpression that was matched earlier in a regular expression is matched again later in the expression. We do this using backreferences. Backreferences are named by the numbers 1 through 99, preceded by the backslash/escape character when used in this manner. These backreferences refer to each successive group in the match pattern, as in (one)(two)(three) \1\2\3. Each numbered backreference refers to the group that, in this example, has the word corresponding to the number.

It is important to note something the example illustrates. What gets matched by a backreference is the same literal string matched the first time, even if the pattern that matched the string could have matched other strings. Simply repeating the same grouped subexpression later in the regular expression does not match the same targets as using a backreference (but you have to decide what it is you actually want to match in either case).

Backreferences refer back to whatever occurred in the previous grouped expressions, in the order those grouped expressions occurred. Up to 99 numbered backreferences may be used. However, Python also allows naming backreferences, which can make it much clearer what the backreferences are pointing to. The initial pattern group must begin with ?P<name>, and the corresponding backreference must contain (?P=name).

```
>>> from re_show import re_show
>>> s2 = '''jkl abc xyz
... jkl xyz abc
... jkl abc abc
... jkl xyz xyz
... '''
>>> re_show(r'(abc|xyz) \1', s2)
jkl abc xyz
jkl xyz abc
jkl {abc abc}
jkl {xyz xyz}

>>> re_show(r'(abc|xyz) (abc|xyz)', s2)
jkl {abc xyz}
jkl {xyz abc}
jkl {abc abc}
jkl {xyz xyz}

>>> re_show(r'(?P<let3>abc|xyz) (?P=let3)', s2)
jkl abc xyz
jkl xyz abc
jkl {abc abc}
jkl {xyz xyz}
```

○ · · ○ · · ○ · · ○ · · ○ · · ○ · · ○ · · ○ · · ○ · · ○ · · ○ · · ○ · · ○

Quantifiers in regular expressions are greedy. That is, they match as much as they possibly can.

Probably the easiest mistake to make in composing regular expressions is to match too much. When you use a quantifier, you want it to match everything (of the right sort) up to the point where you want to finish your match. But when using the *, +, or numeric quantifiers, it is easy to forget that the last bit you are looking for might occur later in a line than the one you are interested in.

```
>>> from re_show import re_show
>>> s2 = '''-- I want to match the words that start
... -- with 'th' and end with 's'.
... this
... thus
... thistle
... this line matches too much
... '''
>>> re_show(r'th.*s', s2)
-- I want to match {the words that s}tart
-- wi{th 'th' and end with 's}'.
{this}
{thus}
{this}tle
{this line matches} too much
```

o ·· o ·· o ·· o ·· o ·· o ·· o ·· o ·· o ·· o ·· o ·· o ·· o ·· o

Often if you find that regular expressions are matching too much, a useful procedure is to reformulate the problem in your mind. Rather than thinking about, "What am I trying to match later in the expression?" ask yourself, "What do I need to avoid matching in the next part?" This often leads to more parsimonious pattern matches. Often the way to avoid a pattern is to use the complement operator and a character class. Look at the example, and think about how it works.

The trick here is that there are two different ways of formulating almost the same sequence. Either you can think you want to keep matching *until* you get to XYZ, or you can think you want to keep matching *unless* you get to XYZ. These are subtly different.

For people who have thought about basic probability, the same pattern occurs. The chance of rolling a 6 on a die in one roll is $1/6$. What is the chance of rolling a 6 in six rolls? A naive calculation puts the odds at $1/6 + 1/6 + 1/6 + 1/6 + 1/6 + 1/6$, or 100 percent. This is wrong, of course (after all, the chance after twelve rolls isn't 200 percent). The correct calculation is, "How do I avoid rolling a 6 for six rolls?" (i.e., $5/6 \times 5/6 \times 5/6 \times 5/6 \times 5/6 \times 5/6$, or about 33 percent). The chance of getting a 6 is the same chance as not avoiding it (or about 66 percent). In fact, if you imagine transcribing a series of die rolls, you could apply a regular expression to the written record, and similar thinking applies.

```
>>> from re_show import re_show
>>> s2 = '''-- I want to match the words that start
... -- with 'th' and end with 's'.
... this
... thus
... thistle
```

```
...  this line matches too much
...  '''
>>> re_show(r'th[^s]*.', s2)
-- I want to match {the words} {that s}tart
-- wi{th 'th' and end with 's}'.
{this}
{thus}
{this}tle
{this} line matches too much
```

○ ·· ○ ·· ○ ·· ○ ·· ○ ·· ○ ·· ○ ·· ○ ·· ○ ·· ○ ·· ○ ·· ○ ·· ○

Not all tools that use regular expressions allow you to modify target strings. Some simply locate the matched pattern; the mostly widely used regular expression tool is probably grep, which is a tool for searching only. Text editors, for example, may or may not allow replacement in their regular expression search facility.

Python, being a general programming language, allows sophisticated replacement patterns to accompany matches. Since Python strings are immutable, *re* functions do not modify string objects in place, but instead return the modified versions. But as with functions in the *string* module, one can always rebind a particular variable to the new string object that results from *re* modification.

Replacement examples in this tutorial will call a function re_new() that is a wrapper for the module function *re.sub()*. Original strings will be defined above the call, and the modified results will appear below the call and with the same style of additional markup of changed areas as re_show() used. Be careful to notice that the curly braces in the results displayed will not be returned by standard *re* functions, but are only added here for emphasis. Simply import the following function in the examples below:

```
re_new.py
```

```
import re
def re_new(pat, rep, s):
    print re.sub(pat, '{'+rep+'}', s)
```

○ ·· ○ ·· ○ ·· ○ ·· ○ ·· ○ ·· ○ ·· ○ ·· ○ ·· ○ ·· ○ ·· ○ ·· ○

Let us take a look at a couple of modification examples that build on what we have already covered. This one simply substitutes some literal text for some other literal text. Notice that *string.replace()* can achieve the same result and will be faster in doing so.

```
>>> from re_new import re_new
>>> s = 'The zoo had wild dogs, bobcats, lions, and other wild cats.'
>>> re_new('cat','dog',s)
The zoo had wild dogs, bob{dog}s, lions, and other wild {dog}s.
```

○ ·· ○ ·· ○ ·· ○ ·· ○ ·· ○ ·· ○ ·· ○ ·· ○ ·· ○ ·· ○ ·· ○ ·· ○

Most of the time, if you are using regular expressions to modify a target text, you will want to match more general patterns than just literal strings. Whatever is matched is what gets replaced (even if it is several different strings in the target):

```
>>> from re_new import re_new
>>> s = 'The zoo had wild dogs, bobcats, lions, and other wild cats.'
>>> re_new('cat|dog','snake',s)
The zoo had wild {snake}s, bob{snake}s, lions, and other wild {snake}s.
>>> re_new(r'[a-z]+i[a-z]*','nice',s)
The zoo had {nice} dogs, bobcats, {nice}, and other {nice} cats.
```

○ · · ○ · · ○ · · ○ · · ○ · · ○ · · ○ · · ○ · · ○ · · ○ · · ○ · · ○ · · ○

It is nice to be able to insert a fixed string everywhere a pattern occurs in a target text. But frankly, doing that is not very context sensitive. A lot of times, we do not want just to insert fixed strings, but rather to insert something that bears much more relation to the matched patterns. Fortunately, backreferences come to our rescue here. One can use backreferences in the pattern matches themselves, but it is even more useful to be able to use them in replacement patterns. By using replacement backreferences, one can pick and choose from the matched patterns to use just the parts of interest.

As well as backreferencing, the examples below illustrate the importance of whitespace in regular expressions. In most programming code, whitespace is merely aesthetic. But the examples differ solely in an extra space within the arguments to the second call—and the return value is importantly different.

```
>>> from re_new import re_new
>>> s = 'A37 B4 C107 D54112 E1103 XXX'
>>> re_new(r'([A-Z])([0-9]{2,4})',r'\2:\1',s)
{37:A} B4 {107:C} {5411:D}2 {1103:E} XXX
>>> re_new(r'([A-Z])([0-9]{2,4}) ',r'\2:\1 ',s)
{37:A }B4 {107:C }D54112 {1103:E }XXX
```

○ · · ○ · · ○ · · ○ · · ○ · · ○ · · ○ · · ○ · · ○ · · ○ · · ○ · · ○ · · ○

This tutorial has already warned about the danger of matching too much with regular expression patterns. But the danger is so much more serious when one does modifications, that it is worth repeating. If you replace a pattern that matches a larger string than you thought of when you composed the pattern, you have potentially deleted some important data from your target.

It is always a good idea to try out regular expressions on diverse target data that is representative of production usage. Make sure you are matching what you think you are matching. A stray quantifier or wildcard can make a surprisingly wide variety of texts match what you thought was a specific pattern. And sometimes you just have to stare at your pattern for a while, or find another set of eyes, to figure out what is really going on even after you see what matches. Familiarity might breed contempt, but it also instills competence.

3.1.4 Advanced Regular Expression Extensions

Some very useful enhancements to basic regular expressions are included with Python (and with many other tools). Many of these do not strictly increase the power of Python's regular expressions, but they *do* manage to make expressing them far more concise and clear.

Earlier in the tutorial, the problems of matching too much were discussed, and some workarounds were suggested. Python is nice enough to make this easier by providing optional "non-greedy" quantifiers. These quantifiers grab as little as possible while still matching whatever comes next in the pattern (instead of as much as possible).

Non-greedy quantifiers have the same syntax as regular greedy ones, except with the quantifier followed by a question mark. For example, a non-greedy pattern might look like: A[A-Z]*?B. In English, this means "match an A, followed by only as many capital letters as are needed to find a B."

One little thing to look out for is the fact that the pattern [A-Z]*?. will always match zero capital letters. No longer matches are ever needed to find the following "any character" pattern. If you use non-greedy quantifiers, watch out for matching too little, which is a symmetric danger.

```
>>> from re_show import re_show
>>> s = '''-- I want to match the words that start
... -- with 'th' and end with 's'.
... this line matches just right
... this # thus # thistle'''
>>> re_show(r'th.*s',s)
-- I want to match {the words that s}tart
-- wi{th 'th' and end with 's}'.
{this line matches jus}t right
{this # thus # this}tle

>>> re_show(r'th.*?s',s)
-- I want to match {the words} {that s}tart
-- wi{th 'th' and end with 's}'.
{this} line matches just right
{this} # {thus} # {this}tle

>>> re_show(r'th.*?s ',s)
-- I want to match {the words }that start
-- with 'th' and end with 's'.
{this }line matches just right
{this }# {thus }# thistle
```

o · · o · · o · · o · · o · · o · · o · · o · · o · · o · · o · · o · · o

Modifiers can be used in regular expressions or as arguments to many of the functions in *re*. A modifier affects, in one way or another, the interpretation of a regular expression pattern. A modifier, unlike an atom, is global to the particular match—in itself, a modifier doesn't match anything, it instead constrains or directs what the atoms match.

When used directly within a regular expression pattern, one or more modifiers begin the whole pattern, as in (?Limsux). For example, to match the word `cat` without regard to the case of the letters, one could use (?i)cat. The same modifiers may be passed in as the last argument as bitmasks (i.e., with a | between each modifier), but only to some functions in the *re* module, not to all. For example, the two calls below are equivalent:

```
>>> import re
>>> re.search(r'(?Li)cat','The Cat in the Hat').start()
4
>>> re.search(r'cat','The Cat in the Hat',re.L|re.I).start()
4
```

However, some function calls in *re* have no argument for modifiers. In such cases, you should either use the modifier prefix pseudo-group or precompile the regular expression rather than use it in string form. For example:

```
>>> import re
>>> re.split(r'(?i)th','Brillig and The Slithy Toves')
['Brillig and ', 'e Sli', 'y Toves']
>>> re.split(re.compile('th',re.I),'Brillig and the Slithy Toves')
['Brillig and ', 'e Sli', 'y Toves']
```

See the *re* module documentation for details on which functions take which arguments.

o · · o · · o · · o · · o · · o · · o · · o · · o · · o · · o · · o · · o

The modifiers listed below are used in *re* expressions. Users of other regular expression tools may be accustomed to a **g** option for "global" matching. These other tools take a line of text as their default unit, and "global" means to match multiple lines. Python takes the actual passed string as its unit, so "global" is simply the default. To operate on a single line, either the regular expressions have to be tailored to look for appropriate begin-line and end-line characters, or the strings being operated on should be split first using *string.split()* or other means.

```
* L (re.L) - Locale customization of \w, \W, \b, \B
* i (re.I) - Case-insensitive match
* m (re.M) - Treat string as multiple lines
* s (re.S) - Treat string as single line
* u (re.U) - Unicode customization of \w, \W, \b, \B
* x (re.X) - Enable verbose regular expressions
```

The single-line option ("s") allows the wildcard to match a newline character (it won't otherwise). The multiple-line option ("m") causes "^" and "$" to match the beginning and end of each line in the target, not just the begin/end of the target as a whole (the default). The insensitive option ("i") ignores differences between the case of letters. The Locale and Unicode options ("L" and "u") give different interpretations to the word-boundary ("\b") and alphanumeric ("\w") escaped patterns—and their inverse forms ("\B" and "\W").

The verbose option ("x") is somewhat different from the others. Verbose regular expressions may contain nonsignificant whitespace and inline comments. In a sense, this is also just a different interpretation of regular expression patterns, but it allows you to produce far more easily readable complex patterns. Some examples follow in the sections below.

○ · · ○ · · ○ · · ○ · · ○ · · ○ · · ○ · · ○ · · ○ · · ○ · · ○ · · ○ · · ○

Let's take a look first at how case-insensitive and single-line options change the match behavior.

```
>>> from re_show import re_show
>>> s = '''MAINE # Massachusetts # Colorado #
... mississippi # Missouri # Minnesota #'''
>>> re_show(r'M.*[ise] ', s)
{MAINE # Massachusetts }# Colorado #
mississippi # {Missouri }# Minnesota #

>>> re_show(r'(?i)M.*[ise] ', s)
{MAINE # Massachusetts }# Colorado #
{mississippi # Missouri }# Minnesota #

>>> re_show(r'(?si)M.*[ise] ', s)
{MAINE # Massachusetts # Colorado #
mississippi # Missouri }# Minnesota #
```

Looking back to the definition of re_show(), we can see it was defined to explicitly use the multiline option. So patterns displayed with re_show() will always be multiline. Let us look at a couple of examples that use *re.findall()* instead.

```
>>> from re_show import re_show
>>> s = '''MAINE # Massachusetts # Colorado #
... mississippi # Missouri # Minnesota #'''
>>> re_show(r'(?im)^M.*[ise] ', s)
{MAINE # Massachusetts }# Colorado #
{mississippi # Missouri }# Minnesota #

>>> import re
>>> re.findall(r'(?i)^M.*[ise] ', s)
['MAINE # Massachusetts ']
>>> re.findall(r'(?im)^M.*[ise] ', s)
['MAINE # Massachusetts ', 'mississippi # Missouri ']
```

○ · · ○ · · ○ · · ○ · · ○ · · ○ · · ○ · · ○ · · ○ · · ○ · · ○ · · ○ · · ○

Matching word characters and word boundaries depends on exactly what gets counted as being alphanumeric. Character codepages for letters outside the (US-English) ASCII range differ among national alphabets. Python versions are configured to a particular locale, and regular expressions can optionally use the current one to match words.

Of greater long-term significance is the *re* module's ability (after Python 2.0) to look at the Unicode categories of characters, and decide whether a character is alphabetic based on that category. Locale settings work OK for European diacritics, but for non-Roman sets, Unicode is clearer and less error prone. The "u" modifier controls whether Unicode alphabetic characters are recognized or merely ASCII ones:

```
>>> import re
>>> alef, omega = unichr(1488), unichr(969)
>>> u = alef +' A b C d '+omega+' X y Z'
>>> u, len(u.split()), len(u)
(u'\u05d0 A b C d \u03c9 X y Z', 9, 17)
>>> ':'.join(re.findall(ur'\b\w\b', u))
u'A:b:C:d:X:y:Z'
>>> ':'.join(re.findall(ur'(?u)\b\w\b', u))
u'\u05d0:A:b:C:d:\u03c9:X:y:Z'
```

o · · o · · o · · o · · o · · o · · o · · o · · o · · o · · o · · o · · o · · o

Backreferencing in replacement patterns is very powerful, but it is easy to use many groups in a complex regular expression, which can be confusing to identify. It is often more legible to refer to the parts of a replacement pattern in sequential order. To handle this issue, Python's *re* patterns allow "grouping without backreferencing."

A group that should not also be treated as a backreference has a question mark colon at the beginning of the group, as in (?:pattern). In fact, you can use this syntax even when your backreferences are in the search pattern itself:

```
>>> from re_new import re_new
>>> s = 'A-xyz-37 # B:abcd:142 # C-wxy-66 # D-qrs-93'
>>> re_new(r'([A-Z])(?:-[a-z]{3}-)([0-9]*)', r'\1\2', s)
{A37} # B:abcd:142 # {C66} # {D93}
>>> # Groups that are not of interest excluded from backref
...
>>> re_new(r'([A-Z])(-[a-z]{3}-)([0-9]*)', r'\1\2', s)
{A-xyz-} # B:abcd:142 # {C-wxy-} # {D-qrs-}
>>> # One could lose track of groups in a complex pattern
...
```

o · · o · · o · · o · · o · · o · · o · · o · · o · · o · · o · · o · · o · · o

Python offers a particularly handy syntax for really complex pattern backreferences. Rather than just play with the numbering of matched groups, you can give them a name. Above we pointed out the syntax for named backreferences in the pattern space; for example, (?P=name). However, a bit different syntax is necessary in replacement patterns. For that, we use the \g operator along with angle brackets and a name. For example:

```
>>> from re_new import re_new
```

```
>>> s = "A-xyz-37 # B:abcd:142 # C-wxy-66 # D-qrs-93"
>>> re_new(r'(?P<prefix>[A-Z])(-[a-z]{3}-)(?P<id>[0-9]*)',
...          r'\g<prefix>\g<id>',s)
{A37} # B:abcd:142 # {C66} # {D93}
```

∘ · · ∘ · · ∘ · · ∘ · · ∘ · · ∘ · · ∘ · · ∘ · · ∘ · · ∘ · · ∘ · · ∘ · · ∘

Another trick of advanced regular expression tools is "lookahead assertions." These are similar to regular grouped subexpression, except they do not actually grab what they match. There are two advantages to using lookahead assertions. On the one hand, a lookahead assertion can function in a similar way to a group that is not backreferenced; that is, you can match something without counting it in backreferences. More significantly, however, a lookahead assertion can specify that the next chunk of a pattern has a certain form, but let a different (more general) subexpression actually grab it (usually for purposes of backreferencing that other subexpression).

There are two kinds of lookahead assertions: positive and negative. As you would expect, a positive assertion specifies that something does come next, and a negative one specifies that something does not come next. Emphasizing their connection with non-backreferenced groups, the syntax for lookahead assertions is similar: `(?=pattern)` for positive assertions, and `(?!pattern)` for negative assertions.

```
>>> from re_new import re_new
>>> s = 'A-xyz37 # B-ab6142 # C-Wxy66 # D-qrs93'
>>> # Assert that three lowercase letters occur after CAP-DASH
...
>>> re_new(r'([A-Z]-)(?=[a-z]{3})([\w\d]*)', r'\2\1', s)
{xyz37A-} # B-ab6142 # C-Wxy66 # {qrs93D-}
>>> # Assert three lowercase letts do NOT occur after CAP-DASH
...
>>> re_new(r'([A-Z]-)(?![a-z]{3})([\w\d]*)', r'\2\1', s)
A-xyz37 # {ab6142B-} # {Wxy66C-} # D-qrs93
```

∘ · · ∘ · · ∘ · · ∘ · · ∘ · · ∘ · · ∘ · · ∘ · · ∘ · · ∘ · · ∘ · · ∘ · · ∘

Along with lookahead assertions, Python 2.0+ adds "lookbehind assertions." The idea is similar—a pattern is of interest only if it is (or is not) preceded by some other pattern. Lookbehind assertions are somewhat more restricted than lookahead assertions because they may only look backwards by a fixed number of character positions. In other words, no general quantifiers are allowed in lookbehind assertions. Still, some patterns are most easily expressed using lookbehind assertions.

As with lookahead assertions, lookbehind assertions come in a negative and a positive flavor. The former assures that a certain pattern does *not* precede the match, the latter assures that the pattern *does* precede the match.

```
>>> from re_new import re_new
>>> re_show('Man', 'Manhandled by The Man')
{Man}handled by The {Man}
```

```
>>> re_show('(?<=The )Man', 'Manhandled by The Man')
Manhandled by The {Man}

>>> re_show('(?<!The )Man', 'Manhandled by The Man')
{Man}handled by The Man
```

    o · · o · · o · · o · · o · · o · · o · · o · · o · · o · · o · · o · · o · · o

In the later examples we have started to see just how complicated regular expressions can get. These examples are not the half of it. It is possible to do some almost absurdly difficult-to-understand things with regular expression (but ones that are nonetheless useful).

There are two basic facilities that Python's "verbose" modifier ("x") uses in clarifying expressions. One is allowing regular expressions to continue over multiple lines (by ignoring whitespace like trailing spaces and newlines). The second is allowing comments within regular expressions. When patterns get complicated, do both!

The example given is a fairly typical example of a complicated, but well-structured and well-commented, regular expression:

```
>>> from re_show import re_show
>>> s = '''The URL for my site is: http://mysite.com/mydoc.html. You
... might also enjoy ftp://yoursite.com/index.html for a good
... place to download files.'''
>>> pat = r'''  (?x)( # verbose identify URLs within text
... (http|ftp|gopher) # make sure we find a resource type
...                :// # ...needs to be followed by colon-slash-slash
...          [^ \n\r]+ # some stuff then space, newline, tab is URL
...                 \w # URL always ends in alphanumeric char
...        (?=[\s\.,]) # assert: followed by whitespace/period/comma
...                  ) # end of match group'''
>>> re_show(pat, s)
The URL for my site is: {http://mysite.com/mydoc.html}. You
might also enjoy {ftp://yoursite.com/index.html} for a good
place to download files.
```

3.2   Some Common Tasks

3.2.1   Problem: Making a text block flush left

For visual clarity or to identify the role of text, blocks of text are often indented— especially in prose-oriented documents (but log files, configuration files, and the like might also have unused initial fields). For downstream purposes, indentation is often irrelevant, or even outright incorrect, since the indentation is not part of the text itself but only a decoration of the text. However, it often makes matters even worse to perform the very most naive transformation of indented text—simply remove leading whitespace from every line. While block indentation may be decoration, the relative indentations of lines within blocks may serve important or essential functions (for example, the blocks of text might be Python source code).

The general procedure you need to take in maximally unindenting a block of text is fairly simple. But it is easy to throw more code at it than is needed, and arrive at some inelegant and slow nested loops of *string.find()* and *string.replace()* operations. A bit of cleverness in the use of regular expressions—combined with the conciseness of a functional programming (FP) style—can give you a quick, short, and direct transformation.

```
flush_left.py
```

```
# Remove as many leading spaces as possible from whole block
from re import findall,sub
# What is the minimum line indentation of a block?
indent = lambda s: reduce(min,map(len,findall('(?m)^ *(?=\S)',s)))
# Remove the block-minimum indentation from each line?
flush_left = lambda s: sub('(?m)^ {%d}' % indent(s),'',s)

if __name__ == '__main__':
    import sys
    print flush_left(sys.stdin.read())
```

The `flush_left()` function assumes that blocks are indented with spaces. If tabs are used—or used combined with spaces—an initial pass through the utility `untabify.py` (which can be found at `$PYTHONPATH/tools/scripts/`) can convert blocks to space-only indentation.

A helpful adjunct to `flush_left()` is likely to be the `reformat_para()` function that was presented in Chapter 2, Problem 2. Between the two of these, you could get a good part of the way towards a "batch-oriented word processor." (What other capabilities would be most useful?)

3.2.2 Problem: Summarizing command-line option documentation

Documentation of command-line options to programs is usually in semi-standard formats in places like manpages, docstrings, READMEs and the like. In general, within documentation you expect to see command-line options indented a bit, followed by a bit more indentation, followed by one or more lines of description, and usually ended by a blank line. This style is readable for users browsing documentation, but is of sufficiently complexity and variability that regular expressions are well suited to finding the right descriptions (simple string methods fall short).

A specific scenario where you might want a summary of command-line options is as an aid to understanding configuration files that call multiple child commands. The file `/etc/inetd.conf` on Unix-like systems is a good example of such a configuration file. Moreover, configuration files themselves often have enough complexity and variability within them that simple string methods have difficulty parsing them.

The utility below will look for every service launched by /etc/inetd.conf and present to STDOUT summary documentation of all the options used when the services are started.

```
┌────────────────┐
│ show_services.py │
└────────────────┘
import re, os, string, sys

def show_opts(cmdline):
    args = string.split(cmdline)
    cmd = args[0]
    if len(args) > 1:
        opts = args[1:]
    # might want to check error output, so use popen3()
    (in_, out_, err) = os.popen3('man %s | col -b' % cmd)
    manpage = out_.read()
    if len(manpage) > 2:           # found actual documentation
        print '\n%s' % cmd
        for opt in opts:
            pat_opt = r'(?sm)^\s*'+opt+r'.*?(?=\n\n)'
            opt_doc = re.search(pat_opt, manpage)
            if opt_doc is not None:
                print opt_doc.group()
            else:                  # try harder for something relevant
                mentions = []
                for para in string.split(manpage,'\n\n'):
                    if re.search(opt, para):
                        mentions.append('\n%s' % para)
                if not mentions:
                    print '\n    ',opt,' '*9,'Option docs not found'
                else:
                    print '\n    ',opt,' '*9,'Mentioned in below para:'
                    print '\n'.join(mentions)
    else:                          # no manpage available
        print cmdline
        print '    No documentation available'

def services(fname):
    conf = open(fname).read()
    pat_srv = r'''(?xm)(?=^[^#])        # lns that are not commented out
                  (?:(?:[\w/]+\s+){6})  # first six fields ignored
                  (.*$)                 # to end of ln is servc launch'''
    return re.findall(pat_srv, conf)

if __name__ == '__main__':
    for service in services(sys.argv[1]):
        show_opts(service)
```

The particular tasks performed by `show_opts()` and `services()` are somewhat specific to Unix-like systems, but the general techniques are more broadly applicable. For example, the particular comment character and number of fields in `/etc/inetd.conf` might be different for other launch scripts, but the use of regular expressions to find the launch commands would apply elsewhere. If the `man` and `col` utilities are not on the relevant system, you might do something equivalent, such as reading in the docstrings from Python modules with similar option descriptions (most of the samples in `$PYTHONPATH/tools/` use compatible documentation, for example).

Another thing worth noting is that even where regular expressions are used in parsing some data, you need not do everything with regular expressions. The simple `string.split()` operation to identify paragraphs in `show_opts()` is still the quickest and easiest technique, even though `re.split()` could do the same thing.

Note: Along the lines of paragraph splitting, here is a thought problem. What is a regular expression that matches every whole paragraph that contains within it some smaller pattern `pat`? For purposes of the puzzle, assume that a paragraph is some text that both starts and ends with doubled newlines ("\n\n").

3.2.3   Problem: Detecting duplicate words

A common typo in prose texts is doubled words (hopefully they have been edited out of this book except in those few cases where they are intended). The same error occurs to a lesser extent in programming language code, configuration files, or data feeds. Regular expressions are well-suited to detecting this occurrence, which just amounts to a backreference to a word pattern. It's easy to wrap the regex in a small utility with a few extra features:

```
dupwords.py
```

```
# Detect doubled words and display with context
# Include words doubled across lines but within paras

import sys, re, glob
for pat in sys.argv[1:]:
    for file in glob.glob(pat):
        newfile = 1
        for para in open(file).read().split('\n\n'):
            dups = re.findall(r'(?m)(^.*(\b\w+\b)\s*\b\2\b.*$)', para)
            if dups:
                if newfile:
                    print '%s\n%s\n' % ('-'*70,file)
                    newfile = 0
                for dup in dups:
                    print '[%s] -->' % dup[1], dup[0]
```

This particular version grabs the line or lines on which duplicates occur and prints them for context (along with a prompt for the duplicate itself). Variations are straightforward. The assumption made by `dupwords.py` is that a doubled word that spans a

line (from the end of one to the beginning of another, ignoring whitespace) is a real
doubling; but a duplicate that spans paragraphs is not likewise noteworthy.

3.2.4   Problem: Checking for server errors

Web servers are a ubiquitous source of information nowadays. But finding URLs that
lead to real documents is largely hit-or-miss. Every Web maintainer seems to reorganize
her site every month or two, thereby breaking bookmarks and hyperlinks. As bad
as the chaos is for plain Web surfers, it is worse for robots faced with the difficult
task of recognizing the difference between content and errors. By-the-by, it is easy to
accumulate downloaded Web pages that consist of error messages rather than desired
content.

In principle, Web servers can and should return error codes indicating server errors.
But in practice, Web servers almost always return dynamically generated results pages
for erroneous requests. Such pages are basically perfectly normal HTML pages that just
happen to contain text like "Error 404: File not found!" Most of the time these pages are
a bit fancier than this, containing custom graphics and layout, links to site homepages,
JavaScript code, cookies, meta tags, and all sorts of other stuff. It is actually quite
amazing just how much many Web servers send in response to requests for nonexistent
URLs.

Below is a very simple Python script to examine just what Web servers return on
valid or invalid requests. Getting an error page is usually as simple as asking for a page
called `http://somewebsite.com/phony-url` or the like (anything that doesn't really
exist). *urllib* is discussed in Chapter 5, but its details are not important here.

---

url_examine.py

```
import sys
from urllib import urlopen

if len(sys.argv) > 1:
    fpin = urlopen(sys.argv[1])
    print fpin.geturl()
    print fpin.info()
    print fpin.read()
else:
    print "No specified URL"
```

Given the diversity of error pages you might receive, it is difficult or impossible to
create a regular expression (or any program) that determines with certainty whether a
given HTML document is an error page. Furthermore, some sites choose to generate
pages that are not really quite errors, but not really quite content either (e.g, generic
directories of site information with suggestions on how to get to content). But some
heuristics come quite close to separating content from errors. One noteworthy heuristic
is that the interesting errors are almost always 404 or 403 (not a sure thing, but good

enough to make smart guesses). Below is a utility to rate the "error probability" of HTML documents:

```
error_page.py
```

```python
import re, sys
page = sys.stdin.read()

# Mapping from patterns to probability contribution of pattern
err_pats = {r'(?is)<TITLE>.*?(404|403).*?ERROR.*?</TITLE>': 0.95,
            r'(?is)<TITLE>.*?ERROR.*?(404|403).*?</TITLE>': 0.95,
            r'(?is)<TITLE>ERROR</TITLE>': 0.30,
            r'(?is)<TITLE>.*?ERROR.*?</TITLE>': 0.10,
            r'(?is)<META .*?(404|403).*?ERROR.*?>': 0.80,
            r'(?is)<META .*?ERROR.*?(404|403).*?>': 0.80,
            r'(?is)<TITLE>.*?File Not Found.*?</TITLE>': 0.80,
            r'(?is)<TITLE>.*?Not Found.*?</TITLE>': 0.40,
            r'(?is)<BODY.*(404|403).*</BODY>': 0.10,
            r'(?is)<H1>.*?(404|403).*?</H1>': 0.15,
            r'(?is)<BODY.*not found.*</BODY>': 0.10,
            r'(?is)<H1>.*?not found.*?</H1>': 0.15,
            r'(?is)<BODY.*the requested URL.*</BODY>': 0.10,
            r'(?is)<BODY.*the page you requested.*</BODY>': 0.10,
            r'(?is)<BODY.*page.{1,50}unavailable.*</BODY>': 0.10,
            r'(?is)<BODY.*request.{1,50}unavailable.*</BODY>': 0.10,
            r'(?i)does not exist': 0.10,
            }
err_score = 0
for pat, prob in err_pats.items():
    if err_score > 0.9: break
    if re.search(pat, page):
        # print pat, prob
        err_score += prob

if err_score > 0.90:   print 'Page is almost surely an error report'
elif err_score > 0.75: print 'It is highly likely page is an error report'
elif err_score > 0.50: print 'Better-than-even odds page is error report'
elif err_score > 0.25: print 'Fair indication page is an error report'
else:                  print 'Page is probably real content'
```

Tested against a fair number of sites, a collection like this of regular expression searches and threshold confidences works quite well. Within the author's own judgment of just what is really an error page, erro_page.py has gotten no false positives and always arrived at at least the lowest warning level for every true error page.

The patterns chosen are all fairly simple, and both the patterns and their weightings were determined entirely subjectively by the author. But something like this weighted hit-or-miss technique can be used to solve many "fuzzy logic" matching problems (most having nothing to do with Web server errors).

Code like that above can form a general approach to more complete applications. But for what it is worth, the scripts `url_examine.py` and `error_page.py` may be used directly together by piping from the first to the second. For example:

```
% python urlopen.py http://gnosis.cx/nonesuch | python ex_error_page.py
Page is almost surely an error report
```

3.2.5   Problem: Reading lines with continuation characters

Many configuration files and other types of computer code are line oriented, but also have a facility to treat multiple lines as if they were a single logical line. In processing such a file it is usually desirable as a first step to turn all these logical lines into actual newline-delimited lines (or more likely, to transform both single and continued lines as homogeneous list elements to iterate through later). A continuation character is generally required to be the *last* thing on a line before a newline, or possibly the last thing other than some whitespace. A small (and very partial) table of continuation characters used by some common and uncommon formats is listed below:

```
\   Python, JavaScript, C/C++, Bash, TCL, Unix config
_   Visual Basic, PAW
&   Lyris, COBOL, IBIS
;   Clipper, TOP
-   XSPEC, NetREXX
=   Oracle Express
```

Most of the formats listed are programming languages, and parsing them takes quite a bit more than just identifying the lines. More often, it is configuration files of various sorts that are of interest in simple parsing, and most of the time these files use a common Unix-style convention of using trailing backslashes for continuation lines.

One *could* manage to parse logical lines with a *string* module approach that looped through lines and performed concatenations when needed. But a greater elegance is served by reducing the problem to a single regular expression. The module below provides this:

logical_lines.py

```
# Determine the logical lines in a file that might have
# continuation characters.  'logical_lines()' returns a
# list.  The self-test prints the logical lines as
# physical lines (for all specified files and options).

import re

def logical_lines(s, continuation='\\', strip_trailing_space=0):
    c = continuation
    if strip_trailing_space:
        s = re.sub(r'(?m)(%s)(\s+)$'%[c], r'\1', s)
    pat_log = r'(?sm)^.*?$(?<!%s)'%[c]   # e.g. (?sm)^.*?$(?<!\\)
    return [t.replace(c+'\n','') for t in re.findall(pat_log, s)]

if __name__ == '__main__':
    import sys
    files, strip, contin = ([], 0, '\\')
    for arg in sys.argv[1:]:
        if arg[:-1] == '--continue=': contin = arg[-1]
        elif arg[:-1] == '-c': contin = arg[-1]
        elif arg in ('--string','-s'): strip = 1
        else: files.append(arg)
    if not files: files.append(sys.stdin)
    for file in files:
        s = open(sys.argv[1]).read()
        print '\n'.join(logical_lines(s, contin, strip))
```

The comment in the pat_log definition shows a bit just how cryptic regular expressions can be at times. The comment is the pattern that is used for the default value of continuation. But as dense as it is with symbols, you can still read it by proceeding slowly, left to right. Let us try a version of the same line with the verbose modifier and comments:

```
>>> pat = r'''
... (?x)       # This is the verbose version
... (?s)       # In the pattern, let "." match newlines, if needed
... (?m)       # Allow ^ and $ to match every begin- and end-of-line
... ^          # Start the match at the beginning of a line
... .*?        # Non-greedily grab everything until the first place
...            # where the rest of the pattern matches (if possible)
... $          # End the match at an end-of-line
... (?<!       # Only count as a match if the enclosed pattern was not
...            # the immediately last thing seen (negative lookbehind)
... \\)        # It wasn't an (escaped) backslash'''
```

3.2.6   Problem: Identifying URLs and email addresses in texts

A neat feature of many Internet and news clients is their automatic identification of
resources that the applications can act upon. For URL resources, this usually means
making the links "clickable"; for an email address it usually means launching a new letter to the person at the address. Depending on the nature of an application, you could
perform other sorts of actions for each identified resource. For a text processing application, the use of a resource is likely to be something more batch-oriented: extraction,
transformation, indexing, or the like.

Fully and precisely implementing RFC1822 (for email addresses) or RFC1738 (for
URLs) is possible within regular expressions. But doing so is probably even more work
than is really needed to identify 99% of resources. Moreover, a significant number of
resources in the "real world" are not strictly compliant with the relevant RFCs—most
applications give a certain leeway to "almost correct" resource identifiers. The utility
below tries to strike approximately the same balance of other well-implemented and
practical applications: get *almost* everything that was intended to look like a resource,
and *almost* nothing that was intended not to:

---

find_urls.py

```
# Functions to identify and extract URLs and email addresses

import re, fileinput

pat_url = re.compile(  r'''
                (?x)( # verbose identify URLs within text
    (http|ftp|gopher) # make sure we find a resource type
                  :// # ...needs to be followed by colon-slash-slash
      (\w+[:.]?){2,} # at least two domain groups, e.g. (gnosis.)(cx)
               (/?| # could be just the domain name (maybe w/ slash)
          [^ \n\r"]+ # or stuff then space, newline, tab, quote
             [\w/]) # resource name ends in alphanumeric or slash
  (?=[\s\.,>)'"\]]) # assert: followed by white or clause ending
                 ) # end of match group
                 ''')
pat_email = re.compile(r'''
              (?xm)  # verbose identify URLs in text (and multiline)
          (?=^.{11}  # Mail header matcher
  (?<!Message-ID:|   # rule out Message-ID's as best possible
      In-Reply-To))  # ...and also In-Reply-To
             (.*?)(  # must grab to email to allow prior lookbehind
  ([A-Za-z0-9-]+\.)? # maybe an initial part: DAVID.mertz@gnosis.cx
       [A-Za-z0-9-]+ # definitely some local user: MERTZ@gnosis.cx
                  @  # ...needs an at sign in the middle
         (\w+\.?){2,} # at least two domain groups, e.g. (gnosis.)(cx)
  (?=[\s\.,>)'"\]]) # assert: followed by white or clause ending
```

```
                    ) # end of match group
                   ''')
extract_urls = lambda s: [u[0] for u in re.findall(pat_url, s)]
extract_email = lambda s: [(e[1]) for e in re.findall(pat_email, s)]

if __name__ == '__main__':
    for line in fileinput.input():
        urls = extract_urls(line)
        if urls:
            for url in urls:
                print fileinput.filename(),'=>',url
        emails = extract_email(line)
        if emails:
            for email in emails:
                print fileinput.filename(),'->',email
```

A number of features are notable in the utility above. One point is that everything
interesting is done within the regular expressions themselves. The actual functions
extract_urls() and extract_email() are each a single line, using the conciseness of
functional-style programming, especially list comprehensions (four or five lines of more
procedural code could be used, but this style helps emphasize where the work is done).
The utility itself prints located resources to STDOUT, but you could do something else
with them just as easily.

A bit of testing of preliminary versions of the regular expressions led me to add a few
complications to them. In part this lets readers see some more exotic features in action;
but in greater part, this helps weed out what I would consider "false positives." For
URLs we demand at least two domain groups—this rules out LOCALHOST addresses,
if present. However, by allowing a colon to end a domain group, we allow for specified
ports such as http://gnosis.cx:8080/resource/.

Email addresses have one particular special consideration. If the files you are scanning for email addresses happen to be actual mail archives, you will also find Message-
ID strings. The form of these headers is very similar to that of email addresses
(In-Reply-To: headers also contain Message-IDs). By combining a negative lookbehind assertion with some throwaway groups, we can make sure that everything that
gets extracted is not a Message-ID: header line. It gets a little complicated to combine
these things correctly, but the power of it is quite remarkable.

3.2.7   Problem: Pretty-printing numbers

In producing human-readable documents, Python's default string representation of numbers leaves something to be desired. Specifically, the delimiters that normally occur
between powers of 1,000 in written large numerals are not produced by the *str()* or
repr() functions—which makes reading large numbers difficult. For example:

```
>>> budget = 12345678.90
>>> print 'The company budget is $%s' % str(budget)
```

```
The company budget is $12345678.9
>>> print 'The company budget is %10.2f' % budget
The company budget is  12345678.90
```

Regular expressions can be used to transform numbers that are already "stringified" (an alternative would be to process numeric values by repeated division/remainder operations, stringifying the chunks). A few basic utility functions are contained in the module below.

> pretty_nums.py

```
# Create/manipulate grouped string versions of numbers

import re

def commify(f, digits=2, maxgroups=5, european=0):
    template = '%%1.%df' % digits
    s = template % f
    pat = re.compile(r'(\d+)(\d{3})([.,]|$)([.,\d]*)')
    if european:
        repl = r'\1.\2\3\4'
    else:   # could also use locale.localeconv()['decimal_point']
        repl = r'\1,\2\3\4'
    for i in range(maxgroups):
        s = re.sub(pat,repl,s)
    return s

def uncommify(s):
    return s.replace(',','')

def eurify(s):
    s = s.replace('.','\000')    # place holder
    s = s.replace(',','.')       # change group delimiter
    s = s.replace('\000',',')    # decimal delimiter
    return s

def anglofy(s):
    s = s.replace(',','\000')    # place holder
    s = s.replace('.',',')       # change group delimiter
    s = s.replace('\000','.')    # decimal delimiter
    return s

vals = (12345678.90, 23456789.01, 34567890.12)
sample = '''The company budget is $%s.
Its debt is $%s, against assets
of $%s'''
```

```
if __name__ == '__main__':
    print sample % vals, '\n-----'
    print sample % tuple(map(commify, vals)), '\n-----'
    print eurify(sample % tuple(map(commify, vals))), '\n-----'
```

The technique used in `commify()` has virtues and vices. It is quick, simple, and it works. It is also slightly kludgey inasmuch as it loops through the substitution (and with the default `maxgroups` argument, it is no good for numbers bigger than a quintillion; most numbers you encounter are smaller than this). If purity is a goal—and it probably should not be—you could probably come up with a single regular expression to do the whole job. Another quick and convenient technique is the "place holder" idea that was mentioned in the introductory discussion of the *string* module.

3.3   Standard Modules

3.3.1   Versions and Optimizations

> Rules of Optimization:
> Rule 1: Don't do it.
> Rule 2 (for experts only): Don't do it yet.
> —M.A. Jackson

Python has undergone several changes in its regular expression support. *regex* was superceded by *pre* in Python 1.5; *pre*, in turn, by *sre* in Python 2.0. Although Python has continued to include the older modules in its standard library for backwards compatibility, the older ones are deprecated when the newer versions are included. From Python 1.5 forward, the module *re* has served as a wrapper to the underlying regular expression engine (*sre* or *pre*). But even though Python 2.0+ has used *re* to wrap *sre*, *pre* is still available (the latter along with its own underlying *pcre* C extension module that can technically be used directly).

Each version has generally improved upon its predecessor, but with something as complicated as regular expressions there are always a few losses with each gain. For example, *sre* adds Unicode support and is faster for most operations—but *pre* has better optimization of case-insensitive searches. Subtle details of regular expression patterns might even let the quite-old *regex* module perform faster than the newer ones. Moreover, optimizing regular expressions can be extremely complicated and dependent upon specific small version differences.

Readers might start to feel their heads swim with these version details. Don't panic. Other than out of historic interest, you really do not need to worry about what implementations underlie regular expression support. The simple rule is just to use the module *re* and not think about what it wraps—the interface is compatible between versions.

The real virtue of regular expressions is that they allow a concise and precise (albeit somewhat cryptic) description of complex patterns in text. Most of the time, regular expression operations are *fast enough*; there is rarely any point in optimizing an application past the point where it does what it needs to do fast enough that speed is not a problem. As Knuth famously remarks, "We should forget about small efficiencies, say about 97% of the time: Premature optimization is the root of all evil." ("Computer Programming as an Art" in *Literate Programming*, CSLI Lecture Notes Number 27, Stanford University Center for the Study of Languages and Information, 1992).

In case regular expression operations prove to be a genuinely problematic performance bottleneck in an application, there are four steps you should take in speeding things up. Try these in order:

1. Think about whether there is a way to simplify the regular expressions involved. Most especially, is it possible to reduce the likelihood of backtracking during pattern matching? You should always test your beliefs about such simplification, however; performance characteristics rarely turn out exactly as you expect.

2. Consider whether regular expressions are *really* needed for the problem at hand. With surprising frequency, faster and simpler operations in the *string* module (or, occasionally, in other modules) do what needs to be done. Actually, this step can often come earlier than the first one.

3. Write the search or transformation in a faster and lower-level engine, especially *mx.TextTools*. Low-level modules will inevitably involve more work and considerably more intense thinking about the problem. But order-of-magnitude speed gains are often possible for the work.

4. Code the application (or the relevant parts of it) in a different programming language. If speed is the absolutely first consideration in an application, Assembly, C, or C++ are going to win. Tools like swig—while outside the scope of this book—can help you create custom extension modules to perform bottleneck operations. There is a chance also that if the problem *really must* be solved with regular expressions that Perl's engine will be faster (but not always, by any means).

3.3.2   Simple Pattern Matching

fnmatch ◇ Glob-style pattern matching

The real purpose of the *fnmatch* module is to match filenames against a pattern. Most typically, *fnmatch* is used indirectly through the *glob* module, where the latter returns lists of matching files (for example to process each matching file). But *fnmatch* does not itself know anything about filesystems, it simply provides a way of checking patterns against strings. The pattern language used by *fnmatch* is much simpler than that used by *re*, which can be either good or bad, depending on your needs. As a plus, most everyone who has used a DOS, Windows, OS/2, or Unix command line is already familiar with the *fnmatch* pattern language, which is simply shell-style expansions.

Four subpatterns are available in *fnmatch* patterns. In contrast to *re* patterns, there is no grouping and no quantifiers. Obviously, the discernment of matches is much less with *fnmatch* than with *re*. The subpatterns are as follows:

> Glob-style subpatterns

```
*      Match everything that follows (non-greedy).
?      Match any single character.
[set]  Match one character from a set.  A set generally
       follows the same rules as a regular expression
       character class.  It may include zero or more ranges
       and zero or more enumerated characters.
[!set] Match any one character that is not in the set.
```

A pattern is simply the concatenation of one or more subpatterns.

FUNCTIONS

fnmatch.fnmatch(s, pat)

Test whether the pattern pat matches the string s. On case-insensitive filesystems, the match is case-insensitive. A cross-platform script should avoid *fnmatch.fnmatch()* except when used to match actual filenames.

```
>>> from fnmatch import fnmatch
>>> fnmatch('this', '[T]?i*')  # On Unix-like system
0

>>> fnmatch('this', '[T]?i*')  # On Win-like system
1
```

SEE ALSO: fnmatch.fnmatchcase() *233*;

fnmatch.fnmatchcase(s, pat)

Test whether the pattern pat matches the string s. The match is case-sensitive regardless of platform.

```
>>> from fnmatch import fnmatchcase
>>> fnmatchcase('this', '[T]?i*')
0
>>> from string import upper
>>> fnmatchcase(upper('this'), upper('[T]?i*'))
1
```

SEE ALSO: fnmatch.fnmatch() *233*;

fnmatch.filter(lst, pat)

Return a new list containing those elements of lst that match pat. The matching behaves like *fnmatch.fnmatch()* rather than like *fnmatch.fnmatchcase()*, so the results can be OS-dependent. The example below shows a (slower) means of performing a case-sensitive match on all platforms.

```
>>> import fnmatch          # Assuming Unix-like system
>>> fnmatch.filter(['This','that','other','thing'], '[Tt]?i*')
['This', 'thing']
>>> fnmatch.filter(['This','that','other','thing'], '[a-z]*')
['that', 'other', 'thing']
>>> from fnmatch import fnmatchcase   # For all platforms
>>> mymatch = lambda s: fnmatchcase(s, '[a-z]*')
>>> filter(mymatch, ['This','that','other','thing'])
['that', 'other', 'thing']
```

For an explanation of the built-in function *filter()* function, see Appendix A.

SEE ALSO: fnmatch.fnmatch() *233*; fnmatch.fnmatchcase() *233*;

SEE ALSO: glob *64*; re *236*;

3.3.3   Regular Expression Modules

pre ◇ Pre-sre module

pcre ◇ Underlying C module for pre

The Python-written module *pre*, and the C-written *pcre* module that implements the actual regular expression engine, are the regular expression modules for Python 1.5–1.6. For complete backwards compatibility, they continue to be included in Python 2.0+. Importing the symbol space of *pre* is intended to be equivalent to importing *re* (i.e., *sre* at one level of indirection) in Python 2.0+, with the exception of the handling of Unicode strings, which *pre* cannot do. That is, the lines below are almost equivalent, other than potential performance differences in specific operations:

```
>>> import pre as re
>>> import re
```

However, there is very rarely any reason to use *pre* in Python 2.0+. Anyone deciding to import *pre* should know far more about the internals of regular expression engines than is contained in this book. Of course, prior to Python 2.0, importing *re* simply imports *pcre* itself (and the Python wrappers later renamed *pre*).

SEE ALSO: re *236*;

---

reconvert ◇ Convert [regex] patterns to [re] patterns

This module exists solely for conversion of old regular expressions from scripts written for pre-1.5 versions of Python, or possibly from regular expression patterns used with tools such as sed, awk, or grep. Conversions are not guaranteed to be entirely correct, but *reconvert* provides a starting point for a code update.

FUNCTIONS

reconvert.convert(s)

Return as a string the modern *re*-style pattern that corresponds to the *regex*-style pattern passed in argument s. For example:

```
>>> import reconvert
>>> reconvert.convert(r'\<\(cat\|dog\)\>')
'\\b(cat|dog)\\b'
>>> import re
>>> re.findall(r'\b(cat|dog)\b', "The dog chased a bobcat")
['dog']
```

SEE ALSO: regex *235*;

---

regex ◇ Deprecated regular expression module

The *regex* module is distributed with recent Python versions only to ensure strict backwards compatibility of scripts. Starting with Python 2.1, importing *regex* will produce a DeprecationWarning:

```
% python -c "import regex"
-c:1: DeprecationWarning:  the regex module is deprecated;
please use the re module
```

For all users of Python 1.5+, *regex* should not be used in new code, and efforts should be made to convert its usage to *re* calls.

SEE ALSO: reconvert *235*;

---

sre ◇ Secret Labs Regular Expression Engine

Support for regular expressions in Python 2.0+ is provided by the module *sre*. The module *re* simply wraps *sre* in order to have a backwards- and forwards-compatible name. There will almost never be any reason to import *sre* itself; some later version of Python might eventually deprecate *sre* also. As with *pre*, anyone deciding to import *sre* itself should know far more about the internals of regular expression engines than is contained in this book.

SEE ALSO: re *236*;

---

re ◇ Regular expression operations

PATTERN SUMMARY

Figure 3.1 lists regular expression patterns; following that are explanations of each pattern. For more detailed explanation of patterns in action, consult the tutorial and/or problems contained in this chapter. The utility function `re_show()` defined in the tutorial is used in some descriptions.

ATOMIC OPERATORS

Plain symbol

Any character not described below as having a special meaning simply represents itself in the target string. An "A" matches exactly one "A" in the target, for example.

Escape: "\"

The escape character starts a special sequence. The special characters listed in this pattern summary must be escaped to be treated as literal character values (including the escape character itself). The letters "A", "b", "B", "d", "D", "s", "S", "w", "W", and "Z" specify special patterns if preceded by an escape. The escape character may also introduce a backreference group with up to two decimal digits. The escape is ignored if it precedes a character with no special escaped meaning.

Since Python string escapes overlap regular expression escapes, it is usually better to use raw strings for regular expressions that potentially include escapes. For example:

```
>>> from re_show import re_show
>>> re_show(r'\$ \\ \^', r'\$ \\ \^ $ \ ^')
\$ \\ \^ {$ \ ^}

>>> re_show(r'\d \w', '7 a 6 # ! C')
{7 a} 6 # ! C
```

Summary of Regular Expression Patterns

Atoms		Quantifiers	
Plain symbol:	. . .	Universal quantifier:	*
Escape:	\	Non-greedy universal quantifier:	*?
Grouping operators:	( )	Existential quantifier:	+
Backreference:	\#, \##	Non-greedy existential quantifier:	+?
Character class:	[ ]	Potentiality quantifier:	?
Digit character class:	\d	Non-greedy potentiality quantifier:	??
Non-digit character class:	\D	Exact numeric quantifier:	{num}
Alphanumeric char class:	\w	Lower-bound quantifier:	{min, }
Non-alphanum char class:	\W	Bounded numeric quantifier:	{min, max}
Whitespace char class:	\s	Non-greedy bounded quantifier:	{min, max}?
Non-whitespace char class:	\S		
Wildcard character:	.	**Group-Like Patterns**	
Beginning of line:	^	Pattern modifiers:	(?Limsux)
Beginning of string:	\A	Comments:	(?#...)
End of line:	$	Non-backreferenced atom:	(?:...)
End of string:	\Z	Positive Lookahead assertion:	(?=...)
Word boundary:	\b	Negative Lookahead assertion:	(?!...)
Non-word boundary:	\B	Positive Lookbehind assertion:	(?<=...)
Alternation operator:	|	Negative Lookbehind assertion:	(?<!...)
		Named group identifier:	(?P<name>)
Constants		Named group backreference:	(?P=name)
re.IGNORECASE	re.I		
re.LOCALE	re.L		
re.MULTILINE	re.M		
re.DOTALL	re.S		
re.UNICODE	re.U		
re.VERBOSE	re.X		

Figure 3.1: Regular expression patterns

Grouping operators: "(", ")"

Parentheses surrounding any pattern turn that pattern into a group (possibly within a larger pattern). Quantifiers refer to the immediately preceding group, if one is defined, otherwise to the preceding character or character class. For example:

```
>>> from re_show import re_show
>>> re_show(r'abc+', 'abcabc abc abccc')
{abc}{abc} {abc} {abccc}

>>> re_show(r'(abc)+', 'abcabc abc abccc')
```

{abcabc} {abc} {abc}cc

Backreference: "\d", "\dd"

A backreference consists of the escape character followed by one or two decimal digits. The first digit in a back reference may not be a zero. A backreference refers to the same string matched by an earlier group, where the enumeration of previous groups starts with 1. For example:

```
>>> from re_show import re_show
>>> re_show(r'([abc])(.*)\1', 'all the boys are coy')
{all the boys a}re coy
```

An attempt to reference an undefined group will raise an error.

Character classes: "[", "]"

Specify a set of characters that may occur at a position. The list of allowable characters may be enumerated with no delimiter. Predefined character classes, such as "\d", are allowed within custom character classes. A range of characters may be indicated with a dash. Multiple ranges are allowed within a class. If a dash is meant to be included in the character class itself, it should occur as the first listed character. A character class may be complemented by beginning it with a caret ("^"). If a caret is meant to be included in the character class itself, it should occur in a noninitial position. Most special characters, such as "$", ".", and "(", lose their special meaning inside a character class and are merely treated as class members. The characters "]", "\", and "-" should be escaped with a backslash, however. For example:

```
>>> from re_show import re_show
>>> re_show(r'[a-fA-F]', 'A X c G')
{A} X {c} G
```

```
>>> re_show(r'[-A$BC\]]', r'A X - \ ] [ $')
{A} X {-} \ {]} [ {$}
```

```
>>> re_show(r'[^A-Fa-f]', r'A X c G')
A{ }{X}{ }c{ }{G}
```

Digit character class: "\d"

The set of decimal digits. Same as "0-9".

Non-digit character class: "\D"

The set of all characters *except* decimal digits. Same as "^0-9".

Alphanumeric character class: "\w"

The set of alphanumeric characters. If re.LOCALE and re.UNICODE modifiers are *not* set, this is the same as [a-zA-Z0-9_]. Otherwise, the set includes any other alphanumeric characters appropriate to the locale or with an indicated Unicode character property of alphanumeric.

Non-alphanumeric character class: "\W"

The set of nonalphanumeric characters. If re.LOCALE and re.UNICODE modifiers are *not* set, this is the same as [^a-zA-Z0-9_]. Otherwise, the set includes any other characters not indicated by the locale or Unicode character properties as alphanumeric.

Whitespace character class: "\s"

The set of whitespace characters. Same as [\t\n\r\f\v].

Non-whitespace character class: "\S"

The set of nonwhitespace characters. Same as [^ \t\n\r\f\v].

Wildcard character: "."

The period matches any single character at a position. If the re.DOTALL modifier is specified, "." will match a newline. Otherwise, it will match anything other than a newline.

Beginning of line: "^"

The caret will match the beginning of the target string. If the re.MULTILINE modifier is specified, "^" will match the beginning of each line within the target string.

Beginning of string: "\A"

The "\A" will match the beginning of the target string. If the re.MULTILINE modifier is *not* specified, "\A" behaves the same as "^". But even if the modifier is used, "\A" will match only the beginning of the entire target.

End of line: "$"

The dollar sign will match the end of the target string. If the re.MULTILINE modifier is specified, "$" will match the end of each line within the target string.

End of string: "\Z"

The "\Z" will match the end of the target string. If the re.MULTILINE modifier is *not* specified, "\Z" behaves the same as "$". But even if the modifier is used, "\Z" will match only the end of the entire target.

Word boundary: "\b"

The "\b" will match the beginning or end of a word (where a word is defined as a sequence of alphanumeric characters according to the current modifiers). Like "^" and "$", "\b" is a zero-width match.

Non-word boundary: "\B"

The "\B" will match any position that is *not* the beginning or end of a word (where a word is defined as a sequence of alphanumeric characters according to the current modifiers). Like "^" and "$", "\B" is a zero-width match.

Alternation operator: "|"

The pipe symbol indicates a choice of multiple atoms in a position. Any of the atoms (including groups) separated by a pipe will match. For example:

```
>>> from re_show import re_show
>>> re_show(r'A|c|G', r'A X c G')
{A} X {c} {G}
```

```
>>> re_show(r'(abc)|(xyz)', 'abc efg xyz lmn')
{abc} efg {xyz} lmn
```

QUANTIFIERS

Universal quantifier: "*"

Match zero or more occurrences of the preceding atom. The "*" quantifier is happy to match an empty string. For example:

```
>>> from re_show import re_show
>>> re_show('a* ', ' a aa aaa aaaa b')
{ }{a }{aa }{aaa }{aaaa }b
```

Non-greedy universal quantifier: "*?"

Match zero or more occurrences of the preceding atom, but try to match as few occurrences as allowable. For example:

```
>>> from re_show import re_show
>>> re_show('<.*>', '<> <tag>Text</tag>')
{<> <tag>Text</tag>}
```

```
>>> re_show('<.*?>', '<> <tag>Text</tag>')
{<>} {<tag>}Text{</tag>}
```

Existential quantifier: "+"

Match one or more occurrences of the preceding atom. A pattern must actually occur in the target string to satisfy the "+" quantifier. For example:

```
>>> from re_show import re_show
>>> re_show('a+ ', ' a aa aaa aaaa b')
 {a }{aa }{aaa }{aaaa }b
```

Non-greedy existential quantifier: "+?"

Match one or more occurrences of the preceding atom, but try to match as few occurrences as allowable. For example

```
>>> from re_show import re_show
>>> re_show('<.+>', '<> <tag>Text</tag>')
{<> <tag>Text</tag>}

>>> re_show('<.+?>', '<> <tag>Text</tag>')
{<> <tag>}Text{</tag>}
```

Potentiality quantifier: "?"

Match zero or one occurrence of the preceding atom. The "?" quantifier is happy to match an empty string. For example:

```
>>> from re_show import re_show
>>> re_show('a? ', ' a aa aaa aaaa b')
{ }{a }a{a }aa{a }aaa{a }b
```

Non-greedy potentiality quantifier: "??"

Match zero or one occurrence of the preceding atom, but match zero if possible. For example:

```
>>> from re_show import re_show
>>> re_show(' a?', ' a aa aaa aaaa b')
{ a}{ a}a{ a}aa{ a}aaa{ }b

>>> re_show(' a??', ' a aa aaa aaaa b')
{ }a{ }aa{ }aaa{ }aaaa{ }b
```

Exact numeric quantifier: "{num}"

Match exactly num occurrences of the preceding atom. For example:

```
>>> from re_show import re_show
>>> re_show('a{3} ', ' a aa aaa aaaa b')
 a aa {aaa }a{aaa }b
```

Lower-bound quantifier: "{min,}"

Match *at least* min occurrences of the preceding atom. For example:

```
>>> from re_show import re_show
>>> re_show('a{3,} ', ' a aa aaa aaaa b')
 a aa {aaa }{aaaa }b
```

Bounded numeric quantifier: "{min,max}"

Match *at least* `min` and *no more than* `max` occurrences of the preceding atom. For example:

```
>>> from re_show import re_show
>>> re_show('a{2,3} ', ' a aa aaa aaaa b')
 a {aa }{aaa }a{aaa }
```

Non-greedy bounded quantifier: "{min,max}?"

Match *at least* `min` and *no more than* `max` occurrences of the preceding atom, but try to match as few occurrences as allowable. Scanning is from the left, so a nonminimal match may be produced in terms of right-side groupings. For example:

```
>>> from re_show import re_show
>>> re_show(' a{2,4}?', ' a aa aaa aaaa b')
 a{ aa}{ aa}a{ aa}aa b
```

```
>>> re_show('a{2,4}? ', ' a aa aaa aaaa b')
 a {aa }{aaa }{aaaa }b
```

GROUP-LIKE PATTERNS

Python regular expressions may contain a number of pseudo-group elements that condition matches in some manner. With the exception of named groups, pseudo-groups are not counted in backreferencing. All pseudo-group patterns have the form "(?...)".

Pattern modifiers: "(?Limsux)"

The pattern modifiers should occur at the very beginning of a regular expression pattern. One or more letters in the set "Limsux" may be included. If pattern modifiers are given, the interpretation of the pattern is changed globally. See the discussion of modifier constants below or the tutorial for details.

Comments: "(?#...)"

Create a comment inside a pattern. The comment is not enumerated in backreferences and has no effect on what is matched. In most cases, use of the "(?x)" modifier allows for more clearly formatted comments than does "(?#...)".

```
>>> from re_show import re_show
>>> re_show(r'The(?#words in caps) Cat', 'The Cat in the Hat')
{The Cat} in the Hat
```

Non-backreferenced atom: "(?:...)"

Match the pattern "...", but do not include the matched string as a backreferencable group. Moreover, methods like *re.match.group()* will not see the pattern inside a non-backreferenced atom.

```
>>> from re_show import re_show
>>> re_show(r'(?:\w+) (\w+).* \1', 'abc xyz xyz abc')
{abc xyz xyz} abc

>>> re_show(r'(\w+) (\w+).* \1', 'abc xyz xyz abc')
{abc xyz xyz abc}
```

Positive Lookahead assertion: "(?=...)"

Match the entire pattern only if the subpattern "..." occurs next. But do not include the target substring matched by "..." as part of the match (however, some other subpattern may claim the same characters, or some of them).

```
>>> from re_show import re_show
>>> re_show(r'\w+ (?=xyz)', 'abc xyz xyz abc')
{abc }{xyz }xyz abc
```

Negative Lookahead assertion: "(?!...)"

Match the entire pattern only if the subpattern "..." does *not* occur next.

```
>>> from re_show import re_show
>>> re_show(r'\w+ (?!xyz)', 'abc xyz xyz abc')
abc xyz {xyz }abc
```

Positive Lookbehind assertion: "(?<=...)"

Match the rest of the entire pattern only if the subpattern "..." occurs immediately prior to the current match point. But do not include the target substring matched by "..." as part of the match (the same characters may or may not be claimed by some prior group(s) in the entire pattern). The pattern "..." must match a fixed number of characters and therefore not contain general quantifiers.

```
>>> from re_show import re_show
>>> re_show(r'\w+(?<=[A-Z]) ', 'Words THAT end in capS X')
Words {THAT }end in {capS }X
```

Negative Lookbehind assertion: "(?<!...)"

Match the rest of the entire pattern only if the subpattern "..." does *not* occur immediately prior to the current match point. The same characters may or may not be claimed by some prior group(s) in the entire pattern. The pattern "..." must match a fixed number of characters and therefore not contain general quantifiers.

```
>>> from re_show import re_show
>>> re_show(r'\w+(?<![A-Z]) ', 'Words THAT end in capS X')
{Words }THAT {end }{in }capS X
```

Named group identifier: "(?P<name>)"

Create a group that can be referred to by the name `name` as well as in enumerated backreferences. The forms below are equivalent.

```
>>> from re_show import re_show
>>> re_show(r'(\w+) (\w+).* \1', 'abc xyz xyz abc')
{abc xyz xyz abc}

>>> re_show(r'(?P<first>\w+) (\w+).* (?P=first)', 'abc xyz xyz abc')
{abc xyz xyz abc}

>>> re_show(r'(?P<first>\w+) (\w+).* \1', 'abc xyz xyz abc')
{abc xyz xyz abc}
```

Named group backreference: "(?P=name)"

Backreference a group by the name `name` rather than by escaped group number. The group name must have been defined earlier by `(?P<name>)`, or an error is raised.

CONSTANTS

A number of constants are defined in the *re* modules that act as modifiers to many *re* functions. These constants are independent bit-values, so that multiple modifiers may be selected by bitwise disjunction of modifiers. For example:

```
>>> import re
>>> c = re.compile('cat|dog', re.IGNORECASE | re.UNICODE)
```

re.I, re.IGNORECASE

Modifier for case-insensitive matching. Lowercase and uppercase letters are interchangeable in patterns modified with this modifier. The prefix `(?i)` may also be used inside the pattern to achieve the same effect.

re.L, re.LOCALE

Modifier for locale-specific matching of \w, \W, \b, and \B. The prefix `(?L)` may also be used inside the pattern to achieve the same effect.

re.M, re.MULTILINE

Modifier to make ^ and $ match the beginning and end, respectively, of *each* line in the target string rather than the beginning and end of the entire target string. The prefix `(?m)` may also be used inside the pattern to achieve the same effect.

re.S, re.DOTALL

Modifier to allow . to match a newline character. Otherwise, . matches every character *except* newline characters. The prefix `(?s)` may also be used inside the pattern to achieve the same effect.

re.U, re.UNICODE

Modifier for Unicode-property matching of \w, \W, \b, and \B. Only relevant for Unicode targets. The prefix (?u) may also be used inside the pattern to achieve the same effect.

re.X, re.VERBOSE

Modifier to allow patterns to contain insignificant whitespace and end-of-line comments. Can significantly improve readability of patterns. The prefix (?x) may also be used inside the pattern to achieve the same effect.

re.engine

The regular expression engine currently in use. Only supported in Python 2.0+, where it normally is set to the string sre. The presence and value of this constant can be checked to make sure which underlying implementation is running, but this check is rarely necessary.

FUNCTIONS

For all *re* functions, where a regular expression pattern pattern is an argument, pattern may be either a compiled regular expression or a string.

re.escape(s)

Return a string with all nonalphanumeric characters escaped. This (slightly scatter-shot) conversion makes an arbitrary string suitable for use in a regular expression pattern (matching all literals in original string).

```
>>> import re
>>> print re.escape("(*@&^$@|")
\(\*\@\&\^\$\@\|
```

re.findall(pattern=..., string=...)

Return a list of all nonoverlapping occurrences of pattern in string. If pattern consists of several groups, return a list of tuples where each tuple contains a match for each group. Length-zero matches are included in the returned list, if they occur.

```
>>> import re
>>> re.findall(r'\b[a-z]+\d-\b', 'abc123 xyz666 lmn-11 def77')
['abc123', 'xyz666', 'def77']
>>> re.findall(r'\b([a-z]+)(\d+)\b', 'abc123 xyz666 lmn-11 def77')
[('abc', '123'), ('xyz', '666'), ('def', '77')]
```

SEE ALSO: re.search() *249*; mx.TextTools.findall() *312*;

re.purge()

Clear the regular expression cache. The *re* module keeps a cache of implicitly compiled regular expression patterns. The number of patterns cached differs between Python versions, with more recent versions generally keeping 100 items in the cache. When the cache space becomes full, it is flushed automatically. You could use *re.purge()* to tune the timing of cache flushes. However, such tuning is approximate at best: Patterns that are used repeatedly are much better off explicitly compiled with *re.compile()* and then used explicitly as named objects.

re.split(pattern=..., string=... [,maxsplit=0])

Return a list of substrings of the second argument `string`. The first argument `pattern` is a regular expression that delimits the substrings. If `pattern` contains groups, the groups are included in the resultant list. Otherwise, those substrings that match `pattern` are dropped, and only the substrings between occurrences of `pattern` are returned.

If the third argument `maxsplit` is specified as a positive integer, no more than `maxsplit` items are parsed into the list, with any leftover contained in the final list element.

```
>>> import re
>>> re.split(r'\s+', 'The Cat in the Hat')
['The', 'Cat', 'in', 'the', 'Hat']
>>> re.split(r'\s+', 'The Cat in the Hat', maxsplit=3)
['The', 'Cat', 'in', 'the Hat']
>>> re.split(r'(\s+)', 'The Cat in the Hat')
['The', ' ', 'Cat', ' ', 'in', ' ', 'the', ' ', 'Hat']
>>> re.split(r'(a)(t)', 'The Cat in the Hat')
['The C', 'a', 't', ' in the H', 'a', 't', '']
>>> re.split(r'a(t)', 'The Cat in the Hat')
['The C', 't', ' in the H', 't', '']
```

See Also: string.split() *142*;

re.sub(pattern=..., repl=..., string=... [,count=0])

Return the string produced by replacing every nonoverlapping occurrence of the first argument `pattern` with the second argument `repl` in the third argument `string`. If the fourth argument `count` is specified, no more than `count` replacements will be made.

The second argument `repl` is most often a regular expression pattern as a string. Backreferences to groups matched by `pattern` may be referred to by enumerated backreferences using the usual escaped numbers. If backreferences in `pattern` are named, they may also be referred to using the form \g<name> (where `name` is the name given the group in `pat`). As well, enumerated backreferences may optionally be referred to using the form \g<num>, where num is an integer between 1 and 99. Some examples:

```
>>> import re
>>> s = 'abc123 xyz666 lmn-11 def77'
>>> re.sub(r'\b([a-z]+)(\d+)', r'\2\1 :', s)
'123abc : 666xyz : lmn-11 77def :'
>>> re.sub(r'\b(?P<lets>[a-z]+)(?P<nums>\d+)', r'\g<nums>\g<1> :', s)
'123abc : 666xyz : lmn-11 77def :'
>>> re.sub('A', 'X', 'AAAAAAAAAA', count=4)
'XXXXAAAAAA'
```

A variant manner of calling *re.sub()* uses a function object as the second argument repl. Such a callback function should take a MatchObject as an argument and return a string. The repl function is invoked for each match of **pattern**, and the string it returns is substituted in the result for whatever **pattern** matched. For example:

```
>>> import re
>>> sub_cb = lambda pat: '('+`len(pat.group())`+')'+pat.group()
>>> re.sub(r'\w+', sub_cb, 'The length of each word')
'(3)The (6)length (2)of (4)each (4)word'
```

Of course, if **repl** is a function object, you can take advantage of side effects rather than (or instead of) simply returning modified strings. For example:

```
>>> import re
>>> def side_effects(match):
...     # Arbitrarily complicated behavior could go here...
...     print len(match.group()), match.group()
...     return match.group()  # unchanged match
...
>>> new = re.sub(r'\w+', side_effects, 'The length of each word')
3 The
6 length
2 of
4 each
4 word
>>> new
'The length of each word'
```

Variants on callbacks with side effects could be turned into complete string-driven programs (in principle, a parser and execution environment for a whole programming language could be contained in the callback function, for example).

SEE ALSO: string.replace() *139*;

re.subn(pattern=..., repl=..., string=...[,count=0])

Identical to *re.sub()*, except return a 2-tuple with the new string and the number of replacements made.

```
>>> import re
>>> s = 'abc123 xyz666 lmn-11 def77'
>>> re.subn(r'\b([a-z]+)(\d+)', r'\2\1 :', s)
('123abc : 666xyz : lmn-11 77def :', 3)
```

SEE ALSO: re.sub() *246*;

CLASS FACTORIES

As with some other Python modules, primarily ones written in C, *re* does not contain true classes that can be specialized. Instead, *re* has several factory-functions that return instance objects. The practical difference is small for most users, who will simply use the methods and attributes of returned instances in the same manner as those produced by true classes.

re.compile(pattern=...[,flags=...])

Return a PatternObject based on pattern string `pattern`. If the second argument `flags` is specified, use the modifiers indicated by `flags`. A PatternObject is interchangeable with a pattern string as an argument to *re* functions. However, a pattern that will be used frequently within an application should be compiled in advance to assure that it will not need recompilation during execution. Moreover, a compiled PatternObject has a number of methods and attributes that achieve effects equivalent to *re* functions, but which are somewhat more readable in some contexts. For example:

```
>>> import re
    >>> word = re.compile('[A-Za-z]+')
>>> word.findall('The Cat in the Hat')
['The', 'Cat', 'in', 'the', 'Hat']
>>> re.findall(word, 'The Cat in the Hat')
['The', 'Cat', 'in', 'the', 'Hat']
```

re.match(pattern=..., string=...[,flags=...])

Return a MatchObject if an initial substring of the second argument `string` matches the pattern in the first argument `pattern`. Otherwise return None. A MatchObject, if returned, has a variety of methods and attributes to manipulate the matched pattern—but notably a MatchObject is *not* itself a string.

Since *re.match()* only matches initial substrings, *re.search()* is more general. *re.search()* can be constrained to itself match only initial substrings by prepending "\A" to the pattern matched.

SEE ALSO: re.search() *249*; re.compile.match() *259*;

re.search(pattern=..., string=... [,flags=...])

Return a MatchObject corresponding to the leftmost substring of the second argument `string` that matches the pattern in the first argument `pattern`. If no match is possible, return None. A matched string can be of zero length if the pattern allows that (usually not what is actually desired). A MatchObject, if returned, has a variety of methods and attributes to manipulate the matched pattern—but notably a MatchObject is *not* itself a string.

SEE ALSO: re.match() *248*; re.compile.search() *250*;

METHODS AND ATTRIBUTES

re.compile.findall(s)

Return a list of nonoverlapping occurrences of the PatternObject in s. Same as `re.findall()` called with the PatternObject.

SEE ALSO *re.findall()*

re.compile.flags

The numeric sum of the flags passed to *re.compile()* in creating the PatternObject. No formal guarantee is given by Python as to the values assigned to modifier flags, however. For example:

```
>>> import re
>>> re.I,re.L,re.M,re.S,re.X
(2, 4, 8, 16, 64)
>>> c = re.compile('a', re.I | re.M)
>>> c.flags
10
```

re.compile.groupindex

A dictionary mapping group names to group numbers. If no named groups are used in the pattern, the dictionary is empty. For example:

```
>>> import re
>>> c = re.compile(r'(\d+)(\[A-Z]+)([a-z]+)')
>>> c.groupindex
{}
>>> c=re.compile(r'(?P<nums>\d+)(?P<caps>\[A-Z]+)(?P<lwrs>[a-z]+)')
>>> c.groupindex
{'nums': 1, 'caps': 2, 'lwrs': 3}
```

re.compile.match(s [,start [,end]])

Return a MatchObject if an initial substring of the first argument s matches the PatternObject. Otherwise, return None. A MatchObject, if returned, has a variety of methods and attributes to manipulate the matched pattern—but notably a MatchObject is *not* itself a string.

In contrast to the similar function *re.match()*, this method accepts optional second and third arguments start and end that limit the match to substring within s. In most respects specifying start and end is similar to taking a slice of s as the first argument. But when start and end are used, "^" will only match the true start of s. For example:

```
>>> import re
>>> s = 'abcdefg'
>>> c = re.compile('^b')
>>> print c.match(s, 1)
None
>>> c.match(s[1:])
<SRE_Match object at 0x10c440>
>>> c = re.compile('.*f$')
>>> c.match(s[:-1])
<SRE_Match object at 0x116d80>
>>> c.match(s,1,6)
<SRE_Match object at 0x10c440>
```

SEE ALSO: re.match() *248*; re.compile.search() *250*;

re.compile.pattern

The pattern string underlying the compiled MatchObject.

```
>>> import re
>>> c = re.compile('^abc$')
>>> c.pattern
'^abc$'
```

re.compile.search(s [,start [,end]])

Return a MatchObject corresponding to the leftmost substring of the first argument string that matches the PatternObject. If no match is possible, return None. A matched string can be of zero length if the pattern allows that (usually not what is actually desired). A MatchObject, if returned, has a variety of methods and attributes to manipulate the matched pattern—but notably a MatchObject is *not* itself a string.

In contrast to the similar function *re.search()*, this method accepts optional second and third arguments start and end that limit the match to a substring within s. In most respects specifying start and end is similar to taking a slice of s as the first argument. But when start and end are used, "^" will only match the true start of s. For example:

```
>>> import re
>>> s = 'abcdefg'
>>> c = re.compile('^b')
>>> c = re.compile('^b')
>>> print c.search(s, 1),c.search(s[1:])
None <SRE_Match object at 0x117980>
>>> c = re.compile('.*f$')
>>> print c.search(s[:-1]),c.search(s,1,6)
<SRE_Match object at 0x51C40> <SRE_Match object at 0x51040>
```

SEE ALSO: re.search() *249*; re.compile.match() *250*;

re.compile.split(s [,maxsplit])

Return a list of substrings of the first argument s. If thePatternObject contains groups, the groups are included in the resultant list. Otherwise, those substrings that match PatternObject are dropped, and only the substrings between occurrences of pattern are returned.

If the second argument maxsplit is specified as a positive integer, no more than maxsplit items are parsed into the list, with any leftover contained in the final list element.

re.compile.split() is identical in behavior to *re.split()*, simply spelled slightly differently. See the documentation of the latter for examples of usage.

SEE ALSO: re.split() *246*;

re.compile.sub(repl, s [,count=0])

Return the string produced by replacing every nonoverlapping occurrence of the PatternObject with the first argument repl in the second argument string. If the third argument count is specified, no more than count replacements will be made.

The first argument repl may be either a regular expression pattern as a string or a callback function. Backreferences may be named or enumerated.

re.compile.sub() is identical in behavior to *re.sub()*, simply spelled slightly differently. See the documentation of the latter for a number of examples of usage.

SEE ALSO: re.sub() *246*; re.compile.subn() *252*;

re.compile.subn()

Identical to *re.compile.sub()*, except return a 2-tuple with the new string and the number of replacements made.

re.compile.subn() is identical in behavior to *re.subn()*, simply spelled slightly differently. See the documentation of the latter for examples of usage.

SEE ALSO: re.subn() *248*; re.compile.sub() *251*;

Note: The arguments to each "MatchObject" method are listed on the *re.match()* line, with ellipses given on the *re.search()* line. All arguments are identical since *re.match()* and *re.search()* return the very same type of object.

re.match.end([group])
re.search.end([group])

The index of the end of the target substring matched by the MatchObject. If the argument **group** is specified, return the ending index of that specific enumerated group. Otherwise, return the ending index of group 0 (i.e., the whole match). If **group** exists but is the part of an alternation operator that is not used in the current match, return -1. If *re.search.end()* returns the same non-negative value as *re.search.start()*, then **group** is a zero-width substring.

```
>>> import re
>>> m = re.search('(\w+)((\d*)| )(\w+)','The Cat in the Hat')
>>> m.groups()
('The', ' ', None, 'Cat')
>>> m.end(0), m.end(1), m.end(2), m.end(3), m.end(4)
(7, 3, 4, -1, 7)
```

re.match.endpos, re.search.endpos

The end position of the search. If *re.compile.search()* specified an **end** argument, this is the value, otherwise it is the length of the target string. If *re.search()* or *re.match()* are used for the search, the value is always the length of the target string.

SEE ALSO: re.compile.search() *250*; re.search() *249*; re.match() *248*;

re.match.expand(template)
re.search.expand(template)

Expand backreferences and escapes in the argument **template** based on the patterns matched by the MatchObject. The expansion rules are the same as for the **repl** argument to *re.sub()*. Any nonescaped characters may also be included as part of the resultant string. For example:

```
>>> import re
>>> m = re.search('(\w+) (\w+)','The Cat in the Hat')
>>> m.expand(r'\g<2> : \1')
'Cat : The'
```

re.match.group([group [,...]])
re.search.group([group [,...]])

Return a group or groups from the MatchObject. If no arguments are specified, return the entire matched substring. If one argument group is specified, return the corresponding substring of the target string. If multiple arguments group1, group2, ... are specified, return a tuple of corresponding substrings of the target.

```
>>> import re
>>> m = re.search(r'(\w+)(/)(\d+)','abc/123')
>>> m.group()
'abc/123'
>>> m.group(1)
'abc'
>>> m.group(1,3)
('abc', '123')
```

SEE ALSO: re.search.groups() *253*; re.search.groupdict() *253*;

re.match.groupdict([defval])
re.search.groupdict([defval])

Return a dictionary whose keys are the named groups in the pattern used for the match. Enumerated but unnamed groups are not included in the returned dictionary. The values of the dictionary are the substrings matched by each group in the MatchObject. If a named group is part of an alternation operator that is not used in the current match, the value corresponding to that key is None, or defval if an argument is specified.

```
>>> import re
>>> m = re.search(r'(?P<one>\w+)((?P<tab>\t)|( ))(?P<two>\d+)','abc 123')
>>> m.groupdict()
{'one': 'abc', 'tab': None, 'two': '123'}
>>> m.groupdict('---')
{'one': 'abc', 'tab': '---', 'two': '123'}
```

SEE ALSO: re.search.groups() *253*;

re.match.groups([defval])
re.search.groups([defval])

Return a tuple of the substrings matched by groups in the MatchObject. If a group is part of an alternation operator that is not used in the current match, the tuple element at that index is None, or defval if an argument is specified.

```
>>> import re
>>> m = re.search(r'(\w+)((\t)|(/))(\d+)','abc/123')
>>> m.groups()
('abc', '/', None, '/', '123')
>>> m.groups('---')
('abc', '/', '---', '/', '123')
```

SEE ALSO: re.search.group() *253*; re.search.groupdict() *253*;

re.match.lastgroup, re.search.lastgroup

The name of the last matching group, or None if the last group is not named or if no groups compose the match.

re.match.lastindex, re.search.lastindex

The index of the last matching group, or None if no groups compose the match.

re.match.pos, re.search.pos

The start position of the search. If *re.compile.search()* specified a start argument, this is the value, otherwise it is 0. If *re.search()* or *re.match()* are used for the search, the value is always 0.

SEE ALSO: re.compile.search() *250*; re.search() *249*; re.match() *248*;

re.match.re, re.search.re

The PatternObject used to produce the match. The actual regular expression pattern string must be retrieved from the PatternObject's `pattern` method:

```
>>> import re
>>> m = re.search('a','The Cat in the Hat')
>>> m.re.pattern
'a'
```

re.match.span([group])
re.search.span([group])

Return the tuple composed of the return values of `re.search.start(group)` and `re.search.end(group)`. If the argument `group` is not specified, it defaults to 0.

```
>>> import re
>>> m = re.search('(\w+)((\d*)| )(\w+)','The Cat in the Hat')
>>> m.groups()
('The', ' ', None, 'Cat')
>>> m.span(0), m.span(1), m.span(2), m.span(3), m.span(4)
((0, 7), (0, 3), (3, 4), (-1, -1), (4, 7))
```

re.match.start([group])
re.search.start([group])

The index of the end of the target substring matched by the MatchObject. If the argument `group` is specified, return the ending index of that specific enumerated group. Otherwise, return the ending index of group 0 (i.e., the whole match). If `group` exists but is the part of an alternation operator that is not used in the current match, return -1. If `re.search.end()` returns the same non-negative value as `re.search.start()`, then group is a zero-width substring.

```
>>> import re
>>> m = re.search('(\w+)((\d*)| )(\w+)','The Cat in the Hat')
>>> m.groups()
('The', ' ', None, 'Cat')
>>> m.start(0), m.start(1), m.start(2), m.start(3), m.start(4)
(0, 0, 3, -1, 4)
```

re.match.string, re.search.string

The target string in which the match occurs.

```
>>> import re
>>> m = re.search('a','The Cat in the Hat')
>>> m.string
'The Cat in the Hat'
```

EXCEPTIONS

re.error

Exception raised when an invalid regular expression string is passed to a function that would produce a compiled regular expression (including implicitly).

Chapter 4

PARSERS AND STATE MACHINES

All the techniques presented in the prior chapters of this book have something in common, but something that is easy to overlook. In a sense, every basic string and regular expression operation treats strings as *homogeneous*. Put another way: String and regex techniques operate on *flat* texts. While said techniques are largely in keeping with the "Zen of Python" maxim that "Flat is better than nested," sometimes the maxim (and homogeneous operations) cannot solve a problem. Sometimes the data in a text has a deeper *structure* than the linear sequence of bytes that make up strings.

It is not entirely true that the prior chapters have eschewed data structures. From time to time, the examples presented broke flat texts into lists of lines, or of fields, or of segments matched by patterns. But the structures used have been quite simple and quite regular. Perhaps a text was treated as a list of substrings, with each substring manipulated in some manner—or maybe even a list of lists of such substrings, or a list of tuples of data fields. But overall, the data structures have had limited (and mostly fixed) nesting depth and have consisted of sequences of items that are themselves treated similarly. What this chapter introduces is the notion of thinking about texts as *trees* of nodes, or even still more generally as graphs.

Before jumping too far into the world of nonflat texts, I should repeat a warning this book has issued from time to time. If you do not *need* to use the techniques in this chapter, you are better off sticking with the simpler and more maintainable techniques discussed in the prior chapters. Solving too general a problem too soon is a pitfall for application development—it is almost always better to do less than to do more. Full-scale parsers and state machines fall to the "more" side of such a choice. As we have seen already, the class of problems you can solve using regular expressions—or even only string operations—is quite broad.

There is another warning that can be mentioned at this point. This book does not attempt to explain parsing theory or the design of parseable languages. There are a lot of intricacies to these matters, about which a reader can consult a specialized text like the so-called "Dragon Book"—Aho. Sethi, and Ullman's *Compilers: Principle, Techniques and Tools* (Addison-Wesley, 1986; ISBN: 0201100886)—or Levine, Mason, and

Brown's *Lex & Yacc* (Second Edition, O'Reilly, 1992; ISBN: 1-56592-000-7). When
Extended Backus-Naur Form (EBNF) grammars or other parsing descriptions are discussed below, it is in a general fashion that does not delve into algorithmic resolution
of ambiguities or big-O efficiencies (at least not in much detail). In practice, everyday
Python programmers who are processing texts—but who are not designing new programming languages—need not worry about those parsing subtleties omitted from this
book.

4.1   An Introduction to Parsers

4.1.1   When Data Becomes Deep and Texts Become Stateful

Regular expressions can match quite complicated patterns, but they fall short when
it comes to matching arbitrarily nested subpatterns. Such nested subpatterns occur
quite often in programming languages and textual markup languages (and other places
sometimes). For example, in HTML documents, you can find lists or tables nested inside
each other. For that matter, character-level markup is also allowed to nest arbitrarily—
the following defines a valid HTML fragment:

```
>>> s = '''<p>Plain text, <i>italicized phrase,
        <i>italicized subphrase</i>, <b>bold
        subphrase</b></i>, <i>other italic
        phrase</i></p>'''
```

The problem with this fragment is that most any regular expression will match either
less or more than a desired `<i>` element body. For example:

```
>>> ital = r'''(?sx)<i>.+</i>'''
>>> for phrs in re.findall(ital, s):
...     print phrs, '\n-----'
...
<i>italicized phrase,
    <i>italicized subphrase</i>, <b>bold
    subphrase</b></i>, <i>other italic
    phrase</i>
-----
>>> ital2 = r'''(?sx)<i>.+?</i>'''
>>> for phrs in re.findall(ital2, s):
...     print phrs, '\n-----'
...
<i>italicized phrase,
    <i>italicized subphrase</i>
-----
<i>other italic
    phrase</i>
-----
```

What is missing in the proposed regular expressions is a concept of *state*. If you imagine reading through a string character-by-character (which a regular expression match must do within the underlying regex engine), it would be useful to keep track of "How many layers of italics tags am I in?" With such a count of nesting depth, it would be possible to figure out which opening tag `<i>` a given closing tag `</i>` was meant to match. But regular expressions are not stateful in the right way to do this.

You encounter a similar nesting in most programming languages. For example, suppose we have a hypothetical (somewhat BASIC-like) language with an IF/THEN/END structure. To simplify, suppose that every condition is spelled to match the regex `cond\d+`, and every action matches `act\d+`. But the wrinkle is that IF/THEN/END structures can nest within each other also. So for example, let us define the following three top-level structures:

```
>>> s = '''
IF cond1 THEN act1 END
-----
IF cond2 THEN
   IF cond3 THEN act3 END
END
-----
IF cond4 THEN
   act4
END
'''
```

As with the markup example, you might first try to identify the three structures using a regular expression like:

```
>>> pat = r'''(?sx)
IF \s+
cond\d+ \s+
THEN \s+
act\d+ \s+
END'''
>>> for stmt in re.findall(pat, s):
...     print stmt, '\n-----'
...
IF cond1 THEN act1 END
-----
IF cond3 THEN act3 END
-----
IF cond4 THEN
   act4
END
-----
```

This indeed finds three structures, but the wrong three. The second top-level structure should be the compound statement that used `cond2`, not its child using `cond3`. It is not too difficult to allow a nested IF/THEN/END structure to optionally substitute for a simple action; for example:

```
>>> pat2 = '''(?sx)(
IF \s+
cond\d+ \s+
THEN \s+
(   (IF \s+ cond\d+ \s+ THEN \s+ act\d+ \s+ END)
 | (act\d+)
) \s+
END
)'''
>>> for stmt in re.findall(pat2, s):
...        print stmt[0], '\n-----'
...
IF cond1 THEN act1 END
-----
IF cond2 THEN
   IF cond3 THEN act3 END
END
-----
IF cond4 THEN
   act4
END
-----
```

By manually nesting a "first order" IF/THEN/END structure as an alternative to a simple action, we can indeed match the example in the desired fashion. But we have assumed that nesting of IF/THEN/END structures goes only one level deep. What if a "second order" structure is nested inside a "third order" structure—and so on, ad infinitum? What we would like is a means of describing arbitrarily nested structures in a text, in a manner similar to, but more general than, what regular expressions can describe.

4.1.2   What Is a Grammar?

In order to parse nested structures in a text, you usually use something called a "grammar." A grammar is a specification of a set of "nodes" (also called "productions") arranged into a strictly hierarchical "tree" data structure. A node can have a name—and perhaps some other properties—and it can also have an ordered collection of child nodes. When a document is parsed under a grammar, no resultant node can ever be a descendent of itself; this is another way of saying that a grammar produces a tree rather than a graph.

In many actual implementations, such as the famous C-based tools `lex` and `yacc`, a grammar is expressed at two layers. At the first layer, a "lexer" (or "tokenizer") produces a stream of "tokens" for a "parser" to operate on. Such tokens are frequently what you might think of as words or fields, but in principle they can split the text differently than does our normal idea of a "word." In any case tokens are nonoverlapping subsequences of the original text. Depending on the specific tool and specification used, some subsequences may be dropped from the token stream. A "zero-case" lexer is one that simply treats the actual input bytes as the tokens a parser operates on (some modules discussed do this, without losing generality).

The second layer of a grammar is the actual parser. A parser reads a stream or sequence of tokens and generates a "parse tree" out of it. Or rather, a tree is generated under the assumption that the underlying input text is "well-formed" according to the grammar—that is, there is a way to consume the tokens within the grammar specification. With most parser tools, a grammar is specified using a variant on EBNF.

An EBNF grammar consists of a set of rule declarations, where each rule allows similar quantification and alternation as that in regular expressions. Different tools use slightly different syntax for specifying grammars, and different tools also differ in expressivity and available quantifiers. But almost all tools have a fairly similar feel in their grammar specifications. Even the DTDs used in XML dialect specifications (see Chapter 5) have a very similar syntax to other grammar languages—which makes sense since an XML dialect is a particular grammar. A DTD entry looks like:

```
<!ELEMENT body  ((example-column | image-column)?, text-column) >
```

In brief, under the sample DTD, a `<body>` element may contain either one or zero occurrences of a "first thing"—that first thing being *either* an `<example-column>` or an `<image-column>`. Following the optional first component, exactly one `<text-column>` must occur. Of course, we would need to see the rest of the DTD to see what can go in a `<text-column>`, or to see what other element(s) a `<body>` might be contained in. But each such rule is similar in form.

A familiar EBNF grammar to Python programmers is the grammar for Python itself. On many Python installations, this grammar as a single file can be found at a disk location like `[...]/Python22/Doc/ref/grammar.txt`. The online and downloadable *Python Language Reference* excerpts from the grammar at various points. As an example, a floating point number in Python is identified by the specification:

```
  EBNF-style description of Python floating point
```

```
floatnumber    ::= pointfloat | exponentfloat
pointfloat     ::= [intpart] fraction | intpart "."
exponentfloat  ::= (intpart | pointfloat) exponent
intpart        ::= digit+
fraction       ::= "." digit+
exponent       ::= ("e" | "E") ["+" | "-"] digit+
digit          ::= "0"..."9"
```

The Python grammar is given in an EBNF variant that allows considerable expressivity. Most of the tools this chapter discusses are comparatively limited (but are still ultimately capable of expressing just as general grammars, albeit more verbosely). Both literal strings and character ranges may be specified as part of a production. Alternation is expressed with "|". Quantifications with both "+" and "*" are used. These features are very similar to those in regular expression syntax. Additionally, optional groups are indicated with square brackets ("[" and "]"), and mandatory groups with parentheses. Conceptually the former is the same as the regex "?" quantifier.

Where an EBNF grammar goes beyond a regular expression pattern is in its use of named terms as parts of patterns. At first glance, it might appear possible simply to substitute regular expression patterns for named subexpressions. In fact, in the floating point pattern presented, we could simply do this as:

> Regular expression to identify a floating point

```
pat = r'''(?x)
    (                      # exponentfloat
      (                    # intpart or pointfloat
        (                  # pointfloat
         (\d+)?[.]\d+      # optional intpart with fraction
         |
         \d+[.]            # intpart with period
        )                  # end pointfloat
        |
        \d+                # intpart
      )                    # end intpart or pointfloat
      [eE][+-]?\d+         # exponent
    )                      # end exponentfloat
    |
    (                      # pointfloat
      (\d+)?[.]\d+         # optional intpart with fraction
      |
      \d+[.]              # intpart with period
    )                      # end pointfloat
    '''
```

As a regular expression, the description is harder to read, even with the documentation added to a verbose regex. The EBNF grammar is more or less self-documenting. Moreover, some care had to be taken about the order of the regular expression—the **exponentfloat** alternative is required to be listed before the **pointfloat** alternative since the latter can form a subsequence of the latter. But aside from the need for a little tweaking and documentation, the regular expression above is exactly as general—and exactly equivalent—to the Python grammar for a floating point number.

You might wonder, therefore, what the point of a grammar is. It turns out that a floating point number is an unusually simple structure in one very specific respect. A **floatnumber** requires no recursion or self-reference in its definition. Everything that makes up a `floatnumber` is something simpler, and everything that makes up one of those simpler components is itself made up of still simpler ones. You reach a bottom in defining a Python floating point number.

In the general case, structures can recursively contain themselves, either directly or by containing other structures that in turn contain the first structures. It is not even entirely absurd to imagine floating point numbers with such a grammar (whatever language had them would not be Python, however). For example, the famous number a "googol" was defined in 1938 by Edward Kasner as 10 to the 100th power (otherwise called "10 dotrigintillion"). As a Python floating point, you could write this as `1e100`. Kasner also defined a "googolplex" as 10 to the googol power (a number much larger than anyone needs for any practical reason). While you can create a Python expression to name a googolplex—for example, `10**1e100`—it is not difficult to conceive a programming language that allowed the term `1e1e100` as a name for a googolplex. By the way: If you try to actually *compute* a googolplex in Python (or any other programming language), you will be in for disappointment; expect a frozen computer and/or some sort of crash or overflow. The numbers you can express in most language grammars are quite a bit more numerous than those your computer can actually do anything with.

Suppose that you wanted to allow these new "extended" floating point terms in a language. In terms of the grammar, you could just change a line of the EBNF description:

```
exponent ::= ("e" | "E") ["+" | "-"] floatnumber
```

In the regular expression, the change is a problem. A portion of the regular expression identifies the (optional) exponent:

```
[eE][+-]?\d+      # exponent
```

In this case, an exponent is just a series of digit characters. But for "extended" floating point terms, the regular expression would need to substitute the entire `pat` regular expression in place of `\d+`. Unfortunately, this is impossible, since each replacement would still contain the insufficient `\d+` description, which would again require substitution. The sequence of substitutions continues ad infinitum, until the regular expression is infinitely long.

4.1.3   An EBNF Grammar for IF/THEN/END Structures

The IF/THEN/END language structure presented above is a more typical and realistic example of nestable grammatical structures than are our "extended" floating point numbers. In fact, Python—along with almost every other programming language—allows precisely such `if` statements inside other `if` statements. It is worthwhile to look at how we might describe our hypothetical simplified IF/THEN/END structure in the same EBNF variant used for Python's grammar.

Recall first our simplified rules for allowable structures: The keywords are IF, THEN, and END, and they always occur in that order within a completed structure. Keywords in this language are always in all capitals. Any whitespace in a source text is insignificant, except that each term is separated from others by at least some whitespace.

Every condition is spelled to match the regular expression `cond\d+`. Every IF "body" either contains an action that matches the regular expression `act\d+`, *or* it contains another IF/THEN/END structure. In our example, we created three IF/THEN/END structures, one of which contained a nested structure:

```
IF cond1 THEN act1 END
-----
IF cond2 THEN
  IF cond3 THEN act3 END
END
-----
IF cond4 THEN
   act4
END
```

Let us try a grammar:

EBNF grammar for IF/THEN/END structures

```
if_expr    ::= "IF" ws cond ws "THEN" ws action ws "END"
whitechar ::= " " | "\t" | "\n" | "\r" | "\f" | "\v"
ws         ::= whitechar+
digit      ::= "0"..."9"
number     ::= digit+
cond       ::= "cond" number
action     ::= simpleact | if_expr
simpleact ::= "act" number
```

This grammar is fairly easy to follow. It defines a few "convenience" productions like `ws` and `number` that consist of repetitions of simpler productions. `whitechar` is defined as an explicit alternation of individual characters, as is `digit` for a continuous range. Taken to the extreme, every production could actually be included in a much more verbose `if_expr` production—you would just substitute all the right-hand sides of nested productions for the names in the `if_expr` production. But as given, the grammar is much easier to read. The most notable aspect of this grammar is the `action` production, since an `action` can itself recursively contain an `if_expr`.

For this problem, the reader is encouraged to develop grammars for some more robust variations on the very simple IF/THEN/END language we have looked at. As is evident, it is difficult to actually do much with this language by itself, even if its actions and conditions are given semantic meaning outside the structure. Readers can invent their own variations, but a few are proposed below.

4.1.4   Pencil-and-Paper Parsing

To test a grammar at this point, just try to expand each successive character into some production that is allowed at that point in the parent production, using pencil and paper. Think of the text of test cases as a tape: Each symbol either completes a production (if so, write the satisfied production down next to the subsequence), or the symbol is added to the "unsatisfied register." There is one more rule to follow with pencil and paper, however: It is better to satisfy a production with a longer subsequence than a shorter one. If a parent production consists of child productions, the children must be satisfied in the specified order (and in the quantity required). For now, assume only one character of lookahead in trying to follow this rule. For example, suppose you find the following sequence in a test case:

```
"IF   cond1..."
```

Your steps with the pencil would be something like this:

1. Read the "I"—no production is satisfied.

2. Read the "F", unsatisfied becomes "I"-"F". Note that "I"-"F" matches the literal term in `if_expr` (a literal is considered a production). Since the literal term contains no quantifiers or alternates, write down the "IF" production. Unsatisfied becomes empty.

3. Read the space, Unsatisfied becomes simply a space. Space satisfies the production `ws`, but hold off for a character since `ws` contains a quantifier that allows a longer substring to satisfy it.

4. Read the second space, unsatisfied becomes space-space. Space-space satisfies the production `ws`. But again hold off for a character.

5. Read the third space, unsatisfied becomes space-space-space. This again satisfies the production `ws`. But keep holding off for the next character.

6. Read the "c", unsatisfied becomes "space-space-space-c". This does not satisfy any production, so revert to the production in 5. Unsatisfied becomes "c".

7. Et cetera.

If you get to the last character, and everything fits into some production, the test case is valid under the grammar. Otherwise, the test case is nongrammatical. Try a few IF/THEN/END structures that you think are and are not valid against the provided grammar.

4.1.5   Exercise: Some variations on the language

1. Create and test an IF/THEN/END grammar that allows multiple actions to occur between the THEN and the END. For example, the following structures are valid under this variation:

```
IF cond1 THEN act1 act2 act3 END
-----
```

```
IF cond2 THEN
  IF cond3 THEN act3 END
  IF cond4 THEN act4 END
END
-----
IF cond5 THEN IF cond6 THEN act6 act7 END act8 END
```

2. Create and test an IF/THEN/END grammar that allows for arithmetic comparisons of numbers as conditions (as an enhancement of variation 1, if you wish). Specifically, a comparison consists of two numbers with one of "<", ">", or "=" between them. There might or might not be any whitespace between a comparison symbol and surrounding numbers. Use your judgment about what a number consists of (the Python floating point grammar might provide an example, but yours could be simpler).

3. Create and test an IF/THEN/END grammar that includes a loop expression as a valid action. A loop consists of the keyword LOOP, followed by a positive integer, followed by action(s), and terminated by the END keyword. Loops should be considered actions, and therefore ifs and loops can be contained inside one another; for example:

```
IF cond1 THEN
  LOOP 100
    IF cond2 THEN
      act2
    END
  END
END
```

You can make this LOOP-enhanced grammar an enhancement of whichever variant you wish.

4. Create and test an IF/THEN/END grammar that includes an optional ELSE keyword. If an ELSE occurs, it is within an IF body, but ELSE might not occur. An ELSE has its own body that can contain action(s). For example (assuming variant 1):

```
IF cond1 THEN
  act1
  act2
ELSE
  act3
  act4
END
```

5. Create and test an IF/THEN/END grammar that may include *zero* actions inside an IF, ELSE, or LOOP body. For example, the following structures are valid under this variant:

```
IF cond1 THEN
ELSE act2
END
-*-
IF cond1 THEN
   LOOP 100 END
ELSE
END
```

4.2 An Introduction to State Machines

State machines, in a theoretical sense, underlay almost everything computer- and programming-related. But a Python programmer does not necessarily need to consider highly theoretical matters in writing programs. Nonetheless, there is a large class of ordinary programming problems where the best and most natural approach is to explicitly code a state machine as the solution. At heart, a state machine is just a way of thinking about the flow control in an application.

A parser is a specialized type of state machine that analyzes the components and meaning of structured texts. Generally a parser is accompanied by its own high-level description language that describes the states and transitions used by the implied state machine. The state machine is in turn applied to text obeying a "grammar."

In some text processing problems, the processing must be *stateful*: How we handle the next bit of text depends upon what we have done so far with the prior text. In some cases, statefulness can be naturally expressed using a parser grammar, but in other cases the state has more to do with the semantics of the prior text than with its syntax. That is, the issue of what grammatical properties a portion of a text has is generally orthogonal to the issue of what predicates it fulfills. Concretely, we might calculate some arithmetic result on numeric fields, or we might look up a name encountered in a text file in a database, before deciding how to proceed with the text processing. Where the parsing of a text depends on semantic features, a state machine is often a useful approach.

Implementing an elementary and generic state machine in Python is simple to do, and may be used for a variety of purposes. The third-party C-extension module *mx.TextTools*, which is discussed later in this chapter, can also be used to create far faster state machine text processors.

4.2.1 Understanding State Machines

A much too accurate description of a state machine is that it is a directed graph, consisting of a set of nodes and a set of transition functions. Such a machine "runs" by responding to a series of events; each event is in the domain of the transition function of the "current" node, where the range is a subset of the nodes. The function return is a "next" (maybe self-identical) node. A subset of the nodes are end-states; if an end-state is reached, the machine stops.

An abstract mathematical description—like the one above—is of little use for most practical programming problems. Equally picayune is the observation that every program in an imperative programming language like Python is a state machine whose nodes are its source lines (but not really in a declarative—functional or constraint-based—language such as Haskell, Scheme, or Prolog). Furthermore, every regular expression is logically equivalent to a state machine, and every parser implements an abstract state machine. Most programmers write lots of state machines without really thinking about it, but that fact provides little guidance to specific programming techniques.

An informal, heuristic definition is more useful than an abstract one. Often we encounter a program requirement that includes a handful of distinct ways of treating clusters of events. Furthermore, it is sometimes the case that individual events need to be put in a context to determine which type of treatment is appropriate (as opposed to each event being "self-identifying"). The state machines discussed in this introduction are high-level machines that are intended to express clearly the programming requirements of a class of problems. If it makes sense to talk about your programming problem in terms of categories of behavior in response to events, it is likely to be a good idea to program the solution in terms of explicit state machines.

4.2.2   Text Processing State Machines

One of the programming problems most likely to call for an explicit state machine is processing text files. Processing a text file very often consists of sequential reading of each chunk of a text file (typically either a character or a line), and doing something in response to each chunk read. In some cases, this processing is "stateless"—that is, each chunk has enough information internally to determine exactly what to do in response to that chunk of text. And in other cases, even though the text file is not 100 percent stateless, there is a very limited context to each chunk (for example, the line number might matter for the action taken, but not much else besides the line number). But in other common text processing problems, the text files we deal with are highly "stateful"—the meaning of a chunk depends on what types of chunks preceded it (and maybe even on what chunks come next). Files like report files, mainframe data-feeds, human-readable texts, programming source files, and other sorts of text files are stateful. A very simple example of a stateful chunk is a line that might occur in a Python source file:*

```
myObject = SomeClass(this, that, other)
```

That line means something very different if it happens to be surrounded by these lines:

```
"""How to use SomeClass:
myObject = SomeClass(this, that, other)
"""
```

That is, we needed to know that we were in a "blockquote" *state* to determine that the line was a comment rather than an action. Of course, a program that deals with Python programs in a more general way will usually use a parser and grammar.

4.2.3   When Not to Use a State Machine

When we begin the task of writing a processor for any stateful text file, the first question we should ask ourselves is "What types of things do we expect to find in the file?" Each type of thing is a candidate for a state. These types should be several in number, but if the number is huge or indefinite, a state machine is probably not the right approach— maybe some sort of database solution is appropriate. Or maybe the problem has not been formulated right if there appear to be that many types of things.

Moreover, we are not quite ready for a state machine yet; there may yet be a simpler approach. It might turn out that even though our text file is stateful there is an easy way to read in chunks where each chunk is a single type of thing. A state machine is really only worth implementing if the transitions between types of text require some calculation based on the content within a single state-block.

An example of a somewhat stateful text file that is nonetheless probably not best handled with a state machine is a Windows-style .ini file (generally replaced nowadays by use of the binary-data-with-API Windows registry). Those files consist of some section headers, some comments, and a number of value assignments. For example:

File: hypothetical.ini

```
; set the colorscheme and userlevel
[colorscheme]
background=red
foreground=blue
title=green

[userlevel]
login=2
; admin=0
title=1
```

This example has no real-life meaning, but it was constructed to indicate some features of the .ini format. (1) In one sense, the type of each line is determined by its first character (either semicolon, left brace, or alphabetic). (2) In another sense, the format is "stateful" insofar as the keyword "title" presumably means something independent when it occurs in each section. You could program a text processor that had a COL-ORSCHEME state and a USERLEVEL state, and processed the value assignments of each state. But that does not seem like the *right* way to handle this problem.

On the one hand, we could simply create the natural chunks in this text file with some Python code like:

> Chunking Python code to process .ini file

```
txt = open('hypothetical.ini').read()
from string import strip, split
nocomm = lambda s: s[0] != ';'          # "no comment" util
eq2pair = lambda s: split(s,'=')        # assignmet -> pair
def assignments(sect):
    name, body = split(sect,']')        # identify name, body
    assigns = split(body,'\n')          # find assign lines
    assigns = filter(strip, assigns)    # remove outside space
    assigns = filter(None, assigns)     # remove empty lines
    assigns = filter(nocomm, assigns)   # remove comment lines
    assigns = map(eq2pair, assigns)     # make name/val pairs
    assigns = map(tuple, assigns)       # prefer tuple pairs
    return (name, assigns)
sects = split(txt,'[')                  # divide named sects
sects = map(strip, sects)               # remove outside newlines
sects = filter(nocomm, sects)           # remove comment sects
config = map(assignments, sects)        # find assigns by sect
pprint.pprint(config)
```

Applied to the `hypothetical.ini` file above, this code produces output similar to:

```
[('colorscheme',
  [('background', 'red'),
   ('foreground', 'blue'),
   ('title', 'green')]),
 ('userlevel',
  [('login', '2'),
   ('title', '1')])]
```

This particular list-oriented data structure may or may not be what you want, but it is simple enough to transform this into dictionary entries, instance attributes, or whatever is desired. Or slightly modified code could generate other data representations in the first place.

An alternative approach is to use a single `current_section` variable to keep track of relevant state and process lines accordingly:

```
for line in open('hypothetical.ini').readlines():
    if line[0] == '[':
        current_section = line[1:-2]
    elif line[0] == ';':
        pass    # ignore comments
    else:
        apply_value(current_section, line)
```

Sidebar: A digression on functional programming

Readers will have noticed that the `.ini` chunking code given in the example above has more of a functional programming (FP) style to it than does most Python code (in this book or elsewhere). I wrote the presented code this way for two reasons. The more superficial reason is just to emphasize the contrast with a state machine approach. Much of the special quality of FP lies in its eschewal of state (see the discussion of functional programming in Chapter 1); so the example is, in a sense, even farther from a state machine technique than would be a coding style that used a few nested loops in place of the `map()` and `filter()` calls.

The more substantial reason I adopted a functional programming style is because I feel that this type of problem is precisely the sort that can often be expressed more compactly and more *clearly* using FP constructs. Basically, our source text document expresses a data structure that is homogeneous at each level. Each section is similar to other sections; and within a section, each assignment is similar to others. A clear—and stateless—way to manipulate these sorts of implicit structures is applying an operation uniformly to each thing at a given level. In the example, we do a given set of operations to find the assignments contained within a section, so we might as well just `map()` that set of operations to the collection of (massaged, noncomment) sections. This approach is more terse than a bunch of nested `for` loops, while simultaneously (in my opinion) better expressing the underlying intention of the textual analysis.

Use of a functional programming style, however, can easily be taken too far. Deeply nested calls to `map()`, `reduce()`, and `filter()` can quickly become difficult to read, especially if whitespace and function/variable names are not chosen carefully. Inasmuch as it is possible to write "obfuscated Python" code (a popular competition for other languages), it is almost always done using FP constructs. Warnings in mind, it is possible to create an even terser and more functional variant of the `.ini` chunking code (that produces identical results). I believe that the following falls considerably short of obfuscated, but will still be somewhat more difficult to read for most programmers. On the plus side, it is half the length of the prior code and is entirely free of accidental side effects:

Strongly functional code to process .ini file

```
from string import strip, split
eq2tup = lambda s: tuple(split(s,'='))
splitnames = lambda s: split(s,']')
parts = lambda s, delim: map(strip, split(s, delim))
useful = lambda ss: filter(lambda s: s and s[0]!=';', ss)
config = map(lambda _:(_[0], map(eq2tup, useful(parts(_[1],'\n')))),
            map(splitnames, useful(parts(txt,'[')))  )
pprint.pprint(config)
```

In brief, this functional code says that a configuration consists of a list of pairs of (1) names plus (2) a list of key/value pairs. Using list comprehensions might make this expression clearer, but the example code is compatible back to Python 1.5. Moreover, the utility function names `useful()` and `parts()` go a long way towards keeping the example readable. Utility functions of this sort are, furthermore, potentially worth saving in a separate module for other use (which, in a sense, makes the relevant .ini chunking code even shorter).

A reader exercise is to consider how the higher-order functions proposed in Chapter 1's section on functional programming could further improve the sort of "stateless" text processing presented in this subsection.

4.2.4   When to Use a State Machine

Now that we have established not to use a state machine if the text file is "too simple," we should look at a case where a state machine is worthwhile. The utility Txt2Html is listed in Appendix D. Txt2Html converts "smart ASCII" files to HTML.

In very brief recap, smart ASCII format is a text format that uses a few spacing conventions to distinguish different types of text blocks, such as headers, regular text, quotations, and code samples. While it is easy for a human reader or writer to visually parse the transitions between these text block types, there is no simple way to chunk a whole text file into its text blocks. Unlike in the .ini file example, text block types can occur in any pattern of alternation. There is no single delimiter that separates blocks in all cases (a blank line *usually* separates blocks, but a blank line within a code sample does not necessarily end the code sample, and blocks need not be separated by blank lines). But we do need to perform somewhat different formatting behavior on each text block type for the correct final XML output. A state machine suggests itself as a natural solution here.

The general behavior of the Txt2Html reader is as follows: (1) Start in a particular state. (2) Read a line of the text file and go to current state context. (3) Decide if conditions have been met to leave the current state and enter another. (4) Failing (3), process the line in a manner appropriate for the current state. This example is about the simplest case you would encounter, but it expresses the pattern described:

A simple state machine input loop in Python

```
global state, blocks, newblock
for line in fpin.readlines():
    if state == "HEADER":        # blank line means new block of ?
        if blankln.match(line):   newblock = 1
        elif textln.match(line):  startText(line)
        elif codeln.match(line):  startCode(line)
        else:
            if newblock: startHead(line)
            else: blocks[-1] += line
    elif state == "TEXT":        # blank line means new block of ?
        if blankln.match(line):   newblock = 1
        elif headln.match(line):  startHead(line)
        elif codeln.match(line):  startCode(line)
        else:
            if newblock: startText(line)
```

```
        else: blocks[-1] += line
elif state == "CODE":          # blank line does not change state
    if blankln.match(line):    blocks[-1] += line
    elif headln.match(line):   startHead(line)
    elif textln.match(line):   startText(line)
    else: blocks[-1] += line
else:
    raise ValueError, "unexpected input block state: "+state
```

The only real thing to notice is that the variable `state` is declared `global`, and its value is changed in functions like `startText()`. The transition conditions—such as `textln.match()`—are regular expression patterns, but they could just as well be custom functions. The formatting itself is actually done later in the program; the state machine just parses the text file into labeled blocks in the `blocks` list. In a sense, the state machine here is acting as a tokenizer for the later block processor.

4.2.5 An Abstract State Machine Class

It is easy in Python to abstract the form of a state machine. Coding in this manner makes the state machine model of the program stand out more clearly than does the simple conditional block in the previous example (which doesn't right away look all that much different from any other conditional). Furthermore, the class presented—and the associated handlers—does a very good job of isolating in-state behavior. This improves both encapsulation and readability in many cases.

File: statemachine.py

```
class InitializationError(Exception): pass

class StateMachine:
    def __init__(self):
        self.handlers = []
        self.startState = None
        self.endStates = []

    def add_state(self, handler, end_state=0):
        self.handlers.append(handler)
        if end_state:
            self.endStates.append(name)

    def set_start(self, handler):
        self.startState = handler

    def run(self, cargo=None):
        if not self.startState:
            raise InitializationError,\
                "must call .set_start() before .run()"
```

```
        if not self.endStates:
            raise InitializationError, \
                    "at least one state must be an end_state"
        handler = self.startState
        while 1:
            (newState, cargo) = handler(cargo)
            if newState in self.endStates:
                newState(cargo)
                break
            elif newState not in self.handlers:
                raise RuntimeError, "Invalid target %s" % newState
            else:
                handler = newState
```

The StateMachine class is really all you need for the form of a state machine. It is a whole lot fewer lines than something similar would require in most languages—mostly because of the ease of passing function objects in Python. You could even save a few lines by removing the target state check and the self.handlers list, but the extra formality helps enforce and document programmer intention.

To actually *use* the StateMachine class, you need to create some handlers for each state you want to use. A handler must follow a particular pattern. Generally, it should loop indefinitely; but in any case it must have some breakout condition(s). Each pass through the state handler's loop should process another event of the state's type. But probably even before handling events, the handler should check for breakout conditions and determine what state is appropriate to transition to. At the end, a handler should pass back a tuple consisting of the target state's name and any cargo the new state handler will need.

An encapsulation device is the use of cargo as a variable in the StateMachine class (not necessarily called cargo by the handlers). This is used to pass around "whatever is needed" by one state handler to take over where the last state handler left off. Most typically, cargo will consist of a file handle, which would allow the next handler to read some more data after the point where the last state handler stopped. But a database connection might get passed, or a complex class instance, or a tuple with several things in it.

4.2.6   Processing a Report with a Concrete State Machine

A moderately complicated report format provides a good example of some processing amenable to a state machine programming style—and specifically, to use of the StateMachine class above. The hypothetical report below has a number of state-sensitive features. Sometimes lines belong to buyer orders, but at other times the identical lines could be part of comments or the heading. Blank lines, for example, are processed differently from different states. Buyers, who are each processed according to different rules, each get their own machine state. Moreover, within each order, a degree of stateful processing is performed, dependent on locally accumulated calculations:

> ┌─────────────────────────────┐
> │ Sample Buyer/Order Report   │
> └─────────────────────────────┘

```
MONTHLY REPORT -- April 2002
==================================================================

Rules:
 - Each buyer has price schedule for each item (func of quantity).
 - Each buyer has a discount schedule based on dollar totals.
 - Discounts are per-order (i.e., contiguous block)
 - Buyer listing starts with line containing ">>", then buyer name.
 - Item quantities have name-whitespace-number, one per line.
 - Comment sections begin with line starting with an asterisk,
   and ends with first line that ends with an asterisk.

>> Acme Purchasing

   widgets      100
   whatzits     1000
   doodads      5000
   dingdongs    20

* Note to Donald: The best contact for Acme is Debbie Franlin, at
* 413-555-0001.  Fallback is Sue Fong (call switchboard). *

>> Megamart

doodads   10k
whatzits  5k

>> Fly-by-Night Sellers
   widgets      500
   whatzits     4
   flazs        1000

* Note to Harry: Have Sales contact FbN for negotiations *

*
Known buyers:
>>   Acme
>>   Megamart
>>   Standard (default discounts)
*

*** LATE ADDITIONS ***

>> Acme Purchasing
widgets       500      (rush shipment)**
```

The code to processes this report below is a bit simplistic. Within each state, almost all the code is devoted merely to deciding when to leave the state and where to go next. In the sample, each of the "buyer states" is sufficiently similar that they could well be generalized to one parameterized state; but in a real-world application, each state is likely to contain much more detailed custom programming for both in-state behavior and out-from-state transition conditions. For example, a report might allow different formatting and fields within different buyer blocks.

```
buyer_invoices.py
```

```python
from statemachine import StateMachine
from buyers import STANDARD, ACME, MEGAMART
from pricing import discount_schedules, item_prices
import sys, string

#-- Machine States
def error(cargo):
    # Don't want to get here! Unidentifiable line
    sys.stderr.write('Unidentifiable line:\n'+ line)

def eof(cargo):
    # Normal termination -- Cleanup code might go here.
    sys.stdout.write('Processing Successful\n')

def read_through(cargo):
    # Skip through headers until buyer records are found
    fp, last = cargo
    while 1:
        line = fp.readline()
        if not line:           return eof, (fp, line)
        elif line[:2] == '>>': return whichbuyer(line), (fp, line)
        elif line[0] == '*':   return comment, (fp, line)
        else:                  continue

def comment(cargo):
    # Skip comments
    fp, last = cargo
    if len(last) > 2 and string.rstrip(last)[-1:] == '*':
        return read_through, (fp, '')
    while 1:
        # could save or process comments here, if desired
        line = fp.readline()
        lastchar = string.rstrip(line)[-1:]
        if not line:           return eof, (fp, line)
        elif lastchar == '*':  return read_through, (fp, line)
```

```
def STANDARD(cargo, discounts=discount_schedules[STANDARD],
                   prices=item_prices[STANDARD]):
    fp, company = cargo
    invoice = 0
    while 1:
        line = fp.readline()
        nextstate = buyerbranch(line)
        if nextstate == 0: continue          # blank line
        elif nextstate == 1:                 # order item
            invoice = invoice + calc_price(line, prices)
        else:                                # create invoice
            pr_invoice(company, 'standard', discount(invoice,discounts))
            return nextstate, (fp, line)

def ACME(cargo, discounts=discount_schedules[ACME],
               prices=item_prices[ACME]):
    fp, company = cargo
    invoice = 0
    while 1:
        line = fp.readline()
        nextstate = buyerbranch(line)
        if nextstate == 0: continue          # blank line
        elif nextstate == 1:                 # order item
            invoice = invoice + calc_price(line, prices)
        else:                                # create invoice
            pr_invoice(company, 'negotiated', discount(invoice,discounts))
            return nextstate, (fp, line)

def MEGAMART(cargo, discounts=discount_schedules[MEGAMART],
                   prices=item_prices[MEGAMART]):
    fp, company = cargo
    invoice = 0
    while 1:
        line = fp.readline()
        nextstate = buyerbranch(line)
        if nextstate == 0: continue          # blank line
        elif nextstate == 1:                 # order item
            invoice = invoice + calc_price(line, prices)
        else:                                # create invoice
            pr_invoice(company, 'negotiated', discount(invoice,discounts))
            return nextstate, (fp, line)

#-- Support function for buyer/state switch
def whichbuyer(line):
    # What state/buyer does this line identify?
    line = string.upper(string.replace(line, '-', ''))
```

```
    find = string.find
    if find(line,'ACME') >= 0:         return ACME
    elif find(line,'MEGAMART')>= 0: return MEGAMART
    else:                              return STANDARD

def buyerbranch(line):
    if not line:                       return eof
    elif not string.strip(line):       return 0
    elif line[0] == '*':               return comment
    elif line[:2] == '>>':             return whichbuyer(line)
    else:                              return 1

#-- General support functions
def calc_price(line, prices):
    product, quant = string.split(line)[:2]
    quant = string.replace(string.upper(quant),'K','000')
    quant = int(quant)
    return quant*prices[product]

def discount(invoice, discounts):
    multiplier = 1.0
    for threshhold, percent in discounts:
        if invoice >= threshhold: multiplier = 1 - float(percent)/100
    return invoice*multiplier

def pr_invoice(company, disctype, amount):
    print "Company name:", company[3:-1], "(%s discounts)" % disctype
    print "Invoice total: $", amount, '\n'

if __name__== "__main__":
    m = StateMachine()
    m.add_state(read_through)
    m.add_state(comment)
    m.add_state(STANDARD)
    m.add_state(ACME)
    m.add_state(MEGAMART)
    m.add_state(error, end_state=1)
    m.add_state(eof, end_state=1)
    m.set_start(read_through)
    m.run((sys.stdin, ''))
```

The body of each state function consists mostly of a `while 1:` loop that sometimes breaks out by returning a new target state, along with a cargo tuple. In our particular machine, `cargo` consists of a file handle and the last line read. In some cases, the line that signals a state transition is also needed for use by the subsequent state. The cargo could contain whatever we wanted. A flow diagram lets you see the set of transitions easily:

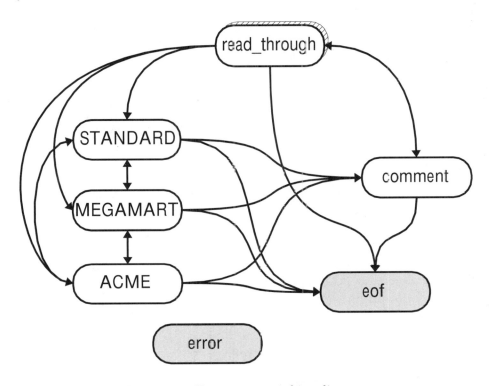

Figure 4.1: Buyer state machine diagram

All of the buyer states are "initialized" using default argument values that are never changed during calls by a normal state machine `.run()` cycle. You could also perhaps design state handlers as classes instead of as functions, but that feels like extra conceptual overhead to me. The specific initializer values are contained in a support module that looks like:

---
pricing.py support data

```
from buyers import STANDARD, ACME, MEGAMART, BAGOBOLTS

# Discount consists of dollar requirement and a percentage reduction
# Each buyer can have an ascending series of discounts, the highest
# one applicable to a month is used.
discount_schedules = {
    STANDARD  : [(5000,10),(10000,20),(15000,30),(20000,40)],
    ACME      : [(1000,10),(5000,15),(10000,30),(20000,40)],
    MEGAMART  : [(2000,10),(5000,20),(10000,25),(30000,50)],
    BAGOBOLTS : [(2500,10),(5000,15),(10000,25),(30000,50)],
  }
item_prices = {
    STANDARD  : {'widgets':1.0, 'whatzits':0.9, 'doodads':1.1,
                 'dingdongs':1.3, 'flazs':0.7},
    ACME      : {'widgets':0.9, 'whatzits':0.9, 'doodads':1.0,
                 'dingdongs':0.9, 'flazs':0.6},
    MEGAMART  : {'widgets':1.0, 'whatzits':0.8, 'doodads':1.0,
                 'dingdongs':1.2, 'flazs':0.7},
    BAGOBOLTS : {'widgets':0.8, 'whatzits':0.9, 'doodads':1.1,
                 'dingdongs':1.3, 'flazs':0.5},
  }
```

In place of reading in such a data structure, a full application might calculate some values or read them from a database of some sort. Nonetheless, the division of data, state logic, and abstract flow into separate modules makes for a good design.

4.2.7   Subgraphs and State Reuse

Another benefit of the state machine design approach is that you can use different start and end states without touching the state handlers at all. Obviously, you do not have complete freedom in doing so—if a state branches to another state, the branch target needs to be included in the list of "registered" states. You can, however, add homonymic handlers in place of target processing states. For example:

Creating end states for subgraphs

```
from statemachine import StateMachine
from BigGraph import *

def subgraph_end(cargo): print "Leaving subgraph..."
foo = subgraph_end
bar = subgraph_end

def spam_return(cargo): return spam, None
baz = spam_return
```

```
if __name__=='__main__':
    m = StateMachine()
    m.add_state(foo, end_state=1)
    m.add_state(bar, end_state=1)
    m.add_state(baz)
    map(m.add_state, [spam, eggs, bacon])
    m.set_start(spam)
    m.run(None)
```

In a complex state machine graph, you often encounter relatively isolated subgraphs. That is, a particular collection of states—i.e., nodes—might have many connections between them, but only a few connections out to the rest of the graph. Usually this occurs because a subgraph concerns a related set of functionality.

For processing the buyer report discussed earlier, only seven states were involved, so no meaningful subgraphs really exist. But in the subgraph example above, you can imagine that the *BigGraph* module contains hundreds or thousands of state handlers, whose targets define a very complex complete graph. Supposing that the states spam, eggs, and bacon define a useful subgraph, and all branches out of the subgraph lead to foo, bar, or baz, the code above could be an entire new application.

The example redefined foo and bar as end states, so processing (at least in that particular StateMachine object) ends when they are reached. However, baz is redefined to transition back into the spam-eggs-bacon subgraph. A subgraph exit need not represent a termination of the state machine. It is actually the end_state flag that controls termination—but if foo was not marked as an end state, it would raise a RuntimeError when it failed to return a valid state target.

If you create large graphs—especially with the intention of utilizing subgraphs as state machines—it is often useful to create a state diagram. Pencil and paper are perfectly adequate tools for doing this; a variety of flow-chart software also exists to do it on a computer. The goal of a diagram is to allow you to identify clustered subgraphs and most especially to help identify paths in and out of a functional subgraph. A state diagram from our buyer report example is given as illustration. A quick look at Figure 4.1, for example, allows the discovery that the error end state is isolated, which might not have been evident in the code itself. This is not a problem, necessarily; a future enhancement to the diagram and handlers might utilize this state, and whatever logic was written into it.

4.2.8   Exercise: Finding other solutions

1. On the face of it, a lot of "machinery" went into processing what is not really that complicated a report above. The goal of the state machine formality was both to be robust and to allow for expansion to larger problems. Putting aside the state machine approach in your mind, how else might you go about processing reports of the presented type (assume that "reasonable" variations occur between reports of the same type).

   Try writing a fresh report processing application that produces the same results as the presented application (or at least something close to it). Test your application against the sample report and against a few variants you create yourself.

What errors did you encounter running your application? Why? Is your application more concise than the presented one? Which modules do you count as part of the presented application? Is your application's code clearer or less clear to follow for another programmer? Which approach would be easier to expand to encompass other report formats? In what respect is your application better/worse than the state machine example?

2. The `error` state is never actually reached in the `buyer_invoices.py` application. What other transition conditions into the `error` state would be reasonable to add to the application? What types of corruption or mistakes in reports do you expect most typically to encounter? Sometimes reports, or other documents, are flawed, but it is still desirable to utilize as much of them as possible. What are good approaches to recover from error conditions? How could you express those approaches in state machine terms, using the presented `StateMachine` class and framework?

4.3   Parser Libraries for Python

4.3.1   Specialized Parsers in the Standard Library

Python comes standard with a number of modules that perform specialized parsing tasks. A variety of custom formats are in sufficiently widespread use that it is convenient to have standard library support for them. Aside from those listed in this chapter, Chapter 5 discusses the *email* and *xml* packages, and the modules *mailbox*, *HTMLParser*, and *urlparse*, each of which performs parsing of sorts. A number of additional modules listed in Chapter 1, which handle and process audio and image formats, in a broad sense could be considered parsing tools. However, these media formats are better considered as byte streams and structures than as token streams of the sort parsers handle (the distinction is fine, though).

The specialized tools discussed under this section are presented only in summary. Consult the *Python Library Reference* for detailed documentation of their various APIs and features. It is worth knowing what is available, but for space reasons, this book does not document usage specifics of these few modules.

ConfigParser

Parse and modify Windows-style configuration files.

```
>>> import ConfigParser
>>> config = ConfigParser.ConfigParser()
>>> config.read(['test.ini','nonesuch.ini'])
>>> config.sections()
['userlevel', 'colorscheme']
>>> config.get('userlevel','login')
```

```
'2'
>>> config.set('userlevel','login',5)
>>> config.write(sys.stdout)
[userlevel]
login = 5
title = 1

[colorscheme]
background = red
foreground = blue
```

difflib
.../Tools/scripts/ndiff.py

The module *difflib*, introduced in Python 2.1, contains a variety of functions and
classes to help you determine the difference and similarity of pairs of sequences.
The API of *difflib* is flexible enough to work with sequences of all kinds, but the
typical usage is in comparing sequences of lines or sequences of characters.

Word similarity is useful for determining likely misspellings and typos and/or edit
changes required between strings. The function *difflib.get_close_matches()* is
a useful way to perform "fuzzy matching" of a string against patterns. The required
similarity is configurable.

```
>>> users = ['j.smith', 't.smith', 'p.smyth', 'a.simpson']
>>> maxhits = 10
>>> login = 'a.smith'
>>> difflib.get_close_matches(login, users, maxhits)
['t.smith', 'j.smith', 'p.smyth']
>>> difflib.get_close_matches(login, users, maxhits, cutoff=.75)
['t.smith', 'j.smith']
>>> difflib.get_close_matches(login, users, maxhits, cutoff=.4)
['t.smith', 'j.smith', 'p.smyth', 'a.simpson']
```

Line matching is similar to the behavior of the Unix `diff` (or `ndiff`) and `patch`
utilities. The latter utility is able to take a source and a difference, and produce the second compared line-list (file). The functions *difflib.ndiff()* and
difflib.restore() implement these capabilities. Much of the time, however, the
bundled `ndiff.py` tool performs the comparisons you are interested in (and the
"patches" with an -r# option).

```
% ./ndiff.py chap4.txt chap4.txt~ | grep '^[+-]'
-: chap4.txt
+: chap4.txt~
+       against patterns.
```

```
    –         against patterns.  The required similarity is configurable.
    –
    –         >>> users = ['j.smith', 't.smith', 'p.smyth', 'a.simpson']
    –         >>> maxhits = 10
    –         >>> login = 'a.smith'
```

There are a few more capabilities in the *difflib* module, and considerable customization is possible.

formatter

Transform an abstract sequence of formatting events into a sequence of callbacks to "writer" objects. Writer objects, in turn, produce concrete outputs based on these callbacks. Several parent formatter and writer classes are contained in the module.

In a way, *formatter* is an "anti-parser"—that is, while a parser transforms a series of tokens into program events, *formatter* transforms a series of program events into output tokens.

The purpose of the *formatter* module is to structure creation of streams such as word processor file formats. The module *htmllib* utilizes the *formatter* module. The particular API details provide calls related to features like fonts, margins, and so on.

For highly structured output of prose-oriented documents, the *formatter* module is useful, albeit requiring learning a fairly complicated API. At the minimal level, you may use the classes included to create simple tools. For example, the following utility is approximately equivalent to `lynx -dump`:

urldump.py

```python
#!/usr/bin/env python
import sys
from urllib import urlopen
from htmllib import HTMLParser
from formatter import AbstractFormatter, DumbWriter
if len(sys.argv) > 1:
    fpin = urlopen(sys.argv[1])
    parser = HTMLParser(AbstractFormatter(DumbWriter()))
    parser.feed(fpin.read())
    print '----------------------------------------------------'
    print fpin.geturl()
    print fpin.info()
else:
    print "No specified URL"
```

SEE ALSO: htmllib *285*; urllib *388*;

htmllib

Parse and process HTML files, using the services of *sgmllib*. In contrast to the *HTMLParser* module, *htmllib* relies on the user constructing a suitable "formatter" object to accept callbacks from HTML events, usually utilizing the *formatter* module. A formatter, in turn, uses a "writer" (also usually based on the *formatter* module). In my opinion, there are enough layers of indirection in the *htmllib* API to make *HTMLParser* preferable for almost all tasks.

SEE ALSO: HTMLParser *384*; formatter *284*; sgmllib *285*;

multifile

The class `multifile.MultiFile` allows you to treat a text file composed of multiple delimited parts as if it were several files, each with their own FILE methods: `.read()`, `.readline()`, `.readlines()`, `.seek()`, and `.tell()` methods. In iterator fashion, advancing to the next virtual file is performed with the method `multifile.MultiFile.next()`.

SEE ALSO: fileinput *61*; mailbox *372*; email.Parser *363*; string.split() *142*; file *15*;

parser
symbol
token
tokenize

Interface to Python's internal parser and tokenizer. Although parsing Python source code is arguably a text processing task, the complexities of parsing Python are too specialized for this book.

robotparser

Examine a `robots.txt` access control file. This file is used by Web servers to indicate the desired behavior of automatic indexers and Web crawlers—all the popular search engines honor these requests.

sgmllib

A partial parser for SGML. Standard Generalized Markup Language (SGML) is an enormously complex document standard; in its full generality, SGML cannot be considered a *format*, but rather a grammar for describing concrete formats. HTML is one particular SGML dialect, and XML is (almost) a simplified subset of SGML.

Although it might be nice to have a Python library that handled generic SGML, *sgmllib* is not such a thing. Instead, *sgmllib* implements just enough SGML parsing to support HTML parsing with *htmllib*. You might be able to coax parsing an XML library out of *sgmllib*, with some work, but Python's standard XML tools are far more refined for this purpose.

SEE ALSO: htmllib *285*; xml.sax *405*;

shlex

A lexical analyzer class for simple Unix shell-like syntaxes. This capability is primarily useful to implement small command language within Python applications.

tabnanny

This module is generally used as a command-line script rather than imported into other applications. The module/script *tabnanny* checks Python source code files for mixed use of tabs and spaces within the same block. Behind the scenes, the Python source is fully tokenized, but normal usage consists of something like:

```
% /sw/lib/python2.2/tabnanny.py SCRIPTS/
SCRIPTS/cmdline.py 165 '\treturn 1\r\n'
'SCRIPTS/HTMLParser_stack.py': Token Error: ('EOF in
                               multi-line string', (3, 7))
SCRIPTS/outputters.py 18 '\tself.writer=writer\r\n'
SCRIPTS/txt2bookU.py 148 '\ttry:\n'
```

The tool is single purpose, but that purpose addresses a common pitfall in Python programming.

SEE ALSO: tokenize *285*;

4.3.2   Low-Level State Machine Parsing

mx.TextTools ◇ Fast Text Manipulation Tools

Marc-Andre Lemburg's *mx.TextTools* is a remarkable tool that is a bit difficult to grasp the gestalt of. *mx.TextTools* can be blazingly fast and extremely powerful. But at the same time, as difficult as it might be to "get" the mindset of *mx.TextTools*, it is still more difficult to get an application written with it working just right. Once it is working, an application that utilizes *mx.TextTools* can process a larger class of text structures than can regular expressions, while simultaneously operating much faster. But debugging an *mx.TextTools* "tag table" can make you wish you were merely debugging a cryptic regular expression!

In recent versions, *mx.TextTools* has come in a larger package with eGenix.com's several other "mx Extensions for Python." Most of the other subpackages add highly efficient C implementations of datatypes not found in a base Python system.

mx.TextTools stands somewhere between a state machine and a full-fledged parser. In fact, the module *SimpleParse*, discussed below, is an EBNF parser library that is built on top of *mx.TextTools*. As a state machine, *mx.TextTools* feels like a lower-level tool than the *statemachine* module presented in the prior section. And yet, *mx.TextTools* is simultaneously very close to a high-level parser. This is how Lemburg characterizes it in the documentation accompanying *mx.TextTools*:

mxTextTools is an extension package for Python that provides several useful functions and types that implement high-performance text manipulation and searching algorithms in addition to a very flexible and extendable state machine, the Tagging Engine, that allows scanning and processing text based on low-level byte-code "programs" written using Python tuples. It gives you access to the speed of C without the need to do any compile and link steps every time you change the parsing description.

Applications include parsing structured text, finding and extracting text (either exact or using translation tables) and recombining strings to form new text.

The Python standard library has a good set of text processing tools. The basic tools are powerful, flexible, and easy to work with. But Python's basic text processing is *not* particularly fast. Mind you, for most problems, Python by itself is as fast as you need. But for a certain class of problems, being able to choose *mx.TextTools* is invaluable.

The unusual structure of *mx.TextTools* applications warrants some discussion of concrete usage. After a few sample applications are presented, a listing of *mx.TextTools* constants, commands, modifiers, and functions is given.

BENCHMARKS

A familiar computer-industry paraphrase of Mark Twain (who repeats Benjamin Disraeli) dictates that there are "Lies, Damn Lies, and Benchmarks." I will not argue with that and certainly do not want readers to put too great an import on the timings suggested. Nonetheless, in exploring *mx.TextTools*, I wanted to get some sense of just how fast it is. So here is a rough idea.

The second example below presents part of a reworked version of the state machine-based `Txt2Html` application reproduced in Appendix D. The most time-consuming aspect of `Txt2Html` is the regular expression replacements performed in the function `Typography()` for smart ASCII inline markup of words and phrases.

In order to get a timeable test case, I concatenated 110 copies of an article I wrote to get a file a bit over 2MB, and about 41k lines and 300k words. My test processes an entire input as one text block, first using an *mx.TextTools* version of `Typography()`, then using the *re* version.

Processing time of the same test file went from about 34 seconds to about 12 seconds on one slowish Linux test machine (running Python 1.5.2). In other words, *mx.TextTools* gave me about a 3x speedup over what I get with the *re* module. This speedup is probably typical, but particular applications might gain significantly more or less from use of *mx.TextTools*. Moreover, 34 seconds is a long time in an interactive application, but is not very long at all for a batch process done once a day, or once a week.

Example: Buyer/Order Report Parsing

Recall (or refer to) the sample report presented in the previous section "An Introduction to State Machines." A report contained a mixture of header material, buyer orders, and comments. The state machine we used looked at each successive line of the file and decided based on context whether the new line indicated a new state should start. It would be possible to write almost the same algorithm utilizing *mx.TextTools* only to speed up the decisions, but that is not what we will do.

A more representative use of *mx.TextTools* is to produce a concrete parse tree of the interesting components of the report document. In principle, you should be able to create a "grammar" that describes every valid "buyer report" document, but in practice using a mixed procedural/grammar approach is much easier, and more maintainable—at least for the test report.

An *mx.TextTools* tag table is a miniature state machine that either matches or fails to match a portion of a string. Matching, in this context, means that a "success" end state is reached, while nonmatching means that a "failure" end state is reached. Falling off the end of the tag table is a success state. Each individual state in a tag table tries to match some smaller construct by reading from the "read-head" and moving the read-head correspondingly. On either success or failure, program flow jumps to an indicated target state (which might be a success or failure state for the tag table as a whole). Of course, the jump target for success is often different from the jump target for failure—but there are only these two possible choices for jump targets, unlike the *statemachine* module's indefinite number.

Notably, one of the types of states you can include in a tag table is another tag table. That one state can "externally" look like a simple match attempt, but internally it might involve complex subpatterns and machine flow in order to determine if the state is a match or nonmatch. Much as in an EBNF grammar, you can build nested constructs for recognition of complex patterns. States can also have special behavior, such as function callbacks—but in general, an *mx.TextTools* tag table state is simply a binary match/nonmatch switch.

Let us look at an *mx.TextTools* parsing application for "buyer reports" and then examine how it works:

buyer_report.py

```
from mx.TextTools import *

word_set = set(alphanumeric+white+'-')
quant_set = set(number+'kKmM')

item    = ( (None, AllInSet, newline_set, +1),        # 1
            (None, AllInSet, white_set, +1),          # 2
            ('Prod', AllInSet, a2z_set, Fail),        # 3
            (None, AllInSet, white_set, Fail),        # 4
            ('Quant', AllInSet, quant_set, Fail),     # 5
            (None, WordEnd, '\n', -5) )               # 6

buyers = ( ('Order', Table,                           # 1
                ( (None, WordEnd, '\n>> ', Fail),     # 1.1
                  ('Buyer', AllInSet, word_set, Fail), # 1.2
```

```
                         ('Item', Table, item, MatchOk, +0) ),    # 1.3
                      Fail, +0), )

comments = ( ('Comment', Table,                                   # 1
                  ( (None, Word, '\n*', Fail),                    # 1.1
                    (None, WordEnd, '*\n', Fail),                 # 1.2
                    (None, Skip, -1) ),                           # 1.3
                  +1, +2),
               (None, Skip, +1),                                  # 2
               (None, EOF, Here, -2) )                            # 3

def unclaimed_ranges(tagtuple):
    starts = [0] + [tup[2] for tup in tagtuple[1]]
    stops = [tup[1] for tup in tagtuple[1]] + [tagtuple[2]]
    return zip(starts, stops)

def report2data(s):
    comtuple = tag(s, comments)
    taglist = comtuple[1]
    for beg,end in unclaimed_ranges(comtuple):
        taglist.extend(tag(s, buyers, beg, end)[1])
    taglist.sort(cmp)
    return taglist

if __name__=='__main__':
    import sys, pprint
    pprint.pprint(report2data(sys.stdin.read()))
```

Several tag tables are defined in *buyer_report*: item, buyers, and comments. State machines such as those in each tag table are general matching engines that can be used to identify patterns; after working with *mx.TextTools* for a while, you might accumulate a library of useful tag tables. As mentioned above, states in tag tables can reference other tag tables, either by name or inline. For example, buyers contains an inline tag table, while this inline tag table utilizes the tag table named item.

Let us take a look, step by step, at what the buyers tag table does. In order to *do* anything, a tag table needs to be passed as an argument to the mx.TextTools.tag() function, along with a string to match against. That is done in the report2data() function in the example. But in general, buyers—or any tag table—contains a list of states, each containing branch offsets. In the example, all such states are numbered in comments. buyers in particular contains just one state, which contains a subtable with three states.

Tag table state in buyers

1. Try to match the subtable. If the match succeeds, add the name Order to the taglist of matches. If the match fails, do not add anything. If the match succeeds, jump back into the one state (i.e., +0). In effect, buyers loops as long as it succeeds, advancing the read-head on each such match.

Subtable states in `buyers`

1. Try to find the end of the "word" `\n>>` in the string. That is, look for two greater-than symbols at the beginning of a line. If successful, move the read-head just past the point that first matched. If this state match fails, jump to `Fail`—that is, the (sub)table as a whole fails to match. No jump target is given for a successful match, so the default jump of +1 is taken. Since `None` is the tag object, do not add anything to the taglist upon a state match.

2. Try to find some `word_set` characters. This set of characters is defined in *buyer_report*; various other sets are defined in *mx.TextTools* itself. If the match succeeds, add the name `Buyer` to the taglist of matches. As many contiguous characters in the set as possible are matched. The match is considered a failure if there is not at least one such character. If this state match fails, jump to `Fail`, as in state (1).

3. Try to match the `item` tag table. If the match succeeds, add the name `Item` to the taglist of matches. What gets added, moreover, includes anything added within the `item` tag table. If the match fails, jump to `MatchOk`—that is, the (sub)table as a whole matches. If the match succeeds, jump +0—that is, keep looking for another `Item` to add to the taglist.

What *buyer_report* actually does is to first identify any comments, then to scan what is left in between comments for buyer orders. This approach proved easier to understand. Moreover, the design of *mx.TextTools* allows us to do this with no real inefficiency. Tagging a string does not involve actually pulling out the slices that match patterns, but simply identifying numerically the offset ranges where they occur. This approach is much "cheaper" than performing repeated slices, or otherwise creating new strings.

The following is important to notice: As of version 2.1.0, the documentation of the `mx.TextTools.tag()` function that accompanies *mx.TextTools* does not match its behavior! If the optional third and fourth arguments are passed to `tag()` they must indicate the start and end offsets within a larger string to scan, *not* the starting offset and length. Hopefully, later versions will fix the discrepancy (either approach would be fine, but could cause some breakage in existing code).

What *buyer_report* produces is a data structure, not final output. This data structure looks something like:

```
 ┌─────────────────────────────────────┐
 │ buyer_report.py data structure      │
 └─────────────────────────────────────┘

$ python ex_mx.py < recs.tmp
[('Order', 0,   638,
  [('Buyer', 547, 562, None),
   ('Item', 562, 583,
    [('Prod', 566, 573, None), ('Quant', 579, 582, None)]),
   ('Item', 583, 602,
    [('Prod', 585, 593, None), ('Quant', 597, 601, None)]),
   ('Item', 602, 621,
    [('Prod', 604, 611, None), ('Quant', 616, 620, None)]),
   ('Item', 621, 638,
    [('Prod', 623, 632, None), ('Quant', 635, 637, None)])]),
 ('Comment', 638, 763, []),
 ('Order', 763, 805,
  [('Buyer', 768, 776, None),
   ('Item', 776, 792,
    [('Prod', 778, 785, None), ('Quant', 788, 791, None)]),
   ('Item', 792, 805,
    [('Prod', 792, 800, None), ('Quant', 802, 804, None)])]),
 ('Order', 805, 893,
  [('Buyer', 809, 829, None),
   ('Item', 829, 852,
    [('Prod', 833, 840, None), ('Quant', 848, 851, None)]),
   ('Item', 852, 871,
    [('Prod', 855, 863, None), ('Quant', 869, 870, None)]),
   ('Item', 871, 893,
    [('Prod', 874, 879, None), ('Quant', 888, 892, None)])]),
 ('Comment', 893, 952, []),
 ('Comment', 952, 1025, []),
 ('Comment', 1026, 1049, []),
 ('Order', 1049, 1109,
  [('Buyer', 1054, 1069, None),
   ('Item',1069, 1109,
    [('Prod', 1070, 1077, None), ('Quant', 1083, 1086, None)])])])]
```

While this is "just" a new data structure, it is quite easy to deal with compared to raw textual reports. For example, here is a brief function that will create well-formed XML out of any taglist. You could even arrange for it to be valid XML by designing tag tables to match DTDs (see Chapter 5 for details about XML, DTDs, etc.):

```
def taglist2xml(s, taglist, root):
    print '<%s>' % root
    for tt in taglist:
        if tt[3]:
            taglist2xml(s, tt[3], tt[0])
        else:
            print '<%s>%s</%s>' % (tt[0], s[tt[1]:tt[2]], tt[0])
    print '</%s>' % root
```

Example: Marking up smart ASCII

The "smart ASCII" format uses email-like conventions to lightly mark features like word emphasis, source code, and URL links. This format—with LATEX as an intermediate format—was used to produce the book you hold (which was written using a variety of plaintext editors). By obeying just a few conventions (that are almost the same as you would use on Usenet or in email), a writer can write without much clutter, but still convert to production-ready markup.

The Txt2Html utility uses a block-level state machine, combined with a collection of inline-level regular expressions, to identify and modify markup patterns in smart ASCII texts. Even though Python's regular expression engine is moderately slow, converting a five-page article takes only a couple seconds. In practice, Txt2Html is more than adequate for my own 20 kilobyte documents. However, it is easy to imagine a not-so-different situation where you were converting multimegabyte documents and/or delivering such dynamically converted content on a high-volume Web site. In such a case, Python's string operations, and especially regular expressions, would simply be too slow.

mx.TextTools can do everything regular expressions can, plus some things regular expressions cannot. In particular, a taglist can contain recursive references to matched patterns, which regular expressions cannot. The utility mxTypography.py utilizes several *mx.TextTools* capabilities the prior example did not use. Rather than create a nested data structure, mxTypography.py utilizes a number of callback functions, each responding to a particular match event. As well, mxTypography.py adds some important debugging techniques. Something similar to these techniques is almost required for tag tables that are likely to be updated over time (or simply to aid the initial development). Overall, this looks like a robust application should.

| mx.TextTools version of Typography() |

```
from mx.TextTools import *
import string, sys

#-- List of all words with  markup, head position, loop count
ws, head_pos, loops = [], None, 0

#-- Define "emitter" callbacks for each output format
def emit_misc(tl,txt,l,r,s):
```

```
        ws.append(txt[l:r])
def emit_func(tl,txt,l,r,s):
    ws.append('<code>'+txt[l+1:r-1]+'</code>')
def emit_modl(tl,txt,l,r,s):
    ws.append('<em><code>'+txt[l+1:r-1]+'</code></em>')
def emit_emph(tl,txt,l,r,s):
    ws.append('<em>'+txt[l+1:r-1]+'</em>')
def emit_strg(tl,txt,l,r,s):
    ws.append('<strong>'+txt[l+1:r-1]+'</strong>')
def emit_titl(tl,txt,l,r,s):
    ws.append('<cite>'+txt[l+1:r-1]+'</cite>')
def jump_count(tl,txt,l,r,s):
    global head_pos, loops
    loops = loops+1
    if head_pos is None: head_pos = r
    elif head_pos == r:
        raise "InfiniteLoopError", \
            txt[l-20:l]+'{'+txt[l]+'}'+txt[l+1:r+15]
    else: head_pos = r


#-- What can appear inside, and what can be, markups?
punct_set = set("'!@#$%^&*()_-+=|\{}[]:;'<>,.?/"+'"')
markable = alphanumeric+whitespace+'''!@#$%^&()+=|\{}:;<>,.?/"+'"'
markable_func = set(markable+"*-_[]'")
markable_modl = set(markable+"*-_'"")
markable_emph = set(markable+"*_'[]'")
markable_strg = set(markable+"-_'[]'")
markable_titl = set(markable+"*-'[]'")
markup_set    = set("-*'[]_")


#-- What can precede and follow markup phrases?
darkins = '(/"'
leadins = whitespace+darkins        # might add from "-*'[]_"
darkouts = '/.),:;?!"'
darkout_set = set(darkouts)
leadouts = whitespace+darkouts     # for non-conflicting markup
leadout_set = set(leadouts)


#-- What can appear inside plain words?
word_set = set(alphanumeric+'{}/@#$%^&-_+=|\><'+darkouts)
wordinit_set = set(alphanumeric+"'$#+\<.&{"+darkins)


#-- Define the word patterns (global so as to do it only at import)
# Special markup
def markup_struct(lmark, rmark, callback, markables, x_post="-"):
    struct = \
```

```
        ( callback, Table+CallTag,
          ( (None, Is, lmark),                    # Starts with left marker
            (None, AllInSet, markables),          # Stuff marked
            (None, Is, rmark),                    # Ends with right marker
            (None, IsInSet, leadout_set,+2,+1),# EITHR: postfix w/ leadout
            (None, Skip, -1,+1, MatchOk),         # ..give back trailng ldout
            (None, IsIn, x_post, MatchFail),      # OR: special case postfix
            (None, Skip, -1,+1, MatchOk)          # ..give back trailing char
          )
        )
    )
    return struct
funcs   = markup_struct("'", "'", emit_func, markable_func)
modules = markup_struct("[", "]", emit_modl, markable_modl)
emphs   = markup_struct("-", "-", emit_emph, markable_emph, x_post="")
strongs = markup_struct("*", "*", emit_strg, markable_strg)
titles  = markup_struct("_", "_", emit_titl, markable_titl)

# All the stuff not specially marked
plain_words = \
 ( ws, Table+AppendMatch,               # AppendMatch only -slightly-
   ( (None, IsInSet,                    #  faster than emit_misc callback
        wordinit_set, MatchFail),       # Must start with word-initial
     (None, Is, "'",+1),                # May have apostrophe next
     (None, AllInSet, word_set,+1),     # May have more word-internal
     (None, Is, "'", +2),               # May have trailing apostrophe
     (None, IsIn, "st",+1),             # May have [ts] after apostrophe
     (None, IsInSet,
        darkout_set,+1, MatchOk),       # Postfixed with dark lead-out
     (None, IsInSet,
        whitespace_set, MatchFail),     # Give back trailing whitespace
     (None, Skip, -1)
   ) )
# Catch some special cases
bullet_point = \
 ( ws, Table+AppendMatch,
   ( (None, Word+CallTag, "* "),        # Asterisk bullet is a word
   ) )
horiz_rule = \
 ( None, Table,
   ( (None, Word, "-"*50),              # 50 dashes in a row
     (None, AllIn, "-"),                # More dashes
   ) )
into_mark = \
 ( ws, Table+AppendMatch,               # Special case where dark leadin
   ( (None, IsInSet, set(darkins)),     #   is followed by markup char
     (None, IsInSet, markup_set),
```

```
                (None, Skip, -1)                # Give back the markup char
         ) )
stray_punct = \
  ( ws, Table+AppendMatch,               # Pickup any cases where multiple
     ( (None, IsInSet, punct_set),       # punctuation character occur
       (None, AllInSet, punct_set),      # alone (followed by whitespace)
       (None, IsInSet, whitespace_set),
       (None, Skip, -1)                  # Give back the whitespace
     ) )
leadout_eater = (ws, AllInSet+AppendMatch, leadout_set)

#-- Tag all the (possibly marked-up) words
tag_words = \
  ( bullet_point+(+1,),
    horiz_rule + (+1,),
    into_mark  + (+1,),
    stray_punct+ (+1,),
    emphs     + (+1,),
    funcs     + (+1,),
    strongs + (+1,),
    modules + (+1,),
    titles  + (+1,),
    into_mark+(+1,),
    plain_words +(+1,),            # Since file is mstly plain wrds, can
    leadout_eater+(+1,-1),         # shortcut by tight looping (w/ esc)
    (jump_count, Skip+CallTag, 0), # Check for infinite loop
    (None, EOF, Here, -13)         # Check for EOF
  )
def Typography(txt):
    global ws
    ws = []    # clear the list before we proceed
    tag(txt, tag_words, 0, len(txt), ws)
    return string.join(ws, '')

if __name__ == '__main__':
    print Typography(open(sys.argv[1]).read())
```

mxTypographify.py reads through a string and determines if the next bit of text
matches one of the markup patterns in tag_words. Or rather, it better match some
pattern or the application just will not know what action to take for the next bit of
text. Whenever a named subtable matches, a callback function is called, which leads to
a properly annotated string being appended to the global list ws. In the end, all such
appended strings are concatenated.

Several of the patterns given are mostly fallback conditions. For example, the
stray_punct tag table detects the condition where the next bit of text is some punctuation symbols standing alone without abutting any words. In most cases, you don't

want smart ASCII to contain such a pattern, but *mxTypographify* has to do *something* with them if they are encountered.

Making sure that every subsequence is matched by some subtable or another is tricky. Here are a few examples of matches and failures for the `stray_punct` subtable. Everything that does not match this subtable needs to match some other subtable instead:

```
-- spam        # matches "--"
& spam         # fails at "AllInSet" since '&' advanced head
#@$ %% spam    # matches "#@$"
**spam         # fails (whitespace isn't encountered before 's')
```

After each success, the read-head is at the space right before the next word "spam" or "%%". After a failure, the read-head remains where it started out (at the beginning of the line).

Like `stray_punct`, `emphs`, `funcs`, `strongs`, `plain_words`, et cetera contain tag tables. Each entry in `tag_words` has its appropriate callback functions (all "emitters" of various names, because they "emit" the match, along with surrounding markup if needed). Most lines each have a "+1" appended to their tuple; what this does is specify where to jump in case of a match failure. That is, even if these patterns fail to match, we continue on— with the read-head in the same position—to try matching against the other patterns.

After the basic word patterns each attempt a match, we get to the "leadout eater" line. For `mxTypography.py`, a "leadout" is the opposite of a "leadin." That is, the latter are things that might precede a word pattern, and the former are things that might follow a word pattern. The `leadout_set` includes whitespace characters, but it also includes things like a comma, period, and question mark, which might end a word. The "leadout eater" uses a callback function, too. As designed, it preserves exactly the whitespace the input has. However, it would be easy to normalize whitespace here by emitting something other than the actual match (e.g., a single space always).

The `jump_count` is extremely important; we will come back to it momentarily. For now, it is enough to say that we *hope* the line never does anything.

The `EOF` line is our flow control, in a way. The call made by this line is to `None`, which is to say that nothing is actually *done* with any match. The command `EOF` is the important thing (`Here` is just a filler value that occupies the tuple position). It succeeds if the read-head is past the end of the read buffer. On success, the whole tag table `tag_words` succeeds, and having succeeded, processing stops. `EOF` failure is more interesting. Assuming we haven't reached the end of our string, we jump -13 states (to `bullet_point`). From there, the whole process starts over, hopefully with the read-head advanced to the next word. By looping back to the start of the list of tuples, we continue eating successive word patterns until the read buffer is exhausted (calling callbacks along the way).

The `tag()` call simply launches processing of the tag table we pass to it (against the read buffer contained in `txt`). In our case, we do not care about the return value of `tag()` since everything is handled in callbacks. However, in cases where the tag table does not loop itself, the returned tuple can be used to determine if there is reason to call `tag()` again with a tail of the read buffer.

DEBUGGING A TAG TABLE

Describing it is easy, but I spent a large number of hours finding the exact collection of tag tables that would match every pattern I was interested in without mismatching any pattern as something it wasn't. While smart ASCII markup seems pretty simple, there are actually quite a few complications (e.g., markup characters being used in nonmarkup contexts, or markup characters and other punctuation appearing in various sequences). Any structured document format that is complicated enough to warrant using *mx.TextTools* instead of *string* is likely to have similar complications.

Without question, the worst thing that can go wrong in a looping state pattern like the one above is that *none* of the listed states match from the current read-head position. If that happens, your program winds up in a tight infinite loop (entirely inside the extension module, so you cannot get at it with Python code directly). I wound up forcing a manual kill of the process *countless* times during my first brush at *mx.TextTools* development.

Fortunately, there is a solution to the infinite loop problem. This is to use a callback like jump_count.

---

mxTypography.py infinite loop catcher

```
def jump_count(taglist,txt,l,r,subtag):
    global head_pos
    if head_pos is None: head_pos = r
    elif head_pos == r:
        raise "InfiniteLoopError", \
            txt[l-20:l]+'{'+txt[l]+'}'+txt[l+1:r+15]
    else: head_pos = r
```

The basic purpose of jump_count is simple: We want to catch the situation where our tag table has been run through multiple times without matching anything. The simplest way to do this is to check whether the last read-head position is the same as the current. If it is, more loops cannot get anywhere, since we have reached the exact same state twice, and the same thing is fated to happen forever. mxTypography.py simply raises an error to stop the program (and reports a little bit of buffer context to see what is going on).

It is also possible to move the read-head manually and try again from a different starting position. To manipulate the read head in this fashion, you could use the Call command in tag table items. But a better approach is to create a nonlooping tag table that is called repeatedly from a Python loop. This Python loop can look at a returned tuple and use adjusted offsets in the next call if no match occurred. Either way, since much more time is spent in Python this way than with the loop tag table approach, less speed would be gained from *mx.TextTools*.

Not as bad as an infinite loop, but still undesirable. is having patterns within a tag table match when they are not supposed to or not match when they are suppose to (but something else has to match, or we would have an infinite loop issue). Using callbacks everywhere makes examining this situation much easier. During development, I frequently create temporary changes to my emit_* callbacks to print or log when certain emitters get called. By looking at output from these temporary `print` statements, most times you can tell where the problem lies.

CONSTANTS

The *mx.TextTools* module contains constants for a number of frequently used collections of characters. Many of these character classes are the same as ones in the *string* module. Each of these constants also has a `set` version predefined; a set is an efficient representation of a character class that may be used in tag tables and other *mx.TextTools* functions. You may also obtain a character set from a (custom) character class using the *mx.TextTools.set()* function:

```
>>> from mx.TextTools import a2z, set
>>> varname_chars = a2z + '_'
>>> varname_set = set(varname_chars)
```

mx.TextTools.a2z
mx.TextTools.a2z_set

> English lowercase letters ("abcdefghijklmnopqrstuvwxyz").

mx.TextTools.A2Z
mx.TextTools.A2Z_set

> English uppercase letters ("ABCDEFGHIJKLMNOPQRSTUVWXYZ").

mx.TextTools.umlaute
mx.TextTools.umlaute_set

> Extra German lowercase hi-bit characters.

mx.TextTools.Umlaute
mx.TextTools.Umlaute_set

> Extra German uppercase hi-bit characters.

mx.TextTools.alpha
mx.TextTools.alpha_set

> English letters (A2Z + a2z).

mx.TextTools.german_alpha
mx.TextTools.german_alpha_set

> German letters (A2Z + a2z + umlaute + Umlaute).

mx.TextTools.number
mx.TextTools.number_set

> The decimal numerals ("0123456789").

mx.TextTools.alphanumeric
mx.TextTools.alphanumeric_set

> English numbers and letters (alpha + number).

mx.TextTools.white
mx.TextTools.white_set

Spaces and tabs (" \t\v"). This is more restricted than *string.whitespace*.

mx.TextTools.newline
mx.TextTools.newline_set

Line break characters for various platforms ("\n\r").

mx.TextTools.formfeed
mx.TextTools.formfeed_set

Formfeed character ("\f").

mx.TextTools.whitespace
mx.TextTools.whitespace_set

Same as *string.whitespace* (white+newline+formfeed).

mx.TextTools.any
mx.TextTools.any_set

All characters (0x00-0xFF).

SEE ALSO: string.digits *130*; string.hexdigits *130*; string.octdigits *130*; string.lowercase *131*; string.uppercase *131*; string.letters *131*; string.punctuation *131*; string.whitespace *131*; string.printable *132*;

COMMANDS

Programming in *mx.TextTools* amounts mostly to correctly configuring tag tables. Utilizing a tag table requires just one call to the *mx.TextTools.tag()*, but inside a tag table is a kind of mini-language—something close to a specialized Assembly language, in many ways.

Each tuple within a tag table contains several elements, of the form:

```
(tagobj, command[+modifiers], argument
        [,jump_no_match=MatchFail [,jump_match=+1]])
```

The "tag object" may be None, a callable object, or a string. If tagobj is None, the indicated pattern may match, but nothing is added to a taglist data structure if so, nor is a callback invoked. If a callable object (usually a function) is given, it acts as a callback for a match. If a string is used, it is used to name a part of the taglist data structure returned by a call to *mx.TextTools.tag()*.

A command indicates a type of pattern to match, and a modifier can change the behavior that occurs in case of such a match. Some commands succeed or fail unconditionally, but allow you to specify behaviors to take if they are reached. An argument is required, but the specific values that are allowed and how they are interpreted depends on the command used.

Two jump conditions may optionally be specified. If no values are given, jump_no_match defaults to MatchFail—that is, unless otherwise specified, failing to match a tuple in a tag table causes the tag table as a whole to fail. If a value *is* given, `jump_no_match` branches to a tuple the specified number of states forward or backward. For clarity, an explicit leading "+" is used in forward branches. Branches backward will begin with a minus sign. For example:

```
# Branch forward one state if next character -is not- an X
# ... branch backward three states if it is an X
tupX = (None, Is, 'X', +1, -3)
# assume all the tups are defined somewhere...
tagtable = (tupA, tupB, tupV, tupW, tupX, tupY, tupZ)
```

If no value is given for `jump_match`, branching is one state forward in the case of a match.

Version 2.1.0 of *mx.TextTools* adds named jump targets, which are often easier to read (and maintain) than numeric offsets. An example is given in the *mx.TextTools* documentation:

```
tag_table = ('start',
             ('lowercase',AllIn,a2z,+1,'skip'),
             ('upper',AllIn,A2Z,'skip'),
             'skip',
             (None,AllIn,white+newline,+1),
             (None,AllNotIn,alpha+white+newline,+1),
             (None,EOF,Here,'start') )
```

It is easy to see that if you were to add or remove a tuple, it is less error prone to retain a jump to, for example, `skip` than to change every necessary +2 to a +3 or the like.

UNCONDITIONAL COMMANDS

mx.TextTools.Fail
mx.TextTools.Jump

Nonmatch at this tuple. Used mostly for documentary purposes in a tag table, usually with the `Here` or `To` placeholder. The tag tables below are equivalent:

```
table1 = ( ('foo', Is, 'X', MatchFail, MatchOk), )
table2 = ( ('foo', Is, 'X', +1, +2),
           ('Not_X', Fail, Here) )
```

The `Fail` command may be preferred if several other states branch to the same failure, or if the condition needs to be documented explicitly.

`Jump` is equivalent to `Fail`, but it is often better self-documenting to use one rather than the other; for example:

```
tup1 = (None, Fail, Here, +3)
tup2 = (None, Jump, To, +3)
```

mx.TextTools.Skip
mx.TextTools.Move

Match at this tuple, and change the read-head position. `Skip` moves the read-head by a relative amount, `Move` to an absolute offset (within the slice the tag table is operating on). For example:

```
# read-head forward 20 chars, jump to next state
tup1 = (None, Skip, 20)
# read-head to position 10, and jump back 4 states
tup2 = (None, Move, 10, 0, -4)
```

Negative offsets are allowed, as in Python list indexing.

MATCHING PARTICULAR CHARACTERS

mx.TextTools.AllIn
mx.TextTools.AllInSet
mx.TextTools.AllInCharSet

Match all characters up to the first that is not included in `argument`. `AllIn` uses a character string while `AllInSet` uses a set as `argument`. For version 2.1.0, you may also use `AllInCharSet` to match `CharSet` objects. In general, the set or CharSet form will be faster and is preferable. The following are functionally the same:

```
tup1 = ('xyz', AllIn, 'XYZxyz')
tup2 = ('xyz', AllInSet, set('XYZxyz'))
tup3 = ('xyz', AllInSet, CharSet('XYZxyz'))
```

At least one character must match for the tuple to match.

mx.TextTools.AllNotIn

Match all characters up to the first that *is* included in `argument`. As of version 2.1.0, *mx.TextTools* does not include an `AllNotInSet` command. However, the following tuples are functionally the same (the second usually faster):

```
from mx.TextTools import AllNotIn, AllInSet, invset
tup1 = ('xyz', AllNotIn, 'XYZxyz')
tup2 = ('xyz', AllInSet, invset('xyzXYZ'))
```

At least one character must match for the tuple to match.

mx.TextTools.Is

Match specified character. For example:

```
tup = ('X', Is, 'X')
```

mx.TextTools.IsNot

Match any one character except the specified character.

```
tup = ('X', IsNot, 'X')
```

mx.TextTools.IsIn
mx.TextTools.IsInSet
mx.TextTools.IsInCharSet

Match exactly one character if it is in `argument`. `IsIn` uses a character string while `IsInSet` use a set as `argument`. For version 2.1.0, you may also use `IsInCharSet` to match `CharSet` objects. In general, the set or CharSet form will be faster and is preferable. The following are functionally the same:

```
tup1 = ('xyz', IsIn, 'XYZxyz')
tup2 = ('xyz', IsInSet, set('XYZxyz'))
tup3 = ('xyz', IsInSet, CharSet('XYZxyz'))
```

mx.TextTools.IsNotIn

Match exactly one character if it is *not* in `argument`. As of version 2.1.0, *mx.TextTools* does not include an `'AllNotInSet` command. However, the following tuples are functionally the same (the second usually faster):

```
from mx.TextTools import IsNotIn, IsInSet, invset
tup1 = ('xyz', IsNotIn, 'XYZxyz')
tup2 = ('xyz', IsInSet, invset('xyzXYZ'))
```

MATCHING SEQUENCES

mx.TextTools.Word

Match a word at the current read-head position. For example:

```
tup = ('spam', Word, 'spam')
```

mx.TextTools.WordStart
mx.TextTools.sWordStart
mx.TextTools.WordEnd
mx.TextTools.sWordEnd

Search for a word, and match up to the point of the match. Searches performed in this manner are extremely fast, and this is one of the most powerful elements of tag tables. The commands `sWordStart` and `sWordEnd` use "search objects" rather than plaintexts (and are significantly faster).

WordStart and sWordStart leave the read-head immediately prior to the matched word, if a match succeeds. WordEnd and sWordEnd leave the read-head immediately after the matched word. On failure, the read-head is not moved for any of these commands.

```
>>> from mx.TextTools import *
>>> s = 'spam and eggs taste good'
>>> tab1 = ( ('toeggs', WordStart, 'eggs'), )
>>> tag(s, tab1)
(1, [('toeggs', 0, 9, None)], 9)
>>> s[0:9]
'spam and '
>>> tab2 = ( ('pasteggs', sWordEnd, BMS('eggs')), )
>>> tag(s, tab2)
(1, [('pasteggs', 0, 13, None)], 13)
>>> s[0:13]
'spam and eggs'
```

SEE ALSO: mx.TextTools.BMS() *307*; mx.TextTools.sFindWord *303*;

mx.TextTools.sFindWord

Search for a word, and match only that word. Any characters leading up to the match are ignored. This command accepts a search object as an argument. In case of a match, the read-head is positioned immediately after the matched word.

```
>>> from mx.TextTools import *
>>> s = 'spam and eggs taste good'
>>> tab3 = ( ('justeggs', sFindWord, BMS('eggs')), )
>>> tag(s, tab3)
(1, [('justeggs', 9, 13, None)], 13)
>>> s[9:13]
'eggs'
```

SEE ALSO: mx.TextTools.sWordEnd *302*;

mx.TextTools.EOF

Match if the read-head is past the end of the string slice. Normally used with placeholder argument Here, for example:

```
tup = (None, EOF, Here)
```

COMPOUND MATCHES

mx.TextTools.Table
mx.TextTools.SubTable

Match if the table given as `argument` matches at the current read-head position. The difference between the `Table` and the `SubTable` commands is in where matches get inserted. When the `Table` command is used, any matches in the indicated table are nested in the data structure associated with the tuple. When `SubTable` is used, matches are written into the current level taglist. For example:

```
>>> from mx.TextTools import *
>>> from pprint import pprint
>>> caps = ('Caps', AllIn, A2Z)
>>> lower = ('Lower', AllIn, a2z)
>>> words = ( ('Word', Table, (caps, lower)),
...           (None, AllIn, whitespace, MatchFail, -1) )
>>> from pprint import pprint
>>> pprint(tag(s, words))
(0,
 [('Word', 0, 4, [('Caps', 0, 1, None), ('Lower', 1, 4, None)]),
  ('Word', 5, 19, [('Caps', 5, 6, None), ('Lower', 6, 19, None)]),
  ('Word', 20, 29, [('Caps', 20, 24, None), ('Lower', 24, 29, None)]),
  ('Word', 30, 35, [('Caps', 30, 32, None), ('Lower', 32, 35, None)])
 ],
 35)
>>> flatwords = ( (None, SubTable, (caps, lower)),
...               (None, AllIn, whitespace, MatchFail, -1) )
>>> pprint(tag(s, flatwords))
(0,
 [('Caps', 0, 1, None),
  ('Lower', 1, 4, None),
  ('Caps', 5, 6, None),
  ('Lower', 6, 19, None),
  ('Caps', 20, 24, None),
  ('Lower', 24, 29, None),
  ('Caps', 30, 32, None),
  ('Lower', 32, 35, None)],
 35)
```

For either command, if a match occurs, the read-head is moved to immediately after the match.

The special constant `ThisTable` can be used instead of a tag table to call the current table recursively.

mx.TextTools.TableInList
mx.TextTools.SubTableInList

Similar to `Table` and `SubTable` except that the `argument` is a tuple of the form (`list_of_tables,index`). The advantage (and the danger) of this is that a list is mutable and may have tables added after the tuple defined—in particular, the containing tag table may be added to `list_of_tables` to allow recursion. Note, however, that the special value `ThisTable` can be used with the `Table` or `SubTable` commands and is usually more clear.

SEE ALSO: mx.TextTools.Table *304*; mx.TextTools.SubTable *304*;

mx.TextTools.Call

Match on any computable basis. Essentially, when the `Call` command is used, control over parsing/matching is turned over to Python rather than staying in the *mx.TextTools* engine. The function that is called must accept arguments `s`, `pos`, and `end`—where `s` is the underlying string, `pos` is the current read-head position, and `end` is ending of the slice being processed. The called function must return an integer for the new read-head position; if the return is different from `pos`, the match is a success.

As an example, suppose you want to match at a certain point only if the next N characters make up a dictionary word. Perhaps an efficient stemmed data structure is used to represent the dictionary word list. You might check dictionary membership with a tuple like:

```
tup = ('DictWord', Call, inDict)
```

Since the function `inDict` is written in Python, it will generally not operate as quickly as does an *mx.TextTools* pattern tuple.

mx.TextTools.CallArg

Same as `Call`, except `CallArg` allows passing additional arguments. For example, suppose the dictionary example given in the discussion of `Call` also allows you to specify language and maximum word length for a match:

```
tup = ('DictWord', Call, (inDict,['English',10]))
```

SEE ALSO: mx.TextTools.Call *305*;

MODIFIERS

mx.TextTools.CallTag

Instead of appending (`tagobj,l,r,subtags`) to the taglist upon a successful match, call the function indicated as the tag object (which must be a function rather than

None or a string). The function called must accept the arguments `taglist`, `s`, `start`, `end`, and `subtags`—where `taglist` is the present taglist, `s` is the underlying string, `start` and `end` are the slice indices of the match, and `subtags` is the nested taglist. The function called *may*, but need not, append to or modify `taglist` or `subtags` as part of its action. For example, a code parsing application might include:

```
>>> def todo_flag(taglist, s, start, end, subtags):
...     sys.stderr.write("Fix issue at offset %d\n" % start)
...
>>> tup = (todo_flag, Word+CallTag, 'XXX')
>>> tag('XXX more stuff', (tup,))
Fix issue at offset 0
(1, [], 3)
```

mx.TextTools.AppendMatch

Instead of appending (`tagobj`,`start`,`end`,`subtags`) to the taglist upon successful matching, append the match found as string. The produced taglist is "flattened" and cannot be used in the same manner as "normal" taglist data structures. The flat data structure is often useful for joining or for list processing styles.

```
>>> from mx.TextTools import *
>>> words = (('Word', AllIn+AppendMatch, alpha),
...          (None, AllIn, whitespace, MatchFail, -1))
>>> tag('this and that', words)
(0, ['this', 'and', 'that'], 13)
>>> join(tag('this and that', words)[1], '-')
'this-and-that'
```

SEE ALSO: string.split() *142*;

mx.TextTools.AppendToTagobj

Instead of appending (`tagobj`,`start`,`end`,`subtags`) to the taglist upon successful matching, call the `.append()` method of the tag object. The tag object must be a list (or a descendent of `list` in Python 2.2+).

```
>>> from mx.TextTools import *
>>> ws = []
>>> words = ((ws, AllIn+AppendToTagobj, alpha),
...          (None, AllIn, whitespace, MatchFail, -1))
>>> tag('this and that', words)
(0, [], 13)
>>> ws
[(None, 0, 4, None), (None, 5, 8, None), (None, 9, 13, None)]
```

SEE ALSO: mx.TextTools.CallTag *305*;

mx.TextTools.AppendTagobj

Instead of appending (tagobj,start,end,subtags) to the taglist upon successful matching, append the tag object. The produced taglist is usually nonstandard and cannot be used in the same manner as "normal" taglist data structures. A flat data structure is often useful for joining or for list processing styles.

```
>>> from mx.TextTools import *
>>> words = (('word', AllIn+AppendTagobj, alpha),
...          (None, AllIn, whitespace, MatchFail, -1))
>>> tag('this and that', words)
(0, ['word', 'word', 'word'], 13)
```

mx.TextTools.LookAhead

If this modifier is used, the read-head position is not changed when a match occurs. As the name suggests, this modifier allows you to create patterns similar to regular expression lookaheads.

```
>>> from mx.TextTools import *
>>> from pprint import pprint
>>> xwords = ((None, IsIn+LookAhead, 'Xx', +2),
...           ('xword', AllIn, alpha, MatchFail, +2),
...           ('other', AllIn, alpha),
...           (None, AllIn, whitespace, MatchFail, -3))
>>> pprint(tag('Xylophone trumpet xray camera', xwords))
(0,
 [('xword', 0, 9, None),
  ('other', 10, 17, None),
  ('xword', 18, 22, None),
  ('other', 23, 29, None)],
 29)
```

CLASSES

mx.TextTools.BMS(word [,translate])
mx.TextTools.FS(word [,translate])
mx.TextTools.TextSearch(word [,translate [,algorithm=BOYERMOORE]])

Create a search object for the string word. This is similar in concept to a compiled regular expression. A search object has several methods to locate its encoded string within another string. The BMS name is short for "Boyer-Moore," which is a particular search algorithm. The name FS is reserved for accessing the "Fast Search" algorithm in future versions, but currently both classes use Boyer-Moore. For *mx.TextTools* 2.1.0+, you are urged to use the .TextSearch() constructor.

If a `translate` argument is given, the searched string is translated during the search. This is equivalent to transforming the string with *string.translate()* prior to searching it.

SEE ALSO: string.translate() *145*;

mx.TextTools.CharSet(definition)

Version 2.1.0 of *mx.TextTools* adds the Unicode-compatible `CharSet` object. `CharSet` objects may be initialized to support character ranges, as in regular expressions; for example, `definition="a-mXYZ"`. In most respects, `CharSet` objects are similar to older sets.

METHODS AND ATTRIBUTES

mx.TextTools.BMS.search(s [,start [,end]])
mx.TextTools.FS.search(s [,start [,end]])
mx.TextTools.TextSearch.search(s [,start [,end]])

Locate as a slice the first match of the search object against `s`. If optional arguments `start` and `end` are used, only the slice `s[start:end]` is considered. Note: As of version 2.1.0, the documentation that accompanies *mx.TextTools* inaccurately describes the `end` parameter of search object methods as indicating the length of the slice rather than its ending offset.

mx.TextTools.BMS.find(s, [,start [,end]])
mx.TextTools.FS.find(s, [,start [,end]])
mx.TextTools.TextSearch.search(s [,start [,end]])

Similar to *mx.TextTools.BMS.search()*, except return only the starting position of the match. The behavior is similar to that of *string.find()*.

SEE ALSO: string.find() *135*; mx.TextTools.find() *312*;

mx.TextTools.BMS.findall(s [,start [,end]])
mx.TextTools.FS.findall(s [,start [,end]])
mx.TextTools.TextSearch.search(s [,start [,end]])

Locate as slices *every* match of the search object against `s`. If the optional arguments `start` and `end` are used, only the slice `s[start:end]` is considered.

```
>>> from mx.TextTools import BMS, any, upper
>>> foosrch = BMS('FOO', upper(any))
>>> foosrch.search('foo and bar and FOO and BAR')
(0, 3)
>>> foosrch.find('foo and bar and FOO and BAR')
0
>>> foosrch.findall('foo and bar and FOO and BAR')
[(0, 3), (16, 19)]
>>> foosrch.search('foo and bar and FOO and BAR', 10, 20)
(16, 19)
```

SEE ALSO: re.findall *245*; mx.TextTools.findall() *312*;

mx.TextTools.BMS.match
mx.TextTools.FS.match
mx.TextTools.TextSearch.match

The string that the search object will look for in the search text (read-only).

mx.TextTools.BMS.translate
mx.TextTools.FS.translate
mx.TextTools.TextSearch.match

The translation string used by the object, or None if no translate string was specified.

mx.TextTools.CharSet.contains(c)

Return a true value if character c is in the CharSet.

mx.TextTools.CharSet.search(s [,direction [,start=0 [,stop=len(s)]]])

Return the position of the first CharSet character that occurs in s[start:end]. Return None if there is no match. You may specify a negative direction to search backwards.

SEE ALSO: re.search() *249*;

mx.TextTools.CharSet.match(s [,direction [,start=0 [,stop=len(s)]]])

Return the length of the longest contiguous match of the CharSet object against substrings of s[start:end].

mx.TextTools.CharSet.split(s [,start=0 [,stop=len(text)]])

Return a list of substrings of s[start:end] divided by occurrences of characters in the CharSet.

SEE ALSO: re.search() *249*;

mx.TextTools.CharSet.splitx(s [,start=0 [,stop=len(text)]])

Like *mx.TextTools.CharSet.split()* except retain characters from CharSet in interspersed list elements.

mx.TextTools.CharSet.strip(s [,where=0 [,start=0 [,stop=len(s)]]])

Strip all characters in s[start:stop] appearing in the character set.

FUNCTIONS

Many of the functions in *mx.TextTools* are used by the tagging engine. A number of others are higher-level utility functions that do not require custom development of tag tables. The latter are listed under a separate heading and generally resemble faster versions of functions in the *string* module.

mx.TextTools.cmp(t1, t2)

Compare two valid taglist tuples on their slice positions. Taglists generated with multiple passes of *mx.TextTools.tag()*, or combined by other means, may not have tuples sorted in string order. This custom comparison function is coded in C and is very fast.

```
>>> import mx.TextTools
>>> from pprint import pprint
>>> tl = [('other', 10, 17, None),
...       ('other', 23, 29, None),
...       ('xword', 0, 9, None),
...       ('xword', 18, 22, None)]
>>> tl.sort(mx.TextTools.cmp)
>>> pprint(tl)
[('xword', 0, 9, None),
 ('other', 10, 17, None),
 ('xword', 18, 22, None),
 ('other', 23, 29, None)]
```

mx.TextTools.invset(s)

Identical to mx.TextTools.set(s, 0).

SEE ALSO: mx.TextTools.set() *310*;

mx.TextTools.set(s [,includechars=1])

Return a bit-position encoded character set. Bit-position encoding makes tag table commands like `InSet` and `AllInSet` operate more quickly than their character-string equivalents (e.g, `In`, `AllIn`).

If `includechars` is set to 0, invert the character set.

SEE ALSO: mx.TextTools.invset() *310*;

mx.TextTools.tag(s, table [,start [,end [,taglist]]])

Apply a tag table to a string. The return value is a tuple of the form (`success`, `taglist`, `next`). `success` is a binary value indicating whether the table matched. `next` is the read-head position after the match attempt. Even on a nonmatch of the table, the read-head might have been advanced to some degree by member tuples matching. The `taglist` return value contains the data structure generated by application. Modifiers and commands within the tag table can alter the composition of `taglist`; but in the normal case, `taglist` is composed of zero or more tuples of the form (`tagname, start, end, subtaglist`).

Assuming a "normal" taglist is created, `tagname` is a string value that was given as a tag object in a tuple within the tag table. `start` and `end` the slice ends of that particular match. `subtaglist` is either `None` or a taglist for a subtable match.

If `start` or `end` are given as arguments to *mx.TextTools.tag()*, application is restricted to the slice `s[start:end]` (or `s[start:]` if only `start` is used). If a `taglist` argument is passed, that list object is used instead of a new list. This allows extending a previously generated taglist, for example. If `None` is passed as `taglist`, no taglist is generated.

See the application examples and command illustrations for a number of concrete uses of *mx.TextTools.tag()*.

UTILITY FUNCTIONS

mx.TextTools.charsplit(s, char, [start [,end]])

Return a list split around each `char`. Similar to *string.split()*, but faster. If the optional arguments `start` and `end` are used, only the slice `s[start:end]` is operated on.

SEE ALSO: string.split() *142*; mx.TextTools.setsplit() *314*;

mx.TextTools.collapse(s, sep=' ')

Return a string with normalized whitespace. This is equivalent to `string.join( string.split(s),sep)`, but faster.

```
>>> from mx.TextTools import collapse
>>> collapse('this and   that','-')
'this-and-that'
```

SEE ALSO: string.join() *137*; string.split() *142*;

mx.TextTools.countlines(s)

Returns the number of lines in s in a platform-portable way. Lines may end with CR (Mac-style), LF (Unix-style), or CRLF (DOS-style), including a mixture of these.

SEE ALSO: FILE.readlines() *17*; mx.TextTools.splitlines() *315*;

mx.TextTools.find(s, search_obj, [start, [,end]])

Return the position of the first match of `search_obj` against `s`. If the optional arguments `start` and `end` are used, only the slice `s[start:end]` is considered. This function is identical to the search object method of the same name; the syntax is just slightly different. The following are synonyms:

```
from mx.TextTools import BMS, find
s = 'some string with a pattern in it'
pos1 = find(s, BMS('pat'))
pos2 = BMS('pat').find(s)
```

SEE ALSO: string.find() *135*; mx.TextTools.BMS.find() *308*;

mx.TextTools.findall(s, search_obj [,start [,end]])

Return as slices *every* match of `search_obj` against `s`. If the optional arguments `start` and `end` are used, only the slice `s[start:end]` is considered. This function is identical to the search object method of the same name; the syntax is just slightly different. The following are synonyms:

```
from mx.TextTools import BMS, findall
s = 'some string with a pattern in it'
pos1 = findall(s, BMS('pat'))
pos2 = BMS('pat').findall(s)
```

SEE ALSO: mx.TextTools.find() *312*; mx.TextTools.BMS.findall() *308*;

mx.TextTools.hex2str(hexstr)

Returns a string based on the hex-encoded string `hexstr`.

```
>>> from mx.TextTools import hex2str, str2hex
>>> str2hex('abc')
'616263'
>>> hex2str('616263')
'abc'
```

SEE ALSO: mx.TextTools.str2hex() *315*;

mx.TextTools.is_whitespace(s [,start [,end]])

Returns a Boolean value indicating whether `s[start:end]` contains only whitespace characters. `start` and `end` are optional, and will default to 0 and `len(s)`, respectively.

mx.TextTools.isascii(s)

Returns a Boolean value indicating whether `s` contains only ASCII characters.

mx.TextTools.join(joinlist [,sep="" [,start [,end]]])

Return a string composed of slices from other strings. `joinlist` is a sequence of tuples of the form (s, start, end, ...) each indicating the source string and offsets for the utilized slice. Negative offsets do not behave like Python slice offsets and should not be used. If a `joinlist` item tuple contains extra entries, they are ignored, but are permissible.

If the optional argument `sep` is specified, a delimiter between each joined slice is added. If `start` and `end` are specified only `joinlist[start:end]` is utilized in the joining.

```
>>> from mx.TextTools import join
>>> s = 'Spam and eggs for breakfast'
>>> t = 'This and that for lunch'
>>> jl = [(s, 0, 4), (s, 9, 13), (t, 0, 4), (t, 9, 13)]
>>> join(jl, '/', 1, 4)
'/eggs/This/that'
```

SEE ALSO: string.join() *137*;

mx.TextTools.lower(s)

Return a string with any uppercase letters converted to lowercase. Functionally identical to *string.lower()*, but much faster.

SEE ALSO: string.lower() *138*; mx.TextTools.upper() *316*;

mx.TextTools.prefix(s, prefixes [,start [,stop [,translate]]])

Return the first prefix in the tuple `prefixes` that matches the end of s. If `start` and `end` are specified, only operate on the slice s[start:end]. Return None if no prefix matches.

If a `translate` argument is given, the searched string is translated during the search. This is equivalent to transforming the string with *string.translate()* prior to searching it.

```
>>> from mx.TextTools import prefix
>>> prefix('spam and eggs', ('spam','and','eggs'))
'spam'
```

SEE ALSO: mx.TextTools.suffix() *316*;

mx.TextTools.multireplace(s ,replacements [,start [,stop]])

Replace multiple nonoverlapping slices in s with string values. `replacements` must be list of tuples of the form (new, left, right). Indexing is always relative to s, even if an earlier replacement changes the length of the result. If `start` and `end` are specified, only operate on the slice s[start:end].

```
>>> from mx.TextTools import findall, multireplace
>>> s = 'spam, bacon, sausage, and spam'
>>> repls = [('X',l,r) for l,r in findall(s, 'spam')]
>>> multireplace(s, repls)
'X, bacon, sausage, and X'
>>> repls
[('X', 0, 4), ('X', 26, 30)]
```

mx.TextTools.replace(s, old, new [,start [,stop]])

Return a string where the pattern matched by search object old is replaced by string new. If start and end are specified, only operate on the slice s[start:end]. This function is much faster than *string.replace()*, since a search object is used in the search aspect.

```
>>> from mx.TextTools import replace, BMS
>>> s = 'spam, bacon, sausage, and spam'
>>> spam = BMS('spam')
>>> replace(s, spam, 'eggs')
'eggs, bacon, sausage, and eggs'
>>> replace(s, spam, 'eggs', 5)
' bacon, sausage, and eggs'
```

SEE ALSO: string.replace() *139*; mx.TextTools.BMS *307*;

mx.TextTools.setfind(s, set [,start [,end]])

Find the first occurence of any character in set. If start is specified, look only in s[start:]; if end is specified, look only in s[start:end]. The argument set must be a set.

```
>>> from mx.TextTools import *
>>> s = 'spam and eggs'
>>> vowel = set('aeiou')
>>> setfind(s, vowel)
2
>>> setfind(s, vowel, 7, 10)
9
```

SEE ALSO: mx.TextTools.set() *310*;

mx.TextTools.setsplit(s, set [,start [,stop]])

Split s into substrings divided at any characters in set. If start is specified, create a list of substrings of s[start:]; if end is specified, use s[start:end]. The argument set must be a set.

SEE ALSO: string.split() *142*; mx.TextTools.set() *310*; mx.TextTools.setsplitx() *315*;

mx.TextTools.setsplitx(text,set[,start=0,stop=len(text)])

Split s into substrings divided at any characters in set. Include the split characters in the returned list. Adjacent characters in set are returned in the same list element. If start is specified, create a list of substrings of s[start:]; if end is specified, use s[start:end]. The argument set must be a set.

```
>>> s = 'do you like spam'
>>> setsplit(s, vowel)
['d', ' y', ' l', 'k', ' sp', 'm']
>>> setsplitx(s, vowel)
['d', 'o', ' y', 'ou', ' l', 'i', 'k', 'e', ' sp', 'a', 'm']
```

SEE ALSO: string.split() *142*; mx.TextTools.set() *310*; mx.TextTools.setsplit() *314*;

mx.TextTools.splitat(s, char, [n=1 [,start [end]]])

Return a 2-element tuple that divides s around the n'th occurence of char. If start and end are specified, only operate on the slice s[start:end].

```
>>> from mx.TextTools import splitat
>>> s = 'spam, bacon, sausage, and spam'
>>> splitat(s, 'a', 3)
('spam, bacon, s', 'usage, and spam')
>>> splitat(s, 'a', 3, 5, 20)
(' bacon, saus', 'ge')
```

mx.TextTools.splitlines(s)

Return a list of lines in s. Line-ending combinations for Mac, PC, and Unix platforms are recognized in any combination. which makes this function more portable than is string.split(s,"\n") or *FILE.readlines()*.

SEE ALSO: string.split() *142*; FILE.readlines() *17*; mx.TextTools.setsplit() *314*; mx.TextTools.countlines() *311*;

mx.TextTools.splitwords(s)

Return a list of whitespace-separated words in s. Equivalent to string.split(s).

SEE ALSO: string.split() *142*;

mx.TextTools.str2hex(s)

Returns a hexadecimal representation of a string. For Python 2.0+, this is equivalent to s.encode("hex").

SEE ALSO: "".encode() *188*; mx.TextTools.hex2str() *312*;

mx.TextTools.suffix(s, suffixes [,start [,stop [,translate]]])

Return the first suffix in the tuple `suffixes` that matches the end of s. If `start` and `end` are specified, only operate on the slice s[start:end]. Return `None` if no suffix matches.

If a `translate` argument is given, the searched string is translated during the search. This is equivalent to transforming the string with *string.translate()* prior to searching it.

```
>>> from mx.TextTools import suffix
>>> suffix('spam and eggs', ('spam','and','eggs'))
'eggs'
```

SEE ALSO: mx.TextTools.prefix() *313*;

mx.TextTools.upper(s)

Return a string with any lowercase letters converted to uppercase. Functionally identical to *string.upper()*, but much faster.

SEE ALSO: string.upper() *146*; mx.TextTools.lower() *313*;

4.3.3   High-Level EBNF Parsing

SimpleParse ◇ A Parser Generator for mx.TextTools

SimpleParse is an interesting tool. To use this module, you need to have the *mx.TextTools* module installed. While there is nothing you can do with *SimpleParse* that cannot be done with *mx.TextTools* by itself, *SimpleParse* is often much easier to work with. There exist other modules to provide higher-level APIs for *mx.TextTools*; I find *SimpleParse* to be the most useful of these, and the only one that this book will present. The examples in this section were written against *SimpleParse* version 1.0, but the documentation is updated to include new features of 2.0. Version 2.0 is fully backward compatible with existing *SimpleParse* code.

SimpleParse substitutes an EBNF-style grammar for the low-level state matching language of *mx.TextTools* tag tables. Or more accurately, *SimpleParse* is a tool for generating tag tables based on friendlier and higher-level EBNF grammars. In principle, *SimpleParse* lets you access and modify tag tables before passing them to *mx.TextTools.tag()*. But in practice, you usually want to stick wholly with *SimpleParse*'s EBNF variant when your processing is amenable to a grammatical description of the text format.

An application based on *SimpleParse* has two main aspects. The first aspect is the grammar that defines the structure of a processed text. The second aspect is the traversal and use of a generated *mx.TextTools* taglist. *SimpleParse* 2.0 adds facilities for the traversal aspect, but taglists present a data structure that is quite easy to work with in any case. The tree-walking tools in *SimpleParse* 2.0 are not covered here, but the examples given in the discussion of *mx.TextTools* illustrate such traversal.

Example: Marking up smart ASCII (Redux)

Elsewhere in this book, applications to process the smart ASCII format are also presented. Appendix D lists the Txt2Html utility, which uses a combination of a state machine for parsing paragraphs and regular expressions for identifying inline markup. A functionally similar example was given in the discussion of *mx.TextTools*, where a complex and compound tag table was developed to recognize inline markup elements. Using *SimpleParse* and an EBNF grammar is yet another way to perform the same sort of processing. Comparing the several styles will highlight a number of advantages that *SimpleParse* has—its grammars are clear and concise, and applications built around it can be extremely fast.

The application simpleTypography.py is quite simple; most of the work of programming it lies in creating a grammar to describe smart ASCII. EBNF grammars are almost self-explanatory to read, but designing one *does* require a bit of thought and testing:

typography.def

```
para            := (plain / markup)+
plain           := (word / whitespace / punctuation)+
<whitespace>    := [ \t\r\n]+
<alphanums>     := [a-zA-Z0-9]+
<word>          := alphanums, (wordpunct, alphanums)*, contraction?
<wordpunct>     := [-_]
<contraction>   := "'", ('am'/'clock'/'d'/'ll'/'m'/'re'/'s'/'t'/'ve')
markup          := emph / strong / module / code / title
emph            := '-', plain, '-'
strong          := '*', plain, '*'
module          := '[', plain, ']'
code            := "'", plain, "'"
title           := '_', plain, '_'
<punctuation>   := (safepunct / mdash)
<mdash>         := '--'
<safepunct>     := [!@#$%^&()+=|\{}:;<>,.?/"]
```

This grammar is almost exactly the way you would describe the smart ASCII language verbally, which is a nice sort of clarity. A paragraph consist of some plaintext and some marked-up text. Plaintext consists of some collection of words, whitespace, and punctuation. Marked-up text might be emphasized, or strongly emphasized, or module names, and so on. Strongly emphasized text is surrounded by asterisks. And so on. A couple of features like just what a "word" really is, or just what a contraction can end with, take a bit of thought, but the syntax of EBNF doesn't get in the way.

Notice that some declarations have their left side surrounded in angle brackets. Those productions will not be written to the taglist—this is the same as using None as a `tagobj` in an *mx.Texttools* tag table. Of course, if a production is not written to the taglist, then its children cannot be, either. By omitting some productions from the resultant taglist, a simpler data structure is produced (with only those elements that interest us).

In contrast to the grammar above, the same sort of rules can be described even more tersely using regular expressions. This is what the `Txt2Html` version of the smart ASCII markup program does. But this terseness is much harder to write and harder still to tweak later. The *re* code below expresses largely (but not precisely) the same set of rules:

Python regexes for smart ASCII markup

```
# [module] names
re_mods =  r"""([\(\s'/">]|^)\[(.*?)\]([<\s\.\),:;'"?!/-])"""
# *strongly emphasize* words
re_strong = r"""([\(\s'/"]|^)\*(.*?)\*([\s\.\),:;'"?!/-])"""
# -emphasize- words
re_emph =  r"""([\(\s'/"]|^)-(.*?)-([\s\.\),:;'"?!/])"""
# _Book Title_ citations
re_title = r"""([\(\s'/"]|^)_(.*?)_([\s\.\),:;'"?!/-])"""
# 'Function()' names
re_funcs = r"""([\(\s/"]|^)'(.*?)'([\s\.\),:;"?!/-])"""
```

If you discover or invent some slightly new variant of the language, it is *a lot* easier to play with the EBNF grammar than with those regular expressions. Moreover, using *SimpleParse*—and therefore *mx.TextTools*—will generally be even faster in performing the manipulations of the patterns.

GENERATING AND USING A TAGLIST

For `simpleTypography.py`, I put the actual grammar in a separate file. For most purposes, this is a good organization to use. Changing the grammar is usually a different sort of task than changing the application logic, and the files reflect this. But the grammar is just read as a string, so in principle you could include it in the main application (or even dynamically generate it in some way).

Let us look at the entire—compact—tagging application:

simpleTypography.py

```
from sys import stdin, stdout, stderr
from simpleparse import generator
from mx.TextTools import TextTools
from typo_html import codes
from pprint import pprint

src = stdin.read()
decl = open('typography.def').read()
parser = generator.buildParser(decl).parserbyname('para')
taglist = TextTools.tag(src, parser)
pprint(taglist, stderr)

for tag, beg, end, parts in taglist[1]:
    if tag == 'plain':
        stdout.write(src[beg:end])
    elif tag == 'markup':
        markup = parts[0]
        mtag, mbeg, mend = markup[:3]
        start, stop = codes.get(mtag, ('<!-- unknown -->',
                                       '<!-- /unknown -->'))
        stdout.write(start + src[mbeg+1:mend-1] + stop)
    else:
        raise TypeError, "Top level tagging should be plain/markup"
```

With version 2.0 of *SimpleParse*, you may use a somewhat more convenient API to create a taglist:

```
from simpleparse.parser import Parser
parser = Parser(open('typography.def').read(), 'para')
taglist = parser.parse(src)
```

Here is what it does. First read in the grammar and create an *mx.TextTools* parser from the grammar. The generated parser is similar to the tag table that is found in the hand-written `mxTypography.py` module discussed earlier (but without the human-friendly comments and structure). Next, apply the tag table/parser to the input source to create a taglist. Finally, loop through the taglist, and emit some new marked-up text. The loop could, of course, do anything else desired with each production encountered.

For the particular grammar used for smart ASCII, everything in the source text is expected to fall into either a "plain" production or a "markup" production. Therefore, it suffices to loop across a single level in the taglist (except when we look exactly one level lower for the specific markup production, such as "title"). But a more free-form grammar—such as occurs for most programming languages—could easily recursively descend into the taglist and look for production names at every level. For example, if the grammar were to allow nested markup codes, this recursive style would probably be used. Readers might enjoy the exercise of figuring out how to adjust the grammar (hint: Remember that productions are allowed to be mutually recursive).

The particular markup codes that go to the output live in yet another file for organizational, not essential, reasons. A little trick of using a dictionary as a `switch` statement is used here (although the `otherwise` case remains too narrow in the example). The idea behind this organization is that we might in the future want to create multiple "output format" files for, say, HTML, DocBook, LATEX, or others. The particular markup file used for the example just looks like:

```
typo_html.py
```

```
codes = \
{ 'emph'     : ('<em>', '</em>'),
  'strong'   : ('<strong>', '</strong>'),
  'module'   : ('<em><code>', '</code></em>'),
  'code'     : ('<code>', '</code>'),
  'title'    : ('<cite>', '</cite>'),
}
```

Extending this to other output formats is straightforward.

THE TAGLIST AND THE OUTPUT

The *tag table* generated from the grammar in `typography.def` is surprisingly complicated and includes numerous recursions. Only the exceptionally brave of heart will want to attempt manual—let alone automated—modification of tag tables created by *SimpleParse*. Fortunately, an average user need not even look at these tags, but simply *use* them, as is done with `parser` in `simpleTypography.py`.

The *taglist* produced by applying a grammar, in contrast, can be remarkably simple. Here is a run of `simpleTypography.py` against a small input file:

```
% python simpleTypography.py < p.txt > p.html
(1,
 [('plain', 0, 15, []),
  ('markup', 15, 27, [('emph', 15, 27, [('plain', 16, 26, [])])]),
  ('plain', 27, 42, []),
  ('markup', 42, 51, [('module', 42, 51, [('plain', 43, 50, [])])]),
  ('plain', 51, 55, []),
  ('markup', 55, 70, [('code', 55, 70, [('plain', 56, 69, [])])]),
  ('plain', 70, 90, []),
  ('markup', 90, 96, [('strong', 90, 96, [('plain', 91, 95, [])])]),
  ('plain', 96, 132, []),
  ('markup', 132, 145, [('title', 132, 145, [('plain',133,144,[])])]),
  ('plain', 145, 174, [])],
 174)
```

Most productions that were satisfied are not written into the taglist, because they are not needed for the application. You can control this aspect simply by defining productions with or without angle braces on the left side of their declaration. The output looks like you would expect:

```
% cat p.txt
Some words are -in italics-, others
name [modules] or 'command lines'.
Still others are *bold* -- that's how
it goes. Maybe some _book titles_.
And some in-fixed dashes.
% cat p.html
Some words are <em>in italics</em>, others
name <em><code>modules</code></em> or <code>command lines</code>.
Still others are <strong>bold</strong> -- that's how
it goes. Maybe some <cite>book titles</cite>.
And some in-fixed dashes.
```

○ · · ○ · · ○ · · ○ · · ○ · · ○ · · ○ · · ○ · · ○ · · ○ · · ○ · · ○ · · ○ · · ○

GRAMMAR

The language of *SimpleParse* grammars is itself defined using a *SimpleParse* EBNF-style grammar. In principle, you could refine the language *SimpleParse* uses by changing the variable `declaration` in `bootstrap.py`, or `simpleparsegrammar.py` in recent versions. For example, extended regular expressions, W3C XML Schemas, and some EBNF variants allow integer occurrence quantification. To specify that three to seven `foo` tokens occur, you could use the following declaration in *SimpleParse*:

```
foos := foo, foo, foo, foo?, foo?, foo?, foo?
```

Hypothetically, it might be more elegant to write something like:

```
foos := foo{3,7}
```

In practice, only someone developing a custom/enhanced parsing module would have any reason to fiddle quite so deeply; "normal" programmers should use the particular EBNF variant defined by default. Nonetheless, taking a look at `simpleparse/bootstrap.py` can be illustrative in understanding the module.

DECLARATION PATTERNS

A *SimpleParse* grammar consists of a set of one or more declarations. Each declaration generally occurs on a line by itself; within a line, horizontal whitespace may be used as desired to improve readability. A common strategy is to align the right sides of declarations, but any other use of internal whitespace is acceptable. A declaration contains a term, followed by the assignment symbol ":=", followed by a definition. An end-of-line comment may be added to a declaration, following an unquoted "#" (just as in Python).

In contrast to most imperative-style programming, the declarations within a grammar may occur in any order. When a parser generator's .parserbyname() method is called, the "top level" of the grammar is given as an argument. The documented API for *SimpleParse* uses a call of the form:

```
from simpleparse import generator
parser = generator.buildParser(decl).parserbyname('toplevel')
from mx.TextTools import TextTools
taglist = TextTools.tag(src, parser)
```

Under *SimpleParse* 2.0, you may simplify this to:

```
from simpleparse.parser import Parser
parser = Parser(decl,'toplevel')
taglist = parser.parse(src)
```

A left side term may be surrounded by angle brackets ("<", ">") to prevent that production from being written into a taglist produced by *mx.TextTools.tag()*. This is called an "unreported" production. Other than in relation to the final taglist, an unreported production acts just like a reported one. Either type of term may be used on the right sides of other productions in the same manner (without angle brackets when occurring on the right side).

In *SimpleParse* 2.0 you may also use reversed angle brackets to report the children of a production, but not the production itself. As with the standard angle brackets, the production functions normally in matching inputs; it differs only in produced taglist. For example:

```
PRODUCTIONS                TAGLIST
----------------------------------------------------------
a   := (b,c)               ('a', 1, r, [
b   := (d,e)                  ('b', 1, r, [...]),
c   := (f,g)                  ('c', 1, r, [...]) ] )
----------------------------------------------------------
a   := (b,c)               ('a', 1, r, [
<b> := (d,e)                  # no b, and no children
c   := (f,g)                  ('c', 1, r, [...]) ] )
----------------------------------------------------------
# Only in 2.0+             ('a', 1, r, [
a   := (b,c)                  # no b, but raise children
>b< := (d,e)                  ('d', 1, r, [...]),
c   := (f,g)                  ('e', 1, r, [...]),
                              ('c', 1, r, [...]) ] )
----------------------------------------------------------
```

The remainder of the documentation of the *SimpleParse* module covers elements that may occur on the right sides of declarations. In addition to the elements listed, a term from another production may occur anywhere any element may. Terms may thus stand in mutually recursive relations to one another.

LITERALS

Literal string

A string enclosed in single quotes matches the exact string quoted. Python escaping may be used for the characters \a, \b, \f, \n, \r, \t, and \v, and octal escapes of one to three digits may used. To include a literal backslash, it should be escaped as \\.

```
foo := "bar"
```

Character class: "[", "]"

Specify a set of characters that may occur at a position. The list of allowable characters may be enumerated with no delimiter. A range of characters may be indicated with a dash ("-"). Multiple ranges are allowed within a class.

To include a "]" character in a character class, make it the first character. Similarly, a literal "-" character must be either the first (after the optional "]" character) or the last character.

```
varchar := [a-zA-Z_0-9]
```

QUANTIFIERS

Universal quantifier: "*"

Match zero or more occurrences of the preceding expression. Quantification has a higher precedence than alternation or sequencing; grouping may be used to clarify quantification scope as well.

```
any_Xs      := "X"*
any_digits := [0-9]*
```

Existential quantifier: "+"

Match one or more occurrences of the preceding expression. Quantification has a higher precedence than alternation or sequencing; grouping may be used to clarify quantification scope as well.

```
some_Xs      := "X"+
some_digits := [0-9]+
```

Potentiality quantifier: "?"

Match at most one occurrence of the preceding expression. Quantification has a higher precedence than alternation or sequencing; grouping may be used to clarify quantification scope as well.

```
maybe_Xs     := "X"?
maybe_digits := [0-9]?
```

Lookahead quantifier: "?"

In *SimpleParse* 2.0+, you may place a question mark *before* a pattern to assert that it occurs, but should not actually claim the pattern. As with regular expressions, you can create either positive or negative lookahead assertions.

```
next_is_Xs         := ?"X"
next_is_not_digits := ?-[0-9]
```

Error on Failure: "!"

In *SimpleParse* 2.0+, you may cause a descriptive exception to be raised when a production does not match, rather than merely stopping parsing at that point.

```
require_Xs   := "X"!
require_code := ([A-Z]+, [0-9])!
contraction := "'", ('clock'/'d'/'ll'/'m'/'re'/'s'/'t'/'ve')!
```

For example, modifying the `contraction` production from the prior discussion could require that every apostrophe is followed by an ending. Since this doesn't hold, you might see an exception like:

```
% python typo2.py < p.txt
Traceback (most recent call last):
[...]
simpleparse.error.ParserSyntaxError:  ParserSyntaxError:
Failed parsing production "contraction" @pos 84 (~line 1:29).
Expected syntax: ('clock'/'d'/'ll'/'m'/'re'/'s'/'t'/'ve')
Got text: 'command lines'.  Still others are *bold*
```

STRUCTURES

Alternation operator: "/"

Match the first pattern possible from several alternatives. This operator allows any of a list of patterns to match. Some EBNF-style parsers will match the *longest* possible pattern, but *SimpleParse* more simply matches the *first* possible pattern. For example:

```
>>> from mx.TextTools import tag
>>> from simpleparse import generator
>>> decl = '''
... short := "foo", " "*
... long  := "foobar", " "*
... sl    := (short / long)*
... ls    := (long / short)*
... '''
>>> parser = generator.buildParser(decl).parserbyname('sl')
>>> tag('foo foobar foo bar', parser)[1]
[('short', 0, 4, []), ('short', 4, 7, [])]
>>> parser = generator.buildParser(decl).parserbyname('ls')
>>> tag('foo foobar foo bar', parser)[1]
[('short', 0, 4, []), ('long', 4, 11, []), ('short', 11, 15, [])]
```

Sequence operator: ","

Match the first pattern followed by the second pattern (followed by the third pattern, if present, ...). Whenever a definition needs several elements in a specific order, the comma sequence operator is used.

```
term := someterm, [0-9]*, "X"+, (otherterm, stillother)?
```

Negation operator: "-"

Match anything that the next pattern *does not* match. The pattern negated can be either a simple term or a compound expression.

```
nonletters   := -[a-zA-Z]
nonfoo       := -foo
notfoobarbaz := -(foo, bar, baz)
```

An expression modified by the negation operator is very similar conceptually to a regular expression with a negative lookahead assertion. For example:

```
>>> from mx.TextTools import tag
>>> from simpleparse import generator
>>> decl = '''not_initfoo := [ \t]*, -"foo", [a-zA-Z ]+'''
>>> p = generator.buildParser(decl).parserbyname('not_initfoo')
>>> tag('  foobar and baz', p)     # no match
(0, [], 0)
>>> tag('  bar, foo and baz', p)   # match on part
(1, [], 5)
>>> tag('  bar foo and baz', p)    # match on all
(1, [], 17)
```

Grouping operators: "(", ")"

Parentheses surrounding any pattern turn that pattern into an expression (possibly within a larger expression). Quantifiers and operators refer to the immediately adjacent expression, if one is defined, otherwise to the adjacent literal string, character class, or term.

```
>>> from mx.TextTools import tag
>>> from simpleparse import generator
>>> decl = '''
... foo       := "foo"
... bar       := "bar"
... foo_bars := foo, bar+
... foobars   := (foo, bar)+
... '''
>>> p1 = generator.buildParser(decl).parserbyname('foobars')
>>> p2 = generator.buildParser(decl).parserbyname('foo_bars')
>>> tag('foobarfoobar', p1)
(1, [('foo', 0, 3, []), ('bar', 3, 6, []),
     ('foo', 6, 9, []), ('bar', 9, 12, [])], 12)
>>> tag('foobarfoobar', p2)
(1, [('foo', 0, 3, []), ('bar', 3, 6, [])], 6)
>>> tag('foobarbarbar', p1)
(1, [('foo', 0, 3, []), ('bar', 3, 6, [])], 6)
>>> tag('foobarbarbar', p2)
(1, [('foo', 0, 3, []), ('bar', 3, 6, []),
     ('bar', 6, 9, []), ('bar', 9, 12, [])], 12)
```

USEFUL PRODUCTIONS

In version 2.0+, *SimpleParse* includes a number of useful productions that may be included in your grammars. See the examples and documentation that accompany *SimpleParse* for details on the many included productions and their usage.

The included productions, at the time of this writing, fall into the categories below:

simpleparse.common.calendar_names

Locale-specific names of months, and days of the week, including abbreviated forms.

simpleparse.common.chartypes

Locale-specific categories of characters, such as digits, uppercase, octdigits, punctuation, locale_decimal_point, and so on.

simpleparse.common.comments

Productions to match comments in a variety of programming languages, such as hash (#) end-of-line comments (Python, Bash, Perl, etc.); C paired comments (/* comment */); and others.

simpleparse.common.iso_date

Productions for strictly conformant ISO date and time formats.

simpleparse.common.iso_date_loose

Productions for ISO date and time formats with some leeway as to common variants in formatting.

simpleparse.common.numbers

Productions for common numeric formats, such as integers, floats, hex numbers, binary numbers, and so on.

simpleparse.common.phonetics

Productions to match phonetically spelled words. Currently, the US military style of "alpha, bravo, charlie, ..." spelling is the only style supported (with some leeway in word spellings).

simpleparse.common.strings

Productions to match quoted strings as used in various programming languages.

simpleparse.common.timezone_names

Productions to match descriptions of timezones, as you might find in email headers or other data/time fields.

GOTCHAS

There are a couple of problems that can easily arise in constructed *SimpleParse* grammars. If you are having problems in your application, keep a careful eye out for these issues:

1. Bad recursion. You might fairly naturally construct a pattern of the form:

   ```
   a := b, a?
   ```

   Unfortunately, if a long string of b rules are matched, the repeated recognition can either exceed the C-stack's recursion limit, or consume inordinate amounts of memory to construct nested tuples. Use an alternate pattern like:

   ```
   a := b+
   ```

   This will grab all the b productions in one tuple instead (you could separately parse out each b if necessary).

2. Quantified potentiality. That is a mouthful; consider patterns like:

   ```
   a := (b? / c)*
   x := (y?, z?)+
   ```

The first alternate b? in the first—and both y? and z? in the second—are happy
to match zero characters (if a b or y or z do not occur at the current position).
When you match "as many as possible" zero-width patterns, you get into an
infinite loop. Unfortunately, the pattern is not always simple; it might not be b
that is qualified as potential, but rather b productions (or the productions *in* b
productions, etc.).

3. No backtracking. Based on working with regular expression, you might expect
SimpleParse productions to use backtracking. They do not. For example:

```
a := ((b/c)*, b)
```

If this were a regular expression, it would match a string of b productions, then
back up one to match the final b. As a *SimpleParse* production, this definition can
never match. If any b productions occur, they will be claimed by (b/c)*, leaving
nothing for the final b to grab.

4.3.4   High-Level Programmatic Parsing

PLY ◇ Python Lex-Yacc

One module that I considered covering to round out this chapter is John Aycock's *Spark*
module. This module is both widely used in the Python community and extremely
powerful. However, I believe that the audience of this book is better served by working
with David Beazley's *PLY* module than with the older *Spark* module.

In the documentation accompanying *PLY*, Beazley consciously acknowledges the in-
fluence of *Spark* on his design and development. While the *PLY* module is far from being
a clone of *Spark*—the APIs are significantly different—there is a very similar *feeling* to
working with each module. Both modules require a very different style of programming
and style of thinking than do *mx.TextTools*, *SimpleParse*, or the state machines discussed
earlier in this chapter. In particular, both *PLY* and *Spark* make heavy use of Python
introspection to create underlying state machines out of specially named variables and
functions.

Within an overall similarity, *PLY* has two main advantages over *Spark* in a text
processing context. The first, and probably greatest, advantage *PLY* has is its far
greater speed. Although *PLY* has implemented some rather clever optimizations—such
as preconstruction of state tables for repeated runs—the main speed difference lies in
the fact that *PLY* uses a far faster, albeit slightly less powerful, parsing algorithm. For
text processing applications (as opposed to compiler development), *PLY*'s LR parsing
is plenty powerful for almost any requirement.

A second advantage *PLY* has over every other Python parsing library that I am aware
of is a flexible and fine-grained error reporting and error correction facility. Again, in a
text processing context, this is particularly important.

For compiling a programming language, it is generally reasonable to allow compilation to fail in the case of even small errors. But for processing a text file full of data fields and structures, you usually want to be somewhat tolerant of minor formatting errors; getting as much data as possible from a text automatically is frequently the preferred approach. *PLY* does an excellent job of handling "allowable" error conditions gracefully.

PLY consists of two modules: a lexer/tokenizer named `lex.py`, and a parser named `yacc.py`. The choice of names is taken from the popular C-oriented tools `lex` and `yacc`, and the behavior is correspondingly similar. Parsing with *PLY* usually consists of the two steps that were discussed at the beginning of this chapter: (1) Divide the input string into a set of nonoverlapping tokens using `lex.py`. (2) Generate a parse tree from the series of tokens using `yacc.py`.

When processing text with *PLY*, it is possible to attach "action code" to any lexing or parsing event. Depending on application requirements, this is potentially much more powerful than *SimpleParse*. For example, each time a specific token is encountered during lexing, you can modify the stored token according to whatever rule you wish, or even trigger an entirely different application action. Likewise, during parsing, each time a node of a parse tree is constructed, the node can be modified and/or other actions can be taken. In contrast, *SimpleParse* simply delivers a completed parse tree (called a "taglist") that must be traversed separately. However, while *SimpleParse* does not provide the fine-tunable event control that *PLY* does, *SimpleParse* offers a higher-level and cleaner grammar language—the choice between the two modules is full of pros and cons.

Example: Marking up smart ASCII (yet again)

This chapter has returned several times to applications for processing smart ASCII: a state machine in Appendix D; a functionally similar example using *mx.TextTools*; an EBNF grammar with *SimpleParse*. This email-like markup format is not in itself all that important, but it presents just enough complications to make for a good comparison between programming techniques and libraries. In many ways, an application using *PLY* is similar to the *SimpleParse* version above—both use grammars and parsing strategies.

GENERATING A TOKEN LIST

The first step in most *PLY* applications is the creation of a token stream. Tokens are identified by a series of regular expressions attached to special pattern names of the form `t_RULENAME`. By convention, the *PLY* token types are in all caps. In the simple case, a regular expression string is merely assigned to a variable. If action code is desired when a token is recognized, the rule name is defined as a function, with the regular expression string as its docstring; passed to the function is a `LexToken` object (with attributes `.value`, `.type`, and `.lineno`), which may be modified and returned. The pattern is clear in practice:

```
wordscanner.py
```

```python
# List of token names.  This is always required.
tokens = [ 'ALPHANUMS','SAFEPUNCT','BRACKET','ASTERISK',
           'UNDERSCORE','APOSTROPHE','DASH' ]

# Regular expression rules for simple tokens
t_ALPHANUMS    = r"[a-zA-ZO-9]+"
t_SAFEPUNCT    = r'[!@#$%^&()+=|\{}:;<>,.?/"]+'
t_BRACKET      = r'[][]'
t_ASTERISK     = r'[*]'
t_UNDERSCORE   = r'_'
t_APOSTROPHE   = r"'"
t_DASH         = r'-'

# Regular expression rules with action code
def t_newline(t):
    r"\n+"
    t.lineno += len(t.value)

# Special case (faster) ignored characters
t_ignore = " \t\r"

# Error handling rule
def t_error(t):
    sys.stderr.write("Illegal character '%s' (%s)\n"
                     % (t.value[0], t.lineno))
    t.skip(1)

import lex, sys
def stdin2tokens():
    lex.input(sys.stdin.read())    # Give the lexer some input
    toklst = []                    # Tokenize
    while 1:
        t = lex.token()
        if not t: break   # No more input
        toklst.append(t)
    return toklst

if __name__=='__main__':
    lex.lex()                      # Build the lexer
    for t in stdin2tokens():
        print '%s<%s>' % (t.value.ljust(15), t.type)
```

You are required to list the token types you wish to recognize, using the `tokens` variable. Each such token, and any special patterns that are not returned as tokens, is defined either as a variable or as a function. After that, you just initialize the lexer, read a string, and pull tokens off sequentially. Let us look at some results:

```
% cat p.txt
-Itals-, [modname]--let's add ~ underscored var_name.
% python wordscanner.py < p.txt
Illegal character '~' (1)
-                  <DASH>
Itals              <ALPHANUMS>
-                  <DASH>
,                  <SAFEPUNCT>
[                  <BRACKET>
modname            <ALPHANUMS>
]                  <BRACKET>
-                  <DASH>
-                  <DASH>
let                <ALPHANUMS>
'                  <APOSTROPHE>
s                  <ALPHANUMS>
add                <ALPHANUMS>
underscored        <ALPHANUMS>
var                <ALPHANUMS>
_                  <UNDERSCORE>
name               <ALPHANUMS>
.                  <SAFEPUNCT>
```

The output illustrates several features. For one thing, we have successfully tagged each nondiscarded substring as constituting some token type. Notice also that the unrecognized tilde character is handled gracefully by being omitted from the token list—you could do something different if desired, of course. Whitespace is discarded as insignificant by this tokenizer—the special `t_ignore` variable quickly ignores a set of characters, and the `t_newline()` function contains some extra code to maintain the line number during processing.

The simple tokenizer above has some problems, however. Dashes can be used either in an m-dash or to mark italicized phrases; apostrophes can be either part of a contraction or a marker for a function name; underscores can occur both to mark titles and within variable names. Readers who have used *Spark* will know of its capability to enhance a lexer or parser by inheritance; *PLY* cannot do that, but it can utilize Python namespaces to achieve almost exactly the same effect:

```
wordplusscanner.py
```

```
"Enhanced word/markup tokenization"
from wordscanner import *
tokens.extend(['CONTRACTION','MDASH','WORDPUNCT'])
t_CONTRACTION   = r"(?<=[a-zA-Z])'(am|clock|d|ll|m|re|s|t|ve)"
t_WORDPUNCT     = r'(?<=[a-zA-Z0-9])[-_](?=[a-zA-Z0-9])'
def t_MDASH(t): # Use HTML style mdash
    r'--'
```

```
        t.value = '&mdash;'
        return t

if __name__=='__main__':
        lex.lex()                              # Build the lexer
        for t in stdin2tokens():
            print '%s<%s>' % (t.value.ljust(15), t.type)
```

Although the tokenization produced by `wordscanner.py` would work with the right choice of grammar rules, producing more specific tokens allows us to simplify the grammar accordingly. In the case of `t_MDASH()`, `wordplusscanner.py` also modifies the token itself as part of recognition:

```
% python wordplusscanner.py < p.txt
Illegal character '~' (1)
–               <DASH>
Itals           <ALPHANUMS>
–               <DASH>
,               <SAFEPUNCT>
[               <BRACKET>
modname         <ALPHANUMS>
]               <BRACKET>
&mdash;         <MDASH>
let             <ALPHANUMS>
's              <CONTRACTION>
add             <ALPHANUMS>
underscored     <ALPHANUMS>
var             <ALPHANUMS>
_               <WORDPUNCT>
name            <ALPHANUMS>
.               <SAFEPUNCT>
```

Parsing a token list

A parser in *PLY* is defined in almost the same manner as a tokenizer. A collection of specially named functions of the form `p_rulename()` are defined, each containing an EBNF-style pattern to match (or a disjunction of several such patterns). These functions receive as argument a `YaccSlice` object, which is list-like in assigning each component of the EBNF declaration to an indexed position.

The code within each function should assign a useful value to `t[0]`, derived in some way from `t[1:]`. If you would like to create a parse tree out of the input source, you can define a `Node` class of some sort and assign each right-hand rule or token as a subnode/leaf of that node; for example:

```
def p_rulename(t):
    'rulename : somerule SOMETOKEN otherrule'
    #            ^            ^          ^
    #  t[0]      t[1]       t[2]       t[3]
    t[0] = Node('rulename', t[1:])
```

Defining an appropriate `Node` class is left as an exercise. With this approach, the final result would be a traversable tree structure.

It is fairly simple to create a set of rules to combine the fairly smart token stream produced by `wordplusscanner.py`. In the sample application, a simpler structure than a parse tree is built. `markupbuilder.py` simply creates a list of matched patterns, interspersed with added markup codes. Other data structures are possible too, and/or you could simply take some action each time a rule is matched (e.g., write to STDOUT).

---

markupbuilder.py

```python
import yacc
from wordplusscanner import *

def p_para(t):
    '''para : para plain
             | para emph
             | para strong
             | para module
             | para code
             | para title
             | plain
             | emph
             | strong
             | module
             | code
             | title '''
    try:    t[0] = t[1] + t[2]
    except: t[0] = t[1]

def p_plain(t):
    '''plain : ALPHANUMS
              | CONTRACTION
              | SAFEPUNCT
              | MDASH
              | WORDPUNCT
              | plain plain '''
    try:    t[0] = t[1] + t[2]
    except: t[0] = [t[1]]

def p_emph(t):
    '''emph : DASH plain DASH'''
    t[0] = ['<i>'] + t[2] + ['</i>']

def p_strong(t):
    '''strong : ASTERISK plain ASTERISK'''
    t[0] = ['<b>'] + t[2] + ['</b>']
```

```
def p_module(t):
    '''module : BRACKET plain BRACKET'''
    t[0] = ['<em><tt>'] + t[2] + ['</tt></em>']

def p_code(t):
    '''code : APOSTROPHE plain APOSTROPHE'''
    t[0] = ['<code>'] + t[2] + ['</code>']

def p_title(t):
    '''title : UNDERSCORE plain UNDERSCORE'''
    t[0] = ['<cite>'] + t[2] + ['</cite>']

def p_error(t):
    sys.stderr.write('Syntax error at "%s" (%s)\n'
                    % (t.value,t.lineno))

if __name__=='__main__':
    lex.lex()                   # Build the lexer
    yacc.yacc()                 # Build the parser
    result = yacc.parse(sys.stdin.read())
    print result
```

The output of this script, using the same input as above, is:

```
% python markupbuilder.py < p.txt
Illegal character '~' (1)
['<i>', 'Itals', '</i>', ',', '<em><tt>', 'modname',
'</tt></em>', '&mdash;', 'let', "'s", 'add', 'underscored',
'var', '_', 'name', '.']
```

One thing that is less than ideal in the *PLY* grammar is that it has no quantifiers. In *SimpleParse* or another EBNF library, we might give, for example, a `plain` declaration as:

```
plain := (ALPHANUMS | CONTRACTION | SAFEPUNCT | MDASH | WORDPUNCT)+
```

Quantification can make declarations more direct. But you can achieve the same effect by using self-referential rules whose left-hand terms also occur on the right-hand side. This style is similar to recursive definitions, for example:

```
plain : plain plain
      | OTHERSTUFF
```

For example, `markupbuilder.py`, above, uses this technique.

If a tree structure were generated in this parser, a `plain` node might wind up being a subtree containing lower `plain` nodes (and terminal leaves of `ALPHANUMS`, `CONTRACTION`, etc.). Traversal would need to account for this possibility. The flat list structure used simplifies the issue, in this case. A particular `plain` object might result from the concatenation of several smaller lists, but either way it is a list by the time another rule includes the object.

LEX

A *PLY* lexing module that is intended as support for a parsing application must do
four things. A lexing module that constitutes a stand-alone application must do two
additional things:

1. Import the *lex* module:

   ```
   import lex
   ```

2. Define a list or tuple variable `tokens` that contains the name of every token type
   the lexer is allowed to produce. A list may be modified in-place should you wish
   to specialize the lexer in an importing module; for example:

   ```
   tokens = ['FOO', 'BAR', 'BAZ', 'FLAM']
   ```

3. Define one or more regular expression patterns matching tokens. Each token type
   listed in `tokens` should have a corresponding pattern; other patterns may be
   defined also, but the corresponding substrings will not be included in the token
   stream.

   Token patterns may be defined in one of two ways: (1) By assigning a regular
   expression string to a specially named variable. (2) By defining a specially named
   function whose docstring is a regular expression string. In the latter case, "action
   code" is run when the token is matched. In both styles, the token name is preceded
   by the prefix `t_`. If a function is used, it should return the `LexToken` object passed
   to it, possibly after some modification, unless you do not wish to include the token
   in the token stream. For example:

   ```
   t_FOO = r"[Ff][Oo]{1,2}"
   t_BAR = r"[Bb][Aa][Rr]"
   def t_BAZ(t):
       r"([Bb][Aa][Zz])+"
       t.value = 'BAZ'   # canonical caps BAZ
       return t
   def t_FLAM(t):
       r"(FLAM|flam)*"
       # flam's are discarded (no return)
   ```

   Tokens passed into a pattern function have three attributes: `.type`, `.value`, and
   `.lineno`. `.lineno` contains the current line number within the string being processed and may be modified to change the reported position, even if the token is
   not returned. The attribute `.value` is normally the string matched by the regular
   expression, but a new string, or a compound value like a tuple or instance, may
   be assigned instead. The `.type` of a LexToken, by default, is a string naming the
   token (the same as the part of the function name after the `t_` prefix).

There is a special order in which various token patterns will be considered. Depending on the patterns used, several patterns could grab the same substring—so it is important to allow the desired pattern first claim on a substring. Each pattern defined with a function is considered in the order it is defined in the lexer file; all patterns defined by assignment to a variable are considered *after* every function-defined pattern. Patterns defined by variable assignment, however, are not considered in the order they are defined, but rather by decreasing length. The purpose of this ordering is to let longer patterns match before their subsequences (e.g., "==" would be claimed before "=", allowing the former comparison operator to match correctly, rather than as sequential assignments).

The special variable `t_ignore` may contain a string of characters to skip during pattern matching. These characters are skipped more efficiently than is a token function that has no return value. The token name `ignore` is, therefore, reserved and may not be used as a regular token (if the all-cap token name convention is followed, it assures no such conflict).

The special function `t_error()` may be used to process illegal characters. The `.value` attribute of the passed-in `LexToken` will contain the remainder of the string being processed (after the last match). If you want to skip past a problem area (perhaps after taking some corrective action in the body of `t_error()`), use the `.skip()` method of the passed-in `LexToken`.

4. Build the lexer. The *lex* module performs a bit of namespace magic so that you normally do not need to name the built lexer. Most applications can use just one default lexer. However, if you wish to—or if you need multiple lexers in the same application—you may bind a built lexer to a name. For example:

```
mylexer = lex.lex()    # named lexer
lex.lex()              # default lexer
mylexer.input(mytext)  # set input for named lexer
lex.input(othertext)   # set input for default lexer
```

5. Give the lexer a string to process. This step is handled by the parser when *yacc* is used in conjunction with *lex*, and nothing need be done explicitly. For stand-alone tokenizers, set the input string using `lex.input()` (or similarly with the `.input()` method of named lexers).

6. Read the token stream (for stand-alone tokenizers) using repeated invocation of the default `lex.token()` function or the `.token()` method of a named lexer. Unfortunately, as of version 1.1, *PLY* does not treat the token stream as a Python 2.2 iterator/generator. You can create an iterator wrapper with:

```
from __future__ import generators
# ...define the lexer rules, etc...
def tokeniterator(lexer=lex):
    while 1:
```

```
        t = lexer.token()
        if t is None:
            raise StopIteration
        yield t
# Loop through the tokens
for t in tokeniterator():
    # ...do something with each token...
```

Without this wrapper, or generally in earlier versions of Python, you should use a `while 1` loop with a break condition:

```
# ...define the lexer rules, etc...
while 1:
    t = lex.token()
    if t is None:    # No more input
        break
    # ...do something with each token...
```

YACC

A *PLY* parsing module must do five things:

1. Import the `yacc` module:

```
import yacc
```

2. Get a token map from a lexer. Suppose a lexer module named `mylexer.py` includes requirements 1 through 4 in the above LEX description. You would get the token map with:

```
from mylexer import *
```

Given the special naming convention `t_*` used for token patterns, the risk of namespace pollution from `import *` is minimal.

You could also, of course, simply include the necessary lexer setup code in the parsing module itself.

3. Define a collection of grammar rules. Grammar rules are defined in a similar fashion to token functions. Specially named functions having a `p_` prefix contain one or more productions and corresponding action code. Whenever a production contained in the docstring of a `p_*()` function matches, the body of that function runs.

   Productions in *PLY* are described with a simplified EBNF notation. In particular, no quantifiers are available in rules; only sequencing and alternation is used (the rest must be simulated with recursion and component productions).

The left side of each rule contains a single rule name. Following the rule name is one or more spaces, a colon, and an additional one or more spaces. The right side of a rule is everything following this. The right side of a rule can occupy one or more lines; if alternative patterns are allowed to fulfill a rule name, each such pattern occurs on a new line, following a pipe symbol ("|"). Within each right side line, a production is defined by a space-separated sequence of terms—which may be either tokens generated by the lexer or parser productions. More than one production may be included in the same p_*() function, but it is generally more clear to limit each function to one production (you are free to create more functions). For example:

```
def p_rulename(t):
    '''rulename   : foo SPACE bar
                  | foo bar baz
                  | bar SPACE baz
        otherrule : this that other
                  | this SPACE that '''
#...action code...
```

The argument to each p_*() function is a YaccSlice object, which assigns each component of the rule to an indexed position. The left side rule name is index position 0, and each term/token on the right side is listed thereafter, left to right. The list-like YaccSlice is sized just large enough to contain every term needed; this might vary depending on which alternative production is fulfilled on a particular call.

Empty productions are allowed by *yacc* (matching zero-width); you never need more than one empty production in a grammar, but this empty production might be a component of multiple higher-level productions. An empty production is basically a way of getting around the absence of (potentiality) quantification in *PLY*; for example:

```
def p_empty(t):
    '''empty : '''
    pass
def p_maybefoo(t):
    '''foo   : FOOTOKEN
             | empty '''
    t[0] = t[1]
def p_maybebar(t):
    '''bar   : BARTOKEN
             | empty '''
    t[0] = t[1]
```

If a fulfilled production is used in other productions (including itself recursively), the action code should assign a meaningful value to index position 0. This position *is* the value of the production. Moreover what is returned by the actual parsing is this position 0 of the top-level production. For example:

```
# Sum N different numbers: "1.0 + 3 + 3.14 + 17"
def p_sum(t):
    '''sum : number PLUS number'''
#          ^           ^        ^
#        t[0]    t[1]   t[2]   t[3]
    t[0] = t[1] + t[3]
def p_number(t):
    '''number : BASICNUMBER
              | sum           '''
#          ^         ^
#        t[0]       t[1]
    t[0] = float(t[1])
# Create the parser and parse some strings
yacc.yacc()
print yacc.parse('1.0')
```

The example simply assigns a numeric value with every production, but it could also assign to position 0 of the YaccSlice a list, Node object, or some other data structure that was useful to higher-level productions.

4. To build the parser the *yacc* module performs a bit of namespace magic so that you normally do not need to name the built parser. Most applications can use just one default parser. However, if you wish to—or if you need multiple parsers in the same application—you may bind a built parser to a name. For example:

```
myparser = yacc.yacc()     # named parser
yacc.yacc()                # default parser
r1 = myparser.parse(mytext) # set input for named parser
r0 = yacc.parse(othertext) # set input for default parser
```

When parsers are built, *yacc* will produce diagnostic messages if any errors are encountered in the grammar.

5. Parse an input string. The lexer is implicitly called to get tokens as needed by the grammar rules. The return value of a parsing action can be whatever thing invocation of matched rules builds. It might be an abstract syntax tree, if a Node object is used with each parse rule; it might be a simple list as in the smart ASCII example; it might be a modified string based on concatenations and modifications during parsing; or the return value could simply be None if parsing was done wholly to trigger side effects in parse rules. In any case, what is returned is index position 0 of the root rule's LexToken.

MORE ON PLY PARSERS

Some of the finer points of *PLY* parsers will not be covered in this book. The documentation accompanying *PLY* contains some additional implementational discussion, and a book devoted more systematically to parsing theory will address theoretical issues. But a few aspects can at least be touched on.

Error Recovery

A *PLY* grammar may contain a special `p_error()` function to catch tokens that cannot be matched (at the current position) by any other rule. The first time `p_error()` is invoked, *PLY* enters an "error-recovery" mode. If the parser cannot process the next three tokens successfully, a traceback is generated. You may include the production `error` in other rules to catch errors that occur at specific points in the input.

To implement recovery within the `p_error()` function, you may use the functions/methods `yacc.token()`, `yacc.restart()`, and `yacc.errok()`. The first grabs the next token from the lexer; if this token—or some sequence of tokens—meets some recovery criteria, you may call `yacc.restart()` or `yacc.errok()`. The first of these, `yacc.restart()`, returns the parser to its initial state—basically, only the final substring of the input is used in this case (however, a separate data structure you have built will remain as it was). Calling `yacc.errok()` tells the parser to stay in its last state and just ignore any bad tokens pulled from the lexer (either via the call to `p_error()` itself, or via calls to `yacc.token()` in the body).

The Parser State Machine

When a parser is first compiled, the files `parsetab.py` and `parser.out` are generated. The first, `parsetab.py`, contains more or less unreadable compact data structures that are used by subsequent parser invocations. These structures are used even during later invocation of the applications; timestamps and signatures are compared to determine if the grammar has been changed. Pregenerating state tables speeds up later operations.

The file `parser.out` contains a fairly readable description of the actual state machine generated by *yacc*. Although you cannot manually modify this state machine, examination of `parser.out` can help you in understanding error messages and undesirable behavior you encounter in your grammars.

Precedence and Associativity

To resolve ambiguous grammars, you may set the variable `precedence` to indicate both the precedence and the associativity of tokens. Absent an explicit indication, *PLY* always shifts a new symbol rather than reduce a rule where both are allowable by some grammar rule.

The *PLY* documentation gives an example of an ambiguous arithmetic expression, such as 3 * 4 + 5. After the tokens 3, *, and 4 have been read from the token list, a `p_mul()` rule might allow reduction of the product. But at the same time, a `p_add()` rule might contain NUMBER PLUS NUMBER, which would allow a lookahead to the PLUS token (since 4 is a NUMBER token). Moreover, the same token can have different meanings in different contexts, such as the unary-minus and minus operators in 3 - 4 * -5.

To solve both the precedence ambiguity and the ambiguous meaning of the token MINUS, you can declare an explicit precedence and associativity such as:

Declaring precedence and associativity

```
precedence = (
    ('left', 'PLUS', 'MINUS'),
    ('left', 'TIMES, 'DIVIDE'),
    ('right', 'UMINUS'),
)
def p_expr_uminus(t):
    'expr : MINUS expr % prec UMINUS'
    t[0] = -1 * t[2]
def p_expr_minus(t):
    'expr : expr MINUS expr'
    t[0] = t[1] - t[3]
def p_expr_plus(t):
    'expr : expr PLUS expr'
    t[0] = t[1] + t[3]
```

Chapter 5

INTERNET TOOLS AND TECHNIQUES

Be strict in what you send, and lenient in what you accept.
—Internet Engineering Task Force

Internet protocols in large measure are descriptions of textual formats. At the lowest level, TCP/IP is a binary protocol, but virtually every layer run on top of TCP/IP consists of textual messages exchanged between servers and clients. Some basic messages govern control, handshaking, and authentication issues, but the information content of the Internet predominantly consists of texts formatted according to two or three general patterns.

The handshaking and control aspects of Internet protocols usually consist of short commands—and sometimes challenges—sent during an initial conversation between a client and server. Fortunately for Python programmers, the Python standard library contains intermediate-level modules to support all the most popular communication protocols: *poplib*, *smtplib*, *ftplib*, *httplib*, *telnetlib*. *gopherlib*, and *imaplib*. If you want to use any of these protocols, you can simply provide required setup information, then call module functions or classes to handle all the lower-level interaction. Unless you want to do something exotic—such as programming a custom or less common network protocol—there is never a need to utilize the lower-level services of the *socket* module.

The communication level of Internet protocols is not primarily a text processing issue. Where text processing comes in is with parsing and production of compliant texts, to contain the *content* of these protocols. Each protocol is characterized by one or a few message types that are typically transmitted over the protocol. For example, POP3, NNTP, IMAP4, and SMTP protocols are centrally means of transmitting texts that conform to RFC-822, its updates, and associated RFCs. HTTP is firstly a means of transmitting Hypertext Markup Language (HTML) messages. Following the popularity of the World Wide Web, however, a dizzying array of other message types also travel over HTTP: graphic and sounds formats. proprietary multimedia plug-ins, executable byte-codes (e.g., Java or Jython), and also more textual formats like XML-RPC and SOAP.

The most widespread text format on the Internet is almost certainly human-readable and human-composed notes that follow RFC-822 and friends. The basic form of such a text is a series of headers, each beginning a line and separated from a value by a colon; after a header comes a blank line; and after that a message body. In the simplest case, a message body is just free-form text; but MIME headers can be used to nest structured and diverse contents within a message body. Email and (Usenet) discussion groups follow this format. Even other protocols, like HTTP, share a top envelope structure with RFC-822.

A strong second as Internet text formats go is HTML. And in third place after that is XML, in various dialects. HTML, of course, is the lingua franca of the Web; XML is a more general standard for defining custom "applications" or "dialects," of which HTML is (almost) one. In either case, rather than a header composed of line-oriented fields followed by a body, HTML/XML contain hierarchically nested "tags" with each tag indicated by surrounding angle brackets. Tags like HTML's `<body>`, `<cite>`, and `<blockquote>` will be familiar already to most readers of this book. In any case, Python has a strong collection of tools in its standard library for parsing and producing HTML and XML text documents. In the case of XML, some of these tools assist with specific XML dialects, while lower-level underlying libraries treat XML sui generis. In some cases, third-party modules fill gaps in the standard library.

Various Python Internet modules are covered in varying depth in this chapter. Every tool that comes with the Python standard library is examined at least in summary. Those tools that I feel are of greatest importance to application programmers (in text processing applications) are documented in fair detail and accompanied by usage examples, warnings, and tips.

5.1   Working with Email and Newsgroups

Python provides extensive support in its standard library for working with email (and newsgroup) messages. There are three general aspects to working with email, each supported by one or more Python modules.

1. Communicating with network servers to actually transmit and receive messages. The modules *poplib*, *imaplib*, *smtplib*, and *nntplib* each address the protocol contained in its name. These tasks do not have a lot to do with text processing per se, but are often important for applications that deal with email. The discussion of each of these modules is incomplete, addressing only those methods necessary to conduct basic transactions in the case of the first three modules/protocols. The module *nntplib* is not documented here under the assumption that email is more likely to be automatically processed than are Usenet articles. Indeed, robot newsgroup posters are almost always frowned upon, while automated mailing is frequently desirable (within limits).

2. Examining the contents of message folders. Various email and news clients store messages in a variety of formats, many providing hierarchical and structured

folders. The module *mailbox* provides a uniform API for reading the messages stored in all the most popular folder formats. In a way, *imaplib* serves an overlapping purpose, insofar as an IMAP4 server can also structure folders, but folder manipulation with IMAP4 is discussed only cursorily—that topic also falls afield of text processing. However, local mailbox folders are definitely text formats, and *mailbox* makes manipulating them a lot easier.

3. The core text processing task in working with email is parsing, modifying, and creating the actual messages. RFC-822 describes a format for email messages and is the lingua franca for Internet communication. Not every Mail User Agent (MUA) and Mail Transport Agent (MTA) strictly conforms to the RFC-822 (and superset/clarification RFC-2822) standard—but they all generally try to do so. The newer *email* package and the older *rfc822*, *rfc1822*, *mimify*, *mimetools*, *MimeWriter*, and *multifile* modules all deal with parsing and processing email messages.

Although existing applications are likely to use *rfc822*, *mimify*, *mimetools*, *MimeWriter*, and *multifile*, the package *email* contains more up-to-date and better-designed implementations of the same capabilities. The former modules are discussed only in synopsis while the various subpackages of *email* are documented in detail.

There is one aspect of working with email that all good-hearted people wish was unnecessary. Unfortunately, in the real-world, a large percentage of email is spam, viruses, and frauds; any application that works with collections of messages practically demands a way to filter out the junk messages. While this topic generally falls outside the scope of this discussion, readers might benefit from my article, "Spam Filtering Techniques," at:

<http://gnosis.cx/publish/programming/filtering-spam.html>

A flexible Python project for statistical analysis of message corpora, based on naive Bayesian and related models, is SpamBayes:

<http://spambayes.sourceforge.net/>

5.1.1   Manipulating and Creating Message Texts

email ◇ Work with email messages

Without repeating the whole of RFC-2822, it is worth mentioning the basic structure of an email or newsgroup message. Messages may themselves be stored in larger text files that impose larger-level structure, but here we are concerned with the structure of a single message. An RFC-2822 message, like most Internet protocols, has a textual format, often restricted to true 7-bit ASCII.

A message consists of a header and a body. A body in turn can contain one or more "payloads." In fact, MIME `multipart/*` type payloads can themselves contain nested payloads, but such nesting is comparatively unusual in practice. In textual terms, each payload in a body is divided by a simple, but fairly long, delimiter; however, the delimiter is pseudo-random, and you need to examine the header to find it. A given payload can either contain text or binary data using base64, quoted printable, or another ASCII encoding (even 8-bit, which is not generally safe across the Internet). Text payloads may either have MIME type `text/*` or compose the whole of a message body (without any payload delimiter).

An RFC-2822 header consists of a series of fields. Each field name begins at the beginning of a line and is followed by a colon and a space. The field value comes after the field name, starting on the same line, but potentially spanning subsequence lines. A continued field value cannot be left aligned, but must instead be indented with at least one space or tab. There are some moderately complicated rules about when field contents can split between lines, often dependent upon the particular type of value a field holds. Most field names occur only once in a header (or not at all), and in those cases their order of occurrence is not important to email or news applications. However, a few field names—notably `Received`—typically occur multiple times and in a significant order. Complicating headers further, field values can contain encoded strings from outside the ASCII character set.

The most important element of the *email* package is the class *email.Message.Message*, whose instances provide a data structure and convenience methods suited to the generic structure of RFC-2822 messages. Various capabilities for dealing with different parts of a message, and for parsing a whole message into an *email.Message.Message* object, are contained in subpackages of the *email* package. Some of the most common facilities are wrapped in convenience functions in the top-level namespace.

A version of the *email* package was introduced into the standard library with Python 2.1. However, *email* has been independently upgraded and developed between Python releases. At the time this chapter was written, the current release of *email* was 2.4.3, and this discussion reflects that version (and those API details that the author thinks are most likely to remain consistent in later versions). I recommend that, rather than simply use the version accompanying your Python installation, you download the latest version of the *email* package from `<http://mimelib.sourceforge.net>` if you intend to use this package. The current (and expected future) version of the *email* package is directly compatible with Python versions back to 2.1. See this book's Web site, `<http://gnosis.cx/TPiP/>`, for instructions on using *email* with Python 2.0. The package is incompatible with versions of Python before 2.0.

CLASSES

Several children of *email.Message.Message* allow you to easily construct message objects with special properties and convenient initialization arguments. Each such class is technically contained in a module named in the same way as the class rather than directly in the *email* namespace, but each is very similar to the others.

email.MIMEBase.MIMEBase(maintype, subtype, **params)

Construct a message object with a `Content-Type` header already built. Generally this class is used only as a parent for further subclasses, but you may use it directly if you wish:

```
>>> mess = email.MIMEBase.MIMEBase('text','html',charset='us-ascii')
>>> print mess
From nobody Tue Nov 12 03:32:33 2002
Content-Type: text/html; charset="us-ascii"
MIME-Version: 1.0
```

email.MIMENonMultipart.MIMENonMultipart(maintype, subtype, **params)

Child of *email.MIMEBase.MIMEBase*, but raises MultipartConversionError on calls to .attach(). Generally this class is used for further subclassing.

email.MIMEMultipart.MIMEMultipart([subtype="mixed" [boundary, [,*subparts [,**params]]]])

Construct a multipart message object with subtype subtype. You may optionally specify a boundary with the argument boundary, but specifying None will cause a unique boundary to be calculated. If you wish to populate the message with payload object, specify them as additional arguments. Keyword arguments are taken as parameters to the Content-Type header.

```
>>> from email.MIMEBase import MIMEBase
>>> from email.MIMEMultipart import MIMEMultipart
>>> mess = MIMEBase('audio','midi')
>>> combo = MIMEMultipart('mixed', None, mess, charset='utf-8')
>>> print combo
From nobody Tue Nov 12 03:50:50 2002
Content-Type: multipart/mixed; charset="utf-8";
        boundary="===============5954819931142521=="
MIME-Version: 1.0

--===============5954819931142521==
Content-Type: audio/midi
MIME-Version: 1.0

--===============5954819931142521==--
```

email.MIMEAudio.MIMEAudio(audiodata [,subtype [,encoder [,**params]]])

Construct a single part message object that holds audio data. The audio data stream is specified as a string in the argument audiodata. The Python standard library module *sndhdr* is used to detect the signature of the audio subtype, but you may explicitly specify the argument subtype instead. An encoder other than base64 may be specified with the encoder argument (but usually should not be). Keyword arguments are taken as parameters to the Content-Type header.

```
>>> from email.MIMEAudio import MIMEAudio
>>> mess = MIMEAudio(open('melody.midi').read())
```

SEE ALSO: sndhdr *397*; .

email.MIMEImage.MIMEImage(imagedata [,subtype [,encoder [,**params]]])

Construct a single part message object that holds image data. The image data
is specified as a string in the argument `imagedata`. The Python standard library
module *imghdr* is used to detect the signature of the image subtype, but you may
explicitly specify the argument `subtype` instead. An encoder other than base64
may be specified with the `encoder` argument (but usually should not be). Keyword
arguments are taken as parameters to the `Content-Type` header.

```
>>> from email.MIMEImage import MIMEImage
>>> mess = MIMEImage(open('landscape.png').read())
```

SEE ALSO: imghdr *396*;

email.MIMEText.MIMEText(text [,subtype [,charset]])

Construct a single part message object that holds text data. The data is specified
as a string in the argument `text`. A character set may be specified in the `charset`
argument:

```
>>> from email.MIMEText import MIMEText
>>> mess = MIMEText(open('TPiP.tex').read(),'latex')
```

FUNCTIONS

email.message_from_file(file [,_class=email.Message.Message [,strict=0]])

Return a message object based on the message text contained in the file-like object
`file`. This function call is exactly equivalent to:

```
email.Parser.Parser(_class, strict).parse(file)
```

SEE ALSO: email.Parser.Parser.parse() *363*;

email.message_from_string(s [,_class=email.Message.Message [,strict=0]])

Return a message object based on the message text contained in the string `s`. This
function call is exactly equivalent to:

```
email.Parser.Parser(_class, strict).parsestr(file)
```

SEE ALSO: email.Parser.Parser.parsestr() *363*;

email.Encoders ◇ Encoding message payloads

The module *email.Encoder* contains several functions to encode message bodies of single part message objects. Each of these functions sets the `Content-Transfer-Encoding` header to an appropriate value after encoding the body. The `decode` argument of the `.get_payload()` message method can be used to retrieve unencoded text bodies.

FUNCTIONS

email.Encoders.encode_quopri(mess)

Encode the message body of message object `mess` using quoted printable encoding. Also sets the header `Content-Transfer-Encoding`.

email.Encoders.encode_base64(mess)

Encode the message body of message object `mess` using base64 encoding. Also sets the header `Content-Transfer-Encoding`.

email.Encoders.encode_7or8bit(mess)

Set the `Content-Transfer-Encoding` to 7bit or 8bit based on the message payload; does not modify the payload itself. If message `mess` already has a `Content-Transfer-Encoding` header, calling this will create a second one—it is probably best to delete the old one before calling this function.

SEE ALSO: email.Message.Message.get_payload() *360*; quopri *162*; base64 *158*:

email.Errors ◇ Exceptions for [email] package

Exceptions within the *email* package will raise specific errors and may be caught at the desired level of generality. The exception hierarchy of *email.Errors* is shown in Figure 5.1.

exceptions.Exception	Root class for all built-in exceptions
MessageError	Base for email exceptions
MessageParseError	Base for message parsing exceptions
BoundaryError	Could not find boundary
HeaderParseError	Problem parsing the header
MultipartConversionError	Also child of `exceptions.TypeError`

Figure 5.1: Standard email.Errors exceptions

SEE ALSO: exceptions *44*;

email.Generator ◇ Create text representation of messages

The module *email.Generator* provides support for the serialization of *email.Message.Message* objects. In principle, you could create other tools to output message objects to specialized formats—for example, you might use the fields of an *email.Message.Message* object to store values to an XML format or to an RDBMS. But in practice, you almost always want to write message objects to standards-compliant RFC-2822 message texts. Several of the methods of *email.Message.Message* automatically utilize *email.Generator*.

CLASSES

email.Generator.Generator(file [,mangle_from_=1 [,maxheaderlen=78]])

Construct a generator instance that writes to the file-like object `file`. If the argument `mangle_from_` is specified as a true value, any occurrence of a line in the body that begins with the string `From` followed by a space is prepended with `>`. This (non-reversible) transformation prevents BSD mailboxes from being parsed incorrectly. The argument `maxheaderlen` specifies where long headers will be split into multiple lines (if such is possible).

email.Generator.DecodedGenerator(file [,mangle_from_ [,maxheaderlen [,fmt]]])

Construct a generator instance that writes RFC-2822 messages. This class has the same initializers as its parent *email.Generator.Generator*, with the addition of an optional argument `fmt`.

The class *email.Generator.DecodedGenerator* only writes out the contents of `text/*` parts of a multipart message payload. Nontext parts are replaced with the string `fmt`, which may contain keyword replacement values. For example, the default value of `fmt` is:

```
[Non-text (%(type)s) part of message omitted, filename %(filename)s]
```

Any of the keywords `type`, `maintype`, `subtype`, `filename`, `description`, or `encoding` may be used as keyword replacements in the string `fmt`. If any of these values is undefined by the payload, a simple description of its unavailability is substituted.

METHODS

email.Generator.Generator.clone()
email.Generator.DecodedGenerator.clone()

Return a copy of the instance with the same options.

email.Generator.Generator.flatten(mess [,unixfrom=0])
email.Generator.DecodedGenerator.flatten(mess [,unixfrom=0])

Write an RFC-2822 serialization of message object mess to the file-like object the
instance was initialized with. If the argument unixfrom is specified as a true value,
the BSD mailbox From_ header is included in the serialization.

email.Generator.Generator.write(s)
email.Generator.DecodedGenerator.write(s)

Write the string s to the file-like object the instance was initialized with. This lets
a generator object itself act in a file-like manner, as an implementation convenience.

SEE ALSO: email.Message *355*; mailbox *372*;

> **email.Header** ◇ **Manage headers with non-ASCII values**

The module *email.Charset* provides fine-tuned capabilities for managing character set
conversions and maintaining a character set registry. The much higher-level interface
provided by *email.Header* provides all the capabilities that almost all users need in a
friendlier form.

The basic reason why you might want to use the *email.Header* module is because
you want to encode multinational (or at least non-US) strings in email headers. Message bodies are somewhat more lenient than headers, but RFC-2822 headers are still
restricted to using only 7-bit ASCII to encode other character sets. The module
email.Header provides a single class and two convenience functions. The encoding of
non-ASCII characters in email headers is described in a number of RFCs, including
RFC-2045, RFC-2046, RFC-2047, and most directly RFC-2231.

CLASSES

email.Header.Header([s="" [,charset [,maxlinelen=76 [,header_name=""
[,continuation_ws=" "]]]]])

Construct an object that holds the string or Unicode string s. You may specify an
optional charset to use in encoding s; absent any argument, either us-ascii or
utf-8 will be used, as needed.

Since the encoded string is intended to be used as an email header, it may be desirable to wrap the string to multiple lines (depending on its length). The argument
maxlinelen specifies where the wrapping will occur; header_name is the name of
the header you anticipate using the encoded string with—it is significant only for its
length. Without a specified header_name, no width is set aside for the header field
itself. The argument continuation_ws specified what whitespace string should be
used to indent continuation lines; it must be a combination of spaces and tabs.

Instances of the class *email.Header.Header* implement a .__str__() method and therefore respond to the built-in *str()* function and the *print* command. Normally the built-in techniques are more natural, but the method *email.Header.Header.encode()* performs an identical action. As an example, let us first build a non-ASCII string:

```
>>> from unicodedata import lookup
>>> lquot = lookup("LEFT-POINTING DOUBLE ANGLE QUOTATION MARK")
>>> rquot = lookup("RIGHT-POINTING DOUBLE ANGLE QUOTATION MARK")
>>> s = lquot + "Euro-style" + rquot + " quotation"
>>> s
u'\xabEuro-style\xbb quotation'
>>> print s.encode('iso-8859-1')
Euro-style quotation
```

Using the string s, let us encode it for an RFC-2822 header:

```
>>> from email.Header import Header
>>> print Header(s)
=?utf-8?q?=C2=ABEuro-style=C2=BB_quotation?=
>>> print Header(s,'iso-8859-1')
=?iso-8859-1?q?=ABEuro-style=BB_quotation?=
>>> print Header(s,'utf-16')
=?utf-16?b?/v8AqwBFAHUAcgBvAC0AcwB0AHkAbABABl?=
 =?utf-16?b?/v8AuwAgAHEAdQBvAHQAYQBOAGkAbwBu?=
>>> print Header(s,'us-ascii')
=?utf-8?q?=C2=ABEuro-style=C2=BB_quotation?=
```

Notice that in the last case, the *email.Header.Header* initializer did not take too seriously my request for an ASCII character set, since it was not adequate to represent the string. However, the class is happy to skip the encoding strings where they are not needed:

```
>>> print Header('"US-style" quotation')
"US-style" quotation
>>> print Header('"US-style" quotation','utf-8')
=?utf-8?q?=22US-style=22_quotation?=
>>> print Header('"US-style" quotation','us-ascii')
"US-style" quotation
```

METHODS

email.Header.Header.append(s [,charset])

Add the string or Unicode string s to the end of the current instance content, using character set charset. Note that the charset of the added text need not be the same as that of the existing content.

```
>>> subj = Header(s,'latin-1',65)
>>> print subj
=?iso-8859-1?q?=ABEuro-style=BB_quotation?=
>>> unicodedata.name(omega), unicodedata.name(Omega)
('GREEK SMALL LETTER OMEGA', 'GREEK CAPITAL LETTER OMEGA')
>>> subj.append(', Greek: ', 'us-ascii')
>>> subj.append(Omega, 'utf-8')
>>> subj.append(omega, 'utf-16')
>>> print subj
=?iso-8859-1?q?=ABEuro-style=BB_quotation?=, Greek:
 =?utf-8?b?zqk=?= =?utf-16?b?/v8DyQ==?=
>>> unicode(subj)
u'\xabEuro-style\xbb quotation, Greek: \u03a9\u03c9'
```

email.Header.Header.encode()
email.Header.Header.__str__()

Return an ASCII string representation of the instance content.

FUNCTIONS

email.Header.decode_header(header)

Return a list of pairs describing the components of the RFC-2231 string held in the header object **header**. Each pair in the list contains a Python string (not Unicode) and an encoding name.

```
>>> email.Header.decode_header(Header('spam and eggs'))
[('spam and eggs', None)]
>>> print subj
=?iso-8859-1?q?=ABEuro-style=BB_quotation?=, Greek:
 =?utf-8?b?zqk=?= =?utf-16?b?/v8DyQ==?=
>>> for tup in email.Header.decode_header(subj): print tup
...
('\xabEuro-style\xbb quotation', 'iso-8859-1')
(', Greek:', None)
('\xce\xa9', 'utf-8')
('\xfe\xff\x03\xc9', 'utf-16')
```

These pairs may be used to construct Unicode strings using the built-in *unicode()* function. However, plain ASCII strings show an encoding of None, which is not acceptable to the *unicode()* function.

```
>>> for s,enc in email.Header.decode_header(subj):
...     enc = enc or 'us-ascii'
...     print `unicode(s, enc)`
```

```
        ...
        u'\xabEuro-style\xbb quotation'
        u', Greek:'
        u'\u03a9'
        u'\u03c9'
```

SEE ALSO: unicode() *423*; email.Header.make_header() *354*;

email.Header.make_header(decoded_seq [,maxlinelen [,header_name [,continuation_ws]]])

Construct a header object from a list of pairs of the type returned by the function *email.Header.decode_header()*. You may also, of course, easily construct the list decoded_seq manually, or by other means. The three arguments maxlinelen, header_name, and continuation_ws are the same as with the *email.Header.Header* class.

```
>>> email.Header.make_header([('\xce\xa9','utf-8'),
...                           ('-man','us-ascii')]).encode()
'=?utf-8?b?zqk=?=-man'
```

SEE ALSO: email.Header.decode_header() *353*; email.Header.Header *351*;

email.Iterators ◇ Iterate through components of messages

The module *email.Iterators* provides several convenience functions to walk through messages in ways different from *email.Message.Message.get_payload()* or *email.Message.Message.walk()*.

FUNCTIONS

email.Iterators.body_line_iterator(mess)

Return a generator object that iterates through each content line of the message object mess. The entire body that would be produced by str(mess) is reached, regardless of the content types and nesting of parts. But any MIME delimiters are omitted from the returned lines.

```
>>> import email.MIMEText, email.Iterators
>>> mess1 = email.MIMEText.MIMEText('message one')
>>> mess2 = email.MIMEText.MIMEText('message two')
>>> combo = email.Message.Message()
>>> combo.set_type('multipart/mixed')
>>> combo.attach(mess1)
```

```
>>> combo.attach(mess2)
>>> for line in email.Iterators.body_line_iterator(combo):
...     print line
...
message one
message two
```

email.Iterators.typed_subpart_iterator(mess [,maintype="text" [,subtype]])

Return a generator object that iterates through each subpart of message whose type matches `maintype`. If a subtype `subtype` is specified, the match is further restricted to `maintype/subtype`.

email.Iterators._structure(mess [,file=sys.stdout])

Write a "pretty-printed" representation of the structure of the body of message `mess`. Output to the file-like object `file`.

```
>>> email.Iterators._structure(combo)
multipart/mixed
    multipart/digest
        image/png
        text/plain
    audio/mp3
    text/html
```

SEE ALSO: email.Message.Message.get_payload() *360*; email.Message.Message.walk() *362*;

---

email.Message ◇ Class representing an email message

A message object that utilizes the *email.Message* module provides a large number of syntactic conveniences and support methods for manipulating an email or news message. The class `email.Message.Message` is a very good example of a customized datatype. The built-in `str()` function—and therefore also the `print` command—cause a message object to produce its RFC-2822 serialization.

In many ways, a message object is dictionary-like. The appropriate magic methods are implemented in it to support keyed indexing and assignment, the built-in `len()` function, containment testing with the `in` keyword, and key deletion. Moreover, the methods one expects to find in a Python dict are all implemented by `email.Message.Message`: `.has_key()`, `.keys()`, `.values()`, `.items()`, and `.get()`. Some usage examples are helpful:

```
>>> import mailbox, email, email.Parser
>>> mbox = mailbox.PortableUnixMailbox(open('mbox'),
...                      email.Parser.Parser().parse)
```

```
>>> mess = mbox.next()
>>> len(mess)               # number of headers
16
>>> 'X-Status' in mess      # membership testing
1
>>> mess.has_key('X-AGENT') # also membership test
0
>>> mess['x-agent'] = "Python Mail Agent"
>>> print mess['X-AGENT']    # access by key
Python Mail Agent
>>> del mess['X-Agent']      # delete key/val pair
>>> print mess['X-AGENT']
None
>>> [fld for (fld,val) in mess.items() if fld=='Received']
['Received', 'Received', 'Received', 'Received', 'Received']
```

This is dictionary-like behavior, but only to an extent. Keys are case-insensitive to match email header rules. Moreover, a given key may correspond to multiple values—indexing by key will return only the first such value, but methods like .keys(), .items(), or .get_all() will return a list of all the entries. In some other ways, an *email.Message.Message* object is more like a list of tuples, chiefly in guaranteeing to retain a specific order to header fields.

A few more details of keyed indexing should be mentioned. Assigning to a keyed field will add an *additional* header, rather than replace an existing one. In this respect, the operation is more like a *list.append()* method. Deleting a keyed field, however, deletes every matching header. If you want to replace a header completely, delete first, then assign.

The special syntax defined by the *email.Message.Message* class is all for manipulating headers. But a message object will typically also have a body with one or more payloads. If the `Content-Type` header contains the value `multipart/*`, the body should consist of zero or more payloads, each one itself a message object. For single part content types (including where none is explicitly specified), the body should contain a string, perhaps an encoded one. The message instance method .get_payload(), therefore, can return either a list of message objects or a string. Use the method .is_multipart() to determine which return type is expected.

As the epigram to this chapter suggests, you should strictly follow content typing rules in messages you construct yourself. But in real-world situations, you are likely to encounter messages with badly mismatched headers and bodies. Single part messages might claim to be multipart, and vice versa. Moreover, the MIME type claimed by headers is only a loose indication of what payloads actually contain. Part of the mismatch comes from spammers and virus writers trying to exploit the poor standards compliance and lax security of Microsoft applications—a malicious payload can pose as an innocuous type, and Windows will typically launch apps based on filenames instead of MIME types. But other problems arise not out of malice, but simply out of application and transport errors. Depending on the source of your processed messages, you might want to be lenient about the allowable structure and headers of messages.

SEE ALSO: UserDict *24*; UserList *28*;

CLASSES

email.Message.Message()

Construct a message object. The class accepts no initialization arguments.

METHODS AND ATTRIBUTES

email.Message.Message.add_header(field, value [,**params])

Add a header to the message headers. The header field is `field`, and its value is `value`.The effect is the same as keyed assignment to the object, but you may optionally include parameters using Python keyword arguments.

```
>>> import email.Message
>>> msg = email.Message.Message()
>>> msg['Subject'] = "Report attachment"
>>> msg.add_header('Content-Disposition','attachment',
...                filename='report17.txt')
>>> print msg
From nobody Mon Nov 11 15:11:43 2002
Subject: Report attachment
Content-Disposition: attachment; filename="report17.txt"
```

email.Message.Message.as_string([unixfrom=0])

Serialize the message to an RFC-2822-compliant text string. If the `unixfrom` argument is specified with a true value, include the BSD mailbox "From_" envelope header. Serialization with *str()* or *print* includes the "From_" envelope header.

email.Message.Message.attach(mess)

Add a payload to a message. The argument `mess` must specify an *email.Message.Message* object. After this call, the payload of the message will be a list of message objects (perhaps of length one, if this is the first object added). Even though calling this method causes the method `.is_multipart()` to return a true value, you still need to separately set a correct **multipart/*** content type for the message to serialize the object.

```
>>> mess = email.Message.Message()
>>> mess.is_multipart()
0
>>> mess.attach(email.Message.Message())
>>> mess.is_multipart()
1
>>> mess.get_payload()
[<email.Message.Message instance at 0x3b2ab0>]
```

```
>>> mess.get_content_type()
'text/plain'
>>> mess.set_type('multipart/mixed')
>>> mess.get_content_type()
'multipart/mixed'
```

If you wish to create a single part payload for a message object, use the method *email.Message.Message.set_payload()*.

SEE ALSO: email.Message.Message.set_payload() *362*;

email.Message.Message.del_param(param [,header="Content-Type" [,requote=1]])

Remove the parameter `param` from a header. If the parameter does not exist, no action is taken, but also no exception is raised. Usually you are interested in the `Content-Type` header, but you may specify a different `header` argument to work with another one. The argument `requote` controls whether the parameter value is quoted (a good idea that does no harm).

```
>>> mess = email.Message.Message()
>>> mess.set_type('text/plain')
>>> mess.set_param('charset','us-ascii')
>>> print mess
From nobody Mon Nov 11 16:12:38 2002
MIME-Version: 1.0
Content-Type: text/plain; charset="us-ascii"

>>> mess.del_param('charset')
>>> print mess
From nobody Mon Nov 11 16:13:11 2002
MIME-Version: 1.0
content-type: text/plain
```

email.Message.Message.epilogue

Message bodies that contain MIME content delimiters can also have text that falls outside the area between the first and final delimiter. Any text at the very end of the body is stored in *email.Message.Message.epilogue*.

SEE ALSO: email.Message.Message.preamble *361*;

email.Message.Message.get_all(field [,failobj=None])

Return a list of all the headers with the field name `field`. If no matches exist, return the value specified in argument `failobj`. In most cases, header fields occur just once (or not at all), but a few fields such as `Received` typically occur multiple times.

The default nonmatch return value of `None` is probably not the most useful choice. Returning an empty list will let you use this method in both `if` tests and iteration context:

```
>>> for rcv in mess.get_all('Received',[]):
...     print rcv
...
About that time
A little earlier
>>> if mess.get_all('Foo',[]):
...     print "Has Foo header(s)"
```

email.Message.Message.get_boundary([failobj=None])

Return the MIME message boundary delimiter for the message. Return `failobj` if no boundary is defined; this *should* always be the case if the message is not multipart.

email.Message.Message.get_charsets([failobj=None])

Return a list of string descriptions of contained character sets.

email.Message.Message.get_content_charset([failobj=None])

Return a string description of the message character set.

email.Message.Message.get_content_maintype()

For message `mess`, equivalent to `mess.get_content_type().split("/")[0]`.

email.Message.Message.get_content_subtype()

For message `mess`, equivalent to `mess.get_content_type().split("/")[1]`.

email.Message.Message.get_content_type()

Return the MIME content type of the message object. The return string is normalized to lowercase and contains both the type and subtype, separated by a /.

```
>>> msg_photo.get_content_type()
'image/png'
>>> msg_combo.get_content_type()
'multipart/mixed'
>>> msg_simple.get_content_type()
'text/plain'
```

email.Message.Message.get_default_type()

Return the current default type of the message. The default type will be used in decoding payloads that are not accompanied by an explicit `Content-Type` header.

email.Message.Message.get_filename([failobj=None])

Return the `filename` parameter of the `Content-Disposition` header. If no such parameter exists (perhaps because no such header exists), `failobj` is returned instead.

email.Message.Message.get_param(param [,failobj [,header=. . . [,unquote=1]]])

Return the parameter `param` of the header `header`. By default, use the `Content-Type` header. If the parameter does not exist, return `failobj`. If the argument `unquote` is specified as a true value, the quote marks are removed from the parameter.

```
>>> print mess.get_param('charset',unquote=1)
us-ascii
>>> print mess.get_param('charset',unquote=0)
"us-ascii"
```

SEE ALSO: email.Message.Message.set_param() *362*;

email.Message.Message.get_params([,failobj=None [,header=. . . [,unquote=1]]])

Return all the parameters of the header `header`. By default, examine the `Content-Type` header. If the header does not exist, return `failobj` instead. The return value consists of a list of key/val pairs. The argument `unquote` removes extra quotes from values.

```
>>> print mess.get_params(header="To")
[('<mertz@gnosis.cx>', '')]
>>> print mess.get_params(unquote=0)
[('text/plain', ''), ('charset', '"us-ascii"')]
```

email.Message.Message.get_payload([i [,decode=0]])

Return the message payload. If the message method `is_multipart()` returns true, this method returns a list of component message objects. Otherwise, this method returns a string with the message body. Note that if the message object was created using *email.Parser.HeaderParser*, then the body is treated as single part, even if it contains MIME delimiters.

Assuming that the message is multipart, you may specify the `i` argument to retrieve only the indexed component. Specifying the `i` argument is equivalent to indexing on the returned list without specifying `i`. If `decode` is specified as a true value, and the payload is single part, the returned payload is decoded (i.e., from quoted printable or base64).

I find that dealing with a payload that may be either a list or a text is somewhat awkward. Frequently, you would like to simply loop over all the parts of a message body, whether or not MIME multiparts are contained in it. A wrapper function can provide uniformity:

```
write_payload_list.py
```
```
#!/usr/bin/env python
"Write payload list to separate files"
import email, sys
def get_payload_list(msg, decode=1):
    payload = msg.get_paylcad(decode=decode)
    if type(payload) in [type(""), type(u"")]:
        return [payload]
    else:
        return payload
mess = email.message_from_file(sys.stdin)
for part,num in zip(get_payload_list(mess),range(1000)):
    file = open('%s.%d' % (sys.argv[1], num), 'w')
    print >> file, part
```

SEE ALSO: email.Parser *363*; email.Message.Message.is_multipart() *361*; email.Message.Message.walk() *362*;

email.Message.Message.get_unixfrom()

Return the BSD mailbox "From_" envelope header. or None if none exists.

SEE ALSO: mailbox *372*;

email.Message.Message.is_multipart()

Return a true value if the message is multipart. Notice that the criterion for being multipart is having multiple message objects in the payload; the Content-Type header is not guaranteed to be multipart/* when this method returns a true value (but if all is well, it *should* be).

SEE ALSO: email.Message.Message.get_payload() *360*;

email.Message.Message.preamble

Message bodies that contain MIME content delimiters can also have text that falls outside the area between the first and final delimiter. Any text at the very beginning of the body is stored in *email.Message.Message.preamble*.

SEE ALSO: email.Message.Message.epilogue *358*;

email.Message.Message.replace_header(field, value)

Replaces the first occurrence of the header with the name field with the value value. If no matching header is found. raise KeyError.

email.Message.Message.set_boundary(s)

Set the boundary parameter of the Content-Type header to s. If the message does not have a Content-Type header, raise HeaderParserError. There is generally no reason to create a boundary manually, since the *email* module creates good unique boundaries on it own for multipart messages.

email.Message.Message.set_default_type(ctype)

Set the current default type of the message to `ctype`. The default type will be used in decoding payloads that are not accompanied by an explicit `Content-Type` header.

email.Message.Message.set_param(param, value [,header="Content-Type" [,requote=1 [,charset [,language]]]])

Set the parameter `param` of the header `header` to the value `value`. If the argument `requote` is specified as a true value, the parameter is quoted. The arguments `charset` and `language` may be used to encode the parameter according to RFC-2231.

email.Message.Message.set_payload(payload [,charset=None])

Set the message payload to a string or to a list of message objects. This method overwrites any existing payload the message has. For messages with single part content, you must use this method to configure the message body (or use a convenience message subclass to construct the message in the first place).

SEE ALSO: email.Message.Message.attach() *357*; email.MIMEText.MIMEText *348*; email.MIMEImage.MIMEImage *348*; email.MIMEAudio.MIMEAudio *347*;

email.Message.Message.set_type(ctype [,header="Content-Type" [,requote=1]])

Set the content type of the message to `ctype`, leaving any parameters to the header as is. If the argument `requote` is specified as a true value, the parameter is quoted. You may also specify an alternative header to write the content type to, but for the life of me, I cannot think of any reason you would want to.

email.Message.Message.set_unixfrom(s)

Set the BSD mailbox envelope header. The argument `s` should include the word `From` and a space, usually followed by a name and a date.

SEE ALSO: mailbox *372*;

email.Message.Message.walk()

Recursively traverse all message parts and subparts of the message. The returned iterator will yield each nested message object in depth-first order.

```
>>> for part in mess.walk():
...     print part.get_content_type()
multipart/mixed
text/html
audio/midi
```

SEE ALSO: email.Message.Message.get_payload() *360*;

email.Parser ◇ Parse a text message into a message object

There are two parsers provided by the *email.Parser* module: *email.Parser.Parser* and its child *email.Parser.HeaderParser*. For general usage, the former is preferred, but the latter allows you to treat the body of an RFC-2822 message as an unparsed block. Skipping the parsing of message bodies can be much faster and is also more tolerant of improperly formatted message bodies (something one sees frequently, albeit mostly in spam messages that lack any content value as well).

The parsing methods of both classes accept an optional headersonly argument. Specifying headersonly has a stronger effect than using the *email.Parser.HeaderParser* class. If headersonly is specified in the parsing methods of either class, the message body is skipped altogether—the message object created has an entirely empty body. On the other hand, if *email.Parser.HeaderParser* is used as the parser class, but headersonly is specified as false (the default), the body is always read as a single part text, even if its content type is multipart/*.

CLASSES

email.Parser.Parser([_class=email.Message.Message [,strict=0]])

Construct a parser instance that uses the class _class as the message object constructor. There is normally no reason to specify a different message object type. Specifying strict parsing with the strict option will cause exceptions to be raised for messages that fail to conform fully to the RFC-2822 specification. In practice, "lax" parsing is much more useful.

email.Parser.HeaderParser([_class=email.Message.Message [,strict=0]])

Construct a parser instance that is the same as an instance of *email.Parser.Parser* except that multipart messages are parsed as if they were single part.

METHODS

email.Parser.Parser.parse(file [,headersonly=0])
email.Parser.HeaderParser.parse(file [,headersonly=0])

Return a message object based on the message text found in the file-like object file. If the optional argument headersonly is given a true value, the body of the message is discarded.

email.Parser.Parser.parsestr(s [,headersonly=0])
email.Parser.HeaderParser.parsestr(s [,headersonly=0])

Return a message object based on the message text found in the string s. If the optional argument headersonly is given a true value, the body of the message is discarded.

email.Utils ◇ Helper functions for working with messages

The module *email.Utils* contains a variety of convenience functions, mostly for working with special header fields.

FUNCTIONS

email.Utils.decode_rfc2231(s)

Return a decoded string for RFC-2231 encoded string s:

```
>>> Omega = unicodedata.lookup("GREEK CAPITAL LETTER OMEGA")
>>> print email.Utils.encode_rfc2231(Omega+'-man@gnosis.cx')
%3A9-man%40gnosis.cx
>>> email.Utils.decode_rfc2231("utf-8''%3A9-man%40gnosis.cx")
('utf-8', '', ':9-man@gnosis.cx')
```

email.Utils.encode_rfc2231(s [,charset [,language]])

Return an RFC-2231-encoded string from the string s. A charset and language may optionally be specified.

email.Utils.formataddr(pair)

Return a formatted address from pair (realname,addr):

```
>>> email.Utils.formataddr(('David Mertz','mertz@gnosis.cx'))
'David Mertz <mertz@gnosis.cx>'
```

email.Utils.formataddr([timeval [,localtime=0]])

Return an RFC-2822-formatted date based on a time value as returned by *time.localtime()*. If the argument localtime is specified with a true value, use the local timezone rather than UTC. With no options, use the current time.

```
>>> email.Utils.formatdate()
'Wed, 13 Nov 2002 07:08:01 -0000'
```

email.Utils.getaddresses(addresses)

Return a list of pairs (realname,addr) based on the list of compound addresses in argument addresses.

```
>>> addrs = ['"Joe" <jdoe@nowhere.lan>','Jane <jroe@other.net>']
>>> email.Utils.getaddresses(addrs)
[('Joe', 'jdoe@nowhere.lan'), ('Jane', 'jroe@other.net')]
```

email.Utils.make_msgid([seed])

Return a unique string suitable for a `Message-ID` header. If the argument `seed` is given, incorporate that string into the returned value; typically a `seed` is the sender's domain name or other identifying information.

```
>>> email.Utils.make_msgid('gnosis')
'<20021113071050.3861.13687.gnosis@localhost>'
```

email.Utils.mktime_tz(tuple)

Return a timestamp based on an *email.Utils.parsedate_tz()* style tuple.

```
>>> email.Utils.mktime_tz((2001, 1, 11, 14, 49, 2, 0, 0, 0, 0))
979224542.0
```

email.Utils.parseaddr(address)

Parse a compound address into the pair (`realname`,`addr`).

```
>>> email.Utils.parseaddr('David Mertz <mertz@gnosis.cx>')
('David Mertz', 'mertz@gnosis.cx')
```

email.Utils.parsedate(datestr)

Return a date tuple based on an RFC-2822 date string.

```
>>> email.Utils.parsedate('11 Jan 2001 14:49:02 -0000')
(2001, 1, 11, 14, 49, 2, 0, 0, 0)
```

SEE ALSO: time *86*;

email.Utils.parsedate_tz(datestr)

Return a date tuple based on an RFC-2822 date string. Same as *email.Utils.parsedate()*, but adds a tenth tuple field for offset from UTC (or None if not determinable).

email.Utils.quote(s)

Return a string with backslashes and double quotes escaped.

```
>>> print email.Utils.quote(r'"MyPath" is d:\this\that')
\"MyPath\" is d:\\this\\that
```

email.Utils.unquote(s)

Return a string with surrounding double quotes or angle brackets removed.

```
>>> print email.Utils.unquote('<mertz@gnosis.cx>')
mertz@gnosis.cx
>>> print email.Utils.unquote('"us-ascii"')
us-ascii
```

5.1.2   Communicating with Mail Servers

imaplib ◇ IMAP4 client

The module *imaplib* supports implementing custom IMAP clients. This protocol is detailed in RFC-1730 and RFC-2060. As with the discussion of other protocol libraries, this documentation aims only to cover the basics of communicating with an IMAP server—many methods and functions are omitted here. In particular, of interest here is merely being able to retrieve messages—creating new mailboxes and messages is outside the scope of this book.

The *Python Library Reference* describes the POP3 protocol as obsolescent and recommends the use of IMAP4 if your server supports it. While this advice is not incorrect technically—IMAP indeed has some advantages—in my experience, support for POP3 is far more widespread among both clients and servers than is support for IMAP4. Obviously, your specific requirements will dictate the choice of an appropriate support library.

Aside from using a more efficient transmission strategy (POP3 is line-by-line, IMAP4 sends whole messages), IMAP4 maintains multiple mailboxes on a server and also automates filtering messages by criteria. A typical (simple) IMAP4 client application might look like the one below. To illustrate a few methods, this application will print all the promising subject lines, after deleting any that look like spam. The example does not itself retrieve regular messages, only their headers.

check_imap_subjects.py

```
#!/usr/bin/env python
import imaplib, sys
if len(sys.argv) == 4:
    sys.argv.append('INBOX')
(host, user, passwd, mbox) = sys.argv[1:]
i = imaplib.IMAP4(host, port=143)
i.login(user, passwd)
resp = i.select(mbox)
if r[0] <> 'OK':
    sys.stderr.write("Could not select %s\n" % mbox)
    sys.exit()
# delete some spam messages
typ, spamlist = i.search(None, '(SUBJECT) "URGENT"')
i.store(','.join(spamlist.split()),'+FLAGS.SILENT','\deleted')
i.expunge()
typ, messnums = i.search(None,'ALL').split()
for mess in messnums:
    typ, header = i.fetch(mess, 'RFC822.HEADER')
    for line in header[0].split('\n'):
        if string.upper(line[:9]) == 'SUBJECT: ':
```

```
        print line[9:]
i.close()
i.logout()
```

There is a bit more work to this than in the POP3 example, but you can also see some additional capabilities. Unfortunately, much of the use of the *imaplib* module depends on passing strings with flags and commands, none of which are well-documented in the *Python Library Reference* or in the source to the module. A separate text on the IMAP protocol is probably necessary for complex client development.

CLASSES

imaplib.IMAP4([host="localhost" [port=143]])

Create an IMAP instance object to manage a host connection.

METHODS

imaplib.IMAP4.close()

Close the currently selected mailbox, and delete any messages marked for deletion. The method *imaplib.IMAP4.logout()* is used to actually disconnect from the server.

imaplib.IMAP4.expunge()

Permanently delete any messages marked for deletion in the currently selected mailbox.

imaplib.IMAP4.fetch(message_set, message_parts)

Return a pair (typ,datalist). The first field typ is either OK or NO, indicating the status. The second field datalist is a list of returned strings from the fetch request. The argument message_set is a comma-separated list of message numbers to retrieve. The message_parts describe the components of the messages retrieved—header, body, date, and so on.

imaplib.IMAP4.list([dirname="" [,pattern="*"]])

Return a (typ,datalist) tuple of all the mailboxes in directory dirname that match the glob-style pattern pattern. datalist contains a list of string names of mailboxes. Contrast this method with *imaplib.IMAP4.search()*, which returns numbers of individual messages from the currently selected mailbox.

imaplib.IMAP4.login(user, passwd)

Connect to the IMAP server specified in the instance initialization, using the authentication information given by user and passwd.

imaplib.IMAP4.logout()

Disconnect from the IMAP server specified in the instance initialization.

imaplib.IMAP4.search(charset, criterion1 [,criterion2 [,. . .]])

Return a (typ,messnums) tuple where messnums is a space-separated string of message numbers of matching messages. Message criteria specified in criterion1, and so on may either be ALL for all messages or flags indicating the fields and values to match.

imaplib.IMAP4.select([mbox="INBOX" [,readonly=0])

Select the current mailbox for operations such as *imaplib.IMAP4.search()* and *imaplib.IMAP4.expunge()*. The argument mbox gives the name of the mailbox, and readonly allows you to prevent modification to a mailbox.

SEE ALSO: email *345*; poplib *368*; smtplib *370*;

---

poplib ◇ A POP3 client class

The module *poplib* supports implementing custom POP3 clients. This protocol is detailed in RFC-1725. As with the discussion of other protocol libraries, this documentation aims only to cover the basics of communicating with a POP3 server—some methods or functions may be omitted here.

The *Python Library Reference* describes the POP3 protocol as obsolescent and recommends the use of IMAP4 if your server supports it. While this advice is not incorrect technically—IMAP indeed has some advantages—in my experience, support for POP3 is far more widespread among both clients and servers than is support for IMAP4. Obviously, your specific requirements will dictate the choice of an appropriate support library.

A typical (simple) POP3 client application might look like the one below. To illustrate a few methods, this application will print all the promising subject lines, and retrieve and delete any that look like spam. The example does not itself retrieve regular messages, only their headers.

new_email_subjects.py

```
#!/usr/bin/env python
import poplib, sys, string
spamlist = []
(host, user, passwd) = sys.argv[1:]
mbox = poplib.POP3(host)
mbox.user(user)
mbox.pass_(passwd)

for i in range(1, mbox.stat()[0]+1):
    # messages use one-based indexing
    headerlines = mbox.top(i, 0)[1]     # No body lines
    for line in headerlines:
        if string.upper(line[:9]) == 'SUBJECT: ':
```

```
            if -1 <> string.find(line,'URGENT'):
                spam = string.join(mbox.retr(i)[1],'\n')
                spamlist.append(spam)
                mbox.dele(i)
            else:
                print line[9:]

mbox.quit()
for spam in spamlist:
    report_to_spamcop(spam)      # assuming this func exists
```

CLASSES

poplib.POP3(host [,port=110])

The *poplib* module provides a single class that establishes a connection to a POP3 server at host host, using port port.

METHODS

poplib.POP3.apop(user, secret)

Log in to a server using APOP authentication.

poplib.POP3.dele(messnum)

Mark a message for deletion. Normally the actual deletion does not occur until you log off with *poplib.POP3.quit()*, but server implementations differ.

poplib.POP3.pass_(password)

Set the password to use when communicating with the POP server.

poplib.POP3.quit()

Log off from the connection to the POP server. Logging off will cause any pending deletions to be carried out. Call this method as soon as possible after you establish a connection to the POP server; while you are connected, the mailbox is locked against receiving any incoming messages.

poplib.POP3.retr(messnum)

Return the message numbered messnum (using one-based indexing). The return value is of the form (resp,linelist,octets), where linelist is a list of the individual lines in the message. To re-create the whole message, you will need to join these lines.

poplib.POP3.rset()

Unmark any messages marked for deletion. Since server implementations differ, it is not good practice to mark messages using *poplib.POP3.dele()* unless you are pretty confident you want to erase them. However, *poplib.POP3.rset()* can usually save messages should unusual circumstances occur before the connection is logged off.

poplib.POP3.top(messnum, lines)

Retrieve the initial lines of message `messnum`. The header is always included, along with `lines` lines from the body. The return format is the same as with *poplib.POP3.retr()*, and you will typically be interested in offset 1 of the returned tuple.

poplib.POP3.stat()

Retrieve the status of the POP mailbox in the format (`messcount,mbox_size`). `messcount` gives you the total number of message pending; `mbox_size` is the total size of all pending messages.

poplib.POP3.user(username)

Set the username to use when communicating with the POP server.

SEE ALSO: email *345*; smtplib *370*; imaplib *366*;

smtplib ◇ SMTP/ESMTP client class

The module *smtplib* supports implementing custom SMTP clients. This protocol is detailed in RFC-821 and RFC-1869. As with the discussion of other protocol libraries, this documentation aims only to cover the basics of communicating with an SMTP server—most methods and functions are omitted here. The modules *poplib* and *imaplib* are used to retrieve incoming email, and the module *smtplib* is used to send outgoing email.

A typical (simple) SMTP client application might look like the one below. This example is a command-line tool that accepts as a parameters the mandatory `To` message envelope header, constructs the `From` using environment variables, and sends whatever text is on STDIN. The `To` and `From` are also added as RFC-822 headers in the message header.

send_email.py

```
#!/usr/bin/env python
import smtplib
from sys import argv, stdin
from os import getenv
host = getenv('HOST', 'localhost')
if len(argv) >= 2:
    to_ = argv[1]
else:
    to_ = raw_input('To: ').strip()
```

```
if len(argv) >=3:
    subject = argv[2]
    body = stdin.read()
else:
    subject = stdin.readline()
    body = subject + stdin.read()
from_ = "%s@%s" % (getenv('USER', 'user'), host)
mess = '''From: %s\nTo: %s\n\n%s' % (to_, from_, body)
server = smtp.SMTP(host)
server.login
server.sendmail(from_, to_, mess)
server.quit()
```

CLASSES

smtplib.SMTP([host="localhost" [,port=25]])

Create an instance object that establishes a connection to an SMTP server at host
host, using port port.

METHODS

smtplib.SMTP.login(user, passwd)

Login to an SMTP server that requires authentication. Raises an error if authentication fails.

Not all—or even most—SMTP servers use password authentication. Modern servers
support direct authentication, but since not all clients support SMTP authentication, the option is often disabled. One commonly used strategy to prevent "open
relays" (servers that allow malicious/spam messages to be sent through them) is
"POP before SMTP." In this arrangement, an IP address is authorized to use an
SMTP server for a period of time after that same address has successfully authenticated with a POP3 server on the same machine. The timeout period is typically
a few minutes to hours.

smtplib.SMTP.quit()

Terminate an SMTP connection.

smtplib.SMTP.sendmail(from_, to_, mess [,mail_options=[] [,rcpt_options=[]]])

Send the message mess with From envelope from_ to recipients to_. The argument
to_ may either be a string containing a single address or a Python list of addresses.
The message should include any desired RFC-822 headers. ESMTP options may be
specified in arguments mail_options and rcpt_options.

SEE ALSO: email *345*; poplib *368*; imaplib *366*;

5.1.3   Message Collections and Message Parts

mailbox ◇ **Work with mailboxes in various formats**

The module *mailbox* provides a uniform interface to email messages stored in a variety of popular formats. Each class in the *mailbox* module is initialized with a mailbox of an appropriate format, and returns an instance with a single method `.next()`. This instance method returns each consecutive message within a mailbox upon each invocation. Moreover, the `.next()` method is conformant with the iterator protocol in Python 2.2+, which lets you loop over messages in recent versions of Python.

By default, the messages returned by `mailbox` instances are objects of the class *rfc822.Mailbox*. These message objects provide a number of useful methods and attributes. However, the recommendation of this book is to use the newer *email* module in place of the older *rfc822*. Fortunately, you may initialize a *mailbox* class using an optional message constructor. The only constraint on this constructor is that it is a callable object that accepts a file-like object as an argument—the *email* module provides two logical choices here.

```
>>> import mailbox, email, email.Parser
>>> mbox = mailbox.PortableUnixMailbox(open('mbox'))
>>> mbox.next()
<rfc822.Message instance at 0x41d770>
>>> mbox = mailbox.PortableUnixMailbox(open('mbox'),
...                        email.message_from_file)
>>> mbox.next()
<email.Message.Message instance at 0x5e43e0>
>>> mbox = mailbox.PortableUnixMailbox(open('mbox'),
...                        email.Parser.Parser().parse)
>>> mbox.next()
<email.Message.Message instance at 0x6ee630>
```

In Python 2.2+ you might structure your application as:

Looping through a mailbox in 2.2+

```
#!/usr/bin/env python
from mailbox import PortableUnixMailbox
from email import message_from_file as mff
import sys
folder = open(sys.argv[1])
for message in PortableUnixMailbox(folder, mff):
    # do something with the message...
    print message['Subject']
```

However, in earlier versions, this same code will raise an `AttributeError` for the missing `.__getitem__()` magic method. The slightly less elegant way to write the same application in an older Python is:

> Looping through a mailbox in any version

```
#!/usr/bin/env python
"Subject printer, older Python and rfc822.Message objects"
import sys
from mailbox import PortableUnixMailbox
mbox = PortableUnixMailbox(open(sys.argv[1]))
while 1:
    message = mbox.next()
    if message is None:
        break
    print message.getheader('Subject')
```

CLASSES

mailbox.UnixMailbox(file [,factory=rfc822.Message])

Read a BSD-style mailbox from the file-like object `file`. If the optional argument `factory` is specified, it must be a callable object that accepts a file-like object as its single argument (in this case, that object is a portion of an underlying file).

A BSD-style mailbox divides messages with a blank line followed by a "Unix From_" line. In this strict case, the "From_" line must have `name` and `time` information on it that matches a regular expression. In most cases, you are better off using *mailbox.PortableUnixMailbox*, which relaxes the requirement for recognizing the next message in a file.

mailbox.PortableUnixMailbox(file [,factory=rfc822.Message])

The arguments to this class are the same as for *mailbox.UnixMailbox*. Recognition of the messages within the mailbox `file` depends only on finding `From` followed by a space at the beginning of a line. In practice, this is as much as you can count on if you cannot guarantee that all mailboxes of interest will be created by a specific application and version.

mailbox.BabylMailbox(file [,factory=rfc822.Message])

The arguments to this class are the same as for *mailbox.UnixMailbox*. Handles mailbox files in Babyl format.

mailbox.MmdfMailbox(file [,factory=rfc822.Message])

The arguments to this class are the same as for *mailbox.UnixMailbox*. Handles mailbox files in MMDF format.

mailbox.MHMailbox(dirname [,factory=rfc822.Message])

The MH format uses the directory structure of the underlying native filesystem to organize mail folders. Each message is held in a separate file. The initializer argument for *mailbox.MHMailbox* is a string giving the name of the directory to be processed. The `factory` argument is the same as with *mailbox.UnixMailbox*.

mailbox.Maildir(dirname [,factory=rfc822.Message])

The QMail format, like the MH format, uses the directory structure of the underlying native filesystem to organize mail folders. The initializer argument for *mailbox.Maildir* is a string giving the name of the directory to be processed. The factory argument is the same as with *mailbox.UnixMailbox*.

SEE ALSO: email *345*; poplib *368*; imaplib *366*; nntplib *397*; smtplib *370*; rfc822 *397*;

---

mimetypes ◇ Guess the MIME type of a file

The *mimetypes* module maps file extensions to MIME datatypes. At its heart, the module is a dictionary, but several convenience functions let you work with system configuration files containing additional mappings, and also query the mapping in some convenient ways. As well as actual MIME types, the *mimetypes* module tries to guess file encodings, for example, compression wrapper.

In Python 2.2+, the *mimetypes* module also provides a *mimetypes.MimeTypes* class that lets instances each maintain their own MIME types mapping, but the requirement for multiple distinct mapping is rare enough not to be worth covering here.

FUNCTIONS

mimetypes.guess_type(url [,strict=0])

Return a pair (typ,encoding) based on the file or Uniform Resource Locator (URL) named by url. If the strict option is specified with a true value, only officially specified types are considered. Otherwise, a larger number of widespread MIME types are examined. If either type or encoding cannot be guessed, None is returned for that value.

```
>>> import mimetypes
>>> mimetypes.guess_type('x.abc.gz')
(None, 'gzip')
>>> mimetypes.guess_type('x.tgz')
('application/x-tar', 'gzip')
>>> mimetypes.guess_type('x.ps.gz')
('application/postscript', 'gzip')
>>> mimetypes.guess_type('x.txt')
('text/plain', None)
>>> mimetypes.guess_type('a.xyz')
(None, None)
```

mimetypes.guess_extension(type [,strict=0])

Return a string indicating a likely extension associated with the MIME type. If multiple file extensions are possible, one is returned (generally the one that is first alphabetically, but this is not guaranteed). The argument strict has the same meaning as in *mimetypes.guess_type()*.

```
>>> print mimetypes.guess_extension('application/EDI-Consent')
None
>>> print mimetypes.guess_extension('application/pdf')
.pdf
>>> print mimetypes.guess_extension('application/postscript')
.ai
```

mimetypes.init([[list-of-files]])

Add the definitions from each filename listed in list-of-files to the MIME type mapping. Several default files are examined even if this function is not called, but additional configuration files may be added as needed on your system. For example, on my MacOSX system, which uses somewhat different directories than a Linux system, I find it useful to run:

```
>>> mimetypes.init(['/private/etc/httpd/mime.types.default',
...                  '/private/etc/httpd/mime.types'])
```

Notice that even if you are specifying only one additional configuration file, you must enclose its name inside a list.

mimetypes.read_mime_types(fname)

Read the single file named fname and return a dictionary mapping extensions to MIME types.

```
>>> from mimetypes import read_mime_types
>>> types = read_mime_types('/private/etc/httpd/mime.types')
>>> for _ in range(5): print types.popitem()
...
('.wbxml', 'application/vnd.wap.wbxml')
('.aiff', 'audio/x-aiff')
('.rm', 'audio/x-pn-realaudio')
('.xbm', 'image/x-xbitmap')
('.avi', 'video/x-msvideo')
```

ATTRIBUTES

mimetypes.common_types

Dictionary of widely used, but unofficial MIME types.

mimetypes.inited

True value if the module has been initialized.

mimetypes.encodings_map

Dictionary of encodings.

mimetypes.knownfiles

List of files checked by default.

mimetypes.suffix_map

Dictionary of encoding suffixes.

mimetypes.types_map

Dictionary mapping extensions to MIME types.

5.2   World Wide Web Applications

5.2.1   Common Gateway Interface

cgi ◇ **Support for Common Gateway Interface scripts**

The module *cgi* provides a number of helpful tools for creating CGI scripts. There are two elements to CGI, basically: (1) Reading query values. (2) Writing the results back to the requesting browser. The first of these elements is aided by the *cgi* module, the second is just a matter of formatting suitable text to return. The *cgi* module contains one class that is its primary interface; it also contains several utility functions that are not documented here because their use is uncommon (and not hard to replicate and customize for your specific needs). See the *Python Library Reference* for details on the utility functions.

A CGI PRIMER

A primer on the Common Gateway Interface is in order. A CGI script is just an application—in any programming language—that runs on a Web server. The server software recognizes a request for a CGI application, sets up a suitable environment, then passes control to the CGI application. By default, this is done by spawning a new process space for the CGI application to run in, but technologies like *FastCGI* and *mod_python* perform some tricks to avoid extra process creation. These latter techniques speed performance but change little from the point of view of the CGI application creator.

A Python CGI script is called in exactly the same way any other URL is. The only difference between a CGI and a static URL is that the former is marked as executable by the Web server—conventionally, such scripts are confined to a `./cgi-bin/` subdirectory (sometimes another directory name is used); Web servers generally allow you to configure where CGI scripts may live. When a CGI script runs, it is expected to output a `Content-Type` header to STDOUT, followed by a blank line, then finally some content of the appropriate type—most often an HTML document. That is really all there is to it.

CGI requests may utilize one of two methods: POST or GET. A POST request sends any associated query data to the STDIN of the CGI script (the Web server sets this up for the script). A GET request puts the query in an environment variable called QUERY_STRING. There is not a lot of difference between the two methods, but GET requests encode their query information in a Uniform Resource Identifier (URI) and may therefore be composed without HTML forms and saved/bookmarked. For example, the following is an HTTP GET query to a script example discussed below:

<http://gnosis.cx/cgi-bin/simple.cgi?this=that&spam=eggs+are+good>

You do not actually *need* the *cgi* module to create CGI scripts. For example, let us look at the script simple.cgi mentioned above:

simple.cgi

```python
#!/usr/bin/python
import os,sys
print "Content-Type: text/html"
print
print "<html><head><title>Environment test</title></head><body><pre>"
for k,v in os.environ.items():
    print k, "::",
    if len(v)<=40: print v
    else:          print v[:37]+"..."
print "&lt;STDIN&gt; ::", sys.stdin.read()
print "</pre></body></html>"
```

I happen to have composed the above sample query by hand, but you will often call a CGI script from another Web page. Here is one that does so:

http://gnosis.cx/simpleform.html

```html
<html><head><title>Test simple.cgi</title></head><body>
<form action="cgi-bin/simple.cgi" method="GET" name="form">
<input type="hidden" name="this" value="that">
<input type="text" value="" name="spam" size="55" maxlength="256">
<input type="submit" value="GET">
</form>
<form action="cgi-bin/simple.cgi" method="POST" name="form">
<input type="hidden" name="this" value="that">
<input type="text" value="" name="spam" size="55" maxlength="256">
<input type="submit" value="POST">
</form>
</body></html>
```

It turns out that the script simple.cgi is moderately useful; it tells the requester exactly what it has to work with. For example, the query above (which could be generated exactly by the GET form on simpleform.html) returns a Web page that looks like the one below (edited):

```
DOCUMENT_ROOT :: /www/gnosis
HTTP_ACCEPT_ENCODING :: gzip, deflate, compress;q=0.9
CONTENT_TYPE :: application/x-www-form-urlencoded
SERVER_PORT :: 80
REMOTE_ADDR :: 151.203.xxx.xxx
SERVER_NAME :: www.gnosis.cx
HTTP_USER_AGENT :: Mozilla/5.0 (Macintosh; U; PPC Mac OS...
REQUEST_URI :: /cgi-bin/simple.cgi?this=that&spam=eg...
QUERY_STRING :: this=that&spam=eggs+are+good
SERVER_PROTOCOL :: HTTP/1.1
HTTP_HOST :: gnosis.cx
REQUEST_METHOD :: GET
SCRIPT_NAME :: /cgi-bin/simple.cgi
SCRIPT_FILENAME :: /www/gnosis/cgi-bin/simple.cgi
HTTP_REFERER :: http://gnosis.cx/simpleform.html
<STDIN> ::
```

A few environment variables have been omitted, and those available will differ between Web servers and setups. The most important variable is QUERY_STRING; you may perhaps want to make other decisions based on the requesting REMOTE_ADDR, HTTP_USER_AGENT, or HTTP_REFERER (yes, the variable name is spelled wrong). Notice that STDIN is empty in this case. However, using the POST form on the sample Web page will give a slightly different response (trimmed):

```
CONTENT_LENGTH :: 28
REQUEST_URI :: /cgi-bin/simple.cgi
QUERY_STRING ::
REQUEST_METHOD :: POST
<STDIN> :: this=that&spam=eggs+are+good
```

The CONTENT_LENGTH environment variable is new, QUERY_STRING has become empty, and STDIN contains the query. The rest of the omitted variables are the same.

A CGI script need not utilize any query data and need not return an HTML page. For example, on some of my Web pages, I utilize a "Web bug"—a 1x1 transparent gif file that reports back who "looks" at it. Web bugs have a less-honorable use by spammers who send HTML mail and want to verify receipt covertly; but in my case, I only want to check some additional information about visitors to a few of my own Web pages. A Web page might contain, at bottom:

```
<img src="http://gnosis.cx/cgi-bin/visitor.cgi">
```

The script itself is:

```
visitor.cgi
```

```
#!/usr/bin/python
import os
from sys import stdout
addr = os.environ.get("REMOTE_ADDR","Unknown IP Address")
agent = os.environ.get("HTTP_USER_AGENT","No Known Browser")
fp = open('visitor.log','a')
fp.write('%s\t%s\n' % (addr, agent))
fp.close()
stdout.write("Content-type: image/gif\n\n")
stdout.write('GIF89a\001\000\001\000\370\000\000\000\000\000\000')
stdout.write('\000\000\000!\371\004\001\000\000\000\000,\000')
stdout.write('\000\000\000\001\000\001\000\000\002\002D\001\000;')
```

CLASSES

The point where the *cgi* module becomes useful is in automating form processing. The class *cgi.FieldStorage* will determine the details of whether a POST or GET request was made, and decode the urlencoded query into a dictionary-like object. You could perform these checks manually, but *cgi* makes it much easier to do.

cgi.FieldStorage([fp=sys.stdin [,headers [,ob [,environ=os.environ [,keep_blank_values=0 [,strict_parsing=0]]]]]])

Construct a mapping object containing query information. You will almost always use the default arguments and construct a standard instance. A *cgi.FieldStorage* object allows you to use name indexing and also supports several custom methods. On initialization, the object will determine all relevant details of the current CGI invocation.

```
import cgi
query = cgi.FieldStorage()
eggs = query.getvalue('eggs','default_eggs')
numfields = len(query)
if query.has_key('spam'):
    spam = query['spam']
[...]
```

When you retrieve a *cgi.FieldStorage* value by named indexing, what you get is not a string, but either an instance of *cgi.FieldStorage* objects (or maybe *cgi.MiniFieldStorage*) or a list of such objects. The string query is in their .value attribute. Since HTML forms may contain multiple fields with the same name, multiple values might exist for a key—a list of such values is returned. The safe way to read the actual strings in queries is to check whether a list is returned:

```
if type(eggs) is type([]):  # several eggs
    for egg in eggs:
        print "<dt>Egg</dt>\n<dd>", egg.value, "</dd>"
else:
    print "<dt>Eggs</dt>\n<dd>", eggs.value, "</dd>"
```

For special circumstances you might wish to change the initialization of the instance by specifying an optional (named) argument. The argument `fp` specifies the input stream to read for POST requests. The argument `headers` contains a dictionary mapping HTTP headers to values—usually consisting of {"Content-Type":...}; the type is determined from the environment if no argument is given. The argument `environ` specified where the environment mapping is found. If you specify a true value for `keep_blank_values`, a key will be included for a blank HTML form field—mapping to an empty string. If `string_parsing` is specified, a `ValueError` will be raised if there are any flaws in the query string.

METHODS

The methods `.keys()`, `.values()`, and `.has_key()` work as with a standard dictionary object. The method `.items()`, however, is not supported.

cgi.FieldStorage.getfirst(key [,default=None])

Python 2.2+ has this method to return exactly one string corresponding to the key `key`. You cannot rely on which such string value will be returned if multiple submitting HTML form fields have the same name—but you are assured of this method returning a string, not a list.

cgi.FieldStorage.getlist(key [,default=None])

Python 2.2+ has this method to return a list of strings whether there are one or several matches on the key `key`. This allows you to loop over returned values without worrying about whether they are a list or a single string.

```
>>> spam = form.getlist('spam')
>>> for s in spam:
...     print s
```

cgi.FieldStorage.getvalue(key [,default=None])

Return a string or list of strings that are the value(s) corresponding to the key `key`. If the argument `default` is specified, return the specified value in case of key miss. In contrast to indexing by name, this method retrieves actual strings rather than storage objects with a `.value` attribute.

```
>>> import sys, cgi, os
>>> from cStringIO import StringIO
```

```
>>> sys.stdin = StringIO("this=that&this=other&spam=good+eggs")
>>> os.environ['REQUEST_METHOD'] = 'POST'
>>> form = cgi.FieldStorage()
>>> form.getvalue('this')
['that', 'other']
>>> form['this']
[MiniFieldStorage('this','that'),MiniFieldStorage('this','other')]
```

ATTRIBUTES

cgi.FieldStorage.file

If the object handled is an uploaded file, this attribute gives the file handle for the file. While you can read the entire file contents as a string from the `cgi.FieldStorage.value` attribute, you may want to read it line-by-line instead. To do this, use the `.readline()` or `.readlines()` method of the file object.

cgi.FieldStorage.filename

If the object handled is an uploaded file, this attribute contains the name of the file. An HTML form to upload a file looks something like:

```
<form action="upload.cgi" method="POST"
      enctype="multipart/form-data">
  Name: <input name="" type="file" size="50">
  <input type="submit" value="Upload">
</form>
```

Web browsers typically provide a point-and-click method to fill in a file-upload form.

cgi.FieldStorage.list

This attribute contains the list of mapping object within a *cgi.FieldStorage* object. Typically, each object in the list is itself a *cgi.MiniStorage* object instead (but this can be complicated if you upload files that themselves contain multiple parts).

```
>>> form.list
[MiniFieldStorage('this', 'that'),
MiniFieldStorage('this', 'other'),
MiniFieldStorage('spam', 'good eggs')]
```

SEE ALSO: cgi.FieldStorage.getvalue() *380*;

cgi.FieldStorage.value
cgi.MiniFieldStorage.value

The string value of a storage object.

SEE ALSO: urllib *388*; cgitb *382*; dict *24*;

cgitb ◇ Traceback manager for CGI scripts

Python 2.2 added a useful little module for debugging CGI applications. You can download it for earlier Python versions from <http://lfw.org/python/cgitb.py>. A basic difficulty with developing CGI scripts is that their normal output is sent to STDOUT, which is caught by the underlying Web server and forwarded to an invoking Web browser. However, when a traceback occurs due to a script error, that output is sent to STDERR (which is hard to get at in a CGI context). A more useful action is either to log errors to server storage or display them in the client browser.

Using the *cgitb* module to examine CGI script errors is almost embarrassingly simple. At the top of your CGI script, simply include the lines:

Traceback enabled CGI script

```
import cgitb
cgitb.enable()
```

If any exceptions are raised, a pretty-formatted report is produced (and possibly logged to a name starting with @).

METHODS

cgitb.enable([display=1 [,logdir=None [context=5]]])

Turn on traceback reporting. The argument `display` controls whether an error report is sent to the browser—you might not want this to happen in a production environment, since users will have little idea what to make of such a report (and there may be security issues in letting them see it). If `logdir` is specified, tracebacks are logged into files in that directory. The argument `context` indicates how many lines of code are displayed surrounding the point where an error occurred.

For earlier versions of Python, you will have to do your own error catching. A simple approach is:

Debugging CGI script in Python

```
import sys
sys.stderr = sys.stdout
def main():
    import cgi
    # ...do the actual work of the CGI...
    # perhaps ending with:
    print template % script_dictionary
print "Content-type: text/html\n\n"
main()
```

This approach is not bad for quick debugging; errors go back to the browser. Unfortunately, though, the traceback (if one occurs) gets displayed as HTML, which means that you need to go to "View Source" in a browser to see the original line breaks in the traceback. With a few more lines, we can add a little extra sophistication.

Debugging/logging CGI script in Python

```
import sys, traceback
print "Content-type: text/html\n\n"
try:                    # use explicit exception handling
    import my_cgi  # main CGI functionality in 'my_cgi.py'
    my_cgi.main()
except:
    import time
    errtime = '--- '+ time.ctime(time.time()) +' ---\n'
    errlog = open('cgi_errlog', 'a')
    errlog.write(errtime)
    traceback.print_exc(None, errlog)
    print "<html>\n<head>"
    print "<title>CGI Error Encountered!</title>\n</head>"
    print "<body><p>A problem was encountered running MyCGI</p>"
    print "<p>Please check the server error log for details</p>"
    print "</body></html>"
```

The second approach is quite generic as a wrapper for any real CGI functionality we might write. Just `import` a different CGI module as needed, and maybe make the error messages more detailed or friendlier.

SEE ALSO: cgi *376*;

5.2.2 Parsing, Creating, and Manipulating HTML Documents

htmlentitydefs ◇ **HTML character entity references**

The module *htmlentitydefs* provides a mapping between ISO-8859-1 characters and the symbolic names of corresponding HTML 2.0 entity references. Not all HTML named entities have equivalents in the ISO-8859-1 character set; in such cases, names are mapped the HTML numeric references instead.

ATTRIBUTES

htmlentitydefs.entitydefs

A dictionary mapping symbolic names to character entities.

```
>>> import htmlentitydefs
>>> htmlentitydefs.entitydefs['omega']
'&#969;'
```

```
>>> htmlentitydefs.entitydefs['uuml']
'\xfc'
```

For some purposes, you might want a reverse dictionary to find the HTML entities for
ISO-8859-1 characters.

```
>>> from htmlentitydefs import entitydefs
>>> iso8859_1 = dict([(v,k) for k,v in entitydefs.items()])
>>> iso8859_1['\xfc']
'uuml'
```

HTMLParser ◇ Simple HTML and XHTML parser

The module *HTMLParser* is an event-based framework for processing HTML files. In
contrast to *htmllib*, which is based on *sgmllib*, *HTMLParser* simply uses some regular
expressions to identify the parts of an HTML document—starttag, text, endtag, comment, and so on. The different internal implementation, however, makes little difference
to users of the modules.

I find the module *HTMLParser* much more straightforward to use than *htmllib*, and
therefore *HTMLParser* is documented in detail in this book, while *htmllib* is not. While
htmllib more or less *requires* the use of the ancillary module *formatter* to operate, there
is no extra difficulty in letting *HTMLParser* make calls to a formatter object. You might
want to do this, for example, if you have an existing formatter/writer for a complex
document format.

Both *HTMLParser* and *htmllib* provide an interface that is very similar to that of SAX
or expat XML parsers. That is, a document—HTML or XML—is processed purely as
a sequence of events, with no data structure created to represent the document as a
whole. For XML documents, another processing API is the Document Object Model
(DOM), which treats the document as an in-memory hierarchical data structure.

In principle, you could use *xml.sax* or *xml.dom* to process HTML documents that con-
formed with XHTML—that is, tightened up HTML that is actually an XML application
The problem is that very little existing HTML is XHTML compliant. A syntactic issue
is that HTML does not require closing tags in many cases, where XML/XHTML requires every tag to be closed. But implicit closing tags can be inferred from subsequent
opening tags (e.g., with certain names). A popular tool like tidy does an excellent job
of cleaning up HTML in this way. The more significant problem is semantic. A whole
lot of actually existing HTML is quite lax about tag matching—Web browsers that
successfully display the majority of Web pages are quite complex software projects.

For example, a snippet like that below is quite likely to occur in HTML you come
across:

```
<p>The <a href="http://ietf.org">IETF admonishes:
   <i>Be lenient in what you <b>accept</i></a>.</b>
```

If you know even a little HTML, you know that the author of this snippet presumably wanted the whole quote in italics, the word **accept** in bold. But converting the snippet into a data structure such as a DOM object is difficult to generalize. Fortunately, *HTMLParser* is fairly lenient about what it will process; however, for sufficiently badly formed input (or any other problem), the module will raise the exception HTMLParser.HTMLParseError.

SEE ALSO: htmllib *285*; xml.sax *405*;

CLASSES

HTMLParser.HTMLParser()

The *HTMLParser* module contains the single class *HTMLParser.HTMLParser*. The class itself is fairly useful, since it does not actually do anything when it encounters any event. Utilizing *HTMLParser.HTMLParser()* is a matter of subclassing it and providing methods to handle the events you are interested in.

If it is important to keep track of the structural position of the current event within the document, you will need to maintain a data structure with this information. If you are certain that the document you are processing is well-formed XHTML, a stack suffices. For example:

HTMLParser_stack.py

```
#!/usr/bin/env python
import HTMLParser
html = """<html><head><title>Advice</title></head><body>
<p>The <a href="http://ietf.org">IETF admonishes:
    <i>Be strict in what you <b>send</b>.</i></a></p>
</body></html>
"""
tagstack = []
class ShowStructure(HTMLParser.HTMLParser):
    def handle_starttag(self, tag, attrs): tagstack.append(tag)
    def handle_endtag(self, tag): tagstack.pop()
    def handle_data(self, data):
        if data.strip():
            for tag in tagstack: sys.stdout.write('/'+tag)
            sys.stdout.write(' >> %s\n' % data[:40].strip())
ShowStructure().feed(html)
```

Running this optimistic parser produces:

```
% ./HTMLParser_stack.py
```

```
/html/head/title >> Advice
/html/body/p >> The
/html/body/p/a >> IETF admonishes:
/html/body/p/a/i >> Be strict in what you
/html/body/p/a/i/b >> send
/html/body/p/a/i >> .
```

You could, of course, use this context information however you wished when processing a particular bit of content (or when you process the tags themselves).

A more pessimistic approach is to maintain a "fuzzy" tagstack. We can define a new object that will remove the most recent starttag corresponding to an endtag and will also prevent <p> and <blockquote> tags from nesting if no corresponding endtag is found. You could do more along this line for a production application, but a class like TagStack makes a good start:

```
class TagStack:
    def __init__(self, lst=[]): self.lst = lst
    def __getitem__(self, pos): return self.lst[pos]
    def append(self, tag):
        # Remove every paragraph-level tag if this is one
        if tag.lower() in ('p','blockquote'):
            self.lst = [t for t in self.lst
                            if t not in ('p','blockquote')]
        self.lst.append(tag)
    def pop(self, tag):
        # "Pop" by tag from nearest pos, not only last item
        self.lst.reverse()
        try:
            pos = self.lst.index(tag)
        except ValueError:
            raise HTMLParser.HTMLParseError, "Tag not on stack"
        del self.lst[pos]
        self.lst.reverse()
tagstack = TagStack()
```

This more lenient stack structure suffices to parse badly formatted HTML like the example given in the module discussion.

METHODS AND ATTRIBUTES

HTMLParser.HTMLParser.close()

Close all buffered data, and treat any current data as if an EOF was encountered.

HTMLParser.HTMLParser.feed(data)

Send some additional HTML data to the parser instance from the string in the argument `data`. You may feed the instance with whatever size chunks of data you wish, and each will be processed, maintaining the previous state.

HTMLParser.HTMLParser.getpos()

Return the current line number and offset. Generally called within a `.handle_*()` method to report or analyze the state of the processing of the HTML text.

HTMLParser.HTMLParser.handle_charref(name)

Method called when a character reference is encountered, such as `&#971;`. Character references may be interspersed with element text, much as with entity references. You can construct a Unicode character from a character reference, and you may want to pass the Unicode (or raw character reference) to *HTMLParser.HTMLParser.handle_data()*.

```
class CharacterData(HTMLParser.HTMLParser):
    def handle_charref(self, name):
        import unicodedata
        char = unicodedata.name(unichr(int(name)))
        self.handle_data(char)
    [...other methods...]
```

HTMLParser.HTMLParser.handle_comment(data)

Method called when a comment is encountered. HTML comments begin with `<!---` and end with `--->`. The argument `data` contains the contents of the comment.

HTMLParser.HTMLParser.handle_data(data)

Method called when content data is encountered. All the text between tags is contained in the argument `data`, but if character or entity references are interspersed with text, the respective handler methods will be called in an interspersed fashion.

HTMLParser.HTMLParser.handle_decl(data)

Method called when a declaration is encountered. HTML declarations with `<!` and end with `>`. The argument `data` contains the contents of the comment. Syntactically, comments look like a type of declaration, but are handled by the *HTMLParser.HTMLParser.handle_comment()* method.

HTMLParser.HTMLParser.handle_endtag(tag)

Method called when an endtag is encountered. The argument `tag` contains the tag name (without brackets).

HTMLParser.HTMLParser.handle_entityref(name)

Method called when an entity reference is encountered, such as `&amp;`. When entity references occur in the middle of an element text, calls to this method are interspersed with calls to *HTMLParser.HTMLParser.handle_data()*. In many cases, you will want to call the latter method with decoded entities; for example:

```
class EntityData(HTMLParser.HTMLParser):
    def handle_entityref(self, name):
        import htmlentitydefs
        self.handle_data(htmlentitydefs.entitydefs[name])
    [...other methods...]
```

HTMLParser.HTMLParser.handle_pi(data)

Method called when a processing instruction (PI) is encountered. PIs begin with **<?** and end with **?>**. They are less common in HTML than in XML, but are allowed. The argument **data** contains the contents of the PI.

HTMLParser.HTMLParser.handle_startendtag(tag, attrs)

Method called when an XHTML-style empty tag is encountered, such as:

```
<img src="foo.png" alt="foo"/>
```

The arguments **tag** and **attrs** are identical to those passed to *HTMLParser.HTMLParser.handle_starttag()*.

HTMLParser.HTMLParser.handle_starttag(tag, attrs)

Method called when a starttag is encountered. The argument **tag** contains the tag name (without brackets), and the argument **attrs** contains the tag attributes as a list of pairs, such as [(``href'',"http://ietf.org")].

HTMLParser.HTMLParser.lasttag

The last tag—start or end—that was encountered. Generally maintaining some sort of stack structure like those discussed is more useful. But this attribute is available automatically. You should treat it as read-only.

HTMLParser.HTMLParser.reset()

Restore the instance to its initial state, lose any unprocessed data (for example, content within unclosed tags).

5.2.3   Accessing Internet Resources

urllib ◇ Open an arbitrary URL

The module *urllib* provides convenient, high-level access to resources on the Internet. While *urllib* lets you connect to a variety of protocols, to manage low-level details of connections—especially issues of complex authentication—you should use the module *urllib2* instead. However, *urllib does* provide hooks for HTTP basic authentication.

The interface to *urllib* objects is file-like. You can substitute an object representing a URL connection for almost any function or class that expects to work with a read-only file. All of the World Wide Web, File Transfer Protocol (FTP) directories, and gopherspace can be treated, almost transparently, as if it were part of your local filesystem.

Although the module provides two classes that can be utilized or subclassed for more fine-tuned control, generally in practice the function *urllib.urlopen()* is the only interface you need to the *urllib* module.

FUNCTIONS

urllib.urlopen(url [,data])

Return a file-like object that connects to the Uniform Resource Locator (URL) resource named in `url`. This resource may be an HTTP, FTP, Gopher, or local file. The optional argument `data` can be specified to make a POST request to an HTTP URL. This data is a urlencoded string, which may be created by the *urllib.urlencode()* method. If no postdata is specified with an HTTP URL, the GET method is used.

Depending on the type of resource specified, a slightly different class is used to construct the instance, but each provides the methods: `.read()`, `.readline()`, `.readlines()`, `.fileno()`, `.close()`, `.info()`, and `.geturl()` (but not `.xreadlines()`, `.seek()`, or `.tell()`).

Most of the provided methods are shared by file objects, and each provides the same interface—arguments and return values—as actual file objects. The method `.geturl()` simply contains the URL that the object connects to, usually the same string as the `url` argument.

The method `.info()` returns *mimetools.Message* object. While the *mimetools* module is not documented in detail in this book, this object is generally similar to an *email.Message.Message* object—specifically, it responds to both the built-in *str()* function and dictionary-like indexing:

```
>>> u = urllib.urlopen('urlopen.py')
>>> print `u.info()`
<mimetools.Message instance at 0x62f800>
>>> print u.info()
Content-Type: text/x-python
Content-Length: 577
Last-modified: Fri, 10 Aug 2001 06:03:04 GMT

>>> u.info().keys()
['last-modified', 'content-length', 'content-type']
>>> u.info()['content-type']
'text/x-python'
```

SEE ALSO: urllib.urlretrieve() *390*; urllib.urlencode() *390*;

urllib.urlretrieve(url [,fname [,reporthook [,data]]])

Save the resources named in the argument url to a local file. If the optional argument fname is specified, that filename will be used; otherwise, a unique temporary filename is generated. The optional argument data may contain a urlencoded string to pass to an HTTP POST request, as with *urllib.urlopen()*.

The optional argument reporthook may be used to specify a callback function, typically to implement a progress meter for downloads. The function reporthook() will be called repeatedly with the arguments bl_transferred, bl_size, and file_size. Even remote files smaller than the block size will typically call reporthook() a few times, but for larger files, file_size will *approximately* equal bl_transferred*bl_size.

The return value of *urllib.urlretrieve()* is a pair (fname,info). The returned fname is the name of the created file—the same as the fname argument if it was specified. The info return value is a *mimetools.Message* object, like that returned by the .info() method of a *urllib.urlopen* object.

SEE ALSO: urllib.urlopen() *389*; urllib.urlencode() *390*;

urllib.quote(s [,safe="/"])

Return a string with special characters escaped. Exclude any characters in the string safe for being quoted.

```
>>> urllib.quote('/~username/special&odd!')
'/%7Eusername/special%26odd%21'
```

urllib.quote_plus(s [,safe="/"])

Same as *urllib.quote()*, but encode spaces as + also.

urllib.unquote(s)

Return an unquoted string. Inverse operation of *urllib.quote()*.

urllib.unquote_plus(s)

Return an unquoted string. Inverse operation of *urllib.quote_plus()*.

urllib.urlencode(query)

Return a urlencoded query for an HTTP POST or GET request. The argument query may be either a dictionary-like object or a sequence of pairs. If pairs are used, their order is preserved in the generated query.

```
>>> query = urllib.urlencode([('hl','en'),
...                           ('q','Text Processing in Python')])
>>> print query
hl=en&q=Text+Processing+in+Python
>>> u = urllib.urlopen('http://google.com/search?'+query)
```

Notice, however, that at least as of the moment of this writing, Google will refuse to return results on this request because a Python shell is not a recognized browser (Google provides a SOAP interface that is more lenient, however). You *could*, but *should not*, create a custom *urllib* class that spoofed an accepted browser.

CLASSES

You can change the behavior of the basic `urllib.urlopen()` and `urllib.urlretrieve()` functions by substituting your own class into the module namespace. Generally this is the best way to use *urllib* classes:

```
import urllib
class MyOpener(urllib.FancyURLopener):
    pass
urllib._urlopener = MyOpener()
u = urllib.urlopen("http://some.url")    # uses custom class
```

urllib.URLopener([proxies [,**x509]])

Base class for reading URLs. Generally you should subclass from the class *urllib.FancyURLopener* unless you need to implement a nonstandard protocol from scratch.

The argument `proxies` may be specified with a mapping if you need to connect to resources through a proxy. The keyword arguments may be used to configure HTTPS authentication; specifically, you should give named arguments `key_file` and `cert_file` in this case.

```
import urllib
proxies = {'http':'http://192.168.1.1','ftp':'ftp://192.168.256.1'}
urllib._urlopener = urllib.URLopener(proxies, key_file='mykey',
                                  cert_file='mycert')
```

urllib.FancyURLopener([proxies [,**x509]])

The optional initialization arguments are the same as for *urllib.URLopener*, unless you subclass further to use other arguments. This class knows how to handle 301 and 302 HTTP redirect codes, as well as 401 authentication requests. The class *urllib.FancyURLopener* is the one actually used by the *urllib* module, but you may subclass it to add custom capabilities.

METHODS AND ATTRIBUTES

urllib.URLFancyopener.get_user_passwd(host, realm)

Return the pair `(user,passwd)` to use for authentication. The default implementation calls the method `.prompt_user_passwd()` in turn. In a subclass you might want to either provide a GUI login interface or obtain authentication information from some other source, such as a database.

urllib.URLopener.open(url [,data])
urllib.URLFancyopener.open(url [,data])

> Open the URL `url`, optionally using HTTP POST query `data`.

> SEE ALSO: urllib.urlopen() *389*;

urllib.URLopener.open_unknown(url [,data])
urllib.URLFancyopener.open_unknown(url [,data])

> If the scheme is not recognized, the `.open()` method passes the request to this method. You can implement error reporting or fallback behavior here.

urllib.URLFancyopener.prompt_user_passwd(host, realm)

> Prompt for the authentication pair (`user,passwd`) at the terminal. You may override this to prompt within a GUI. If the authentication is not obtained interactively, but by other means, directly overriding `.get_user_passwd()` is more logical.

urllib.URLopener.retrieve(url [,fname [,reporthook [,data]]])
urllib.URLFancyopener.retrieve(url [,fname [,reporthook [,data]]])

> Copies the URL `url` to the local file named `fname`. Callback to the progress function `reporthook` if specified. Use the optional HTTP POST query data in `data`.

> SEE ALSO: urllib.urlretrieve() *390*;

urllib.URLopener.version
urllib.URFancyLopener.version

> The User Agent string reported to a server is contained in this attribute. By default it is `urllib/###`, where the *urllib* version number is used rather than `###`.

| urlparse ◇ **Parse Uniform Resource Locators** |

The module *urlparse* support just one fairly simple task, but one that is just complicated enough for quick implementations to get wrong. URLs describe a number of aspects of resources on the Internet: access protocol, network location, path, parameters, query, and fragment. Using *urlparse*, you can break out and combine these components to manipulate or generate URLs. The format of URLs is based on RFC-1738, RFC-1808, and RFC-2396.

Notice that the *urlparse* module does not parse the components of the network location, but merely returns them as a field. For example, the URL `ftp://guest:gnosis@192.168.1.102:21//tmp/MAIL.MSG` is a valid identifier on my local network (at least at the moment this is written). Tools like Mozilla and wget are happy to retrieve this file. Parsing this fairly complicated URL with *urlparse* gives us:

```
>>> import urlparse
>>> url = 'ftp://guest:gnosis@192.168.1.102:21//tmp/MAIL.MSG'
>>> urlparse.urlparse(url)
('ftp', 'guest:gnosis@192.168.1.102:21', '//tmp/MAIL.MSG',
'', '', '')
```

While this information is not incorrect, this network location itself contains multiple
fields; all but the host are optional. The actual structure of a network location, using
square bracket nesting to indicate optional components, is:

```
[user[:password]@]host[:port]
```

The following mini-module will let you further parse these fields:

location_parse.py

```
#!/usr/bin/env python
def location_parse(netloc):
    "Return tuple (user, passwd, host, port) for netloc"
    if '@' not in netloc:
        netloc = ':@' + netloc
    login, net = netloc.split('@')
    if ':' not in login:
        login += ':'
    user, passwd = login.split(':')
    if ':' not in net:
        net += ':'
    host, port = net.split(':')
    return (user, passwd, host, port)

#-- specify network location on command-line
if __name__=='__main__':
    import sys
    print location_parse(sys.argv[1])
```

FUNCTIONS

urlparse.urlparse(url [,def_scheme="" [,fragments=1]])

Return a tuple consisting of six components of the URL url, (scheme, netloc,
path, params, query, fragment). A URL is assumed to follow the pattern
scheme://netloc/path;params?query#fragment. If a default scheme def_scheme
is specified, that string will be returned in case no scheme is encoded in the URL
itself. If fragments is set to a false value, any fragments will not be split from other
fields.

```
>>> from urlparse import urlparse
```

```
>>> urlparse('gnosis.cx/path/sub/file.html#sect', 'http', 1)
('http', '', 'gnosis.cx/path/sub/file.html', '', '', 'sect')
>>> urlparse('gnosis.cx/path/sub/file.html#sect', 'http', 0)
('http', '', 'gnosis.cx/path/sub/file.html#sect', '', '', '')
>>> urlparse('http://gnosis.cx/path/file.cgi?key=val#sect',
...          'gopher', 1)
('http', 'gnosis.cx', '/path/file.cgi', '', 'key=val', 'sect')
>>> urlparse('http://gnosis.cx/path/file.cgi?key=val#sect',
...          'gopher', 0)
('http', 'gnosis.cx', '/path/file.cgi', '', 'key=val#sect', '')
```

urlparse.urlunparse(tup)

Construct a URL from a tuple containing the fields returned by *urlparse.urlparse()*. The returned URL has canonical form (redundancy eliminated) so *urlparse.urlparse()* and *urlparse.urlunparse()* are not precisely inverse operations; however, the composed `urlunparse(urlparse(s))` should be idempotent.

urlparse.urljoin(base, file)

Return a URL that has the same base path as `base` but has the file component `file`. For example:

```
>>> from urlparse import urljoin
>>> urljoin('http://somewhere.lan/path/file.html',
...                    'sub/other.html')
'http://somewhere.lan/path/sub/other.html'
```

In Python 2.2+ the functions *urlparse.urlsplit()* and *urlparse.urlunsplit()* are available. These differ from *urlparse.urlparse()* and *urlparse.urlunparse()* in returning a 5-tuple that does not split out `params` from `path`.

5.3   Synopses of Other Internet Modules

There are a variety of Internet-related modules in the standard library that will not be covered here in their specific usage. In the first place, there are two general aspects to writing Internet applications. The first aspect is the parsing, processing, and generation of messages that conform to various protocol requirements. These tasks are solidly inside the realm of text processing and should be covered in this book. The second aspect, however, are the issues of actually sending a message "over the wire": choosing ports and network protocols, handshaking, validation, and so on. While these tasks are important, they are outside the scope of this book. The synopses below will point you towards appropriate modules, though; the standard documentation, Python interactive help, or other texts can help with the details.

A second issue comes up also, moreover. As Internet standards—usually canonicalized in RFCs—have evolved, and as Python libraries have become more versatile and robust, some newer modules have superceded older ones. In a similar way, for example, the *re* module replaced the older *regex* module. In the interests of backwards compatibility, Python has not dropped any Internet modules from its standard distributions. Nonetheless, the *email* module represents the current "best practice" for most tasks related to email and newsgroup message handling. The modules *mimify*, *mimetools*, *MimeWriter*, *multifile*, and *rfc822* are likely to be utilized in existing code, but for new applications, it is better to use the capabilities in *email* in their stead.

As well as standard library modules, a few third-party tools deserve special mention (at the bottom of this section). A large number of Python developers have created tools for various Internet-related tasks, but a small number of projects have reached a high degree of sophistication and a widespread usage.

5.3.1 Standard Internet-Related Tools

asyncore

Asynchronous socket service clients and servers.

Cookie

Manage Web browser cookies. Cookies are a common mechanism for managing state in Web-based applications. RFC-2109 and RFC-2068 describe the encoding used for cookies, but in practice MSIE is not very standards compliant, so the parsing is relaxed in the *Cookie* module.

SEE ALSO: cgi *376*; httplib *396*;

email.Charset

Work with character set encodings at a fine-tuned level. Other modules within the *email* package utilize this module to provide higher-level interfaces. If you need to dig deeply into character set conversions, you might want to use this module directly.

SEE ALSO: email *345*; email.Header *351*; unicode *423*; codecs *189*;

ftplib

Support for implementing custom File Transfer Protocol (FTP) clients. This protocol is detailed in RFC-959. For a full FTP application, *ftplib* provides a very good starting point; for the simple capability to retrieve publicly accessible files over FTP, `urllib.urlopen()` is more direct.

SEE ALSO: urllib *388*; urllib2 *398*;

gopherlib

Gopher protocol client interface. As much as I am still personally fond of the gopher protocol, it is used so rarely that it is not worth documenting here.

httplib

Support for implementing custom Web clients. Higher-level access to the HTTP and HTTPS protocols than using raw *sockets* on ports 80 or 443, but lower-level, and more communications oriented, than using the higher-level *urllib* to access Web resources in a file-like way.

SEE ALSO: urllib *388*; socket *397*;

ic, icopen

Internet access configuration (Macintosh).

icopen

Internet Config replacement for open() (Macintosh).

imghdr

Recognize image file formats based on their first few bytes.

mailcap

Examine the mailcap file on Unix-like systems. The files /etc/mailcap, /usr/etc/mailcap, /usr/local/etc/mailcap, and $HOME/.mailcap are typically used to configure MIME capabilities in client applications like mail readers and Web browsers (but less so now than a few years ago). See RFC-1524.

mhlib

Interface to MH mailboxes. The MH format consists of a directory structure that mirrors the folder organization of messages. Each message is contained in its own file. While the MH format is in many ways *better*, the Unix mailbox format seems to be more widely used. Basic access to a single folder in an MH hierarchy can be achieved with the *mailbox.MHMailbox* class, which satisfies most working requirements.

SEE ALSO: mailbox *372*; email *345*;

mimetools

Various tools used by MIME-reading or MIME-writing programs.

MimeWriter

Generic MIME writer.

mimify

Mimification and unmimification of mail messages.

netrc

Examine the netrc file on Unix-like systems. The file $HOME/.netrc is typically used to configure FTP clients.

SEE ALSO: ftplib *395*; urllib *388*;

nntplib

Support for Network News Transfer Protocol (NNTP) client applications. This protocol is defined in RFC-977. Although Usenet has a different distribution system from email, the message format of NNTP messages still follows the format defined in RFC-822. In particular, the *email* package, or the *rfc822* module, are useful for creating and modifying news messages.

SEE ALSO: email *345*; rfc822 *397*;

nsremote

Wrapper around Netscape OSA modules (Macintosh).

rfc822

RFC-822 message manipulation class. The *email* package is intended to supercede *rfc822*, and it is better to use *email* for new application development.

SEE ALSO: email *345*; poplib *368*; mailbox *372*; smtplib *370*;

select

Wait on I/O completion, such as sockets.

sndhdr

Recognize sound file formats based on their first few bytes.

socket

Low-level interface to BSD sockets. Used to communicate with IP addresses at the level underneath protocols like HTTP, FTP, POP3, Telnet, and so on.

SEE ALSO: ftplib *395*; gopherlib *395*; httplib *396*; imaplib *366*; nntplib *397*; poplib *368*; smtplib *370*; telnetlib *397*;

SocketServer

Asynchronous I/O on sockets. Under Unix, pipes can also be monitored with *select*. *socket* supports SSL in recent Python versions.

telnetlib

Support for implementing custom telnet clients. This protocol is detailed in RFC-854. While possibly useful for intranet applications, Telnet is an entirely unsecured protocol and should not really be used on the Internet. Secure Shell (SSH) is an encrypted protocol that otherwise is generally similar in capability to Telnet. There is no support for SSH in the Python standard library, but third-party options exist, such as *pyssh*. At worst, you can script an SSH client using a tool like the third-party *pyexpect*.

urllib2

An enhanced version of the *urllib* module that adds specialized classes for a variety of protocols. The main focus of *urllib2* is the handling of authentication and encryption methods.

SEE ALSO: urllib *388*;

Webbrowser

Remote-control interfaces to some browsers.

5.3.2   Third-Party Internet-Related Tools

There are many very fine Internet-related tools that this book cannot discuss, but to which no slight is intended. A good index to such tools is the relevant page at the Vaults of Parnassus:

    <http://py.vaults.ca/apyllo.py/812237977>

Quixote

In brief, *Quixote* is a templating system for HTML delivery. More so than systems like PHP, ASP, and JSP to an extent, *Quixote* puts an emphasis on Web application structure more than page appearance. The home page for *Quixote* is <http://www.mems-exchange.org/software/quixote/>

Twisted

To describe *Twisted*, it is probably best simply to quote from Twisted Matrix Laboratories' Web site <http://www.twistedmatrix.com/>:

> Twisted is a framework, written in Python, for writing networked applications. It includes implementations of a number of commonly used network services such as a Web server, an IRC chat server, a mail server, a relational database interface and an object broker. Developers can build applications using all of these services as well as custom services that they write themselves. Twisted also includes a user authentication system that controls access to services and provides services with user context information to implement their own security models.

While *Twisted* overlaps significantly in purpose with *Zope*, *Twisted* is generally lower-level and more modular (which has both pros and cons). Some protocols supported by *Twisted*—usually both server and client—and implemented in pure Python are SSH; FTP; HTTP; NNTP; SOCKSv4; SMTP; IRC; Telnet; POP3; AOL's instant messaging TOC; OSCAR, used by AOL-IM as well as ICQ; DNS; MouseMan; finger; Echo, discard, chargen, and friends; Twisted Perspective Broker, a remote object protocol; and XML-RPC.

Zope

Zope is a sophisticated, powerful, and just plain *complicated* Web application server. It incorporates everything from dynamic page generation, to database interfaces, to Web-based administration, to back-end scripting in several styles and languages. While the learning curve is steep, experienced Zope developers can develop and manage Web applications more easily, reliably, and faster than users of pretty much any other technology.

The home page for Zope is <http://zope.org/>.

5.4 Understanding XML

Extensible Markup Language (XML) is a text format increasingly used for a wide variety of storage and transport requirements. Parsing and processing XML is an important element of many text processing applications. This section discusses the most common techniques for dealing with XML in Python. While XML held an initial promise of simplifying the exchange of complex and hierarchically organized data, it has itself grown into a standard of considerable complexity. This book will not cover most of the API details of XML tools; an excellent book dedicated to that subject is:

> *Python & XML*, Christopher A. Jones & Fred L. Drake, Jr., O'Reilly 2002. ISBN: 0-596-00128-2.

The XML format is sufficiently rich to represent any structured data, some forms more straightforwardly than others. A task that XML is quite natural at is in representing marked-up text—documentation, books, articles, and the like—as is its parent SGML. But XML is probably used more often to represent *data* than texts—record sets, OOP data containers, and so on. In many of these cases, the fit is more awkward and requires extra verbosity. XML itself is more like a metalanguage than a language—there are a set of syntax constraints that any XML document must obey, but typically particular APIs and document formats are defined as XML *dialects*. That is, a dialect consists of a particular set of tags that are used within a type of document, along with rules for when and where to use those tags. What I refer to as an XML dialect is also sometimes more formally called "an *application* of XML."

THE DATA MODEL

At base, XML has two ways to represent data. Attributes in XML tags map names to values. Both names and values are Unicode strings (as are XML documents as a whole), but values frequently encode other basic datatypes, especially when specified in W3C XML Schemas. Attribute names are mildly restricted by the special characters used for XML markup; attribute values can encode any strings once a few characters are properly escaped. XML attribute values are whitespace normalized when parsed, but whitespace can itself also be escaped. A bare example is:

```
>>> from xml.dom import minidom
>>> x = '''<x a="b" d="e    f g" num="38" />'''
>>> d = minidom.parseString(x)
>>> d.firstChild.attributes.items()
[(u'a', u'b'), (u'num', u'38'), (u'd', u'e    f g')]
```

As with a Python dictionary, no order is defined for the list of key/value attributes of one tag.

The second way XML represents data is by nesting tags inside other tags. In this context, a tag together with a corresponding "close tag" is called an *element*, and it may contain an ordered sequence of *subelements*. The subelements themselves may also contain nested subelements. A general term for any part of an XML document, whether an element, an attribute, or one of the special parts discussed below, is a "node." A simple example of an element that contains some subelements is:

```
>>> x = '''<?xml version="1.0" encoding="UTF-8"?>
... <root>
...     <a>Some data</a>
...     <b data="more data" />
...     <c data="a list">
...         <d>item 1</d>
...         <d>item 2</d>
...     </c>
... </root>'''
>>> d = minidom.parseString(x)
>>> d.normalize()
>>> for node in d.documentElement.childNodes:
...     print node
...
<DOM Text node "
  ">
<DOM Element: a at 7033280>
<DOM Text node "
  ">
<DOM Element: b at 7051088>
<DOM Text node "
  ">
<DOM Element: c at 7053696>
<DOM Text node "
">
>>> d.documentElement.childNodes[3].attributes.items()
[(u'data', u'more data')]
```

There are several things to notice about the Python session above.

1. The "document element," named **root** in the example, contains three ordered subelement nodes, named **a**, **b**, and **c**.

2. Whitespace is preserved within elements. Therefore the spaces and newlines that come between the subelements make up several text nodes. Text and subelements can intermix, each potentially meaningful. Spacing in XML documents is significant, but it is nonetheless also often used for visual clarity (as above).

3. The example contains an XML declaration, `<?xml...?>`, which is optional but generally included.

4. Any given element may contain attributes *and* subelements *and* text data.

OTHER XML FEATURES

Besides regular elements and text nodes, XML documents can contain several kinds of "special" nodes. Comments are common and useful, especially in documents intended to be hand edited at some point (or even potentially). Processing instructions may indicate how a document is to be handled. Document type declarations may indicate expected validity rules for where elements and attributes may occur. A special type of node called CDATA lets you embed mini-XML documents or other special codes inside of other XML documents, while leaving markup untouched. Examples of each of these forms look like:

```
<?xml version="1.0" ?>
<!DOCTYPE root SYSTEM "sometype.dtd">
<root>
<!-- This is a comment -->
This is text data inside the &lt;root&gt; element
<![CDATA[Embedded (not well-formed) XML:
        <this><that> >>string<< </that>]]>
</root>
```

XML documents may be either "well-formed" or "valid." The first characterization simply indicates that a document obeys the proper syntactic rules for XML documents in general: All tags are either self-closed or followed by a matching endtag; reserved characters are escaped; tags are properly hierarchically nested; and so on. Of course, particular documents can also fail to be well-formed—but in that case they are not XML documents sensu stricto, but merely fragments or near-XML. A formal description of well-formed XML can be found at `<http://www.w3.org/TR/REC-xml>` and `<http://www.w3.org/TR/xml11/>`.

Beyond well-formedness, some XML documents are also valid. Validity means that a document matches a further grammatical specification given in a Document Type Definition (DTD), or in an XML Schema. The most popular style of XML Schema is the W3C XML Schema specification, found in formal detail at `<http://www.w3.org/TR/xmlschema-0/>` and in linked documents. There are competing schema specifications, however—one popular alternative is RELAX NG, which is documented at `<http://www.oasis-open.org/committees/relax-ng/>`.

The grammatical specifications indicated by DTDs are strictly structural. For example, you can specify that certain subelements must occur within an element, with a certain cardinality and order. Or, certain attributes may or must occur with a certain tag. As a simple case, the following DTD is one that the prior example of nested subelements would conform to. There are an infinite number of DTDs that the sample *could* match, but each one describes a slightly different *range* of valid XML documents:

```
<!ELEMENT root ((a|OTHER-A)?, b, c*)>
<!ELEMENT a (#PCDATA)>
<!ELEMENT b EMPTY>
<!ATTLIST b data CDATA #REQUIRED
             NOT-THERE (this|that) #IMPLIED>
<!ELEMENT c (d+)>
<!ATTLIST c data CDATA #IMPLIED>
<!ELEMENT d (#PCDATA)>
```

The W3C recommendation on the XML standard also formally specifies DTD rules. A few features of the above DTD example can be noted here. The element `OTHER-A` and the attribute `NOT-THERE` are permitted by this DTD, but were not utilized in the previous sample XML document. The quantifications `?`, `*`, and `+`; the alternation `|`; and the comma sequence operator have similar meaning as in regular expressions and BNF grammars. Attributes may be required or optional as well and may contain any of several specific value types; for example, the `data` attribute must contain any string, while the `NOT-THERE` attribute may contain `this` or `that` only.

Schemas go farther than DTDs, in a way. Beyond merely specifying that elements or attributes must contain strings describing particular datatypes, such as numbers or dates, schemas allow more flexible quantification of subelement occurrences. For example, the following W3C XML Schema might describe an XML document for purchases:

```
<xsd:element name="item">
  <xsd:complexType>
    <xsd:sequence>
      <xsd:element name="USPrice"  type="xsd:decimal"/>
      <xsd:element name="shipDate" type="xsd:date"
                   minOccurs="0" maxOccurs=3 />
    </xsd:sequence>
    <xsd:attribute name="partNum" type="SKU"/>
  </xsd:complexType>
</xsd:element>
<!-- Stock Keeping Unit, a code for identifying products -->
<xsd:simpleType name="SKU">
  <xsd:restriction base="xsd:string">
    <xsd:pattern value="\d{3}-[A-Z]{2}"/>
  </xsd:restriction>
</xsd:simpleType>
```

An XML document that is valid under this schema is:

```
<item partNum="123-XQ">
```

```
<USPrice>21.95</USPrice>
<shipDate>2002-11-26</shipDate>
</item>
```

Formal specifications of schema languages can be found at the above-mentioned URLs; this example is meant simply to illustrate the types of capabilities they have.

In order to check the validity of an XML document to a DTD or schema, you need to use a *validating parser*. Some stand-alone tools perform validation, generally with diagnostic messages in cases of invalidity. As well, certain libraries and modules support validation within larger applications. As a rule, however, *most* Python XML parsers are nonvalidating and check only for well-formedness.

Quite a number of technologies have been built on top of XML, many endorsed and specified by W3C, OASIS, or other standards groups. One in particular that you should be aware of is XSLT. There are a number of thick books available that discuss XSLT, so the matter is too complex to document here. But in shortest characterization, XSLT is a declarative programming language whose syntax is itself an XML application. An XML document is processed using a set of rules in an XSLT stylesheet, to produce a new output, often a different XML document. The elements in an XSLT stylesheet each describe a pattern that might occur in a source document and contain an output block that will be produced if that pattern is encountered. That is the simple characterization, anyway; in the details, "patterns" can have loops, recursions, calculations, and so on. I find XSLT to be more complicated than genuinely powerful and would rarely choose the technology for my own purposes, but you are fairly likely to encounter existing XSLT processes if you work with existing XML applications.

5.4.1   Python Standard Library XML Modules

There are two principle APIs for accessing and manipulating XML documents that are in widespread use: DOM and SAX. Both are supported in the Python standard library, and these two APIs make up the bulk of Python's XML support. Both of these APIs are programming language neutral, and using them in other languages is substantially similar to using them in Python.

The Document Object Model (DOM) represents an XML document as a tree of *nodes*. Nodes may be of several types—a document type declaration, processing instructions, comments, elements, and attribute maps—but whatever the type, they are arranged in a strictly nested hierarchy. Typically, nodes have children attached to them; of course, some nodes are *leaf nodes* without children. The DOM allows you to perform a variety of actions on nodes: delete nodes, add nodes, find sibling nodes, find nodes by tag name, and other actions. The DOM itself does not specify anything about how an XML document is transformed (parsed) into a DOM representation, nor about how a DOM can be serialized to an XML document. In practice, however, all DOM libraries—including *xml.dom*—incorporate these capabilities. Formal specification of DOM can be found at:

```
<http://www.w3.org/DOM/>
```

and:

```
<http://www.w3.org/TR/2000/REC-DOM-Level-2-Core-20001113/>
```

The Simple API for XML (SAX) is an *event-based* API for XML documents. Unlike DOM, which envisions XML as a rooted tree of nodes, SAX sees XML as a sequence of events occurring linearly in a file, text, or other stream. SAX is a very minimal interface, both in the sense of telling you very little inherently about the *structure* of an XML documents, and also in the sense of being extremely memory friendly. SAX itself is forgetful in the sense that once a tag or content is processed, it is no longer in memory (unless you manually save it in a data structure). However, SAX does maintain a basic stack of tags to assure well-formedness of parsed documents. The module *xml.sax* raises exceptions in case of problems in well-formedness; you may define your own custom error handlers for these. Formal specification of SAX can be found at:

```
<http://www.saxproject.org/>
```

○ · · ○ · · ○ · · ○ · · ○ · · ○ · · ○ · · ○ · · ○ · · ○ · · ○ · · ○ · · ○ · · ○

xml.dom

The module *xml.dom* is a Python implementation of most of the W3C Document Object Model, Level 2. As much as possible, its API follows the DOM standard, but a few Python conveniences are added as well. A brief example of usage is below:

```
>>> from xml.dom import minidom
>>> dom = minidom.parse('address.xml')
>>> addrs = dom.getElementsByTagName('address')
>>> print addrs[1].toxml()
<address city="New York" number="344" state="NY" street="118 St."/>
>>> jobs = dom.getElementsByTagName('job-info')
>>> for key, val in jobs[3].attributes.items():
...     print key,'=',val
...
employee-type = Part-Time
is-manager = no
job-description = Hacker
```

SEE ALSO: gnosis.xml.objectify *409*;

xml.dom.minidom

The module *xml.dom.minidom* is a lightweight DOM implementation built on top of SAX. You may pass in a custom SAX parser object when you parse an XML document; by default, *xml.dom.minidom* uses the fast, nonvalidating *xml.parser.expat* parser.

xml.dom.pulldom

The module *xml.dom.pulldom* is a DOM implementation that conserves memory by only building the portions of a DOM tree that are requested by calls to accessor methods. In some cases, this approach can be considerably faster than building an entire tree with *xml.dom.minidom* or another DOM parser; however, the *xml.dom.pulldom* remains somewhat underdocumented and experimental at the time of this writing.

xml.parsers.expat

Interface to the `expat` nonvalidating XML parser. Both the *xml.sax* and the *xml.dom.minidom* modules utilize the services of the fast `expat` parser, whose functionality lives mostly in a C library. You can use *xml.parser.expat* directly if you wish, but since the interface uses the same general event-driven style of the standard *xml.sax*, there is usually no reason to.

xml.sax

The package *xml.sax* implements the Simple API for XML. By default, *xml.sax* relies on the underlying *xml.parser.expat* parser, but any parser supporting a set of interface methods may be used instead. In particular, the validating parser *xmlproc* is included in the *PyXML* package.

When you create a SAX application, your main task is to create one or more callback handlers that will process events generated during SAX parsing. The most important handler is a `ContentHandler`, but you may also define a `DTDHandler`, `EntityResolver`, or `ErrorHandler`. Generally you will specialize the base handlers in *xml.sax.handler* for your own applications. After defining and registering desired handlers, you simply call the .`parse()` method of the parser that you registered handlers with. Or alternately, for incremental processing, you can use the `feed()` method.

A simple example illustrates usage. The application below reads in an XML file and writes an equivalent, but not necessarily identical, document to STDOUT. The output can be used as a canonical form of the document:

```
xmlcat.py
```

```python
#!/usr/bin/env python
import sys
from xml.sax import handler, make_parser
from xml.sax.saxutils import escape

class ContentGenerator(handler.ContentHandler):
    def __init__(self, out=sys.stdout):
        handler.ContentHandler.__init__(self)
        self._out = out
    def startDocument(self):
        xml_decl = '<?xml version="1.0" encoding="iso-8859-1"?>\n'
        self._out.write(xml_decl)
    def endDocument(self):
        sys.stderr.write("Bye bye!\n")
    def startElement(self, name, attrs):
        self._out.write('<' + name)
        name_val = attrs.items()
        name_val.sort()                    # canonicalize attributes
        for (name, value) in name_val:
            self._out.write(' %s="%s"' % (name, escape(value)))
        self._out.write('>')
    def endElement(self, name):
        self._out.write('</%s>' % name)
    def characters(self, content):
        self._out.write(escape(content))
    def ignorableWhitespace(self, content):
        self._out.write(content)
    def processingInstruction(self, target, data):
        self._out.write('<?%s %s?>' % (target, data))

if __name__=='__main__':
    parser = make_parser()
    parser.setContentHandler(ContentGenerator())
    parser.parse(sys.argv[1])
```

xml.sax.handler

The module *xml.sax.handler* defines classes `ContentHandler`, `DTDHandler`, `EntityResolver`, and `ErrorHandler` that are normally used as parent classes of custom SAX handlers.

xml.sax.saxutils

The module *xml.sax.saxutils* contains utility functions for working with SAX events. Several functions allow escaping and munging special characters.

xml.sax.xmlreader

The module *xml.sax.xmlreader* provides a framework for creating new SAX parsers that will be usable by the *xml.sax* module. Any new parser that follows a set of API conventions can be plugged in to the `xml.sax.make_parser()` class factory.

xmllib

Deprecated module for XML parsing. Use *xml.sax* or other XML tools in Python 2.0+.

xmlrpclib
SimpleXMLRPCServer

XML-RPC is an XML-based protocol for remote procedure calls, usually layered over HTTP. For the most part, the XML aspect is hidden from view. You simply use the module *xmlrpclib* to call remote methods and the module *SimpleXMLRPCServer* to implement your own server that supports such method calls. For example:

```
>>> import xmlrpclib
>>> betty = xmlrpclib.Server("http://betty.userland.com")
>>> print betty.examples.getStateName(41)
South Dakota
```

The XML-RPC format itself is a bit verbose, even as XML goes. But it is simple and allows you to pass argument values to a remote method:

```
>>> import xmlrpclib
>>> print xmlrpclib.dumps((xmlrpclib.True,37,(11.2,'spam')))
<params>
<param>
<value><boolean>1</boolean></value>
</param>
<param>
<value><int>37</int></value>
</param>
<param>
<value><array><data>
<value><double>11.199999999999999</double></value>
<value><string>spam</string></value>
</data></array></value>
</param>
</params>
```

SEE ALSO: gnosis.xml.pickle *410*;

5.4.2   Third-Party XML-Related Tools

A number of projects extend the XML capabilities in the Python standard library. I am the principle author of several XML-related modules that are distributed with the *gnosis* package. Information on the current release can be found at:

        <http://gnosis.cx/download/Gnosis_Utils.ANNOUNCE>

The package itself can be downloaded as a *distutils* package tarball from:

        <http://gnosis.cx/download/Gnosis_Utils-current.tar.gz>

The Python XML-SIG (special interest group) produces a package of XML tools known as *PyXML*. The work of this group is incorporated into the Python standard library with new Python releases—not every *PyXML* tool, however, makes it into the standard library. At any given moment, the most sophisticated—and often experimental—capabilities can be found by downloading the latest *PyXML* package. Be aware that installing the latest *PyXML* overrides the default Python XML support and may break other tools or applications.

        <http://pyxml.sourceforge.net/>

Fourthought, Inc. produces the *4Suite* package, which contains a number of XML tools. Fourthought releases *4Suite* as free software, and many of its capabilities are incorporated into the *PyXML* project (albeit at a varying time delay); however, Fourthought is a for-profit company that also offers customization and technical support for *4Suite*. The community page for *4Suite* is:

        <http://4suite.org/index.xhtml>

The Fourthought company Web site is:

        <http://fourthought.com/>

Two other modules are discussed briefly below. Neither of these are XML tools per se. However, both *PYX* and *yaml* fill many of the same requirements as XML does, while being easier to manipulate with text processing techniques, easier to read, and easier to edit by hand. There is a contrast between these two formats, however. *PYX* is semantically identical to XML, merely using a different syntax. YAML, on the other hand, has a quite different semantics from XML—I present it here because in many of the concrete applications where developers might instinctively turn to XML (which has a lot of "buzz"), YAML is a better choice.

   The home page for *PYX* is:

        <http://pyxie.sourceforge.net/>

I have written an article explaining PYX in more detail than in this book at:

        <http://gnosis.cx/publish/programming/xml_matters_17.html>

The home page for YAML is:

    <http://yaml.org>

I have written an article contrasting the utility and semantics of YAML and XML at:

    <http://gnosis.cx/publish/programming/xml_matters_23.html>

○ · · ○ · · ○ · · ○ · · ○ · · ○ · · ○ · · ○ · · ○ · · ○ · · ○ · · ○ · · ○ · · ○

gnosis.xml.indexer

The module *gnosis.xml.indexer* builds on the full-text indexing program presented as an example in Chapter 2 (and contained in the *gnosis* package as *gnosis.indexer*). Instead of file contents, *gnosis.xml.indexer* creates indices of (large) XML documents. This allows for a kind of "reverse XPath" search. That is, where a tool like *4xpath*, in the *4Suite* package, lets you see the contents of an XML node specified by XPath, *gnosis.xml.indexer* identifies the XPaths to the point where a word or words occur. This module may be used either in a larger application or as a command-line tool; for example:

```
% indexer symmetric
./crypto1.xml::/section[2]/panel[8]/title
./crypto1.xml::/section[2]/panel[8]/body/text_column/code_listing
./crypto1.xml::/section[2]/panel[7]/title
./crypto2.xml::/section[4]/panel[6]/body/text_column/p[1]
4 matched wordlist: ['symmetric']
Processed in 0.100 seconds (SlicedZPickleIndexer)

% indexer "-filter=*::/*/title" symmetric
./crypto1.xml::/section[2]/panel[8]/title
./crypto1.xml::/section[2]/panel[7]/title
2 matched wordlist: ['symmetric']
Processed in 0.080 seconds (SlicedZPickleIndexer)
```

Indexed searches, as the example shows, are very fast. I have written an article with more details on this module:

    <http://gnosis.cx/publish/programming/xml_matters_10.html>

gnosis.xml.objectify

The module *gnosis.xml.objectify* transforms arbitrary XML documents into Python objects that have a "native" feel to them. Where XML is used to encode a data structure, I believe that using *gnosis.xml.objectify* is the quickest and simplest way to utilize that data in a Python application.

The Document Object Model defines an OOP model for working with XML, across programming languages. But while DOM is nominally object-oriented, its access methods are distinctly un-Pythonic. For example, here is a typical "drill down" to a DOM value (skipping whitespace text nodes for some indices, which is far from obvious):

```
>>> from xml.dom import minidom
>>> dom_obj = minidom.parse('address.xml')
>>> dom_obj.normalize()
>>> print dom_obj.documentElement.childNodes[1].childNodes[3]\
...                               .attributes.get('city').value
Los Angeles
```

In contrast, *gnosis.xml.objectify* feels like you are using Python:

```
>>> from gnosis.xml.objectify import XML_Objectify
>>> xml_obj = XML_Objectify('address.xml')
>>> py_obj = xml_obj.make_instance()
>>> py_obj.person[2].address.city
u'Los Angeles'
```

gnosis.xml.pickle

The module *gnosis.xml.pickle* lets you serialize arbitrary Python objects to an XML format. In most respects, the purpose is the same as for the *pickle* module, but an XML target is useful for certain purposes. You may process the data in an xml_pickle using standard XML parsers, XSLT processors, XML editors, validation utilities, and other tools.

In several respects, *gnosis.xml.pickle* offers finer-grained control than the standard *pickle* module does. You can control security permissions accurately; you can customize the representation of object types within an XML file; you can substitute compatible classes during the pickle/unpickle cycle; and several other "guru-level" manipulations are possible. However, in basic usage, *gnosis.xml.pickle* is fully API compatible with *pickle*. An example illustrates both the usage and the format:

```
>>> class Container: pass
...
>>> inst = Container()
>>> dct = {1.7:2.5, ('t','u','p'):'tuple'}
>>> inst.this, inst.num, inst.dct = 'that', 38, dct
>>> import gnosis.xml.pickle
>>> print gnosis.xml.pickle.dumps(inst)
<?xml version="1.0"?>
<!DOCTYPE PyObject SYSTEM "PyObjects.dtd">
```

```
<PyObject module="__main__" class="Container" id="5999664">
<attr name="this" type="string" value="that" />
<attr name="dct" type="dict" id="6008464" >
  <entry>
    <key type="tuple" id="5973630" >
      <item type="string" value="t" />
      <item type="string" value="u" />
      <item type="string" value="p" />
    </key>
    <val type="string" value="tuple" />
  </entry>
  <entry>
    <key type="numeric" value="1.7" />
    <val type="numeric" value="2.5" />
  </entry>
</attr>
<attr name="num" type="numeric" value="38" />
</PyObject>
```

SEE ALSO: pickle *93*; cPickle *93*; yaml *415*; pprint *94*;

gnosis.xml.validity

The module *gnosis.xml.validity* allows you to define Python container classes that restrict their containment according to XML validity constraints. Such validity-enforcing classes *always* produce string representations that are valid XML documents, not merely well-formed ones. When you attempt to add an item to a *gnosis.xml.validity* container object that is not permissible, a descriptive exception is raised. Constraints, as with DTDs, may specify quantification, subelement types, and sequence.

For example, suppose you wish to create documents that conform with a "dissertation" Document Type Definition

dissertation.dtd

```
<!ELEMENT dissertation (dedication?, chapter+, appendix*)>
<!ELEMENT dedication (#PCDATA)>
<!ELEMENT chapter (title, paragraph+)>
<!ELEMENT title (#PCDATA)>
<!ELEMENT paragraph (#PCDATA | figure | table)+>
<!ELEMENT figure EMPTY>
<!ELEMENT table EMPTY>
<!ELEMENT appendix (#PCDATA)>
```

You can use *gnosis.xml.validity* to assure your application produced only conformant XML documents. First, you create a Python version of the DTD:

```
dissertation.py
```
```
from gnosis.xml.validity import *
class appendix(PCDATA):    pass
class table(EMPTY):        pass
class figure(EMPTY):       pass
class _mixedpara(Or):      _disjoins = (PCDATA, figure, table)
class paragraph(Some):     _type = _mixedpara
class title(PCDATA):       pass
class _paras(Some):        _type = paragraph
class chapter(Seq):        _order = (title, _paras)
class dedication(PCDATA):  pass
class _apps(Any):          _type = appendix
class _chaps(Some):        _type = chapter
class _dedi(Maybe):        _type = dedication
class dissertation(Seq):   _order = (_dedi, _chaps, _apps)
```

Next, import your Python validity constraints, and use them in an application:

```
>>> from dissertation import *
>>> chap1 = LiftSeq(chapter,('About Validity','It is a good thing'))
>>> paras_ch1 = chap1[1]
>>> paras_ch1 += [paragraph('OOP can enforce it')]
>>> print chap1
<chapter><title>About Validity</title>
<paragraph>It is a good thing</paragraph>
<paragraph>OOP can enforce it</paragraph>
</chapter>
```

If you attempt an action that violates constraints, you get a relevant exception; for example:

```
>>> try:
..       paras_ch1.append(dedication("To my advisor"))
.. except ValidityError, x:
...      print x
Items in _paras must be of type <class 'dissertation.paragraph'>
(not <class 'dissertation.dedication'>)
```

PyXML

The *PyXML* package contains a number of capabilities in advance of those in the Python standard library. *PyXML* was at version 0.8.1 at the time this was written, and as the number indicates, it remains an in-progress/beta project. Moreover, as of this writing, the last released version of Python was 2.2.2, with 2.3 in preliminary stages. When you read this, *PyXML* will probably be at a later number and have new features, and some of the current features will have been incorporated into the standard library. Exactly what is where is a moving target.

Some of the significant features currently available in *PyXML* but not in the standard library are listed below. You may install *PyXML* on any Python 2.0+ installation, and it will override the existing XML support.

• A validating XML parser written in Python called *xmlproc*. Being a pure Python program rather than a C extension, *xmlproc* is slower than *xml.sax* (which uses the underlying *expat* parser).

• A SAX extension called *xml.sax.writers* that will reserialize SAX events to either XML or other formats.

• A fully compliant DOM Level 2 implementation called *4DOM*, borrowed from *4Suite*.

• Support for canonicalization. That is, two XML documents can be semantically identical even though they are not byte-wise identical. You have freedom in choice of quotes, attribute orders, character entities, and some spacing that change nothing about the *meaning* of the document. Two canonicalized XML documents are semantically identical if and only if they are byte-wise identical.

• XPath and XSLT support, with implementations written in pure Python. There are faster XSLT implementations around, however, that call C extensions.

• A DOM implementation, called *xml.dom.pulldom*, that supports lazy instantiation of nodes has been incorporated into recent versions of the standard library. For older Python versions, this is available in *PyXML*.

• A module with several options for serializing Python objects to XML. This capability is comparable to *gnosis.xml.pickle*, but I like the tool I created better in several ways.

PYX

PYX is both a document format and a Python module to support working with that format. As well as the Python module, tools written in C are available to transform documents between XML and PYX format.

The idea behind PYX is to eliminate the need for complex parsing tools like *xml.sax*. Each node in an XML document is represented, in the PYX format on a separate line, using a prefix character to indicate the node type. Most of XML semantics is preserved, with the exception of document type declarations, comments, and namespaces. These features could be incorporated into an updated PYX format, in principle.

Documents in the PYX format are easily processed using traditional line-oriented text processing tools like sed, grep, awk, sort, wc, and the like. Python applications that use a basic *FILE.readline()* loop are equally able to process PYX nodes, one per line. This makes it much easier to use familiar text processing programming styles with PYX than it is with XML. A brief example illustrates the PYX format:

```
% cat test.xml
<?xml version="1.0"?>
<?xml-stylesheet href="test.css" type="text/css"?>
<Spam flavor="pork">
  <Eggs>Some text about eggs.</Eggs>
  <MoreSpam>Ode to Spam (spam="smoked-pork")</MoreSpam>
</Spam>
% ./xmln test.xml
?xml-stylesheet href="test.css" type="text/css"
(Spam
Aflavor pork
-\n
(Eggs
-Some text about eggs.
)Eggs
-\n
(MoreSpam
-Ode to Spam (spam="smoked-pork")
)MoreSpam
-\n
)Spam
```

4Suite

The tools in *4Suite* focus on the use of XML documents for knowledge management. The server element of the *4Suite* software is useful for working with catalogs of XML documents, searching them, transforming them, and so on. The base *4Suite* tools address a variety of XML technologies. In some cases *4Suite* implements standards and technologies not found in the Python standard library or in *PyXML*, while in other cases *4Suite* provides more advanced implementations.

Among the XML technologies implemented in *4Suite* are DOM, RDF, XSLT, XInclude, XPointer, XLink and XPath, and SOAP. Among these, of particular note is *4xslt* for performing XSLT transformations. *4xpath* lets you find XML nodes using concise and powerful XPath descriptions of how to reach them. *4rdf* deals with "meta-data" that documents use to identify their semantic characteristics.

I detail *4Suite* technologies in a bit more detail in an article at:

<http://gnosis.cx/publish/programming/xml_matters_15.html>

yaml

The native data structures of object-oriented programming languages are not straightforward to represent in XML. While XML is in principle powerful enough to represent any compound data, the only inherent mapping in XML is within attributes—but that only maps strings to strings. Moreover, even when a suitable XML format is found for a given data structure, the XML is quite verbose and difficult to scan visually, or especially to edit manually.

The YAML format is designed to match the structure of datatypes prevalent in scripting languages: Python, Perl, Ruby, and Java all have support libraries at the time of this writing. Moreover, the YAML format is extremely concise and unobtrusive—in fact, the acronym cutely stands for "YAML Ain't Markup Language." In many ways, YAML can act as a better pretty-printer than *pprint*, while simultaneously working as a format that can be used for configuration files or to exchange data between different programming languages.

There is no fully general and clean way, however, to convert between YAML and XML. You can use the *yaml* module to read YAML data files, then use the *gnosis.xml.pickle* module to read and write to one particular XML format. But when XML data starts out in other XML dialects than *gnosis.xml.pickle*, there are ambiguities about the best Python native and YAML representations of the same data. On the plus side—and this can be a very big plus—there is essentially a straightforward and one-to-one correspondence between Python data structures and YAML representations.

In the YAML example below, refer back to the same Python instance serialized using *gnosis.xml.pickle* and *pprint* in their respective discussions. As with *gnosis.xml.pickle*—but in this case unlike *pprint*—the serialization can be read back in to re-create an identical object (or to create a different object after editing the text, by hand or by application).

```
>>> class Container: pass
...
>>> inst = Container()
>>> dct = {1.7:2.5, ('t','u','p'):'tuple'}
>>> inst.this, inst.num, inst.dct = 'that', 38, dct
>>> import yaml
>>> print yaml.dump(inst)
--- !!__main__.Container
dct:
    1.7: 2.5
    ?
        - t
        - u
        - p
: tuple
num: 38
this: that
```

SEE ALSO: pprint *94*; gnosis.xml.pickle *410*;

Appendix A

A Selective and Impressionistic Short Review of Python

A reader who is coming to Python for the first time would be well served reading Guido van Rossum's *Python Tutorial*, which can be downloaded from <http://python.org/>, or picking up one of the several excellent books devoted to teaching Python to novices. As indicated in the Preface, the audience of this book is a bit different.

The above said, some readers of this book might use Python only infrequently, or not have used Python for a while, or may be sufficiently versed in numerous other programming languages, that a quick review on Python constructs suffices for understanding. This appendix will briefly mention each major element of the Python language itself, but will not address any libraries (even standard and ubiquitous ones that may be discussed in the main chapters). Not all fine points of syntax and semantics will be covered here, either. This review, however, should suffice for a reader to understand all the examples in this book.

Even readers who are familiar with Python might enjoy skimming this review. The focus and spin of this summary are a bit different from most introductions. I believe that the way I categorize and explain a number of language features can provide a moderately novel—but equally accurate—perspective on the Python language. Ideally, a Python programmer will come away from this review with a few new insights on the familiar constructs she uses every day. This appendix does not shy away from using some abstract terms from computer science—if a particular term is not familiar to you, you will not lose much by skipping over the sentence it occurs in; some of these terms are explained briefly in the Glossary.

A.1 What Kind of Language Is Python?

Python is a byte-code compiled programming language that supports multiple programming paradigms. Python is sometimes called an interpreted and/or scripting language because no separate compilation step is required to run a Python program; in more precise terms, Python uses a virtual machine (much like Java or Smalltalk) to run machine-abstracted instructions. In most situations a byte-code compiled version of an application is cached to speed future runs, but wherever necessary compilation is performed "behind the scenes."

In the broadest terms, Python is an imperative programming language, rather than a declarative (functional or logical) one. Python is dynamically and strongly typed, with very late binding compared to most languages. In addition, Python is an object-oriented language with strong introspective facilities, and one that generally relies on conventions rather than enforcement mechanisms to control access and visibility of names. Despite its object-oriented core, much of the syntax of Python is designed to allow a convenient procedural style that masks the underlying OOP mechanisms. Although Python allows basic functional programming (FP) techniques, side effects are the norm, evaluation is always strict, and no compiler optimization is performed for tail recursion (nor on almost any other construct).

Python has a small set of reserved words, delimits blocks and structure based on indentation only, has a fairly rich collection of built-in data structures, and is generally both terse and readable compared to other programming languages. Much of the strength of Python lies in its standard library and in a flexible system of importable modules and packages.

A.2 Namespaces and Bindings

The central concept in Python programming is that of a namespace. Each context (i.e., scope) in a Python program has available to it a hierarchically organized collection of namespaces; each namespace contains a set of names, and each name is bound to an object. In older versions of Python, namespaces were arranged according to the "three-scope rule" (builtin/global/local), but Python version 2.1 and later add lexically nested scoping. In most cases you do not need to worry about this subtlety, and scoping works the way you would expect (the special cases that prompted the addition of lexical scoping are mostly ones with nested functions and/or classes).

There are quite a few ways of binding a name to an object within the current namespace/scope and/or within some other scope. These various ways are listed below.

A.2.1 Assignment and Dereferencing

A Python statement like x=37 or y="foo" does a few things. If an object—e.g., 37 or "foo"—does not exist, Python creates one. If such an object *does* exist, Python locates it. Next, the name x or y is added to the current namespace, if it does not exist already, and that name is bound to the corresponding object. If a name already exists in the current namespace, it is re-bound. Multiple names, perhaps in multiple scopes/namespaces, can be bound to the same object.

A simple assignment statement binds a name into the current namespace, unless that name has been declared as global. A name declared as global is bound to the global (module-level) namespace instead. A qualified name used on the left of an assignment statement binds a name into a specified namespace—either to the attributes of an object, or to the namespace of a module/package; for example

```
>>> x = "foo"           # bind 'x' in global namespace
>>> def myfunc():       # bind 'myfunc' in global namespace
...     global x, y     # specify namespace for 'x', 'y'
...     x = 1           # rebind global 'x' to 1 object
...     y = 2           # create global name 'y' and 2 object
...     z = 3           # create local name 'z' and 3 object
...
>>> import package.module   # bind name 'package.module'
>>> package.module.w = 4    # bind 'w' in namespace package.module
>>> from mymod import obj   # bind object 'obj' to global namespace
>>> obj.attr = 5            # bind name 'attr' to object 'obj'
```

Whenever a (possibly qualified) name occurs on the right side of an assignment, or on a line by itself, the name is dereferenced to the object itself. If a name has not been bound inside some accessible scope, it cannot be dereferenced; attempting to do so raises a `NameError` exception. If the name is followed by left and right parentheses (possibly with comma-separated expressions between them), the object is invoked/called after it is dereferenced. Exactly what happens upon invocation can be controlled and overridden for Python objects; but in general, invoking a function or method runs some code, and invoking a class creates an instance. For example:

```
>>> pkg.subpkg.func()   # invoke a function from a namespace
>>> x = y               # deref 'y' and bind same object to 'x'
```

A.2.2   Function and Class Definitions

Declaring a function or a class is simply the preferred way of describing an object and binding it to a name. But the `def` and `class` declarations are "deep down" just types of assignments. In the case of functions, the *lambda* operator can also be used on the right of an assignment to bind an "anonymous" function to a name. There is no equally direct technique for classes, but their declaration is still similar in effect:

```
>>> add1 = lambda x,y: x+y # bind 'add1' to function in global ns
>>> def add2(x, y):        # bind 'add2' to function in global ns
...     return x+y
...
>>> class Klass:           # bind 'Klass' to class object
...     def meth1(self):   # bind 'meth1' to method in 'Klass' ns
...         return 'Myself'
```

A.2.3   import Statements

Importing, or importing *from*, a module or a package adds or modifies bindings in the current namespace. The import statement has two forms, each with a bit different effect.

Statements of the forms

```
>>> import modname
>>> import pkg.subpkg.modname
>>> import pkg.modname as othername
```

add a new module object to the current namespace. These module objects themselves define namespaces that you can bind values in or utilize objects within.

Statements of the forms

```
>>> from modname import foo
>>> from pkg.subpkg.modname import foo as bar
```

instead add the names foo or bar to the current namespace. In any of these forms of import, any statements in the imported module are executed—the difference between the forms is simply the effect upon namespaces.

There is one more special form of the import statement; for example:

```
>>> from modname import *
```

The asterisk in this form is not a generalized glob or regular expression pattern, it is a special syntactic form. "Import star" imports every name in a module namespace into the current namespace (except those named with a leading underscore, which can still be explicitly imported if needed). Use of this form is somewhat discouraged because it risks adding names to the current namespace that you do not explicitly request and that may rebind existing names.

A.2.4   for Statements

Although for is a looping construct, the way it works is by binding successive elements of an iterable object to a name (in the current namespace). The following constructs are (almost) equivalent:

```
>>> for x in somelist:   # repeated binding with 'for'
...       print x
...
>>> ndx = 0              # rebinds 'ndx' if it was defined
>>> while 1:             # repeated binding in 'while'
...     x = somelist[ndx]
...     print x
...     ndx = ndx+1
...     if ndx >= len(somelist):
...         del ndx
...         break
```

A.2.5   except Statements

The except statement can optionally bind a name to an exception argument:

```
>>> try:
...     raise "ThisError", "some message"
... except "ThisError", x:    # Bind 'x' to exception argument
...     print x
...
some message
```

A.3   Datatypes

Python has a rich collection of basic datatypes. All of Python's collection types allow you to hold heterogeneous elements inside them, including other collection types (with minor limitations). It is straightforward, therefore, to build complex data structures in Python.

Unlike many languages, Python datatypes come in two varieties: mutable and immutable. All of the atomic datatypes are immutable, as is the collection type tuple. The collections list and dict are mutable, as are class instances. The mutability of a datatype is simply a question of whether objects of that type can be changed "in place"—an immutable object can only be created and destroyed, but never altered during its existence. One upshot of this distinction is that immutable objects may act as dictionary keys, but mutable objects may not. Another upshot is that when you want a data structure—especially a large one—that will be modified frequently during program operation, you should choose a mutable datatype (usually a list).

Most of the time, if you want to convert values between different Python datatypes, an explicit conversion/encoding call is required, but numeric types contain promotion rules to allow numeric expressions over a mixture of types. The built-in datatypes are listed below with discussions of each. The built-in function *type()* can be used to check the datatype of an object.

A.3.1   Simple Types

bool

> Python 2.3+ supports a Boolean datatype with the possible values True and False. In earlier versions of Python, these values are typically called 1 and 0; even in Python 2.3+, the Boolean values behave like numbers in numeric contexts. Some earlier micro-releases of Python (e.g., 2.2.1) include the *names* True and False, but not the Boolean datatype.

int

> A signed integer in the range indicated by the register size of the interpreter's CPU/OS platform. For most current platforms, integers range from (2**31)- 1 to negative (2**31)-1. You can find the size on your platform by examining

sys.maxint. Integers are the bottom numeric type in terms of promotions; nothing gets promoted *to* an integer, but integers are sometimes promoted to other numeric types. A float, long, or string may be explicitly converted to an int using the *int()* function.

SEE ALSO: int *18*;

long

An (almost) unlimited size integral number. A long literal is indicated by an integer followed by an l or L (e.g., 34L, 98765432101). In Python 2.2+, operations on ints that overflow *sys.maxint* are automatically promoted to longs. An int, float, or string may be explicitly converted to a long using the *long()* function.

float

An IEEE754 floating point number. A literal floating point number is distinguished from an int or long by containing a decimal point and/or exponent notation (e.g., 1.0, 1e3, 37., .453e-12). A numeric expression that involves both int/long types and float types promotes all component types to floats before performing the computation. An int, long, or string may be explicitly converted to a float using the *float()* function.

SEE ALSO: float *19*;

complex

An object containing two floats, representing real and imaginary components of a number. A numeric expression that involves both int/long/float types and complex types promotes all component types to complex before performing the computation. There is no way to spell a literal complex in Python, but an addition such as 1.1+2j is the usual way of computing a complex value. A j or J following a float or int literal indicates an imaginary number. An int, long, or string may be explicitly converted to a complex using the *complex()* function. If two float/int arguments are passed to *complex()*, the second is the imaginary component of the constructed number (e.g., complex(1.1,2)).

string

An immutable sequence of 8-bit character values. Unlike in many programming languages, there is no "character" type in Python, merely strings that happen to have length one. String objects have a variety of methods to modify strings, but such methods always return a new string object rather than modify the initial object itself. The built-in *chr()* function will return a length-one string whose ordinal value is the passed integer. The *str()* function will return a string representation of a passed in object. For example:

```
>>> ord('a')
97
```

```
>>> chr(97)
'a'
>>> str(97)
'97'
```

SEE ALSO: string *129*;

unicode

An immutable sequence of Unicode characters. There is no datatype for a single Unicode character, but Unicode strings of length-one contain a single character. Unicode strings contain a similar collection of methods to string objects, and like the latter, Unicode methods return new Unicode objects rather than modify the initial object. See Chapter 2 and Appendix C for additional discussion, of Unicode.

A.3.2 String Interpolation

Literal strings and Unicode strings may contain embedded format codes. When a string contains format codes, values may be *interpolated* into the string using the % operator and a tuple or dictionary giving the values to substitute in.

Strings that contain format codes may follow either of two patterns. The simpler pattern uses format codes with the syntax %[flags][len[.precision]]<type>. Interpolating a string with format codes on this pattern requires % combination with a tuple of matching length and content datatypes. If only one value is being interpolated, you may give the bare item rather than a tuple of length one. For example:

```
>>> "float %3.1f, int %+d, hex %06x" % (1.234, 1234, 1234)
'float 1.2, int +1234, hex 0004d2'
>>> '%e' % 1234
'1.234000e+03'
>>> '%e' % (1234,)
'1.234000e+03'
```

The (slightly) more complex pattern for format codes embeds a name within the format code, which is then used as a string key to an interpolation dictionary. The syntax of this pattern is %(key)[flags][len[.precision]]<type>. Interpolating a string with this style of format codes requires % combination with a dictionary that contains all the named keys, and whose corresponding values contain acceptable datatypes. For example:

```
>>> dct = {'ratio':1.234, 'count':1234, 'offset':1234}
>>> "float %(ratio)3.1f, int %(count)+d, hex %(offset)06x" % dct
'float 1.2, int +1234, hex 0004d2'
```

You *may not* mix tuple interpolation and dictionary interpolation within the same string.

I mentioned that datatypes must match format codes. Different format codes accept a different range of datatypes, but the rules are almost always what you would expect. Generally, numeric data will be promoted or demoted as necessary, but strings and complex types cannot be used for numbers.

One useful style of using dictionary interpolation is against the global and/or local namespace dictionary. Regular bound names defined in scope can be interpolated into strings.

```
>>> s = "float %(ratio)3.1f, int %(count)+d, hex %(offset)06x"
>>> ratio = 1.234
>>> count = 1234
>>> offset = 1234
>>> s % globals()
'float 1.2, int +1234, hex 0004d2'
```

If you want to look for names across scope, you can create an ad hoc dictionary with both local and global names:

```
>>> vardct = {}
>>> vardct.update(globals())
>>> vardct.update(locals())
>>> interpolated = somestring % vardct
```

The flags for format codes consist of the following:

```
0  Pad to length with leading zeros
-  Align the value to the left within its length
_  (space) Pad to length with leading spaces
+  Explicitly indicate the sign of positive values
```

When a length is included, it specifies the *minimum* length of the interpolated formatting. Numbers that will not fit within a length simply occupy more bytes than specified. When a precision is included, the length of those digits to the right of the decimal are included in the total length:

```
>>> '[%f]' % 1.234
'[1.234000]'
>>> '[%5f]' % 1.234
'[1.234000]'
>>> '[%.1f]' % 1.234
'[1.2]'
>>> '[%5.1f]' % 1.234
'[  1.2]'
>>> '[%05.1f]' % 1.234
'[001.2]'
```

The formatting types consist of the following:

```
d  Signed integer decimal
i  Signed integer decimal
o  Unsigned octal
u  Unsigned decimal
x  Lowercase unsigned hexadecimal
X  Uppercase unsigned hexadecimal
e  Lowercase exponential format floating point
E  Uppercase exponential format floating point
f  Floating point decimal format
g  Floating point: exponential format if -4 < exp < precision
G  Uppercase version of 'g'
c  Single character: integer for chr(i) or length-one string
r  Converts any Python object using repr()
s  Converts any Python object using str()
%  The '%' character, e.g.: '%%%d' % (1) --> '%1'
```

One more special format code style allows the use of a `*` in place of a length. In this case, the interpolated tuple must contain an extra element for the formatted length of each format code, preceding the value to format. For example:

```
>>> "%0*d # %0*.2f" % (4, 123, 4, 1.23)
'0123 # 1.23'
>>> "%0*d # %0*.2f" % (6, 123, 6, 1.23)
'000123 # 001.23'
```

A.3.3 Printing

The least-sophisticated form of textual output in Python is writing to open files. In particular, the STDOUT and STDERR streams can be accessed using the pseudo-files *sys.stdout* and *sys.stderr*. Writing to these is just like writing to any other file; for example:

```
>>> import sys
>>> try:
...     # some fragile action
...     sys.stdout.write('result of action\n')
... except:
...     sys.stderr.write('could not complete action\n')
...
result of action
```

You cannot seek within STDOUT or STDERR—generally you should consider these as pure sequential outputs.

Writing to STDOUT and STDERR is fairly inflexible, and most of the time the `print` statement accomplishes the same purpose more flexibly. In particular, methods like *sys.stdout.write()* only accept a single string as an argument, while `print` can

handle any number of arguments of any type. Each argument is coerced to a string
using the equivalent of `repr(obj)`. For example:

```
>>> print "Pi: %.3f" % 3.1415, 27+11, {3:4,1:2}, (1,2,3)
Pi: 3.142 38 {1: 2, 3: 4} (1, 2, 3)
```

Each argument to the `print` statment is evaluated before it is printed, just as when
an argument is passed to a function. As a consequence, the canonical representation of
an object is printed, rather than the exact form passed as an argument. In my example,
the dictionary prints in a different order than it was defined in, and the spacing of the
list and dictionary is slightly different. String interpolation is also peformed and is a
very common means of defining an output format precisely.

There are a few things to watch for with the `print` statement. A space is printed
between each argument to the statement. If you want to print several objects without
a separating space, you will need to use string concatenation or string interpolation to
get the right result. For example:

```
>>> numerator, denominator = 3, 7
>>> print repr(numerator)+"/"+repr(denominator)
3/7
>>> print "%d/%d" % (numerator, denominator)
3/7
```

By default, a `print` statement adds a linefeed to the end of its output. You may
eliminate the linefeed by adding a trailing comma to the statement, but you still wind
up with a space added to the end:

```
>>> letlist = ('a','B','Z','r','w')
>>> for c in letlist: print c,    # inserts spaces
...
a B Z r w
```

Assuming these spaces are unwanted, you must either use *sys.stdout.write()* or
otherwise calculate the space-free string you want:

```
>>> for c in letlist+('\n',): # no spaces
...     sys.stdout.write(c)
...
aBZrw
>>> print ''.join(letlist)
aBZrw
```

There is a special form of the `print` statement that redirects its output somewhere
other than STDOUT. The `print` statement itself can be followed by two greater-than
signs, then a writable file-like object, then a comma, then the remainder of the (printed)
arguments. For example:

```
>>> print >> open('test','w'), "Pi: %.3f" % 3.1415, 27+11
>>> open('test').read()
'Pi: 3.142 38\n'
```

Some Python programmers (including your author) consider this special form overly "noisy," but it *is* occassionally useful for quick configuration of output destinations.

If you want a function that would do the same thing as a `print` statement, the following one does so, but without any facility to eliminate the trailing linefeed or redirect output:

```
def print_func(*args):
    import sys
    sys.stdout.write(' '.join(map(repr,args))+'\n')
```

Readers could enhance this to add the missing capabilities, but using `print` as a statement is the clearest approach, generally.

SEE ALSO: sys.stderr *50*; sys.stdout *51*;

A.3.4 Container Types

tuple

An immutable sequence of (heterogeneous) objects. Being immutable, the membership and length of a tuple cannot be modified after creation. However, tuple elements and subsequences can be accessed by subscripting and slicing, and new tuples can be constructed from such elements and slices. Tuples are similar to "records" in some other programming languages.

The constructor syntax for a tuple is commas between listed items; in many contexts, parentheses around a constructed list are required to disambiguate a tuple for other constructs such as function arguments, but it is the commas not the parentheses that construct a tuple. Some examples:

```
>>> tup = 'spam','eggs','bacon','sausage'
>>> newtup = tup[1:3] + (1,2,3) + (tup[3],)
>>> newtup
('eggs', 'bacon', 1, 2, 3, 'sausage')
```

The function *tuple()* may also be used to construct a tuple from another sequence type (either a list or custom sequence type).

SEE ALSO: tuple *28*;

list

A mutable sequence of objects. Like a tuple, list elements can be accessed by subscripting and slicing; unlike a tuple, list methods and index and slice assignments can modify the length and membership of a list object.

The constructor syntax for a list is surrounding square braces. An empty list may be constructed with no objects between the braces; a length-one list can contain simply an object name; longer lists separate each element object with commas. Indexing and slices, of course, also use square braces, but the syntactic contexts are different in the Python grammar (and common sense usually points out the difference). Some examples:

```
>>> lst = ['spam', (1,2,3), 'eggs', 3.1415]
>>> lst[:2]
['spam', (1, 2, 3)]
```

The function *list()* may also be used to construct a list from another sequence type (either a tuple or custom sequence type).

SEE ALSO: list *28*;

dict

A mutable mapping between immutable keys and object values. At most one entry in a dict exists for a given key; adding the same key to a dictionary a second time overrides the previous entry (much as with binding a name in a namespace). Dicts are unordered, and entries are accessed either by key as index; by creating lists of contained objects using the methods `.keys()`, `.values()`, and `.items()`; or—in recent Python versions—with the `.popitem()` method. All the dict methods generate contained objects in an unspecified order.

The constructor syntax for a dict is surrounding curly brackets. An empty dict may be constructed with no objects between the brackets. Each key/value pair entered into a dict is separated by a colon, and successive pairs are separated by commas. For example:

```
>>> dct = {1:2, 3.14:(1+2j), 'spam':'eggs'}
>>> dct['spam']
'eggs'
>>> dct['a'] = 'b'     # add item to dict
>>> dct.items()
[('a', 'b'), (1, 2), ('spam', 'eggs'), (3.14, (1+2j))]
>>> dct.popitem()
('a', 'b')
>>> dct
{1: 2, 'spam': 'eggs', 3.14: (1+2j)}
```

In Python 2.2+, the function *dict()* may also be used to construct a dict from a sequence of pairs or from a custom mapping type. For example:

```
>>> d1 = dict([('a','b'), (1,2), ('spam','eggs')])
>>> d1
{'a': 'b', 1: 2, 'spam': 'eggs'}
>>> d2 = dict(zip([1,2,3],['a','b','c']))
>>> d2
{1: 'a', 2: 'b', 3: 'c'}
```

SEE ALSO: dict *24*;

sets.Set

Python 2.3+ includes a standard module that implements a set datatype. For earlier Python versions, a number of developers have created third-party implementations of sets. If you have at least Python 2.2, you can download and use the *sets* module from <http://tinyurl.com/2d31> (or browse the Python CVS)—you will need to add the definition True,False=1,0 to your local version, though.

A set is an unordered collection of hashable objects. Unlike a list, no object can occur in a set more than once; a set resembles a dict that has only keys but no values. Sets utilize bitwise and Boolean syntax to perform basic set-theoretic operations; a subset test does not have a special syntactic form, instead using the .issubset() and .issuperset() methods. You may also loop through set members in an unspecified order. Some examples illustrate the type:

```
>>> from sets import Set
>>> x = Set([1,2,3])
>>> y = Set((3,4,4,6,6,2))   # init with any seq
>>> print x, '//', y         # make sure dups removed
Set([1, 2, 3]) // Set([2, 3, 4, 6])
>>> print x | y              # union of sets
Set([1, 2, 3, 4, 6])
>>> print x & y              # intersection of sets
Set([2, 3])
>>> print y-x                # difference of sets
Set([4, 6])
>>> print x ^ y              # symmetric difference
Set([1, 4, 6])
```

You can also check membership and iterate over set members:

```
>>> 4 in y                   # membership check
1
>>> x.issubset(y)            # subset check
0
>>> for i in y:
```

```
...     print i+10,
...
12 13 14 16
>>> from operator import add
>>> plus_ten = Set(map(add, y, [10]*len(y)))
>>> plus_ten
Set([16, 12, 13, 14])
```

sets.Set also supports in-place modification of sets; *sets.ImmutableSet*, naturally, does not allow modification.

```
>>> x = Set([1,2,3])
>>> x |= Set([4,5,6])
>>> x
Set([1, 2, 3, 4, 5, 6])
>>> x &= Set([4,5,6])
>>> x
Set([4, 5, 6])
>>> x ^= Set([4,5])
>>> x
Set([6])
```

A.3.5   Compound Types

class instance

A class instance defines a namespace, but this namespace's main purpose is usually to act as a data container (but a container that also knows how to perform actions; i.e., has methods). A class instance (or any namespace) acts very much like a dict in terms of creating a mapping between names and values. Attributes of a class instance may be set or modified using standard qualified names and may also be set within class methods by qualifying with the namespace of the first (implicit) method argument, conventionally called `self`. For example:

```
>>> class Klass:
...     def setfoo(self, val):
...         self.foo = val
...
>>> obj = Klass()
>>> obj.bar = 'BAR'
>>> obj.setfoo(['this','that','other'])
>>> obj.bar, obj.foo
('BAR', ['this', 'that', 'other'])
>>> obj.__dict__
{'foo': ['this', 'that', 'other'], 'bar': 'BAR'}
```

Instance attributes often dereference to other class instances. thereby allowing hierarchically organized namespace quantification to indicate a data structure. Moreover, a number of "magic" methods named with leading and trailing double-underscores provide optional syntactic conveniences for working with instance data. The most common of these magic methods is .__init__(), which initializes an instance (often utilizing arguments). For example:

```
>>> class Klass2:
...     def __init__(self, *args, **kw):
...         self.listargs = args
...         for key, val in kw.items():
...             setattr(self, key, val)
...
>>> obj = Klass2(1, 2, 3, foo='FOO', bar=Klass2(baz='BAZ'))
>>> obj.bar.blam = 'BLAM'
>>> obj.listargs, obj.foo, obj.bar.baz, obj.bar.blam
((1, 2, 3), 'FOO', 'BAZ', 'BLAM')
```

There are quite a few additional "magic" methods that Python classes may define. Many of these methods let class instances behave more like basic datatypes (while still maintaining special class behaviors). For example. the .__str__() and .__repr__() methods control the string representation of an instance; the .__getitem__() and .__setitem__() methods allow indexed access to instance data (either dict-like named indices, or list-like numbered indices); methods like .__add__(), .__mul__(), .__pow__(), and .__abs__() allow instances to behave in number-like ways. The *Python Reference Manual* discusses magic methods in detail.

In Python 2.2 and above, you can also let instances behave more like basic datatypes by inheriting classes from these built-in types. For example, suppose you need a datatype whose "shape" contains both a mutable sequence of elements and a .foo attribute. Two ways to define this datatype are:

```
>>> class FooList(list):       # works only in Python 2.2+
...     def __init__(self, lst=[], foo=None):
...         list.__init__(self, lst)
...         self.foo = foo
...
>>> foolist = FooList([1,2,3], 'FOO')
>>> foolist[1], foolist.foo
(2, 'FOO')
>>> class OldFooList:           # works in older Pythons
...     def __init__(self, lst=[], foo=None):
...         self._lst, self.foo = lst, foo
...     def append(self, item):
```

```
...                  self._lst.append(item)
...          def __getitem__(self, item):
...                  return self._lst[item]
...          def __setitem__(self, item, val):
...                  self._lst[item] = val
...          def __delitem__(self, item):
...                  del self._lst[item]
...
>>> foolst2 = OldFooList([1,2,3], 'FOO')
>>> foolst2[1], foolst2.foo
(2, 'FOO')
```

If you need more complex datatypes than the basic types, or even than an instance whose class has magic methods, often these can be constructed by using instances whose attributes are bound in link-like fashion to other instances. Such bindings can be constructed according to various topologies, including circular ones (such as for modeling graphs). As a simple example, you can construct a binary tree in Python using the following node class:

```
>>> class Node:
...      def __init__(self, left=None, value=None, right=None):
...          self.left, self.value, self.right = left, value, right
...      def __repr__(self):
...          return self.value
...
>>> tree = Node(Node(value="Left Leaf"),
...            "Tree Root",
...            Node(left=Node(value="RightLeft Leaf"),
...                right=Node(value="RightRight Leaf") ))
>>> tree,tree.left,tree.left.left,tree.right.left,tree.right.right
(Tree Root, Left Leaf, None, RightLeft Leaf, RightRight Leaf)
```

In practice, you would probably bind intermediate nodes to names, in order to allow easy pruning and rearrangement.

SEE ALSO: int *18*; float *19*; list *28*; string *129*; tuple *28*; UserDict *24*; UserList *28*; UserString *33*;

A.4 Flow Control

Depending on how you count it, Python has about a half-dozen flow control mechanisms, which is much simpler than most programming languages. Fortunately, Python's collection of mechanisms is well chosen, with a high—but not obsessively high—degree of orthogonality between them.

From the point of view of this appendix, exception handling is mostly one of Python's flow control techniques. In a language like Java, an application is probably considered "happy" if it does not throw any exceptions at all, but Python programmers find exceptions less "exceptional"—a perfectly good design might exit a block of code *only* when an exception is raised.

Two additional aspects of the Python language are not usually introduced in terms of flow control, but nonetheless amount to such when considered abstractly. Both functional programming style operations on lists and Boolean shortcutting are, at the heart, flow control constructs.

A.4.1 if/then/else Statements

Choice between alternate code paths is generally performed with the `if` statement and its optional `elif` and `else` components. An `if` block is followed by zero or more `elif` blocks; at the end of the compound statement, zero or one `else` blocks occur. An `if` statement is followed by a Boolean expression and a colon. Each `elif` is likewise followed by a Boolean expression and colon. The `else` statement, if it occurs, has no Boolean expression after it, just a colon. Each statement introduces a block containing one or more statements (indented on the following lines or on the same line, after the colon).

Every expression in Python has a Boolean value, including every bare object name or literal. Any empty container (list, dict, tuple) is considered false; an empty string or Unicode string is false; the number 0 (of any numeric type) is false. As well, an instance whose class defines a `.__nonzero__()` or `.__len__()` method is false if these methods return a false value. Without these special methods, every instance is true. Much of the time, Boolean expressions consist of comparisons between objects, where comparisons actually evaluate to the canonical objects "0" or "1". Comparisons are `<, >, ==, >=, <=, <>, !=, is, is not, in`, and `not in`. Sometimes the unary operator `not` precedes such an expression.

Only one block in an "if/elif/else" compound statement is executed during any pass—if multiple conditions hold, the first one that evaluates as true is followed. For example:

```
>>> if 2+2 <= 4:
...     print "Happy math"
...
Happy math
>>> x = 3
>>> if x > 4: print "More than 4'
... elif x > 3: print "More than 3"
... elif x > 2: print "More than 2"
... else: print "2 or less"
...
More than 2
>>> if isinstance(2, int):
...     print "2 is an int"      # 2.2+ test
... else:
```

```
...      print "2 is not an int"
```

Python has no "switch" statement to compare one value with multiple candidate matches. Occasionally, the repetition of an expression being compared on multiple `elif` lines looks awkward. A "trick" in such a case is to use a dict as a pseudo-switch. The following are equivalent, for example:

```
>>> if var.upper() == 'ONE':     val = 1
... elif var.upper() == 'TWO':   val = 2
... elif var.upper() == 'THREE': val = 3
... elif var.upper() == 'FOUR':  val = 4
... else:                        val = 0
...
>>> switch = {'ONE':1, 'TWO':2, 'THREE':3, 'FOUR':4}
>>> val = switch.get(var.upper(), 0)
```

A.4.2   Boolean Shortcutting

The Boolean operators or and and are "lazy." That is, an expression containing or or and evaluates only as far as it needs to determine the overall value. Specifically, if the first disjoin of an or is true, the value of that disjoin becomes the value of the expression, without evaluating the rest; if the first conjoin of an and is false, its value likewise becomes the value of the whole expression.

Shortcutting is formally sufficient for switching and is sometimes more readable and concise than "if/elif/else" blocks. For example:

```
>>> if this:           # 'if' compound statement
...      result = this
... elif that:
...      result = that
... else:
...      result = 0
...
>>> result = this or that or 0  # boolean shortcutting
```

Compound shortcutting is also possible, but not necessarily easy to read; for example:

```
>>> (cond1 and func1()) or (cond2 and func2()) or func3()
```

A.4.3   `for/continue/break` Statements

The `for` statement loops over the elements of a sequence. In Python 2.2+, looping utilizes an iterator object (which may not have a predetermined length)—but standard sequences like lists, tuples, and strings are automatically transformed to iterators in `for` statements. In earlier Python versions, a few special functions like `xreadlines()` and `xrange()` also act as iterators.

Each time a `for` statement loops, a sequence/iterator element is bound to the loop variable. The loop variable may be a tuple with named items, thereby creating bindings for multiple names in each loop. For example:

```
>>> for x,y,z in [(1,2,3),(4,5,6),(7,8,9)]: print x, y, z, '*',
...
1 2 3 * 4 5 6 * 7 8 9 *
```

A particularly common idiom for operating on each item in a dictionary is:

```
>>> for key,val in dct.items():
...     print key, val, '*',
...
1 2 * 3 4 * 5 6 *
```

When you wish to loop through a block a certain number of times, a common idiom is to use the `range()` or `xrange()` built-in functions to create ad hoc sequences of the needed length. For example:

```
>>> for _ in range(10):
...     print "X",      # '_' is not used in body
...
X X X X X X X X X X
```

However, if you find yourself binding over a range just to repeat a block, this often indicates that you have not properly understood the loop. Usually repetition is a way of operating on a collection of related *things* that could instead be explicitly bound in the loop, not just a need to do exactly the same thing multiple times.

If the `continue` statement occurs in a `for` loop, the next loop iteration proceeds without executing later lines in the block. If the `break` statement occurs in a `for` loop, control passes past the loop without executing later lines (except the `finally` block if the `break` occurs in a `try`).

A.4.4 `map()`, `filter()`, `reduce()`, and List Comprehensions

Much like the `for` statement, the built-in functions *map()*, *filter()*, and *reduce()* perform actions based on a sequence of items. Unlike a `for` loop, these functions explicitly return a value resulting from this application to each item. Each of these three functional programming style functions accepts a function object as a first argument and sequence(s) as a subsequent argument(s).

The *map()* function returns a list of items of the same length as the input sequence, where each item in the result is a "transformation" of one item in the input. Where you explicitly want such transformed items, use of *map()* is often both more concise and clearer than an equivalent `for` loop; for example:

```
>>> nums = (1,2,3,4)
>>> str_nums = []
```

```
>>> for n in nums:
...        str_nums.append(str(n))
...
>>> str_nums
['1', '2', '3', '4']
>>> str_nums = map(str, nums)
>>> str_nums
['1', '2', '3', '4']
```

If the function argument of *map()* accepts (or can accept) multiple arguments, multiple sequences can be given as later arguments. If such multiple sequences are of different lengths, the shorter ones are padded with `None` values. The special value `None` may be given as the function argument, producing a sequence of tuples of elements from the argument sequences.

```
>>> nums = (1,2,3,4)
>>> def add(x, y):
...        if x is None: x=0
...        if y is None: y=0
...        return x+y
...
>>> map(add, nums, [5,5,5])
[6, 7, 8, 4]
>>> map(None, (1,2,3,4), [5,5,5])
[(1, 5), (2, 5), (3, 5), (4, None)]
```

The *filter()* function returns a list of those items in the input sequence that satisfy a condition given by the function argument. The function argument must accept one parameter, and its return value is interpreted as a Boolean (in the usual manner). For example:

```
>>> nums = (1,2,3,4)
>>> odds = filter(lambda n: n%2, nums)
>>> odds
(1, 3)
```

Both *map()* and *filter()* can use function arguments that have side effects, thereby making it possible—but not usually desirable—to replace every `for` loop with a *map()* or *filter()* function. For example:

```
>>> for x in seq:
...        # bunch of actions
...        pass
...
>>> def actions(x):
...        # same bunch of actions
...        return 0
```

```
...
>>> filter(actions, seq)
[]
```

Some epicycles are needed for the scoping of block variables and for **break** and **continue** statements. But as a general picture, it is worth being aware of the formal equivalence between these very different-seeming techniques.

The *reduce()* function takes as a function argument a function with two parameters. In addition to a sequence second argument, *reduce()* optionally accepts a third argument as an initializer. For each item in the input sequence, *reduce()* combines the previous aggregate result with the item, until the sequence is exhausted. While *reduce()*—like *map()* and *filter()*—has a loop-like effect of operating on every item in a sequence, its main purpose is to create some sort of aggregation, tally, or selection across indefinitely many items. For example:

```
>>> from operator import add
>>> sum = lambda seq: reduce(add, seq)
>>> sum([4,5,23,12])
44
>>> def tastes_better(x, y):
...     # some complex comparison of x, y
...     # either return x, or return y
...     # ...
...
>>> foods = [spam, eggs, bacon, toast]
>>> favorite = reduce(tastes_better, foods)
```

List comprehensions (listcomps) are a syntactic form that was introduced with Python 2.0. It is easiest to think of list comprehensions as a sort of cross between for loops and the *map()* or *filter()* functions. That is, like the functions, listcomps are expressions that produce lists of items, based on "input" sequences. But listcomps also use the keywords **for** and **if** that are familiar from statements. Moreover, it is typically much easier to read a compound list comprehension expression than it is to read corresponding nested *map()* and *filter()* functions.

For example, consider the following small problem: You have a list of numbers and a string of characters; you would like to construct a list of all pairs that consist of a number from the list and a character from the string, but only if the ASCII ordinal is larger than the number. In traditional imperative style you might write:

```
>>> bigord_pairs = []
>>> for n in (95,100,105):
...     for c in 'aei':
...         if ord(c) > n:
...             bigord_pairs.append((n,c))
...
>>> bigord_pairs
[(95, 'a'), (95, 'e'), (95, 'i'), (100, 'e'), (100, 'i')]
```

In a functional programming style you might write the nearly unreadable:

```
>>> dupelms=lambda lst,n: reduce(lambda s,t:s+t,
...                               map(lambda l,n=n: [l]*n, lst))
>>> combine=lambda xs,ys: map(None,xs*len(ys), dupelms(ys,len(xs)))
>>> bigord_pairs=lambda ns,cs: filter(lambda (n,c):ord(c)>n,
...                                    combine(ns,cs))
>>> bigord_pairs((95,100,105),'aei')
[(95, 'a'), (95, 'e'), (100, 'e'), (95, 'i'), (100, 'i')]
```

In defense of this FP approach, it has not *only* accomplished the task at hand, but also provided the general combinatorial function `combine()` along the way. But the code is still rather obfuscated.

List comprehensions let you write something that is both concise and clear:

```
>>> [(n,c) for n in (95,100,105) for c in 'aei' if ord(c)>n]
[(95, 'a'), (95, 'e'), (95, 'i'), (100, 'e'), (100, 'i')]
```

As long as you have listcomps available, you hardly *need* a general `combine()` function, since it just amounts to repeating the `for` clause in a listcomp.

Slightly more formally, a list comprehension consists of the following: (1) Surrounding square brackets (like a list constructor, which it is). (2) An expression that usually, but not by requirement, contains some names that get bound in the `for` clauses. (3) One or more `for` clauses that bind a name repeatedly (just like a `for` loop). (4) Zero or more `if` clauses that limit the results. Generally, but not by requirement, the `if` clauses contain some names that were bound by the `for` clauses.

List comprehensions may nest inside each other freely. Sometimes a `for` clause in a listcomp loops over a list that is defined by another listcomp; once in a while a nested listcomp is even used inside a listcomp's expression or `if` clauses. However, it is almost as easy to produce difficult-to-read code by excessively nesting listcomps as it is by nesting *map()* and *filter()* functions. Use caution and common sense about such nesting.

It is worth noting that list comprehensions are not as referentially transparent as functional programming style calls. Specifically, any names bound in `for` clauses remain bound in the enclosing scope (or global if the name is so declared). These side effects put a minor extra burden on you to choose distinctive or throwaway names for use in listcomps.

A.4.5   `while/else/continue/break` Statements

The `while` statement loops over a block as long as the expression after the `while` remains true. If an `else` block is used within a compound `while` statement, as soon as the expression becomes false, the `else` block is executed. The `else` block is chosen even if the `while` expression is initially false.

If the `continue` statement occurs in a `while` loop, the next loop iteration proceeds without executing later lines in the block. If the `break` statement occurs in a `while` loop, control passes past the loop without executing later lines (except the `finally` block if the `break` occurs in a `try`). If a `break` occurs in a `while` block, the `else` block is not executed.

If a `while` statement's expression is to go from being true to being false, typically some name in the expression will be re-bound within the `while` block. At times an expression will depend on an external condition, such as a file handle or a socket, or it may involve a call to a function whose Boolean value changes over invocations. However, probably the most common Python idiom for `while` statements is to rely on a `break` to terminate a block. Some examples

```
>>> command = ''
>>> while command != 'exit':
...     command = raw_input('Command > ')
...     # if/elif block to dispatch on various commands
...
Command > someaction
Command > exit
>>> while socket.ready():
...     socket.getdata()  # do something with the socket
... else:
...     socket.close()    # cleanup (e.g. close socket)
...
>>> while 1:
...     command = raw_input('Command > ')
...     if command == 'exit': break
...     # elif's for other commands
...
Command > someaction
Command > exit
```

A.4.6   Functions, Simple Generators, and the `yield` Statement

Both functions and object methods allow a kind of nonlocality in terms of program flow, but one that is quite restrictive. A function or method is called from another context, enters at its top, executes any statements encountered, then returns to the calling context as soon as a `return` statement is reached (or the function body ends). The invocation of a function or method is basically a strictly linear nonlocal flow.

Python 2.2 introduced a flow control construct, called generators, that enables a new style of nonlocal branching. If a function or method body contains the statement `yield`, then it becomes a *generator function* and invoking the function returns a *generator iterator* instead of a simple value. A generator iterator is an object that has a `.next()` method that returns values. Any instance object can have a `.next()` method, but a generator iterator's method is special in having "resumable execution."

In a standard function, once a `return` statement is encountered, the Python interpreter discards all information about the function's flow state and local name bindings. The returned value might contain some information about local values, but the flow

state is always gone. A generator iterator, in contrast, "remembers" the entire flow
state, and all local bindings, between each invocation of its `.next()` method. A value is
returned to a calling context each place a `yield` statement is encountered in the generator function body, but the calling context (or any context with access to the generator
iterator) is able to jump back to the flow point where this last `yield` occurred.

In the abstract, generators seem complex, but in practice they prove quite simple.
For example:

```
>>> from __future__ import generators # not needed in 2.3+
>>> def generator_func():
...     for n in [1,2]:
...         yield n
...     print "Two yields in for loop"
...     yield 3
...
>>> generator_iter = generator_func()
>>> generator_iter.next()
1
>>> generator_iter.next()
2
>>> generator_iter.next()
Two yields in for loop
3
>>> generator_iter.next()
Traceback (most recent call last):
  File "<stdin>", line 1, in ?
StopIteration
```

The object `generator_iter` in the example can be bound in different scopes, and
passed to and returned from functions, just like any other object. Any context invoking `generator_iter.next()` jumps back into the last flow point where the generator
function body yielded.

In a sense, a generator iterator allows you to perform jumps similar to the "GOTO"
statements of some (older) languages, but still retains the advantages of structured
programming. The most common usage for generators, however, is simpler than this.
Most of the time, generators are used as "iterators" in a loop context; for example:

```
>>> for n in generator_func():
...     print n
...
1
2
Two yields in for loop
3
```

In recent Python versions, the `StopIteration` exception is used to signal the end of a
`for` loop. The generator iterator's `.next()` method is implicitly called as many times as

possible by the `for` statement. The name indicated in the `for` statement is repeatedly re-bound to the values the `yield` statement(s) return.

A.4.7 Raising and Catching Exceptions

Python uses exceptions quite broadly and probably more naturally than any other programming language. In fact there are certain flow control constructs that are awkward to express by means other than raising and catching exceptions.

There are two general purposes for exceptions in Python. On the one hand, Python actions can be invalid or disallowed in various ways. You are not allowed to divide by zero; you cannot open (for reading) a filename that does not exist; some functions require arguments of specific types; you cannot use an unbound name on the right side of an assignment; and so on. The exceptions raised by these types of occurrences have names of the form `[A-Z].*Error`. Catching *error* exceptions is often a useful way to recover from a problem condition and restore an application to a "happy" state. Even if such error exceptions are not caught in an application, their occurrence provides debugging clues since they appear in tracebacks.

The second purpose for exceptions is for circumstances a programmer wishes to flag as "exceptional." But understand "exceptional" in a weak sense—not as something that indicates a programming or computer error, but simply as something unusual or "not the norm." For example, Python 2.2+ iterators raise a `StopIteration` exception when no more items can be generated. Most such implied sequences are not infinite length, however; it is merely the case that they contain a (large) number of items, and they run out only once at the end. It's not "the norm" for an iterator to run out of items, but it is often expected that this will happen eventually.

In a sense, raising an exception can be similar to executing a `break` statement—both cause control flow to leave a block. For example, compare:

```
>>> n = 0
>>> while 1:
...     n = n+1
...     if n > 10: break
...
>>> print n
11
>>> n = 0
>>> try:
...     while 1:
...         n = n+1
...         if n > 10: raise "ExitLoop'
... except:
...     print n
...
11
```

In two closely related ways, exceptions behave differently than do `break` statements. In the first place, exceptions could be described as having "dynamic scope," which in most contexts is considered a sin akin to "GOTO," but here is quite useful. That is, you never know at compile time exactly where an exception might get caught (if not anywhere else, it is caught by the Python interpreter). It might be caught in the exception's block, or a containing block, and so on; or it might be in the local function, or something that called it, or something that called the caller, and so on. An exception is a *fact* that winds its way through execution contexts until it finds a place to settle. The upward propagation of exceptions is quite opposite to the downward propagation of lexically scoped bindings (or even to the earlier "three-scope rule").

The corollary of exceptions' dynamic scope is that, unlike `break`, they can be used to exit gracefully from deeply nested loops. The "Zen of Python" offers a caveat here: "Flat is better than nested." And indeed it is so, if you find yourself nesting loops *too* deeply, you should probably refactor (e.g., break loops into utility functions). But if you are nesting *just deeply enough*, dynamically scoped exceptions are just the thing for you. Consider the following small problem: A "Fermat triple" is here defined as a triple of integers (i,j,k) such that "i**2 + j**2 == k**2". Suppose that you wish to determine if any Fermat triples exist with all three integers inside a given numeric range. An obvious (but entirely nonoptimal) solution is:

```
>>> def fermat_triple(beg, end):
...     class EndLoop(Exception): pass
...     range_ = range(beg, end)
...     try:
...         for i in range_:
...             for j in range_:
...                 for k in range_:
...                     if i**2 + j**2 == k**2:
...                         raise EndLoop, (i,j,k)
...     except EndLoop, triple:
...         # do something with 'triple'
...         return i,j,k
...
>>> fermat_triple(1,10)
(3, 4, 5)
>>> fermat_triple(120,150)
>>> fermat_triple(100,150)
(100, 105, 145)
```

By raising the `EndLoop` exception in the middle of the nested loops, it is possible to catch it again outside of all the loops. A simple `break` in the inner loop would only break out of the most deeply nested block, which is pointless. One might devise some system for setting a "satisfied" flag and testing for this at every level, but the exception approach is much simpler. Since the `except` block does not actually *do* anything extra with the triple, it could have just been returned inside the loops; but in the general case, other actions can be required before a `return`.

It is not uncommon to want to leave nested loops when something has "gone wrong" in the sense of an "*Error" exception. Sometimes you might only be in a position to

discover a problem condition within nested blocks, but recovery still makes better sense
outside the nesting. Some typical examples are problems in I/O, calculation overflows,
missing dictionary keys or list indices, and so on. Moreover, it is useful to assign `except`
statements to the calling position that really needs to handle the problems, then write
support functions as if nothing can go wrong. For example:

```
>>> try:
...     result = complex_file_operation(filename)
... except IOError:
...     print "Cannot open file", filename
```

The function `complex_file_operation()` should not be burdened with trying to figure out what to do if a bad `filename` is given to it—there is really nothing to be done
in that context. Instead, such support functions can simply propagate their exceptions
upwards, until some caller takes responsibility for the problem.

The `try` statement has two forms. The `try/except/else` form is more commonly
used, but the `try/finally` form is useful for "cleanup handlers."

In the first form, a `try` block must be followed by one or more `except` blocks. Each
`except` may specify an exception or tuple of exceptions to catch; the last `except` block
may omit an exception (tuple), in which case it catches every exception that is not
caught by an earlier `except` block. After the `except` blocks, you may optionally specify
an `else` block. The `else` block is run only if no exception occurred in the `try` block.
For example:

```
>>> def except_test(n):
...     try: x = 1/n
...     except IOError: print "IO Error"
...     except ZeroDivisionError: print "Zero Division"
...     except: print "Some Other Error"
...     else: print "All is Happy"
...
>>> except_test(1)
All is Happy
>>> except_test(0)
Zero Division
>>> except_test('x')
Some Other Error
```

An `except` test will match either the exception actually listed or any descendent of
that exception. It tends to make sense, therefore, in defining your own exceptions to
inherit from related ones in the *exceptions* module. For example:

```
>>> class MyException(IOError): pass
>>> try:
...     raise MyException
... except IOError:
...     print "got it"
```

```
...
got it
```

In the `try`/`finally` form of the `try` statement, the `finally` statement acts as general cleanup code. If no exception occurs in the `try` block, the `finally` block runs, and that is that. If an exception *was* raised in the `try` block, the `finally` block still runs, but the original exception is re-raised at the end of the block. However, if a `return` or `break` statement is executed in a `finally` block—or if a new exception is raised in the block (including with the `raise` statement)—the `finally` block never reaches its end, and the original exception disappears.

A `finally` statement acts as a cleanup block even when its corresponding `try` block contains a `return`, `break`, or `continue` statement. That is, even though a `try` block might not run all the way through, `finally` is still entered to clean up whatever the `try` *did* accomplish. A typical use of this compound statement opens a file or other external resource at the very start of the `try` block, then performs several actions that may or may not succeed in the rest of the block; the `finally` is responsible for making sure the file gets closed, whether or not all the actions on it prove possible.

The `try`/`finally` form is never strictly needed since a bare `raise` statement will re-raise the last exception. It is possible, therefore, to have an `except` block end with the `raise` statement to propagate an error upward after taking some action. However, when a cleanup action is desired whether or not exceptions were encountered, the `try`/`finally` form can save a few lines and express your intent more clearly. For example:

```
>>> def finally_test(x):
...     try:
...         y = 1/x
...         if x > 10:
...             return x
...     finally:
...         print "Cleaning up..."
...     return y
...
>>> finally_test(0)
Cleaning up...
Traceback (most recent call last):
  File "<stdin>", line 1, in ?
  File "<stdin>", line 3, in finally_test
ZeroDivisionError: integer division or modulo by zero
>>> finally_test(3)
Cleaning up...
0
>>> finally_test(100)
Cleaning up...
100
```

A.4.8   Data as Code

Unlike in languages in the Lisp family, it is *usually* not a good idea to create Python programs that execute data values. It is *possible*, however, to create and run Python strings during program runtime using several built-in functions. The modules *code*, *codeop*, *imp*, and *new* provide additional capabilities in this direction. In fact, the Python interactive shell itself is an example of a program that dynamically reads strings as user input, then executes them. So clearly, this approach is occasionally useful.

Other than in providing an interactive environment for advanced users (who themselves know Python), a possible use for the "data as code" model is with applications that themselves generate Python code, either to run later or to communicate with another application. At a simple level, it is not difficult to write compilable Python programs based on templatized functionality; for this to be useful, of course, you would want a program to contain some customization that was determinable only at runtime.

eval(s [,globals=globals() [,locals=locals()]])

Evaluate the expression in string s and return the result of that evaluation. You may specify optional arguments globals and locals to specify the namespaces to use for name lookup. By default, use the regular global and local namespace dictionaries. Note that only an expression can be evaluated, not a statement suite.

Most of the time when a (novice) programmer thinks of using *eval()* it is to compute some value—often numeric—based on data encoded in texts. For example, suppose that a line in a report file contains a list of dollar amounts, and you would like the sum of these numbers. A naive approach to the problem uses *eval()*:

```
>>> line = "$47   $33   $51   $76"
>>> eval("+".join([d.replace('$','') for d in line.split()]))
207
```

While this approach is generally slow, that is not an important problem. A more significant issue is that *eval()* runs code that is not known until runtime; potentially line could contain Python code that causes harm to the system it runs on or merely causes an application to malfunction. Imagine that instead of a dollar figure, your data file contained os.rmdir("/"). A better approach is to use the safe type coercion functions *int()*, *float()*, and so on.

```
>>> nums = [int(d.replace('$','')) for d in line.split()]
>>> from operator import add
>>> reduce(add, nums)
207
```

exec

The *exec* statement is a more powerful sibling of the *eval()* function. Any valid Python code may be run if passed to the *exec* statement. The format of the *exec* statement allows optional namespace specification, as with *eval()*:

```
exec code [in globals [,locals]]
```

For example:

```
>>> s = "for i in range(10):\n  print i,\n"
>>> exec s in globals(), locals()
0 1 2 3 4 5 6 7 8 9
```

The argument `code` may be either a string, a code object, or an open file object. As with *eval()*, the security dangers and speed penalties of *exec* usually outweigh any convenience provided. However, where `code` is clearly under application control, there are occasionally uses for this statement.

__import__(s [,globals=globals() [,locals=locals() [,fromlist]]])

Import the module named s, using namespace dictionaries `globals` and `locals`. The argument `fromlist` may be omitted, but if specified as a nonempty list of strings—e.g., `[""]`—the fully qualified subpackage will be imported. For normal cases, the *import* statement is the way you import modules, but in the special circumstance that the value of s is not determined until runtime, use *__import__()*.

```
>>> op = __import__('os.path',globals(),locals(),[''])
>>> op.basename('/this/that/other')
'other'
```

input([prompt])

Equivalent to `eval(raw_input(prompt))`, along with all the dangers associated with *eval()* generally. Best practice is to always use *raw_input()*, but you might see *input()* in existing programs.

raw_input([prompt])

Return a string from user input at the terminal. Used to obtain values interactive in console-based applications.

```
>>> s = raw_input('Last Name: ')
Last Name: Mertz
>>> s
'Mertz'
```

A.5   Functional Programming

This section largely recapitulates briefer descriptions elsewhere in this appendix, but a common unfamiliarity with functional programming merits a longer discussion. Additional material on functional programming in Python—mostly of a somewhat exotic nature—can be found in articles at:

```
<http://gnosis.cx/publish/programming/charming_python_13.html>

<http://gnosis.cx/publish/programming/charming_python_16.html>

<http://gnosis.cx/publish/programming/charming_python_19.html>
```

It is hard to find any consensus about exactly what functional programming *is*, among either its proponents or detractors. It is not really entirely clear to what extent FP is a feature of languages, and to what extent a feature of programming styles. Since this is a book about Python, we can leave aside discussions of predominantly functional languages like Lisp, Scheme, Haskell, ML, Ocaml, Clean, Mercury, Erlang, and so on; we can focus on what makes a Python program more or less functional.

Programs that lean towards functional programming, within Python's multiple paradigms, tend to have many of the following features:

1. Functions are treated as first-class objects that are passed as arguments to other functions and methods, and returned as values from same.

2. Solutions are expressed more in terms of *what* is to be computed than in terms of *how* the computation is performed.

3. Side effects, especially rebinding names repeatedly, are minimized. Functions are referentially transparent (see Glossary).

4. Expressions are emphasized over statements; in particular, expressions often describe how a result collection is related to a prior collection—most especially list objects.

5. The following Python constructs are used prevalently: the built-in functions *map()*, *filter()*, *reduce()*, *apply()*, *zip()*, and *enumerate()*; extended call syntax; the *lambda* operator; list comprehensions; and switches expressed as Boolean operators.

Many experienced Python programmers consider FP constructs to be as much of a wart as a feature. The main drawback of a functional programming style (in Python, or elsewhere) is that it is easy to write unmaintainable or obfuscated programming code using it. Too many *map()*, *reduce()*, and *filter()* functions nested inside each other lose all the self-evidence of Python's simple statement and indentation style. Adding unnamed *lambda* functions into the mix makes matters that much worse. The discussion in Chapter 1 of higher-order functions gives some examples.

A.5.1 Emphasizing Expressions Using lambda

The *lambda* operator is used to construct an "anonymous" function. In contrast to the more common def declaration, a function created with *lambda* can only contain a single expression as a result, not a sequence of statements, nested blocks, and so on. There are inelegant ways to emulate statements within a *lambda*, but generally you should think of *lambda* as a less-powerful cousin of def declarations.

Not all Python programmers are happy with the *lambda* operator. There is certainly a benefit in readability to giving a function a descriptive name. For example, the second style below is clearly more readable than the first:

```
>>> from math import sqrt
>>> print map(lambda (a,b): sqrt(a**2+b**2),((3,4),(7,11),(35,8)))
[5.0, 13.038404810405298, 35.902646142032481]
>>> sides = ((3,4),(7,11),(35,8))
>>> def hypotenuse(ab):
...     a,b = ab[:]
...     return sqrt(a**2+b**2)
...
>>> print map(hypotenuse, sides)
[5.0, 13.038404810405298, 35.902646142032481]
```

By declaring a named function `hypotenuse()`, the intention of the calculation becomes much more clear. Once in a while, though, a function used in *map()* or in a callback (e.g., in *Tkinter*, *xml.sax*, or *mx.TextTools*) really is such a one-shot thing that a name only adds noise.

However, you may notice in this book that I fairly commonly use the *lambda* operator to define a name. For example, you might see something like:

```
>>> hypotenuse = lambda (a,b): sqrt(a**2+b**2)
```

This usage is mostly for documentation. A side matter is that a few characters are saved in assigning an anonymous function to a name, versus a `def` binding. But concision is not particularly important. This function definition form documents explicitly that I do not expect any side effects—like changes to globals and data structures—within the `hypotenuse()` function. While the `def` form is also side effect free, that fact is not advertised; you have to look through the (brief) code to establish it. Strictly speaking, there are ways—like calling *setattr()*—to introduce side effects within a *lambda*, but as a convention, I avoid doing so, as should you.

Moreover, a second documentary goal is served by a *lambda* assignment like the one above. Whenever this form occurs, it is possible to literally substitue the right-hand expression anywhere the left-hand name occurs (you need to add extra surrounding parentheses usually, however). By using this form, I am emphasizing that the name is simply a short-hand for the defined expression. For example:

```
>>> hypotenuse = lambda a,b: sqrt(a**2+b**2)
>>> (lambda a,b: sqrt(a**2+b**2))(3,4), hypotenuse(3,4)
(5.0, 5.0)
```

Bindings with `def`, in general, lack substitutability.

A.5.2   Special List Functions

Python has two built-in functions that are strictly operations on sequences, but that are frequently useful in conjunction with the "function-plus-list" built-in functions.

zip(seq1 [,seq2 [,...]])

The *zip()* function, in Python 2.0+, combines multiple sequences into one sequence of tuples. Think of the teeth of a zipper for an image and the source of the name.

The function *zip()* is almost the same as map(None,...), but *zip()* truncates when it reaches the end of the shortest sequence. For example:

```
>>> map(None, (1,2,3,4), [5,5,5])
[(1, 5), (2, 5), (3, 5), (4, None)]
>>> zip((1,2,3,4), [5,5,5])
[(1, 5), (2, 5), (3, 5)]
```

Especially in combination with *apply()*, extended call syntax, or simply tuple unpacking, *zip()* is useful for operating over multiple related sequences at once; for example:

```
>>> lefts, tops = (3, 7, 35), (4, 11, 8)
>>> map(hypotenuse, zip(lefts, tops))
[5.0, 13.038404810405298, 35.902646142032481]
```

A little quirk of *zip()* is that it is *almost* its own inverse. A little use of extended call syntax is needed for inversion, though. The expression zip(*zip(*seq)) is idempotent (as an exercise, play with variations). Consider:

```
>>> sides = [(3, 4), (7, 11), (35, 8)]
>>> zip(*zip(*sides))
[(3, 4), (7, 11), (35, 8)]
```

enumerate(collection)

Python 2.3 adds the *enumerate()* built-in function for working with a sequence and its index positions at the same time. Basically, enumerate(seq) is equivalent to zip(range(len(seq)),seq), but *enumerate()* is a lazy iterator that need not construct the entire list to loop over. A typical usage is:

```
>>> items = ['a','b']
>>> i = 0        # old-style explicit increment
>>> for thing in items:
...      print 'index',i,'contains',thing
...      i += 1
index 0 contains a
index 1 contains b
>>> for i,thing in enumerate(items):
...      print 'index',i,'contains',thing
...
index 0 contains a
index 1 contains b
```

A.5.3   List-Application Functions as Flow Control

I believe that text processing is one of the areas of Python programming where judicious use of functional programming techniques can greatly aid both clarity and conciseness. A strength of FP style—specifically the Python built-in functions *map()*, *filter()*, and *reduce()*—is that they are not merely about *functions*, but also about *sequences*. In text processing contexts, most loops are ways of iterating over chunks of text, frequently over lines. When you wish to do something to a sequence of similar items, FP style allows the code to focus on the action (and its object) instead of on side issues of loop constructs and transient variables.

In part, a *map()*, *filter()*, or *reduce()* call is a kind of flow control. Just as a for loop is an instruction to perform an action a number of times, so are these list-application functions. For example:

```
for x in range(100):
    sys.stdout.write(str(x))
```

and:

```
filter(sys.stdout.write, map(str, range(100)))
```

are just two different ways of calling the str() function 100 times (and the sys.stdout.write() method with each result). The two differences are that the FP style does not bother rebinding a name for each iteration, and that each call to a list-application function returns a value—a list for *map()* and *filter()*, potentially any sort of value for *reduce()*. Functions/methods like *sys.stdout.write* that are called wholly for their side effects almost always return None; by using *filter()* rather than *map()* around these, you avoid constructing a throwaway list—or rather you construct just an empty list.

A.5.4   Extended Call Syntax and apply()

To call a function in a dynamic way, it is sometimes useful to build collections of arguments in data structures prior to the call. Unpacking a sequence containing several positional arguments is awkward, and unpacking a dictionary of keyword arguments simply cannot be done with the Python 1.5.2 standard call syntax. For example, consider the salutation() function:

```
>>> def salutation(title,first,last,use_title=1,prefix='Dear'):
...     print prefix,
...     if use_title: print title,
...     print '%s %s,' % (first, last)
...
>>> salutation('Dr.','David','Mertz',prefix='To:')
To: Dr. David Mertz,
```

Suppose you read names and prefix strings from a text file or database and wish to call salutation() with arguments determined at runtime. You might use:

```
>>> rec = get_next_db_record()
>>> opts = calculate_options(rec)
>>> salutation(rec[0], rec[1], rec[2],
...               use_title=opts.get('use_title',1),
...               prefix=opts.get('prefix','Dear'))
```

This call can be performed more concisely as:

```
>>> salutation(*rec, **opts)
```

Or as:

```
>>> apply(salutation, rec, opts)
```

The calls func(*args,**keywds) and apply(func,args,keywds) are equivalent.
The argument args must be a sequence of the same length as the argument list for
func. The (optional) argument keywds is a dictionary that may or may not contain
keys matching keyword arguments (if not, it has no effect).

In most cases, the extended call syntax is more readable, since the call closely resembles the *declaration* syntax of generic positional and keyword arguments. But in a few
cases—particularly in higher-order functions—the older *apply()* built-in function is
still useful. For example, suppose that you have an application that will either perform
an action immediately or defer it for later, depending on some condition. You might
program this application as:

```
defer_list = []
if some_runtime_condition():
    doIt = apply
else:
    doIt = lambda *x: defer_list.append(x)
#...do stuff like read records and options...
doIt(operation, args, keywds)
#...do more stuff...
#...carry out deferred actions...
map(lambda (f,args,kw): f(*args,**kw), defer_list)
```

Since *apply()* is itself a first-class function rather than a syntactic form, you can
pass it around—or in the example, bind it to a name.

Appendix B

A DATA COMPRESSION PRIMER

B.1 Introduction

See Section 2.2.5 for details on compression capabilities included in the Python standard library. This appendix is intended to provide readers who are unfamiliar with data compression a basic background on its techniques and theory. The final section of this appendix provides a practical example—accompanied by some demonstration code—of a Huffman-inspired custom encoding.

Data compression is widely used in a variety of programming contexts. All popular operating systems and programming languages have numerous tools and libraries for dealing with data compression of various sorts. The right choice of compression tools and libraries for a particular application depends on the characteristics of the data and application in question: streaming versus file; expected patterns and regularities in the data; relative importance of CPU usage, memory usage, channel demands, and storage requirements; and other factors.

Just what is data compression, anyway? The short answer is that data compression removes *redundancy* from data; in information-theoretic terms, compression increases the *entropy* of the compressed text. But those statements are essentially just true by definition. Redundancy can come in a lot of different forms. Repeated bit sequences (11111111) are one type. Repeated byte sequences are another (XXXXXXXX). But more often redundancies tend to come on a larger scale, either regularities of the data set taken as a whole, or sequences of varying lengths that are relatively common. Basically, what data compression aims at is finding algorithmic transformations of data representations that will produce more compact representations given "typical" data sets. If this description seems a bit complex to unpack, read on to find some more practical illustrations.

B.2   Lossless and Lossy Compression

There are actually two fundamentally different "styles" of data compression: lossless and lossy. This appendix is generally about lossless compression techniques, but the reader would be served to understand the distinction first. Lossless compression involves a transformation of the representation of a data set such that it is possible to reproduce *exactly* the original data set by performing a decompression transformation. Lossy compression is a representation that allows you to reproduce something "pretty much like" the original data set. As a plus for the lossy techniques, they can frequently produce far more compact data representations than lossless compression techniques can. Most often lossy compression techniques are used for images, sound files, and video. Lossy compression may be appropriate in these areas insofar as human observers do not perceive the literal bit-pattern of a digital image/sound, but rather more general "gestalt" features of the underlying image/sound.

From the point of view of "normal" data, lossy compression is not an option. We do not want a program that does "about the same" thing as the one we wrote. We do not want a database that contains "about the same" kind of information as what we put into it. At least not for most purposes (and I know of few practical uses of lossy compression outside of what are already approximate mimetic representations of the real world, likes images and sounds).

B.3   A Data Set Example

For purposes of this appendix, let us start with a specific hypothetical data representation. Here is an easy-to-understand example. In the town of Greenfield, MA, the telephone prefixes are 772-, 773-, and 774-. (For non-USA readers: In the USA, local telephone numbers are seven digits and are conventionally represented in the form ###-####; prefixes are assigned in geographic blocks.) Suppose also that the first prefix is the mostly widely assigned of the three. The suffix portions might be any other digits, in fairly equal distribution. The data set we are interested in is "the list of all the telephone numbers currently in active use." One can imagine various reasons why this might be interesting for programmatic purposes, but we need not specify that herein.

Initially, the data set we are interested in comes in a particular data representation: a multicolumn report (perhaps generated as output of some query or compilation process). The first few lines of this report might look like:

```
=============================================================
772-7628     772-8601     772-0113     773-3429     774-9833
773-4319     774-3920     772-0893     772-9934     773-8923
773-1134     772-4930     772-9390     774-9992     772-2314
[...]
```

B.4 Whitespace Compression

Whitespace compression can be characterized most generally as "removing what we are not interested in." Even though this technique is technically a lossy-compression technique, it is still useful for many types of data representations we find in the real world. For example, even though HTML is far more readable in a text editor if incentation and vertical spacing is added, none of this "whitespace" should make any difference to how the HTML document is rendered by a Web browser. If you happen to know that an HTML document is destined only for a Web browser (or for a robot/spider), then it might be a good idea to take out all the whitespace to make it transmit faster and occupy less space in storage. What we remove in whitespace compression never really had any functional purpose to start with.

In the case of our example in this article, it is possible to remove quite a bit from the described report. The row of "=" across the top adds nothing functional, nor do the "-" within numbers, nor the spaces between them. These are all useful for a person reading the original report, but do not matter once we think of it as data. What we remove is not precisely whitespace in traditional terms, but the intent is the same.

Whitespace compression is extremely "cheap" to perform. It is just a matter of reading a stream of data and excluding a few specific values from the output stream. In many cases, no "decompression" step is involved at all. But even where we would wish to re-create something close to the original somewhere down the data stream, it should require little in terms of CPU or memory. What we reproduce may or may not be exactly what we started with, depending on just what rules and constraints were involved in the original. An HTML page typed by a human in a text editor will probably have spacing that is idiosyncratic. Then again, automated tools often produce "reasonable" indentation and spacing of HTML. In the case of the rigid report format in our example, there is no reason that the original representation could not be precisely produced by a "decompressing formatter" down the data stream.

B.5 Run-Length Encoding

Run-length encoding (RLE) is the simplest widely used lossless-compression technique. Like whitespace compression, it is "cheap"—especially to decode. The idea behind it is that many data representations consist largely of strings of repeated bytes. Our example report is one such data representation. It begins with a string of repeated "=", and has strings of spaces scattered through it. Rather than represent each character with its own byte, RLE will (sometimes or always) have an iteration count followed by the character to be repeated.

If repeated bytes are predominant within the expected data representation, it might be adequate and efficient to always have the algorithm specify one or more bytes of iteration count, followed by one character. However, if one-length character strings occur, these strings will require two (or more) bytes to encode them; that is, 00000001 01011000 might be the output bit stream required for just one ASCII "X" of the input stream. Then again, a hundred "X" in a row would be output as 01100100 01011000, which is quite good.

What is frequently done in RLE variants is to selectively use bytes to indicate iterator counts and otherwise just have bytes represent themselves. At least one byte-value has to be reserved to do this, but that can be escaped in the output, if needed. For example, in our example telephone-number report, we know that everything in the input stream is plain ASCII characters. Specifically, they all have bit one of their ASCII value as 0. We could use this first ASCII bit to indicate that an iterator count was being represented rather than representing a regular character. The next seven bits of the iterator byte could be used for the iterator count, and the next byte could represent the character to be repeated. So, for example, we could represent the string "YXXXXXXXX" as:

```
"Y"      Iter(8)  "X"
01001111 10001000 01011000
```

This example does not show how to escape iterator byte-values, nor does it allow iteration of more than 127 occurrences of a character. Variations on RLE deal with issues such as these, if needed.

B.6   Huffman Encoding

Huffman encoding looks at the symbol table of a whole data set. The compression is achieved by finding the "weights" of each symbol in the data set. Some symbols occur more frequently than others, so Huffman encoding suggests that the frequent symbols need not be encoded using as many bits as the less-frequent symbols. There are variations on Huffman-style encoding, but the original (and frequent) variation involves looking for the most common symbol and encoding it using just one bit, say 1. If you encounter a 0, you know you're on the way to encoding a longer variable length symbol.

Let's imagine we apply Huffman encoding to our local phone-book example (assume we have already whitespace-compressed the report). We might get:

Encoding	Symbol
1	7
010	2
011	3
00000	4
00001	5
00010	6
00011	8
00100	9
00101	0
00111	1

Our initial symbol set of digits could already be straightforwardly encoded (with no-compression) as 4-bit sequences (nibbles). The Huffman encoding given will use up to 5-bits for the worst-case symbols, which is obviously worse than the nibble encoding. However, our best case will use only *1* bit, and we know that our best case is also the most frequent case, by having scanned the data set. So we might encode a particular phone number like:

```
772 7628 --> 1 1 010 1 00010 010 00011
```

The nibble encoding would take 28-bits to represent a phone number; in this particular case, our encoding takes 19-bits. I introduced spaces into the example above for clarity; you can see that they are not necessary to unpack the encoding, since the encoding table will determine whether we have reached the end of an encoded symbol (but you have to keep track of your place in the bits).

Huffman encoding is still fairly cheap to decode, cycle-wise. But it requires a table lookup, so it cannot be quite as cheap as RLE, however. The encoding side of Huffman is fairly expensive, though; the whole data set has to be scanned and a frequency table built up. In some cases a "shortcut" is appropriate with Huffman coding. Standard Huffman coding applies to a particular data set being encoded, with the set-specific symbol table prepended to the output data stream. However, if the whole type of data encoded—not just the single data set—has the same regularities, we can opt for a global Huffman table. If we have such a global Huffman table, we can hard-code the lookups into our executables, which makes both compression and decompression quite a bit cheaper (except for the initial global sampling and hard-coding). For example, if we know our data set would be English-language prose, letter-frequency tables are well known and quite consistent across data sets.

B.7   Lempel-Ziv Compression

Probably the most significant lossless-compression technique is Lempel-Ziv. What is explained here is LZ78, but LZ77 and other variants work in a similar fashion. The idea in LZ78 is to encode a streaming byte sequence using a dynamic table. At the start of compressing a bit stream, the LZ table is filled with the actual symbol set, along with some blank slots. Various size tables are used, but for our (whitespace-compressed) telephone number example above, let's suppose that we use a 32-entry table (this should be OK for our example, although much too small for most other types of data). First thing, we fill the first ten slots with our alphabet (digits). As new bytes come in, we first output an existing entry that grabs the longest sequence possible, then fill the next available slot with the N+1 length sequence. In the worst case, we are using 5-bits instead of 4-bits for a single symbol, but we'll wind up getting to use 5-bits for multiple symbols in a lot of cases. For example, the machine might do this (a table slot is noted with square brackets):

```
7 --> Lookup: 7 found        --> nothing to add   --> keep looking
7 --> Lookup: 77 not found   --> add '77' to [11]  --> output [7]=00111
2 --> Lookup: 72 not found   --> add '72' to [12]  --> output [7]=00111
7 --> Lookup: 27 not found   --> add '27' to [13]  --> output [2]=00010
6 --> Lookup: 76 not found   --> add '76' to [14]  --> output [7]=00111
2 --> Lookup: 62 not found   --> add '62' to [15]  --> output [6]=00110
8 --> Lookup: 28 not found   --> add '28' to [16]  --> output [2]=00010
```

So far, we've got nothing out of it, but let's continue with the next phone number:

```
7 --> Lookup: 87 not found   --> add '87' to [17]  --> output [8]=00100
7 --> Lookup: 77 found       --> nothing to add    --> keep looking
2 --> Lookup: 772 not found --> add '772' to [18] --> output [11]=01011
8 --> Lookup: 28 found       --> nothing to add    --> keep looking
6 --> Lookup: 286 not found --> add '286' to [19] --> output [16]=10000
...
```

The steps should suffice to see the pattern. We have not achieved any net compression yet, but notice that we've already managed to use slot 11 and slot 16, thereby getting two symbols with one output in each case. We've also accumulated the very useful byte sequence 772 in slot 18, which would prove useful later in the stream.

What LZ78 does is fill up one symbol table with (hopefully) helpful entries, then write it, clear it, and start a new one. In this regard, 32 entries is still probably too small a symbol table, since that will get cleared before a lot of reuse of 772 and the like is achieved. But the small symbol table is easy to illustrate.

In typical data sets, Lempel-Ziv variants achieve much better compression rates than Huffman or RLE. On the other hand, Lempel-Ziv variants are very pricey cycle-wise and can use large tables in memory. Most real-life compression tools and libraries use a combination of Lempel-Ziv and Huffman techniques.

B.8   Solving the Right Problem

Just as choosing the right algorithm can often create orders-of-magnitude improvements over even heavily optimized wrong algorithms, choosing the right data representation is often even more important than compression methods (which are always a sort of post hoc optimization of desired features). The simple data set example used in this appendix is a perfect case where reconceptualizing the problem would actually be a much better approach than using *any* of the compression techniques illustrated.

Think again about what our data represents. It is not a very general collection of data, and the rigid a priori constraints allow us to reformulate our whole problem. What we have is a maximum of 30,000 telephone numbers (7720000 through 7749999), some of which are active, and others of which are not. We do not have a "duty," as it were, to produce a full representation of each telephone number that is active, but simply to indicate the binary fact that it *is* active. Thinking of the problem this way, we can simply allocate 30,000 bits of memory and storage, and have each bit say "yes" or "no" to the presence of one telephone number. The ordering of the bits in the bit-array can be simple ascending order from the lowest to the highest telephone number in the range.

This bit-array solution is the best in almost every respect. It allocates exactly 3750 bytes to represent the data set; the various compression techniques will use a varying amount of storage depending both on the number of telephone numbers in the set and the efficiency of the compression. But if 10,000 of the 30,000 possible telephone numbers are active, and even a very efficient compression technique requires several bytes per telephone number, then the bit-array is an order-of-magnitude better. In terms of CPU demands, the bit-array is not only better than any of the discussed compression methods, it is also quite likely to be better than the naive noncompression method of listing all the numbers as strings. Stepping through a bit-array and incrementing a "current-telephone-number" counter can be done quite efficiently and mostly within the on-chip cache of a modern CPU.

The lesson to be learned from this very simple example is certainly not that every problem has some magic shortcut (like this one does). A lot of problems genuinely require significant memory, bandwidth, storage, and CPU resources, and in many of those cases compression techniques can help ease—or shift—those burdens. But a more moderate lesson could be suggested: Before compression techniques are employed, it is a good idea to make sure that one's starting conceptualization of the data representation is a good one.

B.9   A Custom Text Compressor

Most styles of compression require a decompression pass before one is able to do something useful with a source document. Many (de)compressors can operate as a stream, producing only the needed bytes of a compressed or decompressed stream in sequence. In some cases, formats even insert recovery or bookkeeping bytes that allow streams to begin within documents (rather than from the very beginning). Programmatic wrappers can make compressed documents or strings look like plaintext ones at the appropriate API layer. Nonetheless, even streaming decompressors require a computational overhead to get at the plaintext content of a compressed document.

An excellent example of a streaming (de)compressor with an API wrapper is *gzip.GzipFile()*. Although not entirely transparent, you can compress and decompress documents without any explicit call to a (de)compression function using this wrapper. *gzip.GzipFile()* provides a file-like interface, but it is also easy to operate on a purely in-memory file using the support of *cStringIO.StringIO()*. For example:

```
>>> from gzip import GzipFile
>>> from cStringIO import StringIO
>>> sio = StringIO()
>>> writer = GzipFile(None, 'wb', 9, sio)
>>> writer.write('Mary had a little lamb\n')
>>> writer.write('its fleece as white as snow\n')
>>> writer.close()
>>> sio.getvalue()[:20]
'\x1f\x8b\x08\xC0k\xc1\x9c<\x02\xff'
>>> reader = GzipFile(None, 'rb', 9, StringIO(sio.getvalue()))
>>> reader.read()[:20]
'Mary had a little la'
>>> reader.seek(30)
>>> reader.read()
'ece as white as snow\n'
```

One thing this example shows is that the underlying compressed string is more or less gibberish. Although the file-like API hides the details from an application programmer, the decompression process is also stateful in its dependence on a symbol table built from the byte sequence in the compressed text. You cannot expect to make sense of a few bytes in the middle of the compressed text without a knowledge of the prior context.

A different approach to compression can have significant advantages in operating on natural-language textual sources. A group of researchers in Brazil and Chile have examined techniques for "word-based Huffman compression." The general strategy of these researchers is to treat whole words as the symbol set for a Huffman table, rather than merely naive byte values. In natural languages, a limited number of (various length, multibyte) words occur with a high frequency, and savings result if such words are represented with shorter byte sequences. In general, such reduced representation is common to all compression techniques, but word-based Huffman takes the additional step of retaining byte boundaries (and uses fixed symbol mapping, as with other Huffman variants).

A special quality of word-based Huffman compressed text is that it need not undergo decompression to be searched. This quality makes it convenient to store textual documents in compressed form, without incurring the requirement to decompress them before they are useful. Instead, if one is searching for words directly contained in the symbol table, one can merely precompress the search terms, then use standard searching algorithms. Such a search can be either against an in-memory string or against a file-like source; in general a search against a precompressed target will be *faster* than one against an uncompressed text. In code, one would use snippets similar to:

```
small_text = word_Huffman_compress(big_text)
search_term = "Foobar"
coded_term = word_Huffman_compress(search_term)
offset = small_text.find(coded_term)
coded_context = small_text[offset-10:offset+10+len(search_term)]
plain_context = word_Huffman_expand(coded_context)
```

A sophisticated implementation of word-based Huffman compression can obtain better compression sizes than does *zlib*. For simplicity, the module below sacrifices optimal compression to the goal of clarity and brevity of code. A fleshed-out implementation could add a number of features.

The presented module *word_huffman* uses a fixed number of bytes to encode each word in the symbol table. This number of bytes can be selected to be 1, 2, or 3 (thereby limiting the table to a generous 2 million entries). The module also separates the generation of a symbol table from the actual compression/decompression. The module can be used in a context where various documents get encoded using the same symbol table—the table presumably generated based on a set of canonical documents. In this situation, the computational requirement of symbol table generation can happen just once, and the symbol table itself need not be transmitted along with each compressed document. Of course, nothing prevents you from treating the document being processed currently as said canonical statistical word source (thereby somewhat improving compression).

In the algorithm utilized by *word_huffman*, only high-bit bytes are utilized in the symbol table. The lower 128 ASCII characters represent themselves as literals. Any

ASCII character sequence that is not in the symbol table is represented as itself—including any short words that would not benefit from encoding. Any high-bit characters that occur in the original source text are escaped by being preceded by an 0xFF byte. As a result, high-bit characters are encoded using two bytes; this technique is clearly only useful for encoding (mostly) textual files, not binary files. Moreover, only character values 0x80-0xFE are used by the symbol table (0xFF *always* signals a literal high-bit character in the encoding).

The *word_huffman* algorithm is not entirely stateless in the sense that not every subsequence in a compressed text can be expanded without additional context. But very little context is required. Any low-bit character always literally represents itself. A high-bit character, however, might be either an escaped literal, a first byte of a symbol table entry, or a non-first byte of a symbol table entry. In the worst case, where a 3-byte symbol table is used, it is necessary to look back two bytes from an arbitrary position in the text to determine the full context. Normally, only one byte lookback is necessary. In any case, words in the symbol table are separated from each other in the uncompressed text by nonalpha low-bit characters (usually whitespace), so parsing compressed entries is straightforward.

---

word_huffman.py

```
wordchars = '-_ABCDEFGHIJKLMNOPQRSTUVWXYZabcdefghijklmnopqrstuvwxyz'

def normalize_text(txt):
    "Convert non-word characters to spaces"
    trans = [' '] * 256
    for c in wordchars: trans[ord(c)] = c
    return txt.translate(''.join(trans))

def build_histogram(txt, hist={}):
    "Incrementally build a histogram table from text source(s)"
    for word in txt.split():
        hist[word] = hist.get(word, 0)+1
    return hist

def optimal_Nbyte(hist, entrylen=2):
    "Build optimal word list for nominal symbol table byte-length"
    slots = 127**entrylen
    words = []
    for word, count in hist.items():
        gain = count * (len(word)-entrylen)
        if gain > 0: words.append((gain, word))
    words.sort()
    words.reverse()
    return [w[1] for w in words[:slots]]

def tables_from_words(words):
```

```
    "Create symbol tables for compression and expansion"
    # Determine ACTUAL best symbol table byte length
    if len(words) < 128: entrylen = 1
    elif len(words) <= 16129: entrylen = 2
    else: entrylen = 3 # assume < ~2M distinct words
    comp_table = {}
    # Escape hibit characters
    for hibit_char in map(chr, range(128,256)):
        comp_table[hibit_char] = chr(255)+hibit_char
    # Literal low-bit characters
    for lowbit_char in map(chr, range(128)):
        comp_table[lowbit_char] = lowbit_char
    # Add word entries
    for word, index in zip(words, range(len(words))):
        comp_table[word] = symbol(index, entrylen)
    # Reverse dictionary for expansion table
    exp_table = {}
    for key, val in comp_table.items():
        exp_table[val] = key
    return (comp_table, exp_table, entrylen)

def symbol(index, entrylen):
    "Determine actual symbol from word sequence and symbol length"
    if entrylen == 1:
        return chr(128+index)
    if entrylen == 2:
        byte1, byte2 = divmod(index, 128)
        return chr(128+byte1)+chr(128+byte2)
    if entrylen == 3:
        byte1, rem = divmod(index, 16129)
        byte2, byte3 = divmod(rem, 128)
        return chr(128+byte1)+chr(128+byte2)+chr(128+byte3)
    raise ValueError, "symbol byte len must be 1 <= S <=3: "+`entrylen`

def word_Huffman_compress(text, comp_table):
    "Compress text based on word-to-symbol table"
    comp_text = []
    maybe_entry = []
    for c in text+chr(0):    # force flush of final word
        if c in wordchars:
            maybe_entry.append(c)
        else:
            word = ''.join(maybe_entry)
            comp_text.append(comp_table.get(word, word))
            maybe_entry = []
            comp_text.append(comp_table[c])
```

```
    return ''.join(comp_text[:-1])

def word_Huffman_expand(text, exp_table, entrylen):
    "Expand text based on symbol-to-word table"
    exp_text = []
    offset = 0
    end = len(text)
    while offset < end:
        c = text[offset]
        if ord(c) == 255:    # escaped highbit character
            exp_text.append(text[offset+1])
            offset += 2
        elif ord(c) >= 128: # symbol table entry
            symbol = text[offset:offset+entrylen]
            exp_text.append(exp_table[symbol])
            offset += entrylen
        else:
            exp_text.append(c)
            offset += 1
    return ''.join(exp_text)

def Huffman_find(pat, comp_text, comp_table):
    "Find a (plaintext) substring in compressed text"
    comp_pat = word_Huffman_compress(pat, comp_table)
    return comp_text.find(comp_pat)

if __name__=='__main__':
    import sys, glob
    big_text = []
    for fpat in sys.argv[1:]:
        for fname in glob.glob(fpat):
            big_text.append(open(fname).read())
    big_text = ''.join(big_text)
    hist = build_histogram(normalize_text(big_text))
    for entrylen in (1, 2, 3):
        comp_words = optimal_Nbyte(hist, entrylen)
        comp_table, exp_table, entrylen_ = tables_from_words(comp_words)
        comp_text = word_Huffman_compress(big_text, comp_table)
        exp_text = word_Huffman_expand(comp_text, exp_table, entrylen_)
        print "Nominal/actual symbol length (entries): %i/%i (%i)" % \
            (entrylen, entrylen_, len(comp_words))
        print "Compression ratio: %i%%" % \
            ((100*len(comp_text))/len(big_text))
        if big_text == exp_text:
            print "*** Compression/expansion cycle successful!\n"
        else:
```

```
        print "*** Failure in compression/expansion cycle!\n"
    # Just for fun, here's a search against compressed text
    pos = Huffman_find('Foobar', comp_text, comp_table)
```

The *word_huffman* module, while simple and fairly short, is still likely to be useful—and it lays the basis for a fleshed-out variant. The compression obtained by the algorithm above is a comparatively modest 50-60 percent of the size of the original text (in informal tests). But given that locality of decompression of subsegments is both possible and cheap, there is nearly no disadvantage to this transformation for stored documents. Word searches become quicker basically in direct proportion to the length reduction.

One likely improvement would be to add run-length compression of whitespace (or generally of nonalpha characters); doing so would lose none of the direct searchability that this algorithm is designed around, and in typical electronic natural-language texts would result in significant additional compression. Moreover, a pleasant side effect of the *word_huffman* transformation is that transformed documents become *more* compressible under Lempel-Ziv-based techniques (i.e., cumulatively). In other words, there is benefit in precompressing documents with *word-huffman* if you intend to later compress them with `gzip`, `zip`, or similar tools.

More aggressive improvements might be obtained by allowing variable byte-length symbol table entries and/or by claiming some additional low-bit control codes for the symbol table (and escaping literals in the original text). You can experiment with such variations, and your results might vary somewhat depending upon the details of application-specific canonical texts.

Search capabilities might also be generalized—but this would require considerably greater effort. In the referenced research article below, the authors show how to generalize to direct regular-expression searching against word-based Huffman encoded texts. The *word_huffman* implementation allows certain straightforward transformations of regular expressions (where literal words occur within them) for searching against compressed documents, but a number of caveats and restrictions apply. Overcoming most such limitations would involve digging into Python's underlying regular expression engine, but it is possible in principle.

B.10   References

A good place to turn for additional theoretical and practical information on compression is at the `<comp.compression>` FAQ:

   `<http://www.faqs.org/faqs/compression-faq/>`

A research article on word-based Huffman encoding inspired my simple example of word-based compression. The article "Fast and Flexible Word Searching on Compressed Text," by Edleno Silva de Moura, Gonzalo Navarro, Nivio Ziviani, and Ricardo Baeza-Yates, can be found at:

   `<http://citeseer.nj.nec.com/silvademoura00fast.html>`

Appendix C

UNDERSTANDING
UNICODE

C.1 Some Background on Characters

Before we see what Unicode is, it makes sense to step back slightly to think about just what it means to store "characters" in digital files. Anyone who uses a tool like a text editor usually just thinks of what they are doing as entering some characters—numbers, letters, punctuation, and so on. But behind the scene a little bit more is going on. "Characters" that are stored on digital media must be stored as sequences of ones and zeros, and some encoding and decoding must happen to make these ones and zeros into characters we see on a screen or type in with a keyboard.

Sometime around the 1960s, a few decisions were made about just what ones and zeros (bits) would represent characters. One important choice that most modern computer users give no thought to was the decision to use 8-bit bytes on nearly all computer platforms. In other words, bytes have 256 possible values. Within these 8-bit bytes, a consensus was reached to represent one character in each byte. So at that point, computers needed a particular *encoding* of characters into byte values; there were 256 "slots" available, but just which character would go in each slot? The most popular encoding developed was Bob Bemers' American Standard Code for Information Interchange (ASCII), which is now specified in exciting standards like ISO-14962-1997 and ANSI-X3.4-1986(R1997). But other options, like IBM's mainframe EBCDIC, linger on, even now.

ASCII itself is of somewhat limited extent. Only the values of the lower-order 7-bits of each byte might contain ASCII-encoded characters. The top 7-bits worth of positions (128 of them) are "reserved" for other uses (back to this). So, for example, a byte that contains "01000001" *might* be an ASCII encoding of the letter "A", but a byte containing "11000001" cannot be an ASCII encoding of anything. Of course, a given byte may or may not *actually* represent a character; if it is part of a text file, it probably does, but if it is part of object code, a compressed archive, or other binary data, ASCII decoding is misleading. It depends on context.

The reserved top 7-bits in common 8-bit bytes have been used for a number of things in a character-encoding context. On traditional textual terminals (and printers, etc.) it has been common to allow switching between *codepages* on terminals to allow display of a variety of national-language characters (and special characters like box-drawing borders), depending on the needs of a user. In the world of Internet communications, something very similar to the codepage system exists with the various ISO-8859-* encodings. What all these systems do is assign a set of characters to the 128 slots that ASCII reserves for other uses. These might be accented Roman characters (used in many Western European languages) or they might be non-Roman character sets like Greek, Cyrillic, Hebrew, or Arabic (or in the future, Thai and Hindi). By using the right codepage, 8-bit bytes can be made quite suitable for encoding reasonable sized (phonetic) alphabets.

Codepages and ISO-8859-* encodings, however, have some definite limitations. For one thing, a terminal can only display one codepage at a given time, and a document with an ISO-8859-* encoding can only contain one character set. Documents that need to contain text in multiple languages are not possible to represent by these encodings. A second issue is equally important: Many ideographic and pictographic character sets have far more than 128 or 256 characters in them (the former is all we would have in the codepage system, the latter if we used the whole byte and discarded the ASCII part). It is simply not possible to encode languages like Chinese, Japanese, and Korean in 8-bit bytes. Systems like ISO-2022-JP-1 and codepage 943 allow larger character sets to be represented using two or more bytes for each character. But even when using these language-specific multibyte encodings, the problem of mixing languages is still present.

C.2   What Is Unicode?

Unicode solves the problems of previous character-encoding schemes by providing a unique code number for *every* character needed, worldwide and across languages. Over time, more characters are being added, but the allocation of available ranges for future uses has already been planned out, so room exists for new characters. In Unicode-encoded documents, no ambiguity exists about how a given character should display (for example, should byte value 0x89 appear as e-umlaut, as in codepage 850, or as the per-mil mark, as in codepage 1004?). Furthermore, by giving each character its own code, there is no problem or ambiguity in creating multilingual documents that utilize multiple character sets at the same time. Or rather, these documents actually utilize the single (very large) character set of Unicode itself.

Unicode is managed by the Unicode Consortium (see Resources), a nonprofit group with corporate, institutional, and individual members. Originally, Unicode was planned as a 16-bit specification. However, this original plan failed to leave enough room for national variations on related (but distinct) ideographs across East Asian languages (Chinese, Japanese, and Korean), nor for specialized alphabets used in mathematics and the scholarship of historical languages.

As a result, the code space of Unicode is currently 32-bits (and anticipated to remain fairly sparsely populated, given the 4 billion allowed characters).

C.3   Encodings

A full 32-bits of encoding space leaves plenty of room for every character we might want to represent, but it has its own problems. If we need to use 4 bytes for every character we want to encode, that makes for rather verbose files (or strings, or streams). Furthermore, these verbose files are likely to cause a variety of problems for legacy tools. As a solution to this, Unicode is itself often encoded using "Unicode Transformation Formats" (abbreviated as UTF-*). The encodings UTF-8 and UTF-16 use rather clever techniques to encode characters in a variable number of bytes, but with the most common situation being the use of just the number of bits indicated in the encoding name. In addition, the use of specific byte value ranges in multibyte characters is designed in such a way as to be friendly to existing tools. UTF-32 is also an available encoding, one that simply uses all four bytes in a fixed-width encoding.

The design of UTF-8 is such that US-ASCII characters are simply encoded as themselves. For example, the English letter "e" is encoded as the single byte 0x65 in both ASCII and in UTF-8. However, the non-English "e-umlaut" diacritic, which is Unicode character 0x00EB, is encoded with the two bytes 0xC3 0xAB. In contrast, the UTF-16 representation of every character is always at least 2 bytes (and sometimes 4 bytes). UTF-16 has the rather straightforward representations of the letters "e" and "e-umlaut" as 0x65 0x00 and 0xEB 0x00, respectively. So where does the odd value for the e-umlaut in UTF-8 come from? Here is the trick: No multibyte encoded UTF-8 character is allowed to be in the 7-bit range used by ASCII, to avoid confusion. So the UTF-8 scheme uses some bit shifting and encodes every Unicode character using up to 6 bytes. But the byte values allowed in each position are arranged in such a manner as not to allow confusion of byte positions (for example, if you read a file nonsequentially).

Let's look at another example, just to see it laid out. Here is a simple text string encoded in several ways. The view presented is similar to what you would see in a hex-mode file viewer. This way, it is easy to see both a likely on-screen character representation (on a legacy, non-Unicode terminal) and a representation of the underlying hexadecimal values each byte contains:

```
┌─────────────────────────────────────────────────┐
│ Hex view of several character string encodings  │
└─────────────────────────────────────────────────┘
------------------- Encoding = us-ascii --------------------------
55 6E 69 63 6F 64 65 20 20 20 20 20 20 20 20 20  | Unicode
------------------- Encoding = utf-8 -----------------------------
55 6E 69 63 6F 64 65 20 20 20 20 20 20 20 20 20  | Unicode
------------------- Encoding = utf-16 ----------------------------
FF FE 55 00 6E 00 69 00 63 00 6F 00 64 00 65 00  |  U n i c o d e
```

C.4   Declarations

We have seen how Unicode characters are actually encoded, at least briefly, but how do applications know to use a particular decoding procedure when Unicode is encountered? How applications are alerted to a Unicode encoding depends upon the type of data stream in question.

Normal text files do not have any special header information attached to them to explicitly specify type. However, some operating systems (like MacOS, OS/2, and BeOS—Windows and Linux only in a more limited sense) have mechanisms to attach extended attributes to files; increasingly, MIME header information is stored in such extended attributes. If this happens to be the case, it is possible to store MIME header information such as:

```
Content-Type: text/plain; charset=UTF-8
```

Nonetheless, having MIME headers attached to files is not a safe, generic assumption. Fortunately, the actual byte sequences in Unicode files provide a tip to applications. A Unicode-aware application, absent contrary indication, is supposed to assume that a given file is encoded with `UTF-8`. A non-Unicode-aware application reading the same file will find a file that contains a mixture of ASCII characters and high-bit characters (for multibyte `UTF-8` encodings). All the ASCII-range bytes will have the same values as if they were ASCII encoded. If any multibyte `UTF-8` sequences were used, those will appear as non-ASCII bytes and should be treated as noncharacter data by the legacy application. This may result in nonprocessing of those extended characters, but that is pretty much the best we could expect from a legacy application (that, by definition, does not know how to deal with the extended characters).

For `UTF-16` encoded files, a special convention is followed for the first two bytes of the file. One of the sequences `0xFF 0xFE` or `0xFE 0xFF` acts as small headers to the file. The choice of which header specifies the endianness of a platform's bytes (most common platforms are little-endian and will use `0xFF 0xFE`). It was decided that the collision risk of a legacy file beginning with these bytes was small and therefore these could be used as a reliable indicator for `UTF-16` encoding. Within a `UTF-16` encoded text file, plain ASCII characters will appear every other byte, interspersed with `0x00` (null) bytes. Of course, extended characters will produce non-null bytes and in some cases double-word (4 byte) representations. But a legacy tool that ignores embedded nulls will wind up doing the right thing with `UTF-16` encoded files, even without knowing about Unicode.

Many communications protocols—and more recent document specifications—allow for explicit encoding specification. For example, an HTTP daemon application (a Web server) can return a header such as the following to provide explicit instructions to a client:

```
HTTP/1.1 200 OK
Content-Type: text/html; charset:UTF-8;
```

Similarly, an NNTP, SMTP/POP3 message can carry a similar `Content-Type:` header field that makes explicit the encoding to follow (most likely as `text/plain` rather than `text/html`, however; or at least we can hope).

HTML and XML documents can contain tags and declarations to make Unicode encoding explicit. An HTML document can provide a hint in a META tag, like:

```
<META HTTP-EQUIV="Content-Type" CONTENT="text/html; charset=UTF-8">
```

However, a META tag should properly take lower precedence than an HTTP header, in a situation where both are part of the communication (but for a local HTML file, such an HTTP header does not exist).

In XML, the actual document declaration should indicate the Unicode encoding, as in:

```
<?xml version="1.0" encoding="UTF-8"?>
```

Other formats and protocols may provide explicit encoding specification by similar means.

C.5   Finding Codepoints

Each Unicode character is identified by a unique codepoint. You can find information on character codepoints on official Unicode Web sites, but a quick way to look at visual forms of characters is by generating an HTML page with charts of Unicode characters. The script below does this:

mk_unicode_chart.py

```
# Create an HTML chart of Unicode characters by codepoint
import sys
head = '<html><head><title>Unicode Code Points</title>\n' +\
       '<META HTTP-EQUIV="Content-Type" ' +\
            'CONTENT="text/html; charset=UTF-8">\n' +\
       '</head><body>\n<h1>Unicode Code Points</h1>'
foot = '</body></html>'
fp = sys.stdout
fp.write(head)
num_blocks = 32  # Up to 256 in theory, but IE5.5 is flaky
for block in range(0,256*num_blocks,256):
    fp.write('\n\n<h2>Range %5d-%5d</h2>' % (block,block+256))
    start = unichr(block).encode('utf-16')
    fp.write('\n<pre>      ')
    for col in range(16): fp.write(str(col).ljust(3))
    fp.write('</pre>')
    for offset in range(0,256,16):
        fp.write('\n<pre>')
        fp.write('+'+str(offset).rjust(3)+' ')
        line = '  '.join([unichr(n+block+offset) for n in range(16)])
        fp.write(line.encode('UTF-8'))
```

```
        fp.write('</pre>')
fp.write(foot)
fp.close()
```

Exactly what you see when looking at the generated HTML page depends on just what Web browser and OS platform the page is viewed on—as well as on installed fonts and other factors. Generally, any character that cannot be rendered on the current browser will appear as some sort of square, dot, or question mark. Anything that *is* rendered is generally accurate. Once a character is visually identified, further information can be generated with the *unicodedata* module:

```
>>> import unicodedata
>>> unicodedata.name(unichr(1488))
'HEBREW LETTER ALEF'
>>> unicodedata.category(unichr(1488))
'Lo'
>>> unicodedata.bidirectional(unichr(1488))
'R'
```

A variant here would be to include the information provided by *unicodedata* within a generated HTML chart, although such a listing would be far more verbose than the example above.

C.6   Resources

More-or-less definitive information on all matters Unicode can be found at:

<http://www.unicode.org/>

The Unicode Consortium:

<http://www.unicode.org/unicode/consortium/consort.html>

Unicode Technical Report #17—Character Encoding Model:

<http://www.unicode.org/unicode/reports/tr17/>

A brief history of ASCII:

<http://www.bobbemer.com/ASCII.HTM>

Appendix D

A STATE MACHINE FOR ADDING MARKUP TO TEXT

This book was written entirely in plaintext editors, using a set of conventions I call "smart ASCII." In spirit and appearance, smart ASCII resembles the informal markup that has developed on email and Usenet. In fact, I have used an evolving version of the format for a number of years to produce articles, tutorials, and other documents. The book required a few additional conventions in the earlier smart ASCII format, but only a few. It was a toolchain that made almost all the individual typographic and layout decisions. Of course, that toolchain only came to exist through many hours of programming and debugging by me and by other developers.

The printed version of this book used tools I wrote in Python to assemble the chapters, frontmatter, and endmatter, and then to add LaTeX markup codes to the text. A moderate number of custom LaTeX macros are included in that markup. From there, the work of other people lets me convert LaTeX source into the PDF format Addison-Wesley can convert into printed copies.

For information on the smart ASCII format, see the discussions of it in several places in this book, chiefly in Chapter 4. You may also download the ASCII text of this book from its Web site at <http://gnosis.cx/TPiP/>, along with a semiformal documentation of the conventions used. Readers might also be interested in a format called "reStructuredText," which is similar in spirit, but both somewhat "heavier" and more formally specified. reStructuredText has a semiofficial status in the Python community since it is now included in the *DocUtils* package; for information see:

<http://docutils.sourceforge.net/rst.html>

In this appendix, I include the full source code for an application that can convert the original text of this book into an HTML document. I believe that this application is a good demonstration of the design and structure of a realistic text processing tool.

In general structure, `book2html.py` uses a line-oriented state machine to categorize lines into appropriate document elements. Under this approach, the "meaning" of a particular line is, in part, determined by the context of the lines that came immediately before it. After making decisions on how to categorize each line with a combination of a state machine and a collection of regular expression patterns, the blocks of document elements are processed into HTML output. In principle, it would not be difficult to substitute a different output format; the steps involved are modular.

The Web site for this book has a collection of utilities similar to the one presented. Over time, I have adapted the skeleton to deal with variations in input and output formats, but there is overlap between all of them. Using this utility is simply a matter of typing something like:

```
% book2html.py "Text Processing in Python" < TPiP.txt > TPiP.html
```

The title is optional, and you may pipe STDIN and STDOUT as usual. Since the target is HTML, I decided it would be nice to colorize source code samples. That capability is in a support module:

colorize.py

```python
#!/usr/bin/python
import keyword, token, tokenize, sys
from cStringIO import StringIO

PLAIN = '%s'
BOLD  = '<b>%s</b>'
CBOLD = '<font color="%s"><b>%s</b></font>'
_KEYWORD = token.NT_OFFSET+1
_TEXT    = token.NT_OFFSET+2
COLORS   = { token.NUMBER:      'black',
             token.OP:          'darkblue',
             token.STRING:      'green',
             tokenize.COMMENT:  'darkred',
             token.NAME:        None,
             token.ERRORTOKEN:  'red',
             _KEYWORD:          'blue',
             _TEXT:             'black'  }

class ParsePython:
    "Colorize python source"
    def __init__(self, raw):
        self.inp  = StringIO(raw.expandtabs(4).strip())
    def toHTML(self):
        "Parse and send the colored source"
        raw = self.inp.getvalue()
        self.out = StringIO()
```

```python
        self.lines = [0,0]       # store line offsets in self.lines
        self.lines += [i+1 for i in range(len(raw)) if raw[i]=='\n']
        self.lines += [len(raw)]
        self.pos = 0
        try:
            tokenize.tokenize(self.inp.readline, self)
            return self.out.getvalue()
        except tokenize.TokenError, ex:
            msg,ln = ex[0],ex[1][0]
            sys.stderr.write("ERROR: %s %s\n" %
                             (msg, raw[self.lines[ln]:]))
            return raw
    def __call__(self,toktype,toktext,(srow,scol),(erow,ecol),line):
        "Token handler"
        # calculate new positions
        oldpos = self.pos
        newpos = self.lines[srow] + scol
        self.pos = newpos + len(toktext)
        if toktype in [token.NEWLINE, tokenize.NL]:   # handle newlns
            self.out.write('\n')
            return
        if newpos > oldpos:      # send the orig whitspce, if needed
            self.out.write(self.inp.getvalue()[oldpos:newpos])
        if toktype in [token.INDENT, token.DEDENT]:
            self.pos = newpos    # skip indenting tokens
            return
        if token.LPAR <= toktype and toktype <= token.OP:
            toktype = token.OP  # map token type to a color group
        elif toktype == token.NAME and keyword.iskeyword(toktext):
            toktype = _KEYWORD
        color = COLORS.get(toktype, COLORS[_TEXT])
        if toktext:              # send text
            txt = Detag(toktext)
            if color is None:    txt = PLAIN % txt
            elif color=='black': txt = BOLD % txt
            else:                txt = CBOLD % (color,txt)
            self.out.write(txt)

Detag = lambda s: \
    s.replace('&','&amp;').replace('<','&lt;').replace('>','&gt;')

if __name__=='__main__':
    parsed = ParsePython(sys.stdin.read())
    print '<pre>'
    print parsed.toHTML()
    print '</pre>'
```

The module *colorize* contains its own self-test code and is perfectly usable as a utility on its own. The main module consists of:

```
book2html.py
```

```python
#!/usr/bin/python
"""Convert ASCII book source files for HTML presentation"

Usage: python book2html.py [title] < source.txt > target.html
"""
__author__=["David Mertz (mertz@gnosis.cx)",]
__version__="November 2002"

from __future__ import generators
import sys, re, string, time
from colorize import ParsePython
from cgi import escape

#-- Define some HTML boilerplate
html_open =\
"""<!DOCTYPE HTML PUBLIC "-//IETF//DTD HTML//EN">
<html>
<head>
<title>%s</title>
<style>
  .code-sample {background-color:#EEEEEE; text-align:left;
                width:90%%; margin-left:auto; margin-right:auto;}
  .module      {color : darkblue}
  .libfunc     {color : darkgreen}
</style>
</head>
<body>
"""
html_title = "Automatically Generated HTML"
html_close = "</body></html>"
code_block = \
"""<table class="code-sample"><tr><td><h4>%s</h4></td></tr>
<tr><td><pre>%s</pre></td></tr>
</table>"""
#-- End of boilerplate

#-- State constants
for s in ("BLANK CHAPTER SECTION SUBSECT SUBSUB MODLINE "
          "MODNAME PYSHELL CODESAMP NUMLIST BODY QUOTE "
          "SUBBODY TERM DEF RULE VERTSPC").split():
    exec "%s = '%s'" % (s,s)
```

```python
markup = {CHAPTER:'h1', SECTION:'h2', SUBSECT:'h3', SUBSUB:'h4',
          BODY:'p', QUOTE:'blockquote', NUMLIST:'blockquote',
          DEF:'blockquote'}
divs = {RULE:'hr', VERTSPC:'br'}

class Regexen:
    def __init__(self):
        # blank line is empty, spaces/dashes only, or proc instruct
        self.blank    = re.compile("^[ -]*$|^  THIS IS [A-Z]+$")
        self.chapter  = re.compile("^(CHAPTER|APPENDIX|FRONTMATTER)")
        self.section  = re.compile("^SECTION ")
        self.subsect  = re.compile("^  (TOPIC|PROBLEM|EXERCISE)")
        self.subsub   = re.compile("^  [A-Z 0-9]+:$") # chk befr body
        self.modline  = re.compile("^  =+$")
        self.pyshell  = re.compile("^ +>>>")
        self.codesamp = re.compile("^ +#[*]?[-=]+ .+ [-=]+#")
        self.numlist  = re.compile("^  \d+[.] ")        # chk befr body
        self.body     = re.compile("^  \S")             # 2 spc indent
        self.quote    = re.compile("^    ?\S")          # 4-5 spc indnt
        self.subbody  = re.compile("^     +")           # 6+ spc indent
        self.rule     = re.compile("^  (-\*-|!!!)$")
        self.vertspc  = re.compile("^  \+\+\+$")

def Make_Blocks(fpin=sys.stdin, r=Regexen()):
    #-- Initialize the globals
    global state, blocks, laststate
    state, laststate = BLANK, BLANK
    blocks = [[BLANK]]
    #-- Break the file into relevant chunks
    for line in fpin.xreadlines():
        line = line.rstrip()            # Normalize line endings
        #-- for "one-line states" just act (no accumulation)
        if r.blank.match(line):
            if inState(PYSHELL):        newState(laststate)
            else:                       blocks[-1].append("")
        elif r.rule.match(line):        newState(RULE)
        elif r.vertspc.match(line):     newState(VERTSPC)
        elif r.chapter.match(line):     newState(CHAPTER)
        elif r.section.match(line):     newState(SECTION)
        elif r.subsect.match(line):     newState(SUBSECT)
        elif r.subsub.match(line):      newState(SUBSUB)
        elif r.modline.match(line):     newState(MODLINE)
        elif r.numlist.match(line):     newState(NUMLIST)
        elif r.pyshell.match(line):
            if not inState(PYSHELL):    newState(PYSHELL)
        elif r.codesamp.match(line):    newState(CODESAMP)
```

```
            #-- now the multi-line states that are self-defining
            elif r.body.match(line):
                if not inState(BODY):        newState(BODY)
            elif r.quote.match(line):
                if inState(MODLINE):         newState(MODNAME)
                elif r.blank.match(line):    newState(BLANK)
                elif not inState(QUOTE):     newState(QUOTE)
            #-- now the "multi-line states" which eat further lines
            elif inState(MODLINE, PYSHELL, CODESAMP, NUMLIST, DEF):
                "stay in this state until we get a blank line"
                "...or other one-line prior type, but shouldn't happen"
            elif r.subbody.match(line):
                "Sub-body is tricky: it might belong with several states:"
                "PYSHELL, CODESAMP, NUMLIST, or as a def after BODY"
                if inState(BODY):            newState(DEF)
                elif inState(BLANK):
                    if laststate==DEF:       pass
                elif inState(DEF, CODESAMP, PYSHELL, NUMLIST, MODNAME):
                    pass
            else:
                raise ValueError, \
                    "unexpected input block state: %s\n%s" %(state,line)
            if inState(MODLINE, RULE, VERTSPC): pass
            elif r.blank.match(line): pass
            else: blocks[-1].append(line)
        return LookBack(blocks)

def LookBack(blocks):
    types = [f[0] for f in blocks]
    for i in range(len(types)-1):
        this, next = types[i:i+2]
        if (this,next)==(BODY,DEF):
            blocks[i][0] = TERM
    return blocks

def newState(name):
    global state, laststate, blocks
    if name not in (BLANK, MODLINE):
        blocks.append([name])
    laststate = state
    state = name

def inState(*names):
    return state in names

def Process_Blocks(blocks, fpout=sys.stdout, title=html_title):
```

```
        fpout.write(html_open % title)
        for block in blocks:           # Massage each block as needed
            typ, lines = block[0], block[1:]
            tag = markup.get(typ, None)
            div = divs.get(typ, None)
            if tag is not None:
                map(fpout.write, wrap_html(lines, tag))
            elif div is not None:
                fpout.write('<%s />\n' % div)
            elif typ in (PYSHELL, CODESAMP):
                fpout.write(fixcode('\n'.join(lines),style=typ))
            elif typ in (MODNAME,):
                mod = '<hr/><h3 class="module">%s</h3>'%'\n'.join(lines)
                fpout.write(mod)
            elif typ in (TERM,):
                terms = '<br />\n'.join(lines)
                fpout.write('<h4 class="libfunc">%s</h4>\n' % terms)
            else:
                sys.stderr.write(typ+'\n')
        fpout.write(html_close)

#-- Functions for start of block-type state
def wrap_html(lines, tag):
    txt = '\n'.join(lines)
    for para in txt.split('\n\n'):
        if para: yield '<%s>%s</%s>\n' %\
                        (tag,URLify(Typography(escape(para))),tag)

def fixcode(block, style=CODESAMP):
    block = LeftMargin(block)            # Move to left
    # Pull out title if available
    title = 'Code Sample'
    if style==CODESAMP:
        re_title = re.compile('^#\*?\-+ (.+) \-+#$', re.M)
        if_title = re_title.match(block)
        if if_title:
            title = if_title.group(1)
            block = re_title.sub('', block)  # take title out of code
    # Decide if it is Python code
    firstline = block[:block.find('\n')]
    if re.search(r'\.py_?|[Pp]ython|>>>', title+firstline):
        # Has .py, py_, Python/python, or >>> on first line/title
        block = ParsePython(block.rstrip()).toHTML()
        return code_block % (Typography(title), block)
    # elif the-will-and-the-way-is-there-to-format-language-X: ...
    else:
```

```
        return code_block % (Typography(title), escape(block).strip())

def LeftMargin(txt):
    "Remove as many leading spaces as possible from whole block"
    for l in range(12,-1,-1):
        re_lead = '(?sm)'+' '*l+'\S'
        if re.match(re_lead, txt): break
    txt = re.sub('(?sm)^'+' '*l, '', txt)
    return txt

def URLify(txt):
    # Conv special IMG URL's: Alt Text: http://site.org/img.png}
    # (don't actually try quite as hard to validate URL though)
    txt = re.sub('(?sm){(.*?):\s*(http://.*)}',
                 '<img src="\\2" alt="\\1">', txt)
    # Convert regular URL's
    txt = re.sub('(?:[^="])((?:http|ftp|file)://(?:[^ \n\r<\)]+))(\s)',
                 '<a href="\\1">\\1</a>\\2', txt)
    return txt

def Typography(txt):
    rc = re.compile      # cut down line length
    MS = re.M | re.S
    # [module] names
    r = rc(r"""([\(\s'/">]|^)\[(.*?)\]([<\s\.\),:;'"?!/-])""", MS)
    txt = r.sub('\\1<i class="module">\\2</i>\\3',txt)
    # *strongly emphasize* words
    r = rc(r"""([\(\s'/"]|^)\*(.*?)\*([\s\.\),:;'"?!/-])""", MS)
    txt = r.sub('\\1<strong>\\2</strong>\\3', txt)
    # -emphasize- words
    r = rc(r"""([\(\s'/"]|^)-(.+?)-([\s\.\),:;'"?!/])""", MS)
    txt = r.sub('\\1<em>\\2</em>\\3', txt)
    # _Book Title_ citations
    r = rc(r"""([\(\s'/"]|^)_(.*?)_([\s\.\),:;'"?!/-])""", MS)
    txt = r.sub('\\1<cite>\\2</cite>\\3', txt)
    # 'Function()' names
    r = rc(r"""([\(\s/"]|^)'(.*?)'([\s\.\),:;"?!/-])""", MS)
    txt = r.sub("\\1<code>\\2</code>\\3", txt)
    # `library.func()` names
    r = rc(r"""([\(\s/"]|^)`(.*?)`([\s\.\),:;"?!/-])""", MS)
    txt = r.sub('\\1<i class="libfunc">\\2</i>\\3', txt)
    return txt

if __name__ == '__main__':
    blocks = Make_Blocks()
    if len(sys.argv) > 1:
```

```
        Process_Blocks(blocks, title=sys.argv[1])
    else:
        Process_Blocks(blocks)
```

Appendix E

GLOSSARY

Asymmetrical Encryption:

Encryption using a pair of keys—the first encrypts a message that the second decrypts. In the most common protocol, the decryption key is kept secret but the encryption key may be widely revealed. For example, you might publish your encryption—or "public"—key, which lets anyone encrypt a message that only you can decrypt. The person who first creates the message, of course, has initial access to it, but any third-party without the decryption—or "private"—key cannot access the message. See Section 2.2.4 for a discussion of cryptographic capabilities.

Big-O Notation, Complexity:

Big-O notation is a way of describing the governing asymptotic complexity of an algorithm. Often such complexity is described using a capital "O" with an expression on "n" following in parentheses. Textbooks often use a bold letter or a special typeface for the "O". The "O" is originally associated with "order" of complexity.

The insight behind big-O notation is that many problems require a calculation time that can be expressed as a formula involving the size of the data set or domain at issue. For the most important complexity orders, constant startup times and even speed multipliers are *overpowered* by the underlying complexity. For example, suppose that you have an algorithm that takes 100 seconds to initialize some data structures and $10*(N^2)$ seconds to perform the main calculation. If you have N=4 objects, the total runtime will be 260 seconds; saving that 100 seconds initialization might seem worthwhile, if possible. However, if you also need to deal with N=10 objects, you are looking at 1,100 seconds in total, and the initialization is a minor component. Moreover, you might think it significant to go from $10*(N^2)$ seconds to only $2*(N^2)$ seconds—say, by using a faster CPU or programming language. Once you consider the 100,100 seconds it will take to calculate for N=100, even the multiplier is not all that important. In particular if you had a better algorithm that took, for example, $50*N$ seconds (bigger multiplier), you would be a lot better off only needing 50,000 seconds.

In noting complexity orders, constants and multipliers are conventionally omitted, leaving only the dominant factor. Compexities one often sees are:

```
O(1)                constant
O(log(n))           logarithmic
O((log(n))^c)       polylogarithmic
O(n)                linear
O(n*log(n))         frequent in sorts and other problems
O(n^2)              quadratic
O(n^c)              polynomial
O(c^n)              exponential (super-polynomial)
```

Birthday Paradox:

The name "birthday paradox" comes from the fact—surprising to many people—that in a room with just 23 people there is a 50 percent chance of two of them sharing a birthday. A naive hunch is often that, since there are 365 days, it should instead take something like 180 people to reach this likelihood.

In a broader sense the probability of collision of two events, where N outcomes are possible, reaches 50 percent when approximately sqrt(N) items are collected. This is a concern when you want hashes, random selections, and the like to consist of only distinct values.

Cryptographic Hash:

A hash with a strong enough noncollision property that a tamperer cannot produce a false message yielding the same hash as does an authentic message. See Section 2.2.4 for a discussion of cryptographic capabilities.

Cyclic Redundancy Check (CRC32):

See Hash. Based on mod 2 polynomial operations, CRC32 produces a 32-bit "fingerprint" of a set of data.

Digital Signatures:

A means of proving the authenticity of a message. As with asymmetric encryption, digital signatures involve two keys. The signing key is kept secret, but a published validation key can be used to show that the owner of the signing key used it to authenticate a message. See Section 2.2.4 for a discussion of cryptographic capabilities.

Hash:

A short value that is used as a "fingerprint" of a larger collection of data. It should be unlikely that two data sets will yield the same hash value. Hashes can be used to check for data errors, by comparing data to an indicated hash value (mismatch suggests data error). Some hashes have sufficient noncollision properties to be used cryptographically.

Idempotent Function:

The property that applying a function to its return value returns an identical value. That is, if and only if F is idempotent then `F(x)==F(F(x))`, for every x. In a nod to Chaos Theory, we can observe that if some function defined by finite repetitions of composition with F is idempotent, then F has an attractor—that is, if G is idempotent for `G=lambda x:F(F(F((x)...)))`. This interesting fact is completely unnecessary to understand the rest of this book.

Immutable:

Literally, "cannot be changed." Some data collection objects—notably tuples and strings, in Python—consist of a set of items, and the membership cannot change over the life of the object. In contrast, mutable objects like lists and dictionaries can continue to be the same object, while changing their membership. Since you generally access objects in Python via names (and index positions), it is sometimes easy to confuse the mere name—which can be used at different times to point to different objects—with the underlying objects. For example, a pattern with tuples like the one below is common:

```
>>> tup = (1,2,3)
>>> id(tup)
248684
>>> tup = tup+(4,5,6)
>>> tup
(1, 2, 3, 4, 5, 6)
>>> id(tup)
912076
```

Even though the name `tup` is re-bound during the run, the identity of the bound object changes. Moreover, creating a tuple with the same objects later produces the same identity:

```
>>> tup2 = (1,2,3)
>>> id(tup2)
248684
```

Immutable objects are particularly useful as dictionary keys, since they will continue to hash the same way over program run. However, "hashability" is a stricter constraint than immutability—it is necessary that every member of an immutable object itself be (recursively) immutable in order to be hashable.

Mutable:

Literally, "can be changed." Data collection objects like lists, dictionaries, and arrays from the *array* module are mutable. The identity of these objects stays the same, even as their membership changes. Mutable objects are not (usually) suitable as dictionary keys, however. Conceptually, lists are often used to hold *records* of a data collection, where tuples are used to hold *fields* within a record. The insight underlying this distinction is that if a record contained different field data, it would not be the same record. But individual self-identical records can be added or subtracted from a collection, depending on outside events and purposes.

Public-key Encryption:

See Assymmetrical Encryption.

Referential Transparency:

The property of a function or block construct such that it will produce the same value every time it is called with the same arguments. Mathematical functions are referentially transparent, by definition, but functions whose results depend on global state, external context, or local mutable values are *referentially opaque*.

Shared-key Encryption:

See Symmetrical Encryption.

Structured Text Database:

A text file that is used to encode multiple records of data, each record composed of the same fields. Records and fields are also often called rows and columns, respectively. A structured text database might be any textual format that contains little or no explicit markup; the most common variants are delimited files and fixed-width files, both widely used on mainframes and elsewhere. Most of the time, structured text databases are line oriented, with one conceptual record per line; but at times, devices like indentation are used to indicate dependent subrecords.

Symmetrical Encryption:

Encryption using a single "key" that must be shared between parties. See Section 2.2.4 for a discussion of cryptographic capabilities.

INDEX

M

N